Implementing E

This book provides a comprehensive assessment of the effectiveness of Mobility Partnerships and their consequences for third countries.

Mobility partnerships between the EU and third countries are usually viewed as reflecting asymmetric power relations where development aid, trade relations and visa policies are made conditional upon the cooperation by third countries with an EU agenda of migration control. This book argues that three main factors condition the relevance of Mobility Partnerships: the state of relations between EU Member States and a third country and, in particular, the role of postcolonial ties; the power of negotiation of a third country, which is linked to its geopolitical importance for the EU; and its administrative capacity, which is understood as the capacity of a state to define and implement policies and to legislate and enforce the law. The work combines a comparative legal analysis of the development of the legal and policy frameworks in the cases of Morocco and Cape Verde with an empirical study of the implementation of Mobility Partnerships' projects. The analysis demonstrates that Mobility Partnerships, despite their non-binding nature, have legal and policy relevance for these third countries with regard to the regulation of migration, asylum, human trafficking and even labour law. As such, this book makes a contribution to the understanding of the interplay between the interests of EU, Member State and third country actors in the implementation of the Mobility Partnerships.

The book will be a key resource for academics and students focusing on Migration Law, EU Studies, Geopolitics and African Studies. The empirical approach will also appeal to policy-makers, international organisation representatives and NGOs alike.

Fanny Tittel Mosser is affiliated to the Research Centre for Justice and Governance (JusGov) of the University of Minho, Portugal, where she completed in 2018 a Marie Curie PhD in law. Fanny has experience in research, comparative studies, monitoring and evaluation as well as a deep knowledge of migration issues in the MENA Region and West Africa. Dr Tittel-Mosser previously worked on various migration-related issues with IOM, the UN Alliance of Civilizations, ICMPD and NGOs. Her research interests include migration governance, EU External Action, EU-Africa relations and EU-UN relations.

Law and Migration

Series Editor

Satvinder S. Juss, King's College London, UK

Migration and its subsets of refugee and asylum policy are rising up the policy agenda at national and international level. Current controversies underline the need for rational and informed debate of this widely misrepresented and little understood area.

Law and Migration contributes to this debate by establishing a monograph series to encourage discussion and help to inform policy in this area. The series provides a forum for leading new research principally from the Law and Legal Studies area but also from related social sciences. The series is broad in scope, covering a wide range of subjects and perspectives.

Other titles in this series:

Refugee Law and Durability of Protection
Temporary Residence and Cessation of Status
Maria O'Sullivan

Implementing EU Mobility Partnership
Putting Soft Law into Practice
Fanny Tittel-Mosser

Persecution, International Refugee Law and Refugees
A Feminist Approach
Mathilde Crépin

Human Rights and The Revision of Refugee Law
Romit Bhandari

Refugees, Democracy and the Law
A Deficit of Rights
Dana Schmalz

For more information about this series, please visit: www.routledge.com/Law-and-Migration/book-series/LAWANDMIG

Implementing EU Mobility Partnerships

Putting Soft Law into Practice

Fanny Tittel-Mosser

Routledge
Taylor & Francis Group
LONDON AND NEW YORK

First published 2020
by Routledge
2 Park Square, Milton Park, Abingdon, Oxon OX14 4RN

and by Routledge
52 Vanderbilt Avenue, New York, NY 10017

Routledge is an imprint of the Taylor & Francis Group, an informa business

British Library Cataloguing-in-Publication Data
A catalogue record for this book is available from the British Library

Library of Congress Cataloging-in-Publication Data
Names: Tittel-Mosser, Fanny, author.
Title: Implementing EU mobility partnerships : putting soft law into practice / Fanny Tittel-Mosser.
Description: Abingdon, Oxon ; New York, NY : Routledge, 2020. |
Series: Law and migration | Based on author's thesis (doctoral - Universidade do Minho, Escola de Direito, 2018) issued under title: The legal and policy relevance of EU mobility partnerships : a comparative study of Morocco and Cape Verde. | Includes bibliographical references and index.
Identifiers: LCCN 2020006048 (print) | LCCN 2020006049 (ebook) |
ISBN 9780367444303 (hardback) | ISBN 9781003009665 (ebook)
Subjects: LCSH: Emigration and immigration law--European Union countries. |
European Union countries--Foreign relations--Law and legislation. |
European Union countries--Foreign relations--Morocco. |
European Union countries--Foreign relations--Cabo Verde. |
Morocco--Foreign relations--European Union countries. |
Cabo Verde--Foreign relations--European Union countries.
Classification: LCC KJE6044 .T58 2020 (print) |
LCC KJE6044 (ebook) | DDC 342.2408/2--dc23
LC record available at https://lccn.loc.gov/2020006048
LC ebook record available at https://lccn.loc.gov/2020006049

ISBN: 978-0-367-44430-3 (hbk)
ISBN: 978-0-367-49353-0 (pbk)
ISBN: 978-1-003-00966-5 (ebk)

Typeset in Galliard
by Taylor & Francis Books

A Mireille et Christophe, merci de m'avoir donné des ailes
A Aldo, pour m'avoir transmis l'amour des livres
To Raul, for your unfailing support

This research has been supported by the European Union under the Marie Curie Initial Training Network (ITN), Transnational Migration, Citizenship and the Circulation of Rights and Responsibilities (TRANSMIC) (Project number No. 608417).

Contents

Tables

Abbreviations

ACP	African, Caribbean and Pacific
ANAPEC	*Agence Nationale pour la Promotion de l'Emploi et des Compétences*/National Agency for the Promotion of Employment and Skills
BRA	*Bureau des réfugiés et apatrides*/Office for Refugees and the Stateless
BTC	Belgian Development Cooperation
CAMM	Common Agendas for Migration and Mobility
CAMPO	Centre for Migrant Support at the Country of Origin
CFSP	Common Foreign and Security Policy
CJEU	Court of Justice of the European Union
CIMI	*Comissão Interministerial para o Estudo e Proposição das Bases da Política de Imigração*/Interministerial Commission for the Study and Proposition for the Bases of Immigration Policy
CNDH	*Comissão Nacional de Direitos Humanos* (in Cape Verde)/ National Commission on Human Rights
CNDH	*Conseil national des droits de l'Homme* (in Morocco)/National Human Rights Council
CoE	Council of Europe
DCFTA	Deep and Comprehensive Free Trade Agreement
DEF	*Direcção de Estrangeiros e Fronteiras*/Directorate for Foreigners and Borders
DG Devco	Directorate-General for International Cooperation and Development
DG Home Affairs	Directorate General Migration and Home Affairs
DGI	Directorate-General of Immigration
DG NEAR	Directorate-General for Neighbourhood and Enlargement Negotiations
DGT	*Direção Geral do Trabalho*/General Directory for Labour
DIDH	*Délégation Interministérielle aux Droits de l'Homme*/Interministerial Delegation for Human Rights
EAM	European Agenda on Migration

EASO	European Asylum Support Office
EC	European Communities
ECJ	European Court of Justice
ECOWAS	Economic Community of West African States
EEAS	European External Action Service
EEC	European Economic Community
ENP	European Neighbourhood Policy
ETF	European Training Foundation
EU	European Union
EURA	EU Readmission Agreement
FTA	Free Trade Area
FRONTEX	European External Borders Agency
GAM	Global Approach to Migration
GAMM	Global Approach to Migration and Mobility
GADEM	*Groupe Antiraciste de Défense et d'Accompagnement des Etrangers et Migrants*/Antiracist Defence and Support Group for Foreigners and Migrants
GAREC	General Affairs and External Relations Council
GATT	General Agreement on Tariffs and Trade
GCIM	Global Commission on International Migration
GIZ	*Gesellschaft für Internationale Zusammenarbeit*
HOMERe	High Opportunity for Mediterranean Executive Recruitment
ICCPR	International Covenant on Civil and Political Rights
ICESCR	International Covenant on Economic, Social and Cultural Rights
ICJ	International Court of Justice
ICMPD	International Centre for Migration Policy Development
ICRMW	International Convention on the Protection of the Rights of All Migrant Workers and Members of Their Families
IEFP	Institute for Employment and Vocational Training
INS	Immigration and Naturalisation Service
IOM	International Organisation for Migration
MCMREAM	*Ministère chargé des MRE et des affaires de la Migration*/Ministry in charge of Moroccans Residing Abroad and Migration Affairs
MENA	Middle East and North Africa
MIEUX	MIgration EU eXpertise
MoU	Memorandum of Understanding
MPF	Migration Partnership Framework
MSF	*Médecins Sans Frontières*/Doctors without borders
NGO	Non-Governmental Organisation
NIP	National Immigration Policy (Cape Verde)
NIS	National Immigration Strategy (Cape Verde)
NSIA	National Strategy for Immigration and Asylum (Morocco)
OECD	Organisation for Economic Co-operation and Development

OFPPT	*Office de la Formation Professionnelle et de la Promotion du Travail*/Office for Vocational Training and the Promotion of Employment and Work
OMC	Open Method of Coordination
PALIM	Pilot Project Addressing Labour Shortages through Innovative Labour Migration Models
RAMED	*Régime d'assistance médicale*/Medical assistance plan
RDPP NA	Regional Development and Protection Programme for North Africa
RPP	Regional Protection Programme
SALT II	Second Strategic Arms Limitations Treaty
SICJ	Statute of the International Court of Justice
SPRING	Support for the Partnership, Reforms and Inclusive Growth
TFEU	Treaty on the Functioning of the European Union
UCI	*Unidade de Coordenação da Imigração*/Immigration Coordination Unit
UNCLOS	UN Convention on the Law of the Sea
UNDP	United Nations Development Programme
UNEP	United Nations Environmental Programme
UNESCO	United Nations Educational, Scientific and Cultural Organization
UNFPA	United Nations Population Fund
UNHCR	United Nations High Commissioner for Refugees

Annex I Interview List

0 DG Home Affairs, Brussels, 27 June 2015
1 DG Devco, Brussels (by phone), 28 October 2015
2 EEAS, Brussels (by phone), 15 October 2015
3 DG Home Affairs, Brussels, 18 November 2015
4 Council of Europe, Strasbourg, 21 December 2015
5 AMERM, University Mohammed V, Rabat, 12 January 2016
6 EU Delegation, Rabat, 13 January 2016
7 EU Delegation, Rabat, 13 January 2016
8 French Embassy, Rabat, 14 January 2016
9 UNHCR, Rabat, 15 January 2016
10 Expertise France, Rabat, 15 January 2016
11 Portuguese Embassy, Rabats, 18, January 2016
12 Council of Europe, Rabat, 19 January 2016
13 Moroccan Ministry of Labour, Rabat, 19 January 2016
14 GIZ*, Rabat, 20 January 2016
15 IOM*, Rabat, 20 January 2016
16 MCMREAM*, Rabat, 21 January 2016
17 Spanish Embassy*, Rabat, 22 January 2016
18 ICMPD, Brussels, 13 May 2016
19 Belgian Embassy, Rabat, 12 April 2016
20 CEI, Rabat, 15 April 2016
21 CCSM, Rabat, 15 April 2016
22 FASED**, Rabat, 19 April 2016
23 CNDH*, Rabat, 21 April 2016
24 Red Chabaka*, Tanger, 22 April 2016
25 APIMA, Rabat, 23 April 2016
26 CEI, Rabat, 25 April 2016
27 Collectif des travailleurs migrants au Maroc, Rabat, 25 April 2016
28 DG Home Affairs, Brussels, 20 October 2016
29 DG Home Affairs, Brussels, 26 October 2016
30 DG Near, Brussels, 27 October 2016
31 ICMPD, Brussels, 27 October 2016
32 ICMPD, Brussels, 28 October 2016

33 Direção Geral das Comunidades, Praia, 23 February 2016
34 Centro Comum de Vistos/Portuguese Consulate, Praia, 23 February 2016
35 DGI, Praia, 23 February 2026
36 MIREX, Praia, 23 February 2016
37 CAMPO, Praia, 24 February 2016
38 IOM, Praia, 24 February 2016
39 EU Delegation*, Praia, 25 February 2016
40 Institute of Social and Legal Sciences of Cape Verde, Praia, 26 February 2016
41 Luxembourg Embassy, Praia, 2016
42 CNDH*, Praia, 26 February 2016
43 Associação dos Guineenses Residentes em Cabo Verde, Praia, 14 November 2016
44 Associação dos Filhos e Amigos para o Desenvolvimento Integrado da Região de Bafatá, Praia, 16 November 2016
45 Ex-Secretário de Estado dos Negócios Estrangeiros/Former Ambassador, Praia, 16 November 2016
46 Associação dos Serraleoneses Residentes em Cabo Verde, Praia, 17 November 2016
47 Associação dos Estudantes e investigados Guineenses, Praia, 17 November 2016
48 Associação de Guineenses, Boa Vista, 24 November 2016
49 Camara Municipal, Boa Vista, 25 November 2016
50 Plataforma das Communidades Africanas Residentes em Cabo Verde, Boa Vista, 29 November 2016
51 Association des Senegalais, Boa Vista, 29 November 2016
52 Associação dos Emigrantes Senegaleses Residentes em Cabo Verde, Praia, 2 December 2016
53 Associação Esperança Africana, Praia, 2 December 2016
54 Association des Senegalais, Praia, 2 December 2016
55 Association avenir école Cape – Vert, Paris, 18 December 2016
56 Association Cap – Vert Amiens, Amiens, 19 December 2016
57 Association Cap – Vert Amiens, Amiens, 19 December 2016
58 Alliance et Echanges, Creil, 19 December 2016
59 Section des femmes du Secteur France du Parti africain pour l'indépendance du Cap Vert (PAICV), Paris, 20 December 2016
60 Association des femmes d'Asnieres, 20 December 2016
61 Calima, Strasbourg, 1 June 2017
62 ATMF, Strasbourg, 2 June 2017
63 Conseil de la communauté marocaine à l'étranger, Rabat (by phone), 12 June 2017
64* Associação Essalam, Porto, 11 October 2017
65 Associação Cabo-Verdiana de Setubal, Setubal, 3 November 2017
66 Associação Girassol Solidario, Lisbon, 4 November 2017
67* Associação da Comunidade Marroquina em Portugal, Lisbon, 4 November 2017
68* Associação dos Antigos Alunos do Ensino Secundario de Cabo Verde, Lisbon, 4 November 2017

69 Congresso dos Quadros Cabo-Verdianos da Diaspora/Universidade do Minho, Braga, 5 December 2017
70 ICMPD, Brussels, 3 December 2019

Note

* Two respondents attended the same Interview.
**Three respondents attended the same Interview.

Introduction

The first developments of the external dimension of migration policy date back to 1985 with the adoption of a decision by the Commission of the European Communities 'Setting Up a Prior Communication and Consultation Procedure on Migration Policies in Relation to Non-Member Countries'.[1] The entry into force of the Amsterdam Treaty in 1999 marks the beginning of the communitarisation of EU migration policy. The same year (1999), the Tampere programme was launched as the main framework for the development of a Common EU asylum and migration policy that was presented by the Commission in an official communication in 2000.[2] The conclusions of the General Affairs and External Relations Council (GAREC) of 2002 followed the same trend and repeated the need to 'intensify cooperation on the management of migration flows with third countries'[3] and to 'intensify EU partnership with countries and regions of particular relevance'.[4] The African and Mediterranean regions have been a political priority for the EU in terms of the fight against irregular migration and particularly for border control and readmission agreements.[5] Emma Haddad observes that external developments of migration policy are more likely than internal developments, because 'everything is somehow less sensitive when it takes place in another country'.[6] This means that Member States are more hesitant to consent to internal legal developments at the EU level than to developments in the external dimension of migration policy. This should not be surprising, since this way Member States and the EU can share the 'burden' of asylum seekers and refugees

1 Commission of the European Communities, Commission Decision of 8 July 1985 setting up a prior communication and consultation procedure on migration policies in relation to non-member countries, 85/381/EEC OJ L 217, 14.8.1985 26.

2 European Commission, A Community Immigration Policy, COM(2000) 757 final, Brussels 22 November 2000.

3 General Affairs and External Relations Council, 2463rd Meeting of the General and External Relations Council, 14183/02, Brussels 18 November 2002, V.

4 Ibid.

5 Sergio Carrera and Raül Hernández I Sagrera, 'The externalisation of the EU's labour immigration policy: Towards mobility or insecurity partnerships?' (2009) CEPS Working Document 321 1, 31.

6 Emma Haddad, 'The External Dimension of EU Refugee Policy: A new Approach to Asylum?' (2008) 43(2) *Gov Oppos* 190, 197.

with neighbouring third countries, requiring their help to reinforce borders and prevent migrants from entering their territory irregularly.[7]

The externalisation of migration control is not a new phenomenon and has existed since the fall of the Soviet bloc in the 1990s, slowly shifting from the East towards EU's neighbourhood in the South.[8] Sandra Lavenex argues that the 'external dimension' of EU asylum and immigration policies has 'always' existed involving non-European countries to 'share the burden of migration control'.[9] Additionally, several authors have argued that the EU uses a strategy of externalisation to fight against irregular migration flows[10] and that the externalisation of EU's migration policy trend will not stop.[11] Christina Boswell, for example, argues that the EU externalises 'traditional tools of domestic or EU migration control', such as the strengthening of border controls, the fight against human trafficking and readmission agreements.[12] Moreover, she argues that the EU also uses 'preventive' tools in order to allow asylum seekers to make an asylum application 'closer to home' or to guarantee more rights to immigrants and refugees in third countries.

From the GAM to the GAMM

EU migration policy orientations were in practice embodied in the Global Approach to Migration (GAM), introduced at the Hampton Court's European Council, in October 2005. Three weeks after the Hampton Court's European Council, the Commission adopted a Communication on the priority actions for responding to the challenges of migration[13] – the 'First follow up to Hampton Court' – in which the idea of win-win was presented for the first time. The Commission stressed 'the benefits of migration for all partners',[14] the EU, the

7 Sandra Lavenex, 'Shifting Up and Out: The Foreign Policy of European Immigration Control' (2006) 29(2) *West Eur Politics* 329, 337–338; Virginie Guiraudon, 'European Integration and Migration Policy: Vertical Policy-making as Venue Shopping' (2000) 38(2) *JCMS* 251, 251; Sandra Lavenex and Nicole Wichmann, 'The External Governance of EU Internal Security' (2008) 31(1) *J Eur Integr* 83, 91.

8 Sandra Lavenex (n7) 330.

9 Ibid 335.

10 Joanne van Selm, 'Immigration and Asylum or Foreign Policy: The EU's Approach to Migrants and Their Countries of Origin' 143 in Sandra Lavenex and Emek M. Uçarer (eds), *Migration and the Externalities of European Integration* (Lanham MD: Lexington Books 2002); Christina Boswell, 'The "External Dimension" of EU Immigration and Asylum Policy' (2003) 79(3) *International Affairs* 619.

11 Sandra Lavenex and Emek M. Uçarer, 'The External Dimension of Europeanization: The Case of Immigration Policies' (2004) *Cooperation and Conflict* 39(4) 417; Virginie Guiraudon (n7) 252.

12 Christina Boswell (n10) 620.

13 Commission of the European Communities, 'Priority actions for responding to the challenges of migration: First follow-up to Hampton Court', COM(2005) 621 final, Brussels, 30 November 2005.

14 Ibid 5.

Member States and the partner third country. The launch of the GAM was the first key step towards the realisation of the political discourse in vogue since 1999.

Since 2005, the GAM is the predominant framework for the external dimension of the migration and asylum policy.[15] In November 2006, the Commission made a first evaluation of the implementation of the GAM focusing on the efforts made by the EU to discuss migration issues with African countries.[16] The Commission proposed to add legal migration and integration to the GAM.[17] The Commission in the Communication on a Common Immigration Policy for Europe: Principles, Actions and Tools presented the need to refocus the GAM towards a more coordinate and coherent approach.[18] The Commission described in this document its vision of a common migration policy organised around three main axes 'prosperity, security and solidarity'.[19] In two further documents of 2009, the cooperation between the Member States on migration issues was highlighted by the Commission as well as by the Council.[20]

Later, with the Arab Spring in 2011, a renewed focus was given to migration but this time with a more comprehensive perspective. In 2011, the GAM became the Global Approach to Migration and Mobility (GAMM).[21] In the Communication on the GAMM, the Commission argues that the focus should not only be on the fight against irregular migration but also on mobility.[22] By fully including the idea of mobility, the GAM evolved into a more strategic approach to migration management; this is when the notion of mobility was fully integrated into EU migration policy. With the GAMM, the EU tries to put forth a more balanced and attractive framework for cooperation with third countries, by enhancing possibilities for legal migration and migration and development initiatives.[23] International protection has also been included in the GAMM.[24] Several factors can explain this evolution. The first factor is the entry into force of the Lisbon Treaty which extends the ordinary legislative procedure to immigration and integration issues. Following the entry into force of the Lisbon treaty, migration was considered as a

15 Commission of the European Communities, 'Strengthening the Global Approach to Migration: Increasing Coordination, Coherence and Synergies' COM(2008) 611 final, Brussels, 8 October 2008, 1.

16 Ibid.

17 Ibid 4–5.

18 Commission of the European Communities, 'Common Immigration Policy for Europe: Principles, Actions and Tools' COM(2008) 359 final, Brussels, 17 June 2008, 1.

19 Ibid 4.

20 Commission of the European Communities, 'Mobility Partnerships as a tool of the Global Approach to Migration' SEC(2009) 124 final, Brussels, 18 September 2009, 9; Council of the European Union, 'Brussels European Council 18–19 June 2009: Presidency Conclusions', 112252/2/09 Brussels, 10 July 2009, 1, 14.

21 European Commission, 'The Global Approach to Migration and Mobility' COM (2011) 743 Brussels, 18 November 2011, 1.

22 Ibid.

23 Ibid.

24 James Hampshire, 'European Migration Governance since the Lisbon Treaty: Introduction to the Special Issue' (2016) 42(4) *J Ethn Migr Stud* 537, 540.

priority area and included as such in the Stockholm programme.[25] Additionally, Catherine Wihtol de Wenden, argues that the GAMM was proposed by the EU as a reaction to the influx of migrants and refugees after the start of the Arab Spring uprisings in Southern Mediterranean countries in 2011.[26] Accordingly, Sergio Carrera, Leonhard den Hertog and Joanna Parkin argue that with the Arab Spring, the EU had to adapt its migration policy by considering the increasing migration flows coming from the region as well as the potential security threats that could arise from the political unrest.[27] The Communication on a Partnership for Democracy and Shared Prosperity of 2011 stated the justification of EU's shift in its migration policy, emphasising that a 'radically changing political landscape in the Southern Mediterranean requires a change in the EU's approach to the region'.[28] The GAMM is implemented through two specific instruments: the Common Agendas for Migration and Mobility (CAMM) and the Mobility Partnerships.

In 2014, the Commission established the Asylum, Migration and Integration Fund[29] with a total of EUR 3.137 billion for 2014–2020, highlighting the importance of Mobility Partnerships as the main strategic, comprehensive and long-term cooperation framework for migration management with third countries and invited the EU to pursue and increase the use of this tool. The Commission suggests in the 'European Agenda on Migration' that the EU and the Member States should 'work together with partner countries to put in place concrete measures to prevent hazardous journeys'.[30] Subsequently, the EU put forth a communication establishing a new Migration Partnership Framework (MPF) with third countries under the 'European Agenda on Migration', stating the importance of providing 'capacity building to the host communities and relevant institutions'.[31]

The introduction of the Mobility Partnership tool

In 2007, the Commission introduced Mobility Partnerships as an innovating tool to achieve the Global Approach to Migration's objectives of enhanced dialogue and

25 Council of the European Union, 'The Stockholm Programme: An Open and Secure Europe Serving and Protecting Citizens' 2010/C 115/01, 4 May 2010, 1.
26 Catherine Wihtol de Wenden, 'Révolutions arabes et migrations: Schengen face aux accords bilatéraux de contrôle des frontières', *Esprit* 2011/8 (August/September) 162.
27 Sergio Carrera, Leonhard den Hertog and Joanna Parkin, 'EU Migration Policy in the wake of the Arab Spring: What prospects for EU-Southern Mediterranean Relations?' (2012) MEDPRO Technical Report No. 15/August 2012, 1, 1.
28 European Commission, 'A Partnership for Democracy and Shared Prosperity with the Southern Mediterranean' COM(2011) 200 final Brussels, 8 March 2011, 3.
29 For more information see: https://ec.europa.eu/home-affairs/financing/fundings/migration-asylum-borders/asylum-migration-integration-fund_en (accessed 15 January 2018).
30 European Commission, 'A European Agenda on Migration' COM(2015) 240, Brussels, 13 May 2015.
31 European Commission, 'Establishing a New Partnership Framework with Third Countries Under the European Agenda on Migration' COM(2016) 385 final, Strasbourg, 7 June 2016, 1, 6.

cooperation with third countries.[32] In 2008 the first two pilot Mobility Partnerships were concluded with Cape Verde and Moldova, followed by Georgia (2009), Armenia (2011), Azerbaijan (2013), Morocco (2013), Tunisia (2014), Jordan (2014) and Belarus (2016). Mobility Partnerships are Joint Declarations in which the objectives are set following the objectives of the GAM/GAMM. Mobility Partnerships are composed of the text of the Joint Declaration and an Annex which is a list of projects designed to implement the Mobility Partnership. Mobility Partnerships projects' topics are directly linked to the different pillars of the GAM(M). The first pillar of the GAMM[33] covers mobility, legal migration and integration; the second pillar includes cooperation on border management, the fight against illegal migration and trafficking in human beings; the third pillar consist of international protection; and finally the forth pillar comprises migration and development. The list of projects proposed in the Annex to the Joint Declaration can evolve in line with emerging policy priorities and new projects can be proposed if new policy priorities arise. Therefore, Mobility Partnerships can play a role in continuing discussions between the EU and third countries. The number of projects and the number of Member States participating in any Mobility Partnership varies.

The notion of circular migration has been closely related to the Mobility Partnership tool.[34] Before the launch of the first Mobility Partnerships, academics and policy makers welcomed the new tool with enthusiasm. Circular migration was perceived as 'an important shift in migration patterns' for countries of origin.[35] However, with the conclusion of the first Mobility Partnerships criticism started to be raised. It is often assumed that Mobility Partnerships are unfair tools created in favour of the EU and its Member States, failing to provide new opportunities for legal migration to third country nationals.[36] Mobility Partnerships have also been criticised for achieving EU's 'disguised' externalisation of migration control.[37] Stefan Brocza and Katharina Paulhart[38] concur with this argument and describe Mobility Partnerships' first interests as expanding EU's migration scope of influence and externalisation of its borders.

Mobility Partnerships are non-binding instruments concluded between the EU, interested Member States and a third country. They are widely presented in the

32 European Commission, 'On circular migration and Mobility Partnerships between the European Union and third countries' COM(2007) 248, Brussels, 15 May 2007.

33 European Commission (n21).

34 Ibid 4.

35 Global Commission on International Migration (GCIM), 'Migration in an Interconnected World: New Directions for Action', Report of the Global Commission on International Migration, 5 October 2005, 1, 31.

36 Sergio Carrera and Raül Hernández I Sagrera, 'Mobility Partnerships: "Insecurity Partnerships" for Policy Coherence and Migrant Workers Human Rights in the EU', 97 in Rahel Kunz, Sandra Lavenex and Marion Panizzon (eds), *Multilayered Migration Governance: The Promise of Partnership* (London, New York: Routledge 2011) 101.

37 Euromed Rights, 'EU-Morocco Mobility Partnership: Border control at the expense of human lives?' (2014) http://www.euromedrights.org/publication/eu-morocco-mobility-partnership-border-control-at-the-expense-of-human-lives (accessed 20 August 2017).

38 Stefan Brocza and Katharina Paulhart, 'EU Mobility Partnerships: A Smart Instrument for the Externalization of Migration Control' (2015) 15(3) *Eur J Futures Res* 1, 6.

literature as soft law instruments or defined as being of 'soft legal nature' or of 'non-legal nature'.[39] Some accounts are less straightforward and refer to Mobility Partnerships as having a 'complex legal nature'.[40] Traditionally, bilateral and binding agreements have been the legal instrument of choice in the field of international migration with the disadvantage of leading to sometimes incoherent regulations. In parallel to the development of legal instruments, the EU resorts to non-binding instruments to cooperate with third countries on migration and asylum issues.

The relevance of Mobility Partnerships

The term *relevance* implies some 'reasonable connection' with something.[41] In the Oxford dictionary, relevance is defined as '[t]he quality or state of being closely connected or appropriate'. According to the Cambridge dictionary, relevance is 'the degree to which something is related or useful to what is happening or being talked about'. In this book we are discussing to what extend the implementation of Mobility Partnerships' projects are linked to the legal and policy developments occurring in a third country (Morocco and Cape Verde). Despite its non-binding nature, several authors have observed that Mobility Partnerships can have concrete legal implications especially regarding visa facilitation and readmission.[42] The logic behind this is that Mobility Partnerships often combine interests from both the EU (e.g.: an effective readmission policy of third countries) and third countries (e. g.: access for its nationals to the territory of the EU through visa facilitation).[43] These could be considered as direct intended effects. The projects designed to achieve these specific goals are the exception.

Despite the absence of enforcement mechanisms in Mobility Partnerships, their *quid pro quo* nature may ensure sufficient political will on the part of the partner third country to implement the required legal changes in its domestic legal orders.

39 Sergio Carrera and Raül Hernández I Sagrera (n5) 28; Sergio Carrera and Raül Hernández I Sagrera (n36) 97. Panos Koutrakos, *European Foreign Policy: Legal and Political Perspectives* (Cheltenham, UK: Edward Elgar 2011) 164–165; Bart Van Vooren, *EU External Relations Law and the European Neighbourhood Policy: A Paradigm for Coherence* (London, New York: Routledge 2012) 209–210.

40 European Commission (n18) 3.

41 Fanny Tittel-Mosser, 'The Unintended Legal and Policy Relevance of EU Mobility Partnerships: A Comparative Implementation Analysis of Morocco and Cape Verde' (2018) 20 *EJML* 314, 317–321.

42 Sergio Carrera and others, 'Labour Immigration Policy in the EU: A Renewed Agenda for Europe 2020' (2011) Policy Brief No 240, CEPS 1, 6; Linda Senden, 'Soft Law, Self-regulation and Co-regulation in European Law: Where do they Meet?' (2005) 9(1) *EJCL* 1, 23; Filippa Chatzistavrou, 'L'usage du soft law dans le système juridique international et ses implications sémantiques et pratiques sur la notion de règle de droit' (2005) http://leportique.revues.org/591 (accessed 17 January 2018) 1, 7; Francis Snyder, 'Interinstitutional Agreements: Forms and Constitutional Limitations' 453 in Gerd Winter (ed.), *Sources and Categories of European Union Law: A Comparative and Reform Perspective* (Baden-Baden, Germany: Nomos 1996) 461–463.

43 Fanny Tittel-Mosser, 'Reversed Conditionality in EU External Migration Policy: The Case of Morocco' (2018) 14(4) *JCER* 349, 350.

In this book I argue that legal and policy relevance can be consequences of Mobility Partnerships. Hussein Kassim and Patrick Le Galès argue that not only can the consequences of policy instruments change, but also the power structure between the different parties.[44] They add that the 'adoption of instruments is likely to produce unintended consequences'.[45] Sarah Wolff adds that migration policy instruments 'do not always respond to the original intended effect and can escape the objectives assigned to them'.[46] The negotiation of Mobility Partnerships means that political priorities are translated into projects, to which resources are allocated and which aim at creating results. This has two implications. First, these political priorities can change over time which can explain the inclusion of new projects. Second, the expected results of the implementation may be different from the intended ones and unintended consequences can occur.

In a recent paper, Olga Burlyuk unpacks the notion of unintended consequences of EU External Action going beyond the typical narrow interpretation of this term in the literature.[47] She builds on de Zwart's work, explaining that beyond the usual understanding of unintended consequences equating to unanticipated consequences there are more ways to apprehend this notion. In this book, the understanding of unintended consequences of Mobility Partnerships for third countries follows Burlyuk's broad definition.

When looking at the content of all nine Joint Declarations on a Mobility Partnership concluded so far, they all refer to similar goals, which are directly related to the four pillars of the GAMM which Mobility Partnerships aim to embody.[48] The objectives stated in the text of the Mobility Partnerships are vague and standard therefore opening the way for unintended consequences. One of the main issues when discussing unintended consequences is to determine the intent behind an action.[49] Olga Burlyuk argues that the 'EU's own stated objectives for a particular external action or policy [...], derived from EU formal documents, constitute a ready-to-be-examined proxy for EU intent'. Moreover, she adds that the analysis of these documents should be complemented, for example, by the analysis of EU working documents, interviews and taking into account the broader context.[50] In this book we follow the same methodology. Starting from the content of the Joint

44 Hussein Kassim and Patrick Le Galès, 'Exploring Governance in a Multi-Level Polity: A Policy Instruments Approach' (2010) 33(1) *West Eur Politics* 1, 7–8.

45 Ibid 13.

46 Sarah Wolff, 'The Politics of Negotiating EU Readmission Agreements. Insights from Morocco and Turkey' (2014) 16 *EJML* 69, 94.

47 Olga Burlyuk, 'The "Oops!" of EU Engagement Abroad: Analyzing Unintended Consequences of EU External Action' (2017) *JCMS* 1.

48 European Commission, 'Dialogue for Migration, Mobility and Security with the Southern Mediterranean Countries' COM(2011) 292 final, Brussels, 24 May 2011, 1, 11.

49 Robert Merton, 'The unanticipated consequences of purposive social action' (1936) 1 (6) *Am Sociol Rev* 894, 896; Benjamin Buckland, 'Neither Seen not Heard: The Unintended Consequences of Counter-Trafficking and Counter-Smuggling' in Christopher Daase and Cornelius Friesendort (eds) *Rethinking Security Governance: The Problem of Unintended Consequences* (London: Routledge, 2010) 137, 138.

50 Olga Burlyuk (n47) 5.

Declarations on a Mobility Partnership, we attempt to understand the actual intend of the EU and Member States by analysing EU policy documents and contextualising the negotiation and implementation of the Mobility Partnerships.

It should also be pointed out that usually there are multiple intentions behind one action.[51] With Mobility Partnerships this was clearly the case, as the list of projects in Annex to the Mobility Partnerships materialises not only the EU's interests but also the interests of each participating EU Member States and sometimes the interests of third countries. The vast majority of projects proposed in the frame of a Mobility Partnership are bilateral initiatives between one EU Member State and the third country.[52] Another important point to note is that unintended consequences are not automatically adverse. Several authors, on the contrary, argue that unintended consequences can have unexpected positive benefits[53] or that they can also just lead to unexpected consequences that are distinct to the original purpose of the action.[54]

Merton also adds that unintended consequences can differ depending on who the impact is on (for example, the targets of the action or third parties).[55] In this book I am particularly focusing on the consequences of Mobility Partnerships for two groups: the third country that concluded a Mobility Partnership and its nationals and immigrants staying in these countries. Only the first group is a direct target of Mobility Partnerships. All consequences on immigrants staying in these third countries are unintended as no mention is made in the content of the Joint Declarations particularly in regard to the rights of immigrants in the third country. Additionally, Olga Burlyuk underlines that when analysing unintended consequences, scholars should also take into account unintended consequences that are not associated only to the EU.[56] This plays a key role in my analysis, mainly in the case of Morocco, as we will see that the legal and policy changes happening there, supported through the Mobility Partnership, are not primarily the result of the intent of the EU but rather of the intent of the third country itself.

Factors influencing the relevance of Mobility Partnerships

Brocza and Paulhart argue that it is impossible to solely link developments in the third country to the implementation of the Mobility Partnership and that 'surrounding factors' can influence these developments.[57] Several factors have been

51 Patrick Baert, 'Unintended Consequences: A Typology and Examples' (1991) 6(2) *Int Sociol* 201, 202.
52 See the annexes to the different Mobility Partnerships.
53 Patrich Baert (n51) 204; Florian Kohstall, 'Strengthening Autocracy: The World Bank and Social Reform in Egypt' in Christopher Daase and Cornelius Friesendorf (eds) *Rethinking Security Governance: The Problem of Unintended Consequences* (London: Routledge, 2010) 21.
54 Olga Burlyuk (n47) 6.
55 Robert Merton (n49) 895.
56 Olga Burlyuk (n47) 6.
57 Stefan Brocza and Katharina Paulhart (n38) 4.

observed in the literature which can potentially condition the way Mobility Partnerships are relevant and the extent to which legal and policy developments are influenced by the EU and Member States.[58] In this book the focus will be put on the three factors I considered as being the most influential.

The first factor is the State of relations between third countries and EU Member States. Several EU Member States are former colonial empires, which keep privileged relations with their former colonies, through cultural, political and economic cooperation. The enduring relevance of postcolonial ties has been questioned in the literature. Vezzoli argues that time can affect the relevance of postcolonial ties.[59] Geographical location also explains a strong interest of Southern European countries for Northern Africa and the Mediterranean region.[60] Finally, postcolonial ties have strongly influenced the political system of their former colonies.[61] This means that not only can postcolonial ties influence the level of administrative capacity of a third country but also influence policies that are being developed and implemented in these countries. The second factor is the power of negotiation. It may be said that there are two opposite scenarios for the position of third countries vis-à-vis the EU: either the third country has a high geopolitical importance for the EU's migration policy, which gives it a strong negotiating position, or it has low geopolitical importance placing it in a weak negotiating position.[62] Such a situation where the third country takes over the bargaining initiative and demands financial and political support in return for cooperation with the EU can be seen as 'reversed conditionality'.[63] In this configuration, the third country can also influence the content of the Mobility Partnership. The use of 'reversed conditionality' thus can lead to more dynamic

58 See, for example, Daniel Wunderlich, 'The Limits of External Governance: Implementing EU External Migration Policy' (2012) 19(9) *JEPP* 1414; Natasja Reslow, 'EU "Mobility" Partnerships: An Initial Assessment of Implementation Dynamics' (2015) 3(2) *Politics and Governance* 117; Meng-Hsuan Chou, 'European Union Migration Strategy Towards West Africa: The Origin and Outlook of "Mobility Partnerships" with Cape Verde and Senegal' (2009) EUSA Working Paper 1; Jean-Pierre Cassarino, 'A Reappraisal of the EU's Expending Readmission System' (2014) 49(4) *The International Spectator* 130.

59 Simona Vezzoli, 'The role of the State in international migration: Exploring the transition from colony to independence' (2014) IMI Working Papers Series (102) 1, 13.

60 James Hampshire, 'Speaking With One Voice? The European Union's Global Approach to Migration and Mobility and the Limits of International Migration Cooperation' (2016) 42(4) *J Ethn Migr Stud* 571, 576; Jean-Pierre Cassarino, 'Dealing with Unbalanced Reciprocities: Cooperation on Readmission and Implications' 1 in Jean-Pierre Cassarino, (ed.), *Unbalanced Reciprocities: Cooperation on Readmission in the Euro-Mediterranean Area* (Washington, DC: Middle East Institute 2010) 14.

61 Joy Asongazoh Alemazung, 'Post-Colonial Colonialism: An Analysis of International Factors and Actors Marring African Socio-Economic and Political Development' (2010) 3(10) *JPAS* 62; Rollin F. Tusalem, 'The Colonial Foundations of State Fragility and Failure' (2016) 48(8) *Polity* 445.

62 Frank R. Pfetsch, 'Power in International Negotiations: Symmetry and Asymmetry' (2011/2) *Négociations* 16, 39.

63 Jean-Pierre Cassarino, 'Informalising Readmission Agreements in the EU Neighbourhood' (2007) *The International Spectator* 42(2) 179, 192; Fanny Tittel-Mosser (n43).

relations between the EU and a third country than what is often pictured. On the other hand, if a third country has low migration fluxes towards the EU or is not located on a major migration route, it will have low geopolitical importance for the EU. This third country will therefore have a low level of negotiation power with the EU. If the third country agrees to conclude a Mobility Partnership under these terms, the content of the Mobility Partnership will presumably be mainly influenced by the EU and the Member States. The third factor is the administrative capacity of a third country. There is no commonly accepted definition of administrative capacity and it is often assumed that measuring it is extremely complex,[64] but, for the purposes of this study, it is suffice to say that administrative capacity refers to the capacity of a state to define and implement policies and to legislate and enforce the law. The way these three factors condition the relevance of Mobility Partnerships is twofold: they condition the development and implementation of legally or politically relevant projects and they condition the extent to which the EU and the Member States influence the content of new policies or laws being developed in the framework of the Mobility Partnership.

Methodology

The geographical focus of this book is Africa and the research specifically focuses on the case studies of Morocco and Cape Verde. Mobility Partnerships were concluded with several countries in Africa: Cape Verde (2008), Morocco (2013) and Tunisia (2014). To be able to examine the influence of postcolonial ties, it was important in the case selection to choose third countries that were former colonies. Out of the third countries which concluded a Mobility Partnership, Cape Verde, Morocco and Tunisia have postcolonial ties with an EU Member State. Cape Verde is a former Portuguese colony while Morocco and Tunisia were both French Protectorates. Both France and Portugal are participants in the Mobility Partnerships with these three countries. As such, Cape Verde was chosen as it is the only third country that concluded a Mobility Partnership and has postcolonial ties with Portugal. As Moroccans represent a larger group of migrants in France and Portugal than Tunisians, the second case study chosen was Morocco. The existence of a Moroccan and Cape Verdean diaspora population in France and Portugal would allow us to study the mobility possibilities from the third country to Europe. Moreover, Morocco concluded its Mobility Partnership in 2013 whereas Tunisia only concluded it in 2014, leaving less time for the implementation process, which can be an issue in the evaluation of the implementation stage of projects. Additionally, these two countries are interesting case studies to observe the two other factors that may influence the relevance of Mobility Partnerships: the power of negotiation and administrative capacity of a third country. According

64 Helen J. Addison, 'Is Administrative Capacity a Useful Concept? Review of the Application, Meaning and Observation of Administrative Capacity in Political Science Literature' (2009) LSE Research Paper 1, 4.

to an official from the EU Delegation in Cape Verde, the reasons why Cape Verde was chosen as a pilot Mobility Partnership are its small size, its geographic location, its small population, the fact that it is not a big threat for migration flows and that it is culturally close to the EU because of its historical ties with Portugal. Oppositely, the EU has considered Morocco as a 'gate-keeper' for over a decade in the externalisation of its migration control to neighbouring third countries.[65] This gives the two countries a different geopolitical importance for the EU, conferring them, more or less, power of negotiation. Moreover, Miller argues that developing countries are usually lacking administrative capacity.[66] Following Miller's argumentation, as both Morocco and Cape Verde are developing countries, I argue that they are lacking administrative capacity, though to different degrees.[67]

While the literature on Mobility Partnerships is fairly extensive,[68] few studies cover their implementation. Daniel Wunderlich, for example, discusses the coherence in the implementation of EU External Migration Policy but only takes Mobility Partnerships as examples among other instruments.[69] Natasja Reslow conducted an analysis of the implementation of the Mobility Partnership in Cape Verde at the starting phase of the implementation.[70] She also analysed the implementation of Mobility Partnerships but focused on the process used to assess the success or failure of the implementation itself.[71] To date, no comprehensive overview of the implementation of the Mobility Partnership with Morocco exists and this book aims at filling this gap by providing a detailed empirical analysis of its implementation. Giving an overview of the implementation of Mobility Partnerships not only allows

65 Lavenex (n7) 94.

66 Jonathan Miller, 'A Typology of Legal Transplants: Using Sociology, Legal History and Argentine Examples to Explain the Transplants Process' (2003) 51(4) *Am J Comp L* 839, 857.

67 Ibid.

68 See, for example: Sergio Carrera and Raül Hernández I Sagrera (n5) 28; Sergio Carrera and Raül Hernández I Sagrera (n36) 97; Stefan Brocza and Katharina Paulhart (n38); Panos Koutrakos (n39) 164–165; Bart Van Vooren (n39) 209–210; Jean-Pierre Cassarino, 'EU Mobility Partnerships: Expression of a New Compromise' (2009) Migration Policy Institute; Natasja Reslow, 'Migration and Development? An Assessment of Recent EU Initiatives' (2010) 6(1) *JCER* 3; Natasja Reslow, 'Deciding on EU External Migration Policy: The Member States and the Mobility Partnerships' (2012) 34(3) *JEI* 223; Natasja Reslow, 'The Role of Third Countries in EU Migration Policy: The Mobility Partnerships' (2012) 14 *EJML* 393; Meng-Hsuan Chou and Marie Gibert, 'The EU-Senegal Mobility Partnership: From Launch to Suspension and Negotiation Failure' (2012) 8(4) *JCER* 408; Steffen Angenendt, 'EU Mobility Partnerships: the "most innovative and sophisticated tool" of European migration policy?' (2014) migration strategy group policy brief; Julia Maisenbacher, 'The Political Economy of Mobility Partnerships – Structural Power in the EU's External Migration Policy' (2015) 20(6) *NPE* 871.

69 Daniel Wunderlich, 'Towards Coherence of EU External Migration Policy? Implementing a Complex Policy' (2013) *Int Migr* 51, 26.

70 Natasja Reslow, *Partnering for Mobility? Three-level Games in EU External Migration Policy* (Maastricht, The Netherlands: Datawyse/Universitaire Pers Maastricht 2013).

71 Natasja Reslow (n58); Natasja Reslow, '"Not everything that counts can be counted": Assessing "Success" of EU External Migration Policy' (2017) *Int Migr* 1.

us to answer the question of what Mobility Partnerships deliver, but, it also allows us to potentially link the projects' implementation to legal and policy developments in the third country, in the case where Mobility Partnerships are legally and policy relevant. Finally, the present book aims to contribute to the development of a methodology for the empirical analysis of the implementation of Mobility Partnerships that might be replicated in other third countries which are (current or future) parties to Mobility Partnerships with the EU.

There has been little empirical research into the possible relevance of soft law instruments for third countries and even less on the relevance of Mobility Partnerships for external legal and policy developments. The questioning about the type of instrument that Mobility Partnerships really are is particularly novel as it has largely been neglected in the literature and can have particularly important consequences. Another novelty of this book is the discussion about the relevance of Mobility Partnerships for the legal and policy framework of a third country. There have been few empirical investigations into 'external effects' of soft law instruments and even fewer on the relevance of Mobility Partnerships on external legal and policy developments. The relation between administrative capacity and Mobility Partnerships, the relation between the Member States and third countries and the negotiation of Mobility Partnerships or the relation between conditionality, 'reversed conditionality' and Mobility Partnerships have already been studied.[72] But what is novel in the approach of this book is that these criteria are looked at in relation to the relevance of Mobility Partnerships and the potential intertwining of the three criteria.

Whilst some studies have been carried out on Mobility Partnerships, there is still insufficient scientific understanding of the consequences of their implementation. First, it is striking that the last evaluation of Mobility Partnerships conducted by the EU dates back to 2009.[73] In this evaluation the European Commission concluded that Mobility Partnerships are a 'promising, innovative and comprehensive tool' and 'the most innovative and sophisticated tool' of the GAM.[74] This description shows the importance that the Commission gave to Mobility Partnerships. In the Commission's view, it should have been extended and applied to two or three more countries. Subsequently, seven more Mobility Partnerships have been concluded. Today, nine Mobility Partnerships have been signed but with the exception of Moldova in 2012,[75] no other third country participated in an official

72 See, for example, on administrative capacity and Mobility Partnerships: Natasja Reslow and Maarten Vink, 'Three-Level Games in EU External Migration Policy: Negotiating Mobility Partnerships in West Africa' (2014) 53(4) *JCMS* 857; on the relation between Member States and third countries and the negotiation of Mobility Partnerships: Meng-Hsuan Chou and Marie Gibert (n68); on conditionality, reversed conditionality and Mobility Partnerships: Jean-Pierre Cassarino (n68).

73 Commission of the European Communities (n20) 4.

74 Ibid.

75 In Moldova, an evaluation was conducted by an expert contracted by the IOM Mission to Moldova. The evaluation was jointly agreed on by the Moldovan government, EU and Member States officials at the High-Level Mobility Partnership Meeting in 2011. The evaluation report can be found here: http://www.mfa.gov.md/img/docs/eu-moldova-mobility-partnership-evaluation.pdf (accessed 29 January 2018).

evaluation by the EU, nor an independent assessment of the implementation of its Mobility Partnership since 2009. The 2009 evaluation focused on the conclusion process and the content of Mobility Partnerships, rather than on their actual implementation. However, now that the oldest Partnerships have been in place for over ten years, it is time to conduct an analysis of the implementation of Mobility Partnerships and to discuss their relevance for third countries. This evaluation is crucial to learn 'what' Mobility Partnerships are concretely delivering so far and whether they keep their promises in terms of 'mobility'. To gain an in-depth understanding of the implementation of Mobility Partnerships, it is essential to look at the specific content of the projects being implemented. This book does not only contribute to filling the knowledge gap on the implementation dynamics and relevance of the Mobility Partnerships but can also benefit the negotiations and implementation of more novel instruments such as the MPF and EU Compacts by drawing best practices and providing a better understanding of the geopolitical context and the interplay between different interests.

To address the questions raised in this book, a legal analysis of the developments on the legal framework in both countries has been conducted in parallel with the empirical analysis of the projects being proposed and implemented in the framework of the Mobility Partnership. It is the connection between the legal analysis, the empirical analysis and the data obtained during the extensive fieldwork conducted in Cape Verde, Morocco, Belgium, Portugal and France (70 interviews) that allowed us to provide a comprehensive overview of the implementation of Mobility Partnerships, their relevance for third countries and the role and interests of the different actors involved in the negotiation and implementation of Mobility Partnerships. The interviews were conducted with EU officials and policy makers belonging to the EU, Member States and third countries, the staff of implementing organisations, as well as migrants' representatives in Cape Verde, Morocco, Portugal and France. Interviewing migrants' representatives helped to have insights into the way potential legal and policy changes are perceived by the target population. Furthermore, this book aims to provide an overview of the evolution of the legal framework and policies in Cape Verde and Morocco and link these developments to concrete Mobility Partnership projects to discuss the existing connections between them and clarify the relevance of Mobility Partnerships in these developments.

Chapter 1 highlights the importance of understanding the legal nature of Mobility Partnerships. It provides an important opportunity to advance the understanding of the Mobility Partnership instrument itself, its functioning and its potential relevance. In the last subsection, the different criteria that can influence the relevance of Mobility Partnerships, are discussed. The aim of Chapter 2 is to better understand the Mobility Partnership tool via the cases of Morocco and Cape Verde from their conclusion to their implementation. This chapter discusses the context of the adoption of the Mobility Partnerships with Cape Verde and Morocco and the content of both Mobility Partnerships. It also provides an overview of the implementation of both Mobility Partnerships. The aim of Chapter 3 is to analyse the legal and policy developments that occurred in Morocco and Cape Verde since the conclusion of their respective Mobility Partnership. A set of legal provisions in relation to migration, including the access to socio-economic and political rights for migrants is reviewed. The analysis considers distinct phases of the migration process: emigration, staying in a foreign country and returning home. This analysis also helps us to have a better understanding of immigrants' access to rights in the third country and whether these rights were affected, positively or negatively, by the implementation of a Mobility Partnership. Chapter 4 puts in context the analysis of the implementation of the Mobility Partnerships in Morocco and Cape Verde and the comparative analysis of the legal and policy developments in both countries by giving first-hand insight to the complexity and interaction of several factors and actors. Finally, Chapter 5 gives us an overview of the current position of Mobility Partnerships and where they fit in the plethora of new instruments implemented since the 'migrants' crisis' of 2015. In this last chapter, I also present a new instrument, pilot projects, that could be the next type of Mobility Partnerships.

1 Mobility Partnerships in the context of EU External Migration Governance

Mobility Partnerships are presented as non-binding instruments, soft law instruments or as having a soft legal nature.[1] But few studies have examined what that exactly means in concrete terms. Beyond the shared understanding of Mobility Partnerships as being a soft law instrument, a notion which is often simply taken for granted, few authors have questioned what Mobility Partnerships actually are (what type of instrument they are) and what consequences they can have. This chapter highlights the importance of understanding the legal nature of Mobility Partnerships. It will help to better understand the instrument itself, its functioning and its potential relevance.

1.1 Origin, rationale and expectations surrounding Mobility Partnerships

The Commission introduced the 'Mobility Package'[2] tool aiming at facilitating the management of EU's migration policy with third countries based on the Franco-German initiative for a 'New European Migration Policy'.[3] Nicolas Sarkozy and Wolfgang Schäuble presented this initiative during the G6 in July 2006. They proposed to use circular migration to decrease irregular migration towards the EU.[4] The Franco-German initiative foresaw the conclusion of partnerships

1 Sergio Carrera and Raül Hernández I Sagrera, 'The externalisation of the EU's labour immigration policy: Towards mobility or insecurity partnerships?' (2009) CEPS Working Document 321 1, 28; Sergio Carrera and Raül Hernández I Sagrera, 'Mobility Partnerships: "Insecurity Partnerships" for Policy Coherence and Migrant Workers Human Rights in the EU', 97 in Rahel Kunz, Sandra Lavenex and Marion Panizzon (eds), *Multilayered Migration Governance: The Promise of Partnership* (London, New York: Routledge 2011) 97; Panos Koutrakos, *European Foreign Policy. Legal and Political Perspectives* (Cheltenham, UK. Edward Elgar 2011) 164–165; Bart Van Vooren, *EU External Relations Law and the European Neighbourhood Policy: A Paradigm for Coherence* (London, New York: Routledge 2012) 209–210.

2 Jean-Pierre Cassarino, 'EU Mobility Partnerships: Expression of a New Compromise' (2009) Migration Policy Institute.

3 Nicolas Sarkozy and Wolfgang Schäuble, 'New European Migration Policy, a Franco-German plan presented by Nicolas Sarkozy and Wolfgang Schäuble to G6 immigration ministers meeting in the UK', 26 October 2006, 1.

4 Ibid 4.

between Member States and a third country leading to a 'European partnership' composed of the sum of all the bilateral partnerships.[5] Steffen Angenendt as well as Sergio Carrera and Räul Hernández I Sagrera consider that the Franco-German initiative for a 'New European Migration Policy' provided a solid basis to the development of Mobility Partnerships.[6] When the Commission first proposed Mobility Partnerships (still called 'Mobility Packages' at the time) it already recommended that they should

> provide the overall framework for managing such movements[7] and would bring together the opportunities offered by the Member States and the European Community, while fully respecting the division of competences as provided by the Treaty.[8]

Legal migration was already a central element of 'Mobility Packages'. Franco Frattini is said to have been the one who mentioned 'Mobility Partnerships' for the first time, instead of 'Mobility Packages', during the Africa-EU Summit in Tripoli.[9] Subsequently, in the 2006 evaluation of the GAM, the Commission declared that 'Mobility Packages' should be a central goal when discussing legal migration issues.[10] The European Council in 2006 invited the Commission to incorporate legal migration 'into the Union's external policies in order to develop a balanced partnership with third countries' and 'to present detailed proposals on how to better organise and inform about the various forms of legal movement between the EU and third countries by June 2007'.[11] According to the Commission, thanks to Mobility Partnerships and circular migration schemes, the EU could solve the problem of labour market shortages by allowing the entry into the labour market of legal labour migrants proportionally to their needs.[12] This explains why legal migration was presented as one of the main goals of Mobility Partnerships.

5 Sergio Carrera and Räul Hernández I Sagrera (2009) (n1) 12.
6 Steffen Angenendt, 'Circular Migration: A Sustainable Concept for Migration Policy?' (2007) Stiftung Wissenschaft und Politik (SWP) Comments 11 Berlin; Sergio Carrera and Räul Hernández I Sagrera (2009) (n2).
7 "Such movements" referring to legal migration.
8 Commission of the European Communities, 'The Global Approach to Migration One Year On: Towards a Comprehensive European Migration Policy' COM(2006) 735 final, Brussels, 30 November 2006, 1, 7.
9 Franco Frattini, 'Migration and Development: Time for creative and courageous approaches, Speech to the EU-Africa Ministerial Conference on Migration and Development', Tripoli, 22 November 2006.
10 Commission of the European Communities (n8) 7.
11 Council of the European Union, 'Brussels European Council 14–15 December 2006 – Presidency conclusions 16879/1/06', Brussels, 12 February 2007, 1, 9.
12 Anna Triandafyllidou, 'Circular migration: Introductory remarks', 1 in Anna Triandafyllidou, *Circular Migration Between Europe and Its Neighbourhood: Choice or Necessity?* (Oxford: Oxford University Press 2013) 7.

Legal migration is a highly sensitive issue as it touches upon Member States' sovereignty, which explains why the Member States never sought to include the issue into the 'common' EU migration policy. By covering legal migration issues, Mobility Partnerships raised the question of competence.[13] The principle of conferred powers is fundamental in EU law as it defines what the competences of the EU are and what competences remain those of the Member States. This principle is formulated in Articles 4 and 5 of the Treaty on European Union.[14] It is clear that the EU should only act within the framework of its competences, as stipulated in Article 5. Article 5 rules that

> in areas which do not fall within its exclusive competence, the Union shall act only if and in so far as the objectives of the proposed action cannot be sufficiently achieved by the Member States, either at central level or at regional and local level, but can rather, by reason of the scale or effects of the proposed action, be better achieved at Union level.

Both Articles 4 and 5 establish that 'competences not conferred upon the Union in the Treaties remain with the Member States'. It is therefore important to distinguish between EU competences, shared competences and competences of the Member States. The principle of conferred powers guarantees that new legislation is adopted by the competent authority in conformity with the division of powers.[15] If a competence has not been transferred to the EU, the national authorities must adopt the legal provisions. If it is a shared competence, it is the Council and the authorities of the Member States that have to agree on the legal provisions and if it is an EU competence, the Council and the European Parliament can adopt the act autonomously. In practice, there are many areas of shared competences between the EU and the Member States. Article 5 adds that 'the use of Union competences is governed by the principles of subsidiarity and proportionality', which means that the actions taken have to be suitable to achieve a given goal but 'should not exceed what is necessary'. Several authors have stressed the importance of the notion of proportionality.[16] Article 1 of the Protocol on the application of the subsidiarity and proportionality principles confirms that 'each institution shall ensure constant respect for the principles of subsidiarity and proportionality'.[17]

13 Commission of the European Communities (n8) 7; Commission of the European Communities (n51) 2.
14 European Union, Treaty on European Union (Consolidated version), Treaty of Maastricht, 7 February 1992, *Official Journal of the European Communities* C325/5.
15 Linda Senden, *Soft Law in European Community Law Modern Studies in European Law* (Portland, OR: Bloomsbury 2004) 78.
16 Gráinne de Búrca, 'The Principle of Proportionality and its Application in EC Law' 105 in Ami Barav and Derrick Arthur Wyatt (eds), *YBEL* 13 (Oxford: Oxford University Press 1993) 117; Jan Jans, 'Proportionality Revisited' (2000) 27(3) *Legal Issues of Economic Integration* 239, 240.
17 Protocol (No 2) on the application of the principles of subsidiarity and proportionality, annexed to the Treaty on European Union and the Treaty on the Functioning of the European Union by the Treaty of Lisbon of 13 December 2007.

As noted by Piet Van Nuffel, the principle of subsidiarity has been at the centre of debates on the defence of Member States' competences in decision-making at the national level against the 'ever-expanding action' of the EU.[18] The application of the principle of subsidiarity raises several important questions, such as that of knowing when a Member State cannot sufficiently achieve the objectives of an action proposed by the EU, and when is the EU better able to reach these objectives than the Member States. It should be noted that, in order to evaluate the ability of Member States to reach the objective on their own, it is not the political will that is evaluated but the actual resources and capacity of Member States to reach the objective.[19] Moreover, determining that the EU is better able to reach the objective than the Member States means that the EU has to prove its added value over Member States' actions.[20] Several authors argue that, if the results obtained by the EU are merely equal to (not better than) those achieved by the Member States, there is not enough reason for the EU to act.[21] However, only few cases involving issues of subsidiarity have been presented to the European Court of Justice (ECJ) and the ECJ has consistently supported EU's action.[22] Some authors claim that the judicial activism of the ECJ was pivotal in the enlargement of EU competences, namely in fundamental rights matters.[23]

The first case presented to the ECJ where the principle of subsidiarity was raised was the *SPO* Case,[24] in 1995. The *SPO* Case concerned the validity of a decision applying competition rules. The SPO argued that the Commission was not competent to decide in the field of competition and therefore it was against the principle of subsidiarity. The ECJ refused to recognise the principle of subsidiarity in that case because it 'did not, before the entry into force of the Treaty on European Union, constitute a general principle of law by reference to which the legality of Community acts should be reviewed'.[25] Therefore, the principle of subsidiarity could not be used in court before the entry into force of the Maastricht Treaty. In the *Working Time Directive* Case,[26] where the United Kingdom requested the ECJ to annul a directive limiting working time throughout Europe,

18 Piet Van Nuffel, 'The Protection of Member States' Regions Through the Subsidiarity Principle' 55 in Carlo Panara and Alexander De Becker (eds), *The Role of the Regions in EU Governance* (Heidelberg, Germany: Springer Science and Business Media 2010) 55.
19 Ibid 59.
20 Ibid 60; Aurélien Portuese, 'The Case for a Principled Approach to Law and Economics: Efficiency Analysis and General Principles of EU Law' 275 in Klaus Mathis (ed.), *Law and Economics in Europe: Foundations and Applications* (Dordrecht, The Netherlands: Springer Science and Business Media 2013) 290.
21 Trevor C Hartley, *The Foundations of European Union Law* (Oxford: Oxford University Press 2010) 122; Aurélien Portuese (n339) 290.
22 Carlo Panara, *The Sub-National Dimension of the EU: A Legal Study of Multilevel Governance* (Heidelberg, Germany: Springer 2015) 82.
23 Jessica Guth, 'Transforming the European Legal Order: The European Court of Justice at 60+' (2016) 12(1) *JCER* 455; Sionaidh Douglas-Scott, 'A Tale of Two Courts: Luxembourg, Strasbourg and the Growing European Human Rights Acquis' (2006) *Common Mark Law Rev* 629.
24 Case T-29/92 (1995) *SPO and others v Commission*, II-289.
25 Ibid II-293 para 12.
26 Case C-84/94 (1996) *United Kingdom v Council*, I-5793.

the Court argued that it was not in a position to evaluate the benefits of the directive.[27] In the *Germany v European Parliament and Council* Case,[28] Germany argued that a Directive on credit institution was not valid because it did not explicitly state in its text why the Council was competent to vote this Directive and therefore was in breach of the principle of subsidiarity. The ECJ decided that the Directive was not adopted in breach of the principle of subsidiarity and that even though the text of the Directive did not specifically state why the Council was competent rather than Member States it was clear that action at the EU level could best achieve its objectives.[29]

In the more recent *Vodafone Ltd and others v Secretary of State for Business Enterprise and Regulatory Reform* Case,[30] the Court took a stance. It would favour EU legislation over national legislation as it would effectively lead to harmonisation and the strengthening of the common market.[31] This Case was about Regulation No 717/2007 adopted by the UK and Northern Ireland relating to the prices payable by users of public mobile telephone networks for retail roaming services. The Regulation declares a maximum limit for the rooming costs. The regulation also imposes a ceiling for roaming costs paid by the consumer's network to the foreign network which that consumer uses. According to the Court, the fixation of a maximum limit for roaming costs would protect consumers against excessive costs.[32] Moreover, a common approach at the EU level was necessary to avoid the distortion in the EU market as operators would act within a comprehensible regulatory framework.[33]

The principle of subsidiarity had already been examined in relation to the Open Method of Coordination (OMC), some viewing it as non-democratic because of the exclusion of the European Parliament from the process.[34] In a 2007 resolution,[35] the European Parliament expressed its concerns about soft law as leading to abuses of power by the executive[36] and being non-democratic.[37] Understandably, the European Parliament has usually been against the use of soft law,[38] arguing that it is being used to circumvent the decision-making process. The text of the motion stressed that the concept of soft law was not clearly and commonly

27 Ibid I-5802 para 23.
28 C-233/94 (1997) *Germany v European Parliament and Council*, I-2441.
29 Ibid I-2953 para 28.
30 Case C-58/08 (2010) *Vodafone Ltd and others v Secretary of State for Business Enterprise and Regulatory Reform*, I-4999.
31 Ibid para 38 and 48.
32 Ibid para 38.
33 Ibid para 47.
34 Fabien Terpan, 'Soft Law in the European Union – The Changing Nature of EU Law' (2015) 21 *ELJ* 68, 82.
35 Resolution of the European Parliament, *Non-legislative Resolution on Institutional and Legal Implication of the use of "Soft Law" Instruments*, 2007/2028 (INI) (2007).
36 Ibid, para 17.
37 Ibid, preamble para I, X.
38 Oana Andrea Stefan, 'European Soft law: New Developments Concerning the Divide between Legally Binding Force and Legal effects' (2012) 75(5) *Mod Law Rev* 879, 888.

defined and that therefore it 'should not be used in any documents of the Community institutions'.[39] This coincided with the Commission's push for the use of soft law instruments, such as Mobility Partnerships, to deal with sensitive issues in the area of migration. The Opinion of the Committee on Culture and Education reiterated this stance.[40]

Mobility Partnerships were introduced in 2007 by the EU Commission with the aim to 'give operational substance to the EU's Global Approach to Migration'.[41] The Commission's Communication on 'Circular Migration and Mobility Partnerships between the European Union and Third Countries' recognised Mobility Partnerships as 'novel approaches to improve the management of legal movements of people between the EU and third countries'.[42] Mobility Partnerships would be negotiated with 'third countries that have committed themselves to cooperating actively with the EU on management of migration flows, including by fighting against illegal migration, and that are interested in securing better access to EU territory for their citizens'.[43] Accordingly, the Commission lists a set of commitments that third countries are expected to be willing to fulfil when agreeing to participate in a Mobility Partnership. This list includes the commitment to conclude a Readmission Agreement including nationals of other third countries and the fight against irregular migration and human trafficking.[44] A list of commitments that the EU has to observe is also included in the communication and covers the creation of legal migration channels, financial and technical assistance, circular migration schemes and the conclusion of visa facilitation agreements.[45] In practice, Mobility Partnerships would give perspectives of mobility and legal migration to third countries, including circular migration, in exchange for their cooperation in the fight against irregular immigration, the intensification of border management and their consent to start negotiations on Readmission Agreements.[46]

According to the Commission, the content of the Mobility partnerships will vary from country to country according to their specific context as well as EU Member States' interests. The Council in its conclusions on extending and enhancing the GAM describes the topics that can be covered by Mobility Partnerships, namely:

> the offer of legal migration opportunities, adapted in particular to the specific Member States' labour market needs, while fully respecting the competences

39 Ibid A of the Motion for a European Parliament Resolution.
40 Ibid B of the Committee on Culture and Education.
41 Commission of the European Communities, 'Circular Migration and Mobility Partnerships between the European Union and Third Countries' COM(2007) 248 final, Brussels, 15 May 2007, 1, 2.
42 Ibid 2.
43 Ibid 3.
44 Ibid 4.
45 Ibid 5–8.
46 Ibid; Council of the European Union, Brussels European Council 14 December 2007: Presidency Conclusions 16616/1/07 REV 1, Brussels, 14 February 2008.

> of the Member States and the principle of Community preference on the one hand, and a genuine cooperation on preventing and combating illegal immigration, trafficking in and smuggling of human beings as well as effective readmission and return policy while respecting the protection of human rights, on the other hand.[47]

The context of the adoption of the first Mobility Partnerships was highly influenced by economic considerations. The EU wanted to use this new tool in order to support the market needs for cheap and flexible workers and to enhance the single market's competitiveness.[48] Circular migration was at the heart of the discussions when Mobility Partnerships were developed, and they were considered the ideal tool to support legal migration opportunities for third country workers.[49]

Since 2008, nine Mobility Partnerships have been concluded with the following countries: Cape Verde and Moldova in 2008, Georgia in 2009, Armenia in 2011, Morocco and Azerbaijan in 2013, Tunisia and Jordan in 2014 and Belarus in 2016. Mobility Partnerships have been proposed to Senegal, Egypt and Ghana but have either been rejected or negotiations have stalled.[50] Mobility Partnerships are concluded between the EU, interested Member States and a third country. This means that all member States do not have to be party of a Mobility Partnership. The number of Member States participating in a Mobility Partnership can vary, since no Member State is obliged to participate. Cape Verde is the Mobility Partnership with the lowest number of Member States participating (only five). In general, it can be said that Mobility Partnerships concluded with countries of the Eastern Partnership have more Member States participating than Mobility Partnerships with countries of the Southern Mediterranean. In the Mobility Partnership with Azerbaijan, 8 countries participated, 10 with Armenia, 15 with Moldova, 16 with Georgia and only 7 for the new Mobility Partnership with Belarus. In the South, 9 Member States concluded the Mobility Partnership with Morocco, 10 for Tunisia and 12 for Jordan.

47 Council of the European Union, Council Conclusions on Extending and Enhancing the Global Approach to Migration (2007), Luxembourg, 17–18 June 2007, 3 para 10.

48 Julia Maisenbacher, 'Political Economy of Mobility Partnerships: Structural Power in the EU's External Migration Policy' (2015) 20(6) *New Political Economy* 871.

49 Anna Triandafyllidou (n12) 7; Meng-Hsuan Chou and Marie Gibert, 'The EU-Senegal Mobility Partnership: From Launch to Suspension and Negotiation Failure' (2012) 8(4) *JCER* 408, 409.

50 On the proposition of a Mobility Partnership to Senegal and Ghana see: Meng-Hsuan Chou and Marie Gibert, (n49); Tine Van Criekinge, 'The EU-Africa migration partnership: A case study of the EU's migration dialogue with Ghana and Senegal' (2010) EUI Migration Working Group, European University Institute, Florence, Italy; Natasja Reslow and Maarten Vink, 'Three-level Games in EU External Migration Policy: Negotiating Mobility Partnerships in West Africa' (2015) 53(4) *JCMS* 857. On the proposition of a Mobility Partnership to Egypt see: Peter Seeberg, 'Mobility Partnerships and the EU, Part I: Where are we regarding implementation and what will be the consequences?' (2014) Center for Contemporary Middle East Studies.

Since the launch of the Mobility Partnerships, the EU Commission has been enthusiastic about the use of this migration management tool and describes it as 'the most innovative and sophisticated tool' of the GAM.[51] In the early evaluation of the two pilot Mobility Partnerships (with Cape Verde and Moldova), the Commission declared that the tool is 'promising, innovative and comprehensive' which 'merit being further developed, improved and replicated' and that it

> may represent a valuable framework for increasing transparency, enhancing synergies, triggering cooperation and ensuring more cost-efficient operations between partners, between the Commission and Member States, and inside them, between various ministries and departments involved.[52]

Additionally, the Stockholm Programme predicts 'continued and expanded use of the Mobility partnership instrument as the main strategic, comprehensive and long-term cooperation framework for migration management with third countries'.[53]

The literature concerning Mobility Partnerships is prolific, many of it being published early, in 2008 and 2009, at the time of the negotiation and conclusion of the pilot Mobility Partnerships. Most of the literature at the time concerns both the content and structure[54] of Mobility Partnerships, the way they have been concluded[55] or their place in the broader context of EU's External policies.[56] Roderick Parkes, for example, links Mobility Partnerships and the European Neighbourhood Policy (ENP).[57] He criticises the soft law nature of Mobility Partnerships considering that there is no guarantee that they will effectively be implemented.[58] According to Parkes, the legal migration opportunities in Mobility Partnerships seem to be limited and there is no real joint ownership of the projects, as they are mostly imposed by the EU and Member States to third countries. He also criticises the fact that not all Member States have to participate to a Mobility Partnership, leading to 'fragmented schemes'.[59] However, not all authors

51 Commission of the European Communities, 'Mobility Partnerships as a Tool of the Global Approach to Migration' SEC (2009) 124 final, Brussels, 18 September 2009, 1, 4.
52 Ibid 8.
53 Council of the European Union, 'The Stockholm Programme: And open and secure Europe serving and protecting the citizens, 17024/09', Brussels, 2 December 2009, 1, 62.
54 Sandra Lavenex and Rachel Stucky, 'Partnering for migration in EU external relations' 116 in Rahel Kunz, Sandra Lavenex and Marion Panizzon (eds), *Multilayered Migration Governance: The Promise of Partnership* (London: Routledge 2011), 127–134.
55 Sergio Carrera and Räul Hernández I Sagrera (2011) (n1) 100.
56 Roderick Parkes, 'EU Mobility Partnerships: A Model of Policy Coordination?' (2009) 11(4) *EJML* 327; Katharina Eisele, *The External Dimension of the EU's Migration Policy: Different Legal Positions of Third-Country Nationals in the EU: A Comparative Perspective* (Leiden, The Netherlands: Nijhoff 2014).
57 Roderick Parkes, 'Mobility Partnerships: Valuable addition to the ENP repertoire?' (2009) SWP Working Papers FG 1 2009/03 Berlin: Stiftung Wissenschaft und Politik.
58 Roderick Parkes (n56) 331.
59 Roderick Parkes (n56) 344.

were pessimistic about Mobility Partnerships. For example, Natasha Ward compared Mobility Partnerships and the Economic Partnership Agreement concluded between the EU and the Caribbean Forum countries and she argues that the provisions on legal migration seem to be more promising to third country nationals than the provisions on legal migration included in the Economic Partnership Agreement.[60] Even after the conclusion and implementation of several Mobility Partnerships, Natasha Ward still stayed positive towards Mobility Partnerships concluding that Mobility Partnerships have the capacity to enable mobility.[61] Jean-Pierre Cassarino also sees Mobility Partnerships from a positive angle and considers them as 'a new generation of temporary labour-migration schemes'.[62]

The Commission explicitly underlined the non-binding nature of Mobility Partnerships in the 2009 working document on 'Mobility Partnerships as a tool of the Global Approach to Migration'[63] and the recurring reason offered for favouring this type of instrument is its flexibility. Additionally, Mobility Partnerships are widely presented in the literature as soft law instruments or defined as being of 'soft legal nature' or of 'non-legal nature'.[64] First, non-binding instruments offer a safe way to deal with uncertainty[65] as they are flexible,[66] which means that these instruments can be adapted to changes in policy priorities and circumstances.[67] In the EU context, flexibility is an important feature and becomes increasingly so as the EU grows, and the legislative process becomes more burdensome.[68] When the impact of an agreement is not known, non-binding instruments help to deal with the uncertainty as the States will not have to commit themselves to an obligation that might have negative effects for them in the future.[69] Michael Bothe agrees with this

60 Natasha Ward, 'Comparing EU-Mobility Partnerships and the provisions for temporary movement of labour in the Cariforum-EC Economic Partnership, Paper presented at the conference Swiss migration and EU mobility partnerships: Unveiling the promise' (2008) Bern, 12–13 December as cited in Natasja Reslow, *Partnering for Mobility? Three-level Games in EU External Migration Policy* (Maastricht, The Netherlands: Datawyse/Universitaire Pers Maastricht 2013).

61 Natasha Ward, 'Facilitating the temporary movement of natural persons: Economic partnership agreements versus bilateral migration agreements and Mobility Partnerships' 143 in Rahel Kunz, Sandra Lavenex and Marion Panizzon (eds) *Multilayered Migration Governance: The promise of partnership* (London: Routledge 2011).

62 Jean-Pierre Cassarino (n2).

63 Commission of the European Communities (n51) 4.

64 Sergio Carrera and Räul Hernández I Sagrera (2009) (n1) 28; Sergio Carrera and Raül Hernández I Sagrera (2011) (n1) 97; Panos Koutrakos (n1) 164–165; Bart Van Vooren (n1) 209–210.

65 Pierre-Marie Dupuy, 'Soft Law and the International Law of the Environment' (1991) 12 *Mich J Int'l L* 420, 423.

66 Paula Garcia Andrade, 'The legal Feasibility of the EU's External Action on Legal Migration: The Internal and the External Intertwined' (2013) 15(3) *EJML* 263, 277.

67 Bart Van Vooren (n1) 209.

68 Fabien Terpan (n34) 89.

69 Kenneth Abbott and Duncan Snidal, 'Hard and Soft Law in International Governance' (2000) 54(1) *Int Organ* 421, 423.

line of argumentation and claims that it is only when a State is sure that it can fulfil its obligations that it accepts to be bound by them.[70] Moreover, the 'voluntary nature' of Mobility Partnerships is considered favourable by the Commission as it believes that Mobility Partnerships 'w[ould] be supported by motivated signatories'.[71]

Second, non-binding instruments are perceived to be a 'tool of compromise'.[72] It is easier to negotiate a non-binding agreement than a legally binding one. Favouring non-binding content can allow the different partners to propose more significant measures, which would not be accepted in the case of the negotiation of a binding agreement. Besides, in some cases, a non-binding agreement is the only solution available as no binding agreement would be reached.[73] This can be seen as the advantage of low 'contracting costs'.[74] Abbott adds that it can also lead to 'mutually beneficial cooperation' without favouring only the powerful States.[75] The question of power is also raised as Mobility Partnerships can be perceived as unbalanced and mostly in favour of the EU and the Member States to the detriment of the third country. For example, it is sometimes argued that Mobility Partnerships only represent ways for the EU to strengthen the control on irregular migration and push for readmission agreements while promising legal migration opportunities that are rarely put into practice.[76]

Third, non-binding instruments have the advantage of lowering the sovereignty costs associated with highly sensitive issues by dispensing with the often long and difficult national ratification procedures.[77] Abbott argues that sovereignty costs are high on topics that are directly linked to territory, citizenship or security, which are the intrinsic symbols of sovereignty.[78] Migration and asylum issues are clearly part of these 'high sovereignty costs' topics, which is why non-binding instruments are so common in the EU in these particular fields. Member States would like for the EU to take relevant measures on delicate issues such as migration but do not want to lose or concede sovereignty.[79] For example, Bart Van Vooren argues that the non-binding nature of Mobility Partnerships was seen as a way to overcome the EU's division of competence in migration matters.[80] Mobility Partnerships

70 Michael Bothe, 'Legal and Non-Legal Norms – A Meaningful Distinction in International Relations?' (1980) 11 *NYIL* 65, 91.
71 Commission of the European Communities (n51) 4.
72 Kenneth Abbott and Duncan Snidal (n69) 444.
73 Hartmut Hillgenberg, 'A fresh look at soft law' (1999) 10(3) *EJIL* 499, 501.
74 David M Trubek and others, '"Soft Law", "Hard Law", and European Integration: Toward a Theory of Hybridity' (2005) University of Wisconsin Law School Legal Studies Research Paper Series 1002 1, 11–12.
75 Kenneth Abbott and Duncan Snidal (n69) 423.
76 Sandra Lavenex and Rahel Kunz, 'The migration–development nexus in EU external relations' (2008) 30(3) *J Eur Integr* 439; Sergio Carrera and Räul Hernández I Sagrera (n2); Meng-Hsuan Chou, 'European Union migration strategy towards West Africa: The origin and outlook of "Mobility Partnerships" with Cape Verde and Senegal' (2009) EUSA Working Paper 1.
77 David M Trubek and others (n74) 11–12.
78 Kenneth Abbott and Duncan Snidal (n69) 436–437.
79 Fabien Terpan (n34) 89.
80 Bart Van Vooren (n1) 210.

could include a broader spectrum of actions than a binding agreement could and enhance the coherence of EU external relations on migration, including labour migration.[81]

In the literature, one of the main criticisms directed against the use of non-binding instruments pertains to the power imbalance that these instruments may create. Prosper Weil raises the issue of power in the relationship between States and argues that binding instruments are a shield for weaker States.[82] It is noted that binding instruments, by definition, force all parties to abide by the rules, whereas non-binding instruments favour powerful States that have 'greater control over international outcomes'.[83] Kenneth Abbott and Duncan Snidal, for instance, argue that non-binding instruments tend to reinforce the perspectives and interests of powerful countries.[84]

The question of the 'triple win' claim in relation to migration related policies or tools has been extensively debated in the literature.[85] Triple win includes both parties to an agreement plus the migrants potentially affected by the agreement. According to the Commission, the core of the debate on this issue relates to labour and economic migration.[86] In the EU migration policy, the notion of circular migration has been closely related to the Mobility Partnership tool.[87] A novelty in the EU discourse in 2011 was the idea that Mobility Partnerships would result in a triple win situation.[88] In a Communication on a Dialogue for Migration, Mobility and Security with the Southern Mediterranean countries, the Commission argued that Mobility Partnerships are

81 Ibid.
82 Prosper Weil, 'Towards Relative Normativity in International Law?' (1983) 77 *Am J Int Law* 413, 442.
83 Kenneth Abbott and Duncan Snidal (n69) 448.
84 Ibid 450.
85 Rahel Kunz, Sandra Lavenex and Marion Panizzon, 'Introduction: governance through partnerships' 1 in Rahel Kuntz, Sandra Lavenex and Marion Panizzon (eds), *Multilayered Migration Governance: The Promise for Partnerships* (London: Routledge 2012) 2 and 12; Stephen Castles and Derya Ozkul, 'Circular Migration: Triple Win, or a New Label for Temporary Migration?' 27 in Battistella Grazianno (ed.), *Global Migration Issues Vol. 4: Global and Asian Perspectives on International Migration* (London: Springer 2014) 27; particularly about Mobility Partnerships: Natasha Ward (n61) 147; Martin Geiger and others, 'The Politics of International Migration Management' 1 in Martin Geiger and Antoine Pécoud (eds), *The Politics of International Migration Management* (Basingstoke, UK. Palgrave Macmillan 2010) 1–2 on the notion of "international migration management".
86 Commission of the European Communities, 'Green Paper on an EU Approach to Managing Economic Migration' COM(2004) 811 final, 11 January 2005; Commission of the European Communities, 'Policy Plan on Legal Migration' COM(2005) 669 final, Brussels, 21 December 2005.
87 Commission of the European Communities (n41) 4.
88 European Commission, 'Dialogue for Migration, Mobility and Security with the Southern Mediterranean Countries' COM(2011) 292 final, Brussels, 24 May 2011, 1.

> a crucial tool, beneficial for both sides to ensure better and more effectively managed migration and mobility, *not only of the citizens of partner countries but also for the nationals of other countries*, in particular those of sub-Saharan Africa and of the Middle East, who increasingly reside on or transit through the territory of the Southern Mediterranean countries.[89]

In other words, the Commission suggested that Member States in need of workers, would have access to foreign labour markets thanks to legal labour migration schemes. Migrant workers could be a response to the need of workforce in some EU Member States. Migrant workers would also benefit of new labour mobility opportunities. Additionally, the sending countries, would benefit from these schemes since migrants would contribute to the country's development by sending remittances and making investments in their country of origin from abroad. However, the triple-win approach quickly lost its momentum as circular migration was widely criticised and labour needs in Member States decreased.[90] The literature contests the EU's claim that circular migration is beneficial for sending countries and migrants. For example, Carrera and Hernández I Sagrera were critical of the inclusion of circular migration schemes into Mobility Partnerships rather than long term legal migration schemes.[91] They argue that Mobility Partnerships are 'insecurity partnerships' where third-country nationals are considered as economic units rather than human rights holders.[92] In 2011 Carrera and Hernández I Sagrera published another article in which they further criticised circular migration opportunities provided by the Mobility Partnerships with Moldova, Cape Verde and Georgia.[93] They argued that concretely these Mobility Partnerships gave 'few tangible examples of effective 'circular migration' initiatives'.[94]

In 2011, the Commission presents Mobility Partnerships as the primary tool to translate the GAMM into practice, defining them as a 'long-term framework based on political dialogue and operational cooperation'.[95] Later in 2011, the Commission presented Mobility Partnerships as the main framework for cooperation with third countries.[96] Contrary to the position of the Commission, most of the literature is pessimistic concerning the effectivity of Mobility Partnerships and, at best, academics consider that it is an empty shell that will have no influence on migrants' mobility rights,[97] at worst, it is a tool to provide EU Member States with access to a dispensable work force,[98] or simply a migration management tool, hindering the access

89 Ibid 7 (emphasis added).
90 Stephen Castles and Derya Ozkul (n85) 27; Piyasiri Wickramasekara, 'Circular Migration: A Triple Win or a Dead End' (2011) International Labour Organization.
91 Sergio Carrera and Räul Hernández I Sagrera (2009) (n1).
92 Ibid.
93 Sergio Carrera and Räul Hernández I Sagrera (2011) (n1).
94 Ibid 101.
95 European Commission (n88) 11.
96 European Commission, 'The Global Approach to Migration and Mobility' COM (2011) 743 Brussels, 18 November 2011, 1, 10.
97 Sandra Lavenex and Rahel Kunz (n76).
98 Sergio Carrera and Räul Hernández I Sagrera (2009) (n1) 33.

of third-country nationals to Europe.[99] Mobility Partnerships were presented by the Commission as offering partner third countries access to more development opportunities and to offer economic migrants increasing opportunities for legal migration[100] but Meng-Hsuan Chou for example, refutes this argument.[101] She argues that projects proposed or implemented in third countries (she takes the specific examples of Cape Verde and Senegal) are 'primarily benefit[ing] the Union at the expenses of migrants, countries of origin or transit and other private actors'.[102]

Even though Mobility Partnerships are depicted by the Commission as being cooperation tools offering a balanced partnership and said to be established only in cases where they are likely to bring added value compared to existing agreements,[103] several authors criticise these arguments.[104] Several authors argue that Mobility Partnerships are not balanced partnerships and that there is no real cooperation between the EU and Member States and the third country. Meng-Hsuan Chou and Marie Gibert, for example, argue that the EU uses an 'one-size-fits-all' approach with third countries or what Reslow and Vink would call a 'take it or leave it' approach.[105] Reslow highlights the 'take it or leave it' approach taken in the cases of Moldova, Cape Verde and Senegal, where the same Mobility Partnership text was unilaterally proposed by the EU to these third countries with little room for negotiation.[106] This view is supported by Lavenex and Stucky who argue that Mobility Partnerships are not balanced and that there is a higher number of projects aimed at fighting irregular migration and controlling migration flows than projects on legal migration or migration and development, which would be in the interest of third countries.[107] They also underline that the 'scope for third countries to express their concerns [is] limited' in the negotiations of the Mobility Partnerships.[108] Sergio Carrera and Raül Hernández I Sagrera concur with this argument and note that there is a clear focus on the issues of irregular migration and border control.[109] Anna Triandafyllidou argues that Mobility Partnerships replicate power relations 'where the EU sets the rules of the game and third countries have to abide by these rules'.[110] She also argues that the language used in the Communication introducing Mobility Partnerships[111]

99 Meng-Hsuan Chou (n76) 20–22.
100 Council of the European Union, Commission Staff Working Document – Mobility partnerships as a tool of the Global Approach to Migration 13489/09 Brussels, 21 September 2009, 1, 4.
101 Meng-Hsuan Chou (n76) 5.
102 Ibid 8.
103 Council of the European Union (n100) 2.
104 See for example: Sandra Lavenex and Rahel Kunz (n76); Sergio Carrera and Räul Hernández I Sagrera (n2); Meng-Hsuan Chou (n76).
105 Meng-Hsuan Chou and Marie Gibert (n49); Natasja Reslow and Maarten Vink (n50).
106 Natasja Reslow, 'The role of Third Countries in EU Migration Policy: The Mobility Partnerships' (2012) 14 *EJML* 393, 395.
107 Sandra Lavenex and Rachel Stucky (n54).
108 Ibid 132.
109 Sergio Carrera and Räul Hernández I Sagrera (2009) (n2).
110 Anna Triandafyllidou (n12) 8.
111 Commission of the European Communities (n41).

is highly unequal.[112] Another reason put forth in the argument that relations between the EU and the partner third country are being one sided, is that Mobility Partnerships make development aid, trade relations and visa policies conditional upon the cooperation of third countries with an EU agenda of migration control.[113] It is generally agreed in the literature that Mobility Partnerships put more pressure on the third country than on participating Member States.[114]

The first Mobility Partnerships were concluded with third countries with a weak leverage vis-à-vis the EU and only after the Arab Spring did this pattern change. Nevertheless, the relations between different parties to a Mobility Partnership may be more dynamic than what is often assumed.[115] Beyond their conflicting interests, the EU, Member States and third countries can share a common objective on migration management.[116] Natasja Reslow argues that third countries are prominent players in the EU's migration policy.[117] Taking the example of Cape Verde and Senegal, she discusses the role of domestic preferences of the third country in its decision to participate in a Mobility Partnership with the EU and the cost/benefit calculation of their cooperation with the EU. Others have also pointed out that third countries have their own priorities when negotiating with the EU and the Member States.[118] The stated overall goal of Mobility Partnership is to create a 'balanced partnership with third countries adapted to specific EU Member States' labour markets'.[119] This goal links legal migration and the fight against irregular migration through border management, migration control and readmission agreements.[120]

The added value of Mobility Partnerships can be diverse. Agnieszka Weinar, for example, argues that projects with added value could be proposed by two actors: a group of Member States or by the European Commission.[121] This would mean

112 Anna Triandafyllidou (n12) 8.

113 Sergio Carrera and others, 'EU-Morocco Cooperation on Readmission, Borders and Protection: A Model to Follow?' (2016) *CEPS Papers in Liberty and Security in Europe*; Sergio Carrera, Leonhard den Hertog and Joanna Parkin, 'EU Migration Policy in the Wake of the Arab Spring, What prospects for EU-Southern Mediterranean Relations?' (2012) MEDPRO Technical Report No 15/August 2012, 1, 15; Stefan Brocza and Katharina Paulhart, 'EU Mobility Partnerships: A Smart Instrument for the Externalization of Migration Control' (2015) 3(15) *Eur J Futures Res* 1.

114 Carrera and Hernández I Sagrera (2009) (n2) 321; Carrera and Hernández I Sagrera (2011) (n2); Mohamed Limam and Rafaella Del Sarto, 'Periphery under Pressure: Morocco, Tunisia and the European Union's Mobility Partnership on migration' (2015) EUI Working Paper RSCAS 2015/75.

115 Fanny Tittel-Mosser, 'Reversed Conditionality in EU External Migration Policy: The Case of Morocco' 14(4) (2018) *JCER* 349.

116 Ibid.

117 Natasja Reslow (n106) 394.

118 Abdelmalek Sayad, *The suffering of the Immigrant* (Cambridge: Wiley 2004).

119 Commission of the European Communities (n41) 2.

120 Ibid 3.

121 Agnieszka Weinar, 'Mobility Partnerships – what impact do they have on legal migration and mobility?' The Migration Policy Centre, European University Institute, Florence, available at: http://www.migrationpolicycenter.eu/publication/mobility-partnerships-what-impact-do-they-have-on-legal-migration-and-mobility (accessed 25 August 2017).

that bilateral projects proposed by a Member State to the third country without including other Member States or the EU are usually not adding value to the existing relationship with the third country. The existence of added value of Mobility Partnerships has been doubted by Paula Garcia Andrade as she observed that the Member States tend to include projects in the Annex that have already been proposed bilaterally.[122] Another type of added value can be related to legal migration. As we saw previously in this section, legal migration was presented as one of the novelties of the Mobility Partnership. Agnieszka Weinar argues that a Member State modifying its legal order to open new legal migration channels would be a 'clear value added of a Mobility Partnership'.[123] Sergio Carrera and Raül Hernández I Sagrera argue that Mobility Partnerships have little added value in enabling legal migration opportunities for citizens from third countries.[124] One of the main criticism towards Mobility Partnerships is that they do not fulfil the promises of enhanced legal migration towards Europe.[125]

Finally, in 2014, the Commission established the Asylum, Migration and Integration Fund[126] with a total of EUR 3.137 billion for 2014–2020, highlighting the particular importance of Mobility Partnerships as the main strategic, comprehensive and long-term cooperation framework for migration management with third countries and invited the EU to pursue and increase the use of this tool. Moreover, the launch of a Mobility Partnership Facility[127] in 2016, designed to secure specific funding for some Mobility Partnerships' initiatives, suggests that the enthusiasm from the Commission towards this instrument is not declining.

1.2 Content of Mobility Partnerships

Mobility Partnerships are Joint Declarations concluded between the EU, interested Member States and a third country. They are composed of a Joint Declaration text and, except for the Mobility Partnerships with Tunisia and Jordan, an Annex with a list of projects designed for the implementation of the Mobility Partnership.

The Joint Declaration starts with a preamble that summarises the relations between the EU and the third country and lists the regional or bilateral dialogues that the third country is part of or the existence of legal instruments such as Association Agreements. Then, it establishes the goals of the Mobility Partnership,

122 Paula García Andrade and Ivan Martín, 'EU Cooperation with Third Countries in the field of Migration', Study, DG for Internal Policies, Policy Department C, European Parliament, PE 536.469, 2015, available at: http://www.europarl.europa.eu/RegData/etudes/STUD/2015/536469/IPOL_STU(2015)536469_EN.pdf (accessed 1 February 2018) Annex II, 141 ff, 1, 33.

123 Agnieszka Weinar (n121).

124 Sergio Carrera and Raül Hernández I Sagrera (2009) (n2).

125 Sergio Carrera and Raül Hernández I Sagrera (2011) (n2) 101.

126 For more information see: https://ec.europa.eu/home-affairs/financing/fundings/migration-asylum-borders/asylum-migration-integration-fund_en (accessed 15 January 2018).

127 For more information see: https://www.icmpd.org/our-work/capacity-building/multi-thematic-programmes/mobility-partnership-facility-mpf (accessed 15 January 2018).

taking into consideration the context of the third country. The content of the Joint Declaration does usually not differ extensively from one Mobility Partnership to the other and the goals are always phrased around the four pillars of the GAMM. Once the general objectives are set, a list of specific objectives is presented under each of the four pillars of the GAMM. It should be noted that asylum and international protection did not exist under the GAM which means that the Mobility Partnerships concluded before the entry into force of the GAMM do not include objectives related to this topic (this is the case of the Mobility Partnerships with Cape Verde, Moldova and Georgia). The list of projects in the Annex is designed to translate the objectives in practical terms.

The last section of the Joint Declaration is about the implementation of the Mobility Partnership. Some key points should be underlined here. First, Mobility Partnerships are 'conceived as a long-term cooperation framework', which means that the content of the Mobility Partnership will evolve over time and according to the context and relations with the third country. What evolves is not so much the text of the Joint Declaration but rather the projects listed in its Annex. Moreover, the number of Member States party to the Mobility Partnership can also change, as Member States can decide to join at a later stage (e.g. the Netherlands joined the Mobility Partnership with Cape Verde when it was already in effect). There are no provisions about a Member State 'leaving' the Mobility Partnership, nor has this question been raised in the literature. As the proposal and implementation of projects by a Member State is not mandatory, its inaction could have the same result as if it would be leaving the Mobility Partnership. The second point is that Mobility Partnerships are 'based on political dialogue', which means that the Joint Declaration is a 'political' document, rather than a legal document and therefore does not aim at being legally binding. This also appears clearly in the 'disclaimer' clause that usually appears at the end of the Joint Declaration and which mentions that 'the provisions of this joint declaration and its Annex are not designed to create legal rights or obligations under international law'.[128] Even though non-binding, the text of the Joint Declaration still foresees that all parties to the Mobility Partnership 'confirm their intention to cooperate at an operational level', arguably creating a moral obligation. The Mobility Partnerships with Morocco, Jordan and Belarus include a clause that does not exist in the six other Mobility Partnerships. This clause states that the partner third country 'will take action to ensure that the objectives of this partnership are attained, taking account of the technical and financial means available'. The clause also includes the notion of 'balanced' partnership and of 'visa facilitation and readmission package', which are not present in the other Joint Declarations.

The Annex is considered a living document, which is expected to evolve over time according to the interests of the different parties to the partnership. The projects can be proposed either by the EU, one or several Member States, the

128 All Joint Declarations can be found here: https://ec.europa.eu/home-affairs/what-we-do/policies/international-affairs/global-approach-to-migration_en (accessed 15 January 2018).

third country, or a combination of these. Save for the Mobility Partnerships with Cape Verde, Moldova and Georgia,[129] as noted earlier, the projects are divided into the four thematic categories of the GAMM: enhancing legal migration, fighting against irregular migration, migration and development, and international protection. From a review of the projects listed in the Mobility Partnerships entered into so far, it seems clear that there are usually few projects related to asylum and international protection. The three other categories seem to have a more balanced number of projects, even though the focus on irregular migration and border control is clear when we look at the content of the projects. Therefore, it is important to look at each project in order to see what it really covers. For example, it may seem that the number of projects related to legal migration is similar to that of projects related to border management and the fight against irregular migration but, in reality, the projects aiming at enhancing the possibilities for legal migration can be almost inexistent. It is not uncommon that projects clearly designed to fight against irregular migration end up being categorised as legal migration projects. This is the case with the Mobility Partnership with Cape Verde, in which an important project aiming at fighting irregular migration and supporting return initiatives is included under the legal migration heading. In the case of Morocco, this is even more apparent because projects linked to border management are included under the legal migration heading. Several studies have argued for the need to look beyond the statistics in this respect and pointed out that, even if the number of projects under the heading 'legal migration' is high, the fact is that most of these projects do not result in an increase in legal channels for migration.[130] Most commonly, these projects serve to provide information to potential migrants on the risks of irregular migration or on the existing options for legal migration.[131] It should be added that the overwhelming majority of projects result from bilateral initiatives between individual Member States and the third country and only a few are joint projects proposed by several Member States together. Significantly, in every Mobility Partnership, the Annex includes projects on the negotiation of a readmission agreement and visa facilitation agreement, which comes as no surprise since one of the preconditions for a third country to

129 In these countries, projects are divided into three thematic categories, excluding international protection.

130 Paula García Andrade and Ivan Martín (n122); IOM, 'The European Union-Moldova Mobility Partnership 2008–2011: Evaluation Report' (2012), available at: http://www.mfa.gov.md/img/docs/eu-moldova-mobility-partnership-evaluation.pdf (accessed 31 October 2017) 11; European Training Foundation, 'Migration Support Measures from an Employment and Skills Perspective', Tunisia (2015), available at: http://www.etf.europa.eu/webatt.nsf/0/2938DD5003574A3EC1257E9A002BF071/$file/MISMES%20Tunisia.pdf (accessed 30 October 2017) 1, 8.

131 Paula García Andrade and Ivan Martín (n122); IOM (n130); European Training Foundation, 'Migration Support Measures from an Employment and Skills Perspective: Georgia' (2015), available at: http://cadmus.eui.eu/bitstream/handle/1814/36841/MISMES_Georgia.pdf?sequence=1&isAllowed=y (accessed 10 August 2017) 1, 4.

enter a Mobility Partnership is that it accepts to start negotiations of such agreements with the EU.

The context of adoption and aim of each Mobility Partnership depends on the state of the relations between the EU, participating Member States and the third country. Several authors have observed that Member States decide to participate in a Mobility Partnership because the aim of the negotiations is in line with their own national policies and the projects they propose reflect their policy preferences.[132] The list of projects proposed in the Annex to the Joint Declaration is constantly evolving and new projects can be proposed if new policy priorities arise. Therefore, the Mobility Partnership can play a role in continuing discussions among the EU, its Member States and partner third countries.[133] New policy priorities on the part of both the EU and third countries can lead to negotiations about the implementation of new initiatives.[134]

1.3 Monitoring and evaluation mechanisms

The Commission (particularly DG Home Affairs) oversees the general management of the Mobility Partnerships, but it does not implement the projects.[135] The Member States are the ones in charge of the projects' implementation. The Commission organises senior official meetings with the representatives of all countries party to the Mobility Partnership. The meetings are, in principle, supposed to be held on a bi-annual basis, but, depending on the dynamism of the implementation of the Mobility Partnership and its stage of implementation, the meetings can occur less often. For example, the Mobility Partnership with Cape Verde is not dynamic and the last two meetings occurred in 2014 and 2017. The monitoring of the implementation of Mobility Partnerships is conducted by a Mobility Partnership task force in Brussels comprised of representatives of the Commission and the Member States and through 'cooperation platforms' in third countries composed of Member States' embassies, the EU Delegation and the third country's representatives.[136] The cooperation platform coordinates the activities in the Partner Country and monitors the implementation of the Mobility Partnership.[137] In the case of Cape Verde, for example, the cooperation platform is the 'Groupe Local de Suivi', which existed prior to the conclusion of the Mobility Partnership. According to Paula Garcia Andrade, the involvement of Member States in the monitoring of the implementation of Mobility Partnerships is feeble.[138]

132 Ibid 31; Natasja Reslow, 'Deciding on EU External Migration Policy: The Member States and the Mobility Partnerships' (2012) 24(3) *J Eur Integr* 223, 226–227.
133 Fanny Tittel-Mosser (n115).
134 Ibid.
135 Interview 3, DG Home Affairs, Brussels, 18 November 2015.
136 Natasja Reslow, 'EU "Mobility" Partnerships: An Initial Assessment of Implementation Dynamics' (2015) 3(2) *Politics and Governance* 117, 118.
137 Council of the European Union (n100) 5–6.
138 Paula García Andrade and Ivan Martín (n122) 104.

The Commission is also in charge of overseeing the updating of the scoreboard.[139] The scoreboard is the only monitoring tool for Mobility Partnerships that exists so far. The scoreboards in the different Mobility Partnerships are all based on the same model: a list of projects with information on their stage of implementation, the country or entity which proposed the project, as well as those responsible for its implementation and some budgetary information. Depending on the scoreboard, this information is sometimes only approximate, not available or not up to date.[140] Moreover, scoreboards are not easily accessible from open sources/databases and have to be requested from DG Home Affairs. On the contrary, the scoreboard for Moldova is accessible to all as it is online (it is the only scoreboard available online), it is regularly updated and includes a fair amount of information.[141]

It is important to note that Mobility Partnerships (except those with Morocco, Tunisia and Jordan) foresee the possibility to conduct an evaluation 'whenever necessary'. This possibility is still largely unexplored as the only official evaluation so far was conducted by the Commission in 2009.[142] The 2009 evaluation exercise focused on the conclusion process and on the content of the existing Mobility Partnerships, rather than on their actual implementation. Now that the first Partnerships have been in place for almost ten years, it is arguable that an analysis of the implementation of Mobility Partnerships needs to be conducted in order to assess their actual impact. In particular, given the political importance of Mobility Partnerships.

In any case, the non-binding nature of Mobility Partnerships means that, even if one party to the agreement does not implement the projects and the purported goals are not met, it is not possible to impose sanctions on any of the partners.[143] It should be mentioned, however, in this respect, that the European Court of Auditors oversees the inspection of external migration expenditure including the funds allocated to the implementation of Mobility Partnership projects. The European Court of Auditors has completed a Special Report in 2016 relating to the spending on migration under two external funding instruments: the European Neighbourhood Policy Instrument and the Thematic Programme on Migration and Asylum under the Development Cooperation Instrument.[144] The Court found that there was a lack of overview of the funded actions and that a proper assessment of what was occurring was sometimes difficult considering the limited or unclear information

139 Council of the European Union (n100) 5.
140 We will discuss this point in more details in Chapter 2.
141 You can find the scoreboard for Moldova here: http://scoreboard.mfa.gov.md (accessed 15 January 2018).
142 Commission of the European Communities (n51).
143 Ian Bache and Stephen George, *Politics in the European Union* (Oxford: Oxford University Press 2006) 35.
144 European Court of Auditors, Special Report No 9/2016, EU external migration spending in Southern Mediterranean and Eastern Neighbourhood countries until 2014, Luxembourg, 2016.

available.[145] The Court concluded therefore that '[t]he total amount of expenditure charged to the EU budget could not be established during the audit'.[146] Moreover, the Court of Auditors stressed the point that more information is needed on what exactly is being funded and implemented, as the various categories and descriptions of projects are often vague and/or overlapping.[147] The Court also noted that the fund allocation seemed to be privileging projects related to the fight against irregular migration.[148] This confirms the existing criticisms found in the literature that I mentioned above and raises to interrogations about how 'balanced' the approach underlying Mobility Partnerships really is.

1.4 The legal nature of Mobility Partnerships

Mobility Partnerships have been portrayed as soft law instruments, but little research has been conducted on where they fit in the EU legal architecture. It is however key to have a clear understanding of the type of instrument that Mobility Partnerships are, as this can influence the existence of legal and policy relevance. Subsequently, drawing from the literature, I will present the three main factors that could influence the relevance of Mobility Partnerships.

1.4.1 Mobility Partnerships in the EU legal architecture

The Communication on circular migration and Mobility Partnerships between the European Union and third countries, which introduced the Mobility Partnership concept, stated that 'Mobility partnerships will necessarily have a *complex legal nature* as they will involve a series of components, some of which will fall in the Community's remit and others in the Member States'.[149] However, the Commission never specified what it meant by a 'complex legal nature'. Are Mobility Partnerships EU legal acts? Or are they something else?

First, we should recall the inclusion of the 'disclaimer' clause in every Mobility Partnership stating that 'the provisions of this joint declaration and its Annex are not designed to create legal rights or obligations under international law'. This clause makes it clear that the authors of the Joint Declaration do not intend to create rights and obligations. This is an important first point as, without a clearly stated 'will of the authors' to the opposite effect, Mobility Partnerships could be considered as an international agreement due to its structure and content. It is widely held in the international law literature and case law that the main conditions for the existence of legal effects are the aim and identity of the authors, as well as the content of the instrument, and not the type of instrument in itself.[150] For example, in the International Court of

145 Ibid.
146 Ibid 7.
147 Ibid.
148 Ibid, see figures 4 and 5 of the Special Report.
149 Commission of the European Communities (n41) 3 (emphasis added).
150 See for example Linda Senden (n15) 249.

Justice Case *New Zealand v France*, of 1974, on the conduction of nuclear tests by France in the South Pacific, the ruling of the International Court of Justice (ICJ) was that the simple declaration by France of its commitment to stop conducting nuclear tests in the South Pacific was legally binding because of 'the intention and circumstances in which it was made'.[151] In this case, several public declarations had been made by French representatives announcing that they would stop conducting nuclear tests in the South Pacific. The declarations were made through a communiqué from the President of the Republic's Office, a diplomatic note addressed to the Ministry of Foreign Affairs of New Zealand, a letter from the President of the Republic to the Prime Minister of New Zealand, a statement at a press conference by the French Ministry of Defence and a speech at the General Assembly of the United Nations given by the Minister for Foreign Affairs.[152] These declarations taken all together imply the good faith of the different 'authors', which can lead to the expectation by other States that France would keep its promise. It must be noted, however, that the aim of the authors does not always determine if a soft law instrument can have legal effects. In the case concerning the *Maritime Delimitation and Territorial Questions between Qatar and Bahrain*,[153] the International Court of Justice ruled that the minutes of a meeting held between government officials of Qatar and Bahrain and the letters exchanged between both governments were to be considered as legally binding instruments, even though it was established that the government official of Bahrain had only had the intention to give a political significance to the meeting and the exchange of letters.[154]

According to Sergio Carrera,

> Mobility Partnerships are political declarations that fall outside the classical remits of European law or international law. They need to be seen as an experimental method of external governance on migration management as they are not enforceable (legally binding) upon the EU member states.[155]

The Commission, on its part, acknowledges that Mobility Partnerships, being Joint Declarations, do not fit into any type of EU legal act and that they are negotiated under political guidelines set by the Council.[156] It was noted by several authors that the procedure of negotiation and signature of Mobility Partnerships does not really diverge much from the procedure adopted to conclude mixed agreements.[157] Mixed agreements are international agreements

151 Case *New Zealand v France* [1974] ICJ Rep 253 477.
152 Eighth report, A/CN4/557, paras 71 and 72.
153 Case *Qatar v Bahrain* [1994] ICJ Rep 112, 112.
154 Ibid 116–122.
155 Sergio Carrera, 'The EU's Dialogue on Migration, Mobility and Security with the Southern Mediterranean: Filling the Gaps in the Global Approach to Migration' (2011) CEPS Liberty and Security in Europe, 4.
156 Commission of the European Communities (n41) 3.
157 Paula García Andrade and Ivan Martín (n122) 32; Uyen Do and Thomas Huddleston, 'Negotiating Migration' 277 in *the Euro Mediterranean: The Potential for EC Mobility*

concluded between the EU and its Member States and one or various third countries.[158] They are concluded in areas were the EU does not have full competency. Mobility Partnerships are negotiated by the Commission, the Presidency of the Council, representatives of the interested Member States and representatives of the third country. It is not consistent who signs a Mobility Partnership on behalf of the EU. In the case of the Mobility Partnership with Belarus, it was signed by the Commissioner for Migration, Home Affairs and Citizenship, Dimitris Avramopoulos.[159] In the case of Cape Verde, Louis Michel, the Commissioner responsible for development policy and Jacques Barrot, the Vice-President of the European Commission responsible for justice, freedom and security signed the Mobility Partnership.[160] In the case of Moldova and Georgia, three signatures on behalf of the EU appeared on the Mobility Partnerships. They were signed by Jacques Barrot, Benita Ferrero-Waldner, the European Commissioner for External Relations and European Neighbourhood Policy and Tobias Billström, Sweden's Minister for Migration and Asylum Policy (for the Mobility Partnership with Georgia)[161] or Dragutin Mate, the Slovenian Minister for Home Affairs (for the Mobility Partnership with Moldova).[162] EU Commissioner for Home Affairs, Cecilia Malmström signed alone the Mobility Partnerships with Jordan,[163] Tunisia,[164] Morocco[165] and Azerbaijan[166] but co-signed the Mobility partnership with Armenia with Jerzy Miller, Poland's Minister of the Interior and Administration.[167] When a

Partnerships (IEMed-CIDOB Mediterranean Yearbook 2009), available at: http://www.migpolgroup.com/public/docs/163.NegotiatingMigrationintheEuro-Med.pdf (accessed 8 January 2018).

158 Allan Rosas, 'The European Union and mixed agreements' 200 in Alan Dashwood, Christophe Hillion (eds), *The General Law of EC External Relations* (London: Sweet and Maxwell 2000); Henry G Schermers, 'A typology of mixed agreements' 23 in David O'Keeffe and Henry G Schermers (eds), *Mixed Agreements* (Deventer, The Netherlands: Kluwer 1983).

159 European Commission, Press release, 'EU launches Mobility Partnership with Belarus', Luxembourg, 13 October 2016.

160 Commission of the European Communities, Press release, 'The European Union and Cape Verde enter into a Mobility Partnership', Luxembourg/Brussels, 5 June 2008.

161 Commission of the European Communities, Press release, 'The European Union and Georgia enter into a Mobility partnership', Brussels 30 November 2009.

162 Council of the European Union, Joint Declaration on a Mobility Partnerships between the European Union and the Republic of Moldova 9460/08 ADD1 Brussels, 21 May 2008.

163 European Commission, Press release, 'EU-Jordan: A new partnership to better manage mobility and migration', Brussels 9 October 2014.

164 European Commission, Press release, 'EU and Tunisia establish their Mobility Partnership', Brussels, 3 March 2014.

165 European Commission, Press release, 'Migration and Mobility Partnership signed between the EU and Morocco', Brussels, 7 June 2013.

166 European Commission, Press release, 'Mobility Partnership signed between the EU and Azerbaijan', Brussels, 5 December 2013.

167 Council of the European Union, Joint Declaration on a Mobility Partnership between the European Union and Armenia 14963/11 ADD1 Brussels, 6 October 2011.

minister of a Member State co-signed a Mobility Partnership it was because the country he represents was holding the Presidency of the Council of the European Union.

Concerning the content of Mobility Partnerships, they combine initiatives on legal economic migration, which is the exclusive competence of Member States, with the proposition of the conclusion of a visa facilitation agreement which is the exclusive competence of the EU. Additionally, most of the projects aimed at fighting irregular migration such as border control and readmission are shared competences. This hints towards the argument that Mobility Partnerships could be mixed agreements, if they were hard law, but that the soft law nature has been preferred by the EU for several reasons that were exposed earlier, including flexibility and rapidity of conclusion.

As Mobility Partnerships are not hard law mixed agreements, Member States do not ratify them, and the European Parliament is excluded from its adoption process. A report of 2015 by the European Parliament qualifies Mobility Partnerships as 'non-conventional concerted acts or non-normative agreements'[168] because they lack (*a priori*)[169] scrutiny by the ECJ and because they do not aim at creating rights and obligations. Sergio Carrera, for instance, has expressed concern over the fact that Mobility Partnerships lack 'democratic control by the European Parliament and judicial scrutiny by the Court of Justice in Luxembourg'.[170] He had previously argued that Member States purposely chose the soft law nature of Mobility Partnerships so that the ECJ would be excluded.[171] Mobility Partnerships might escape juridical control, but as we saw in the previous section, they are under financial accountability as the Court of Auditors is in charge of examining spending on migration, including funds used to finance Mobility Partnership projects.

In what pertains to judicial scrutiny by the ECJ it is worth noting that this possibility is not entirely off the table. The Court is competent to rule on the legality of a measure adopted by the Council, whatever the nature or form of this measure, as long as it has legal effects.[172] In this book I discuss the relevance of Mobility Partnerships. I argue that even though an instrument is non-binding, it does not mean that it cannot have legal relevance. Legal relevance includes potential legal effects. As I will discuss later in this section, legal effects of Mobility Partnerships may be difficult to prove. Nevertheless, if legal effects can be attributed to Mobility Partnerships, then the ECJ would be competent to judge their legality. This possibility should therefore not be entirely dismissed and the question of the jurisdiction of the ECJ might be posed in the future.

168 Paula García Andrade and Ivan Martín (n122) 32.
169 Ibid.
170 Sergio Carrera and Räul Hernández I Sagrera (2009) (n2) 4.
171 Ibid.
172 Sergio Carrera, Leonhard den Hertog and Marco Stefan, 'It wasn't me! The Luxembourg Court Orders on the EU-Turkey Refugee Deal' (2017) CEPS Policy Insights No 2017 15, 1, 4.

1.4.2 Mobility Partnerships as soft law

Soft law is not a new topic of interest and has already been widely discussed in the literature. According to René-Jean Dupuy, Arnold McNair first used the concept of soft law, in the 1930s.[173] However, McNair used the term soft law distinctively from the way it is used today. He considered as being 'soft', the legal principles that were not precise and were, therefore, challenging to apply in court, but he did not consider soft law as something different from hard law.[174] Today, there is still no consensus about what exactly is soft law and what instruments can be classified as soft law instruments, but it is now generally agreed that soft law means 'not legally binding' and a tentative list is likely to include guidelines, resolutions, conclusions, communications, declarations, memoranda of understanding, strategies, action plans, reports, etc.

With the adoption of the Universal Declaration of Human Rights (UDHR), by the General Assembly of the United Nations, in 1948, probably one of the most influential soft law instruments to date, the concept started to be used more frequently.[175] It was in the 1970s that the term soft law started to be widely used, mainly in the field of international environmental law, following the 1972 Stockholm Conference. Similarly, the Stockholm Declaration is a soft law instrument which is legally significant as it is generally considered as the basis of international environmental law.[176] Additional outcomes of the Stockholm Conference were the creation of the United Nations Environmental Programme (UNEP) and the enhanced action of Non-Governmental Organisations (NGOs) that led to the development of numerous other soft law instruments in the field of environment protection,[177] making it the most prolific field in terms of soft law in international law at the time, greatly contributing to the development of this field of international law.

Classical international law literature on the subject is dominated by a debate between authors not recognising soft law as any kind of law (the legal positivists) and those considering it as a source of international law (the rationalists).[178] In the

173 René-Jean Dupuy, 'Declaratory Law and Programmatory Law: From Revolutionary Custom to "Soft Law"' 247, in Robert Akkerman, Peter van Krieken and Charles Pannenborg (eds), *Declarations on Principles: A Quest for World Peace* (Leiden, The Netherlands: Sijthoff 1977) 252.

174 Jean d'Aspremont, 'Softness in International Law: A Self-Serving Quest for New Legal Materials' (2008) 19(5) *EJIL* 1075, 1081.

175 Michele Olivier, 'The Relevance of "Soft Law" as a source of international human rights' (2002) 35(3) *Comp Int Law J South Afr* 289, 298.

176 Pierre-Marie Dupuy (n65) 422.

177 Ibid 433–423.

178 About legal positivism, see, for example: Prosper Weil (n82); Jan Klabbers, 'Informal Instruments before the European Court of Justice', (1994) 31 *Common Mark Law Rev* 997. About rationalism, see, for example: Gregory Shaffer and Mark Pollack, 'Hard vs Soft Law: Alternatives, Complements and Antagonists in International Governance' (2010) 94 *Minn Law Rev* 706, 707; Richard Baxter, 'International Law in "Her" Infinite Variety' (1980) 29(4) *ICLQ* 549; Kenneth Abbott and Duncan Snidal (n69) 421.

positivists' camp, for example, Prosper Weil[179] argues that soft law does not exist as there is either law or no law at all. According to Weil, there is a 'normativity threshold' between non-legal and legal and between what is a norm and what is not.[180] Soft law is problematic because it does not fit neatly into any of the two categories (law/no law) and, by not allowing a clear distinction, it can, according to Prosper Weil, 'destabilize the whole international normative system'.[181] In a similar vein, Jan Klabbers argues that the recognition of soft law would mean the end of public international law because of the difficult distinction between soft law and hard law.[182] Klabbers does not consider soft law as 'real law' but does nevertheless consider that soft law may have legal effects.[183] Indeed, he concedes that soft law cannot be of total legal insignificance.[184] Jan Klabbers considers that soft law is meant to become hard law over time and so he argues that soft law can be seen as 'presumptive law'.[185] Presumptive law means that an act is presumed to be hard law unless it is proved otherwise; if it is proven not to be hard law then it is non-law.[186]

On the rationalist camp, Kenneth Abbott and others identify three types of legalisation depending on 'the degree of *obligation*, *precision*, and *delegation* involved in a legal regime' and argues that the distinction is not so much between hard and soft law, but between harder law and softer law.[187] In order to have hard law all three criteria have to be present. 'Hard legalisation' corresponds to a situation when at least the *obligation* and *delegation* criteria are high.[188] In other words, for 'hard legalisation' the instrument must be legally binding and subject to judicial review and enforcement. When none of the criteria is met, there is no legalisation. According to Abbot, soft law corresponds to everything in between hard law and no legalisation, with various degrees of one or several criteria (but one criterion must be strong). 'Hard legalisation' is the hardest degree of soft law, the one that is the closest to hard law. It is the fact that all criteria do not have to be met that leads to the adoption of soft law in cases where hard law would be too costly for the parties involved.[189] Similarly, Richard Baxter argues that soft law is a source of international law that can have various levels of 'intensity'.[190]

The question of whether soft law is a source of international law has also been disputed in the literature. It is widely accepted that Article 38 of the Statute of the

179 Prosper Weil (n82).
180 Ibid 415.
181 Ibid 423.
182 Jan Klabbers (n178) 998–999.
183 Jan Klabbers, 'The Redundancy of Soft Law' (1996) 65 2 *NJIL* 167.
184 Ibid 167.
185 Jan Klabbers, 'Law-making and Constitutionalism' 81 in Jan Klabbers, Anne Peters and Geir Ulfstein (eds), *The Constitutionalization of International Law* (Oxford: Oxford University Press 2009) 115–116.
186 Ibid 111–121.
187 Kenneth Abbott and others, 'The Concept of Legalization' (2000) 54(3) *Int Organ* 401.
188 Ibid 402.
189 Ibid.
190 Richard Baxter (n178) 566.

International Court of Justice (SICJ), which lists the sources of international law, is not exhaustive.[191] As we saw earlier, Declarations adopted by the General Assembly of the United Nations can have considerable significance in the development of whole branches of international law, and they are not mentioned as such in Article 38. Besides, States have increasingly committed themselves to instruments that are not listed as sources of international law in Article 38.

Article 38 rules that:

1 The Court, whose function is to decide in accordance with international law such disputes as are submitted to it, shall apply:

  a international conventions, whether general or particular, establishing rules expressly recognized by the contesting states;
  b international custom, as evidence of a general practice accepted as law;
  c the general principles of law recognized by civilized nations;
  d subject to the provisions of Article 59, judicial decisions and the teachings of the most highly qualified publicists of the various nations, as subsidiary means for the determination of rules of law.

2 This provision shall not prejudice the power of the Court to decide a case *ex aequo et bono*, if the parties agree thereto.

Treaties are agreements concluded between States or International Organisations. Parties to a treaty are bound to certain obligations for which they are held accountable. International custom is defined in Article 38(1)(b) as 'evidence of a general practice accepted as law'. There are two distinct types of customary law; the first type is *jus cogens*, which is a norm from which no derogation is permitted[192] and that is globally accepted as such by the international community. The second type of customary law is not binding on all States but only on a group of States and covers general practice and the recognition of an instrument as law by a group of States.[193] Article 38 does not make the distinction between the distinct types of customary law. The notion of *jus cogens* was recognised later on by the Vienna Convention on the Law of Treaties of 1969.[194]

191 Jean d'Aspremont, *Formalism and the Sources of International Law* (Oxford: Oxford University Press 2011) 149; Joost Pauwelyn, 'Is It International Law or Not, and Does it Even Matter?' 125 in Joost Pauwelyn, *Informal International Lawmaking* (Oxford: Oxford University Press 2012) 133; Hemme Battjes, *European Asylum Law and International Law* (Leiden, The Netherlands; Boston, MA: Nijhoff 2006) 328; Hugh Thirlway, *The Sources of International Law* (Oxford: Oxford University Press 2014) 6.

192 United Nations, *Vienna Convention on the Law of Treaties*, 23 May 1969, United Nations, Treaty Series, 1155 331, para 53. *Jus cogens* is a "peremptory normal of general international law".

193 Restatement (Third) of the Foreign Relations Law of the United States § 102(2) (1986). The exact definition given here is "customary practice of States followed from a sense of legal obligation".

194 United Nations (n192).

In the case of judicial decisions or scholarly works, they are not direct sources of international law, but they contribute to recognising and developing rules that exist already. According to Article 38, they are 'subsidiary means for the determination of rules of law'. Per Article 59 SICJ, 'the decision of the Court has no binding force except between the parties and in respect of a particular case'. Article 94(1) of the United Nations Charter adds that 'each Member of the United Nations undertakes to comply with the decision of the International Court of Justice in any case to which it is a party'.[195] The Court has no means to enforce its decisions. The UN Security Council can decide to enforce a ruling from the Court according to Chapter XIV of the United Nations Charter,[196] but permanent members of the Security Council can use their veto in order to make the enforcement of such a decision impossible. The enforcement of the International Court of Justice ruling in the case *Nicaragua v United States*[197] was made impossible due to the use by the United States of its veto power.[198] Besides, the Security Council can only request the enforcement of a decision if 'international peace and security' are at risk.[199] This shows that, in practice, the decisions of the International Court of Justice are not binding and usually do not create law. For this reason, Andrew Guzman and Timothy Meyer argue that the rulings of the International Court of Justice are soft law.[200]

The discussion about the use and meaning of soft law instruments is more recent in EU law than in international law, even though the first mention of soft law instruments can be found as far back as 1962 in relation to competition law.[201] In EU law there are three types of sources.[202] Primary sources are composed of Treaties and Related Acts and they have priority over the other categories of sources of law.[203] Secondary sources are composed of EU legislation including Regulations, Directives and Decisions. The label 'tertiary sources' is sometimes used to categorise soft law instruments.[204] Soft law has to conform to primary and secondary sources as their non-binding nature puts them at the bottom of the legal hierarchy.[205] Soft law as a source of EU law is not unanimously recognised.[206] Article 288 of the

195 United Nations, *Charter of the United Nations*, 24 October 1945, 1 UNTS XVI.
196 Ibid.
197 *Case Concerning Military and Paramilitary Activities In and Against Nicaragua (Nicaragua v United States of America)*, Merits, International Court of Justice (ICJ), 27 June 1986.
198 Attila Tanzi, 'Problems of Enforcement of Decisions of the International Court of Justice and the Law of the United Nations' (1995) 6 *EJIL* 539, 544–545.
199 United Nations (1945).
200 Andrew Guzman and Timothy Meyer, 'International Soft Law' (2010) 2(1) *JLA* 171, 172.
201 Oana Andreea Ştefan, 'European Competition Soft Law in European Courts: A Matter of Hard Principles?' (2008) 14(6) *ELJ* 753, 758.
202 EUR-Lex – l14534 – EN, Sources of European Union law, available at: http://eur-lex.europa.eu/legal-content/EN/ALL/?uri=LEGISSUM:l14534 (accessed 1 November 2017); Ursula Smartt, *Optimize Public Law* (New York: Routledge 2014) 41.
203 Linda Senden (n15) 37.
204 Ibid 55.
205 Ibid 56.
206 Ibid.

Treaty on the Functioning of the European Union (TFEU)[207] lists regulations, decisions and directives as binding legal acts adding that recommendations and opinions are not binding. We can infer from the fact that Treaties are not cited as a source of hard law that this list is not exhaustive. No mention of soft law is explicitly made in this article. It can be difficult to establish the difference between hard law and soft law in EU law as terminology is not sufficient to determine the legal nature of an act or instrument. Automatically associating the name and the nature of the act should be avoided.[208] Soft law instruments can be comprised of guidelines, resolutions, conclusions, communications, declarations, memoranda of understanding, strategies, action plans and reports etc. This list is not exhaustive and only gives examples of what can be considered as soft law, not meaning that all these instruments, in each particular case, fulfil the criteria to be considered as such.

Since the early 1990s the EU was in favour of a deregulation in EU law-making.[209] The necessity to use soft law to ensure flexibility within the EU has been underlined in the Commission's White Paper on Governance of 2001, putting the accent on 'opening up the policy-making process' to promote 'better involvement and more openness' as well as more responsibility.[210] The same year, the Commission suggested to apply the OMC to migration issues.[211] In this Communication, the Commission already declared that 'an open procedure for coordination will lead to the identification of common objectives' aiming towards a common policy on asylum and immigration. Linda Senden argues similarly, underlining that the EU is aiming at restraining the creation of hard law to the strict minimum[212] attempting to use alternative instruments such as soft law[213] to achieve this goal. The use of soft law is also seen as beneficial by the legal service team of the European Commission who argue in favour of a more extensive use of soft law.[214] According to the legal service, soft law is considered as a way to 'guide' the transposition of secondary law at the Member States level and to insure uniformisation between Member States.[215] The European Parliament, on the other hand, has been against the use of soft law since only a few years after its first

207 Consolidated Version of the Treaty on the Functioning of the European Union Article 288, 2008 OJ C 115/47.

208 Filippa Chatzistavrou, 'L'usage du soft law dans le système juridique international et ses implications sémantiques et pratiques sur la notion de règle de droit' (2005), available at: http://leportique.revues.org/591 (accessed 17 January 2018) 1, 7.

209 Council Resolution (EC) C 224/5 on legislative and administrative simplification in the field of the internal market, OJ 1996.

210 Commission of the European Communities, 'European Governance: A White Paper' COM(2011) 428, Brussels, 25 July 2011, 1, 3–5.

211 Commission of the European Communities, 'An Open Method of Coordination for the Community Immigration Policy' COM(2001) 387, Brussels, 11 July 2011.

212 Linda Senden, 'Soft Law, Self-regulation and Co-regulation in European Law: Where do they Meet?' (2005) 9(1) *EJCL* 1, 7.

213 Ibid 8.

214 European Commission, Service Juridique, 'Quality of Legislation team, Complexity of EU law in domestic implementing process', Brussels, 3 July 2014.

215 Ibid 8.

appearance in EU law, arguing that it was being used to circumvent the decision-making process.[216]

The different criteria proposed in the literature to identify soft law instruments and norms are not uniform and some criteria contradict each other. This is not surprising as there is no commonly agreed upon definition of soft law and authors often put forward their own definitions and criteria in relation to their own field of law. The main criteria used to distinguish soft law from hard law and from non-law are *obligation*, *bindingness*, *delegation*, *enforcement*, *precision*, *voluntary compliance* and *the aim of the authors*. These criteria are not necessarily alternative, and they are often combined in the literature.

Obligation

Usually, the existence of an *obligation* suggests that a norm legally binds the parties.[217] Kenneth Abbott and Duncan Snidal[218] and later Fabien Terpan[219] use the criterion of *obligation* in order to determine if an instrument is of a soft law nature or not. We saw previously that Kenneth Abbott and others were using a combination of three criteria to determine if an instrument was hard law, soft law or non-law. These criteria are *Obligation*, *Delegation* and *Precision*. According to Kenneth Abbott and others, when there is hard law then *obligation* must be high, as hard law involves the existence of a binding obligation and it has to be combined with *delegation*. When there is no law then there is no *obligation*. In the case of soft law, the terms of the instrument somehow bind parties. This means that the degree of legal *obligation* is lower than in the case of hard law and that there might be no combination with the *delegation* criteria.

According to Fabien Terpan, there are two types of soft law that can be taken from the literature. The first type of soft law is when there is a binding norm (*obligation*) with a soft dimension and the second type of soft law is a non-binding norm (no *obligation*) with legal relevance. Soft law is opposed to hard law where the norm is strictly binding. It is also opposed to non-law when there is a non-binding norm that is also without legal relevance.[220] According to Fabien Terpan, an obligation can have a soft dimension, this means that either the source or the content of the obligation is soft.[221] The source can be soft when the obligation is not included in a binding legal act, such as a Treaty, or if the way they are expressed is not clear. He gives the example of an 'obligation to achieve a particular result' being stronger than a 'best effort obligation'.[222] The only existence of an obligation is not sufficient in order to define soft law as the norm has to be enforceable. If the *obligation* is binding without a soft dimension, then it is hard

216 Oana Andrea Stefan (n38) 888.
217 Ibid 888.
218 Kenneth Abbott and Duncan Snidal (n69) 423.
219 Fabien Terpan (n31) 72–73
220 Ibid 71.
221 Ibid 71–72.
222 Ibid 73.

law. The criterion of *obligation* is not used by Fabien Terpan to differentiate soft law from non-law.

Soft obligations can be subjective, which means that a State can still decide to what extent to abide by such obligations, if it does it at all.[223] This is what happens with international agreements that can be characterised as 'political treaties'.[224] The latter are mainly related to war matters, as was the case with the Yalta Agreement and the Atlantic Charter,[225] and, in case of non-compliance by a State, there is no real possibility of enforcement. These agreements are still considered as being soft law. Richard Baxter adds to this list 'joint statements of policy',[226] arguing that the non-compliance with the soft obligations that they create cannot be seen as a 'violation' and therefore cannot be enforceable, since they are only based on the *will of the parties* to comply.

Bindingness

Many definitions of soft law consider the criterion of *bindingness.* For example, Linda Senden, Daniel Thürer, Francis Snyder and Gustaaf Brochardt and Karel Wellens consider *bindingness* as a criterion to distinguish hard law from soft law.[227] Francis Snyder and Linda Senden consider rules of conduct, which are non-legally binding, as soft law instruments.[228] Gustaaf Brochardt and Karel Wellens also define soft law as rules of conduct that are *non-binding*, in the sense of justiciability, but which aim at having practical effects (and maybe legal effects).[229] Alan Boyle, for example, defines soft law as non-legally binding instruments used by States and international organisations.[230] If an instrument is binding, it means that the parties to the agreement have to adhere to the obligations expressed in the instrument and any non-compliance with these obligations can lead to enforceable sanctions. If an instrument is binding in this sense, then it is hard law. Soft law instruments are usually non-binding; it can be difficult to distinguish between what is binding and what is not. It depends on the content of

223 Tadeusz Gruchalla-Wesierski, 'A Framework for Understanding "Soft Law"' (1984) 30 *McGill Law J* 37, 73; Baxter (n178) 551.

224 Arnold McNair, *The Law of the Treaties* (1961) 513.

225 Baxter (n178) 550.

226 Ibid 551.

227 Linda Senden (n212) 23–24; Daniel Thürer, 'The Role of Soft Law in the Actual Process of European Integration' 131 in Olivier Jacot-Guillarmod (eds), *L'avenir du libre-échange en Europe: vers un Espace économique européen?* (Zürich, Switzerland: Schulthess Polygraphischer Verlag, 1990) 132; Gustaaf Borchardt and Karel Wellens, 'Soft Law in European Community law' (1989) 14(5) *Eur L Rev* 267, 285; Francis Snyder, 'Soft law and institutional practice in the European Community' 198 in Stephen Martin (ed.), *The Construction of Europe* (Dordrecht, The Netherlands; Boston, MA: Springer 1994) 198.

228 Linda Senden (n212) 23; Snyder (n227) 198.

229 Borchardt and Wellens (n227) 285.

230 Alan Boyle, 'Soft Law in International Law-Making' 118 in Malcolm D Evans (ed.), *International Law* (Oxford: Oxford University Press 2005) 141–157.

the instrument as well as the context in which the instrument is adopted. According to the ECJ Case, *French Republic v Commission of the European Communities*, it is the intention of the parties that determines whether or not an instrument is binding.[231] The International Court of Justice does not share this understanding, as we saw in the case *Qatar v Bahrain*.[232]

As we saw previously, Fabien Terpan uses the notion of *bindingness* to define hard law (fully binding norm), non-law (fully non-binding or non-binding without any legal relevance) and soft law (binding with a soft dimension or non-binding but with legal relevance).[233] In other words, soft law can cover binding and non-binding instruments according to him. However, he does not use *bindingness* as a criterion as such but uses bindingness in relation to the criterion *obligation*. He gives the examples of the OMC and the declarations and strategic documents of the Common Foreign and Security Policy (CFSP).[234] He further remarks that if the instrument is non-binding there must be 'an incentive to act in a specific way'.[235] He differentiates between *bindingness* and justiciability and takes the example of the instruments adopted in the fields of Justice and Home Affairs and of the Common Foreign and Security Policy. The policies adopted here aim to be considered as binding but, since they are not conveyed by 'hard law' instruments, they cannot be brought in front of the ECJ (or any other court). In this case, soft law instruments include binding norms which create only soft *obligations*.

This criterion does not distinguish soft law from hard law because hard law is always binding but soft law instruments can be binding too, depending on their content or the intention of the parties, for example. Moreover, it does not distinguish soft law from non-law as non-law is non-binding like most of soft law instruments.

Delegation

Kenneth Abbott and several other authors use the criteria of *delegation* to identify soft law.[236] To exist, hard law must combine at least a high level of *obligation* and *delegation*. Without *delegation* there is no hard law according to Kenneth Abbott and others Abbott and others also argue that in the case of soft law, there is no need for delegation, but delegation can define soft law as long as it is not combined with a hard obligation. Abbott's *delegation* is a broad term that does not presuppose the *enforcement* of the rule. According to Oana Stefan, '[d]elegation means that the implementation, interpretation, application of the rules and conflict resolution is to be entrusted to third parties'.[237] Under *delegation*, third parties

231 Case C-233/02 *French Republic v Commission of the European Communities* [2004] I-02759 para 42.
232 Case *Qatar v Bahrain* [1994] ICJ Rep 112.
233 Fabien Terpan (n34) 71.
234 Ibid 77.
235 Ibid.
236 Kenneth Abbott and others (n187) 406.
237 Oana Andrea Stefan, 'Soft Law and Enforcement of EU Law' 200 in András Jakab and Dimitry Kochenov (eds), *The Enforcement of EU Law and Values: Ensuring Member States' Compliance* (Oxford: Oxford University Press 2017) 212.

may be qualified to explain and apply rules and find solutions to disagreements.[238] This criterion does not consider the content of the instrument as such, but rather the way disputes are settled in case of non-compliance to a norm or a set of norms. If there is no delegation and no other of the three criteria presented by Abbott and others, then there is no law. The criterion of *delegation* was replaced, by Fabien Terpan for example, by *enforcement*.

Enforcement

Hard law is directly *enforceable* in front of a court, whereas soft law and non-law are not. Usually, the *enforcement* mechanism in case of non-compliance with an obligation is foreseen in the instrument itself. This is, for example, the case of the UN Convention on the Law of the Sea (UNCLOS) that provides a specific dispute-settlement procedure.[239] According to Fabien Terpan, *enforcement* encompasses monitoring as well as more forceful instruments, such as judicial review and sanctions.[240] He distinguishes between 'hard enforcement, soft enforcement and the absence of any enforcement mechanism'.[241] Hard enforcement covers cases where rules are under judicial review or under non-judicial control by international organisations (such as the World Trade Organisation for example) using a monitoring mechanism and specific conflict resolution procedures.[242] Soft enforcement concerns methods intended to guarantee conformity with the engagement taken without using pressure or coercion. This means that non-compliance will not be sanctioned by a court but rather could be brought before specialised committees such as the UN Human Rights Committee for non-compliance with human rights treaties. No enforcement covers the cases where the compliance only depends on the will of the parties. According to Fabien Terpan, *obligation* and *enforcement* must be analysed jointly. If both criteria are present then it is hard law, if none of the criteria is present then it is non-law, and if some level of *obligation* and/or *enforcement* exists then it is soft law.[243] On the other hand, Anthony D'Amato argues that soft law is not enforceable and that:

> A soft law system will allow an infraction to be cost-effective: that is, a violator of a norm of soft law may suffer a reputational loss, but reputational damage may be well worth the benefits that are derived from non-compliance with the norm.[244]

238 Daniel Sokol, 'International Antitrust Institutions' 187 in Andrew T Guzmán (ed.), *Cooperation, Comity, and Competition Policy* (Oxford: Oxford University Press 2011) 196–197.
239 Alan Boyle, 'Dispute Settlement and the Law of the Sea Convention: Problems of Fragmentation and Jurisdiction' (1997) 46 *ICLQ* 37, 38.
240 Fabien Terpan (n34) 73.
241 Ibid 73–74.
242 Ibid 74.
243 Ibid.
244 Anthony D'Amato, 'Softness in International Law: A Self-Serving Quest for New Legal Materials: A Reply to Jean d'Aspremont' (2009) 20 *EJIL* 897, 902.

The absence of *enforcement* does not distinguish soft law from non-law and the notion of *enforcement* is directly linked to the criteria of *bindingness* and *obligation* that characterise hard law.

Precision

Precision refers to the way provisions are written in a given document. For example, they can be vague and ambiguous, in which case it is usually agreed that there cannot be an *obligation* resulting from them but only objectives, and therefore they are soft law and not hard law.[245] Applied to the hard law/soft law/non-law distinction, it is usually agreed that if an instrument is not precise then it is soft law.[246] For example, Michele Olivier defines soft law as an instrument with a 'vague content' and an 'imprecise scope'.[247] Soft law provisions are often imprecise to allow for interpretation and flexibility, but this is not always the case and some soft law instruments can be precise, such as for example, the decisions of the UN Human Rights Committee. Andrew Guzman and Timothy Meyer argue that the decisions of the UN Human Rights Committee are impacting States because they are drafted in a precise manner.[248] These instruments are soft law instruments even though they are *precise* in their wording. Moreover, *precision* is not a feature of all the provisions of hard law instruments[249] and all hard law provisions are open to interpretation by a court. Richard Baxter gave a broad definition of soft law, including legal acts having no real obligations due to the lack of precision of their content.[250] Other authors, such as Fabien Terpan, do not make any use of the *precision* criterion.[251]

Lack of *precision* can be found in soft law instruments, but also in non-law and hard law instruments in some cases, consequently, this criterion does not help to differentiate soft law instruments from hard or non-law.

Ulrika Mörth's argues that the criteria of *obligation, precision, delegation* and *enforcement* cannot be used to understand soft law because they only work in combination with each other and the combinations are too numerous.[252] I argue that the criteria are of some use even if they must be combined in order to determine whether an instrument is soft law or not. Additionally, as put forth by Martha Finnemore and

245 Jay Ellis, 'Shades of Grey: Soft Law and the Validity of Public International law' (2011) 25(2) *LJIL* 313, 317.

246 Richard Baxter (n178); Jean d'Aspremont (n174) 1075; Alan Boyle, 'Some Reflections on the Relationship of Treaties and Soft Law' (1999) 48 *ICLQ* 901, 906.

247 Michele Olivier (n175) 294

248 Andrew Guzman and Timothy Meyer (n200) 172.

249 For example, the use of the term "good faith", which is a vague term in hard law instruments.

250 Richard Baxter (n178) 549.

251 Fabien Terpan (n34) 73.

252 Ulrika Mörth, *Soft Law I Governance and Regulation. An interdisciplinary Analysis* (2004) 6.

Stephen Toope, these criteria fail to capture the way 'a sense of obligation might be generated'.[253] The next two criteria will try to grasp this concept.

Voluntary compliance

Usually, hard law implies the compliance to an obligation and the non-compliance to this obligation can be sanctioned. The difference between soft law and hard law is the notion of '*voluntary*'. In hard law, the compliance is not voluntary, and the non-compliance is sanctioned while in soft law parties abide by the rules because they want to. In the facts though, v*oluntary compliance* is a feature of many international treaties, for example in the fields of human rights or environment.[254] These treaties are usually considered to be hard law. This criterion does not always clearly differentiate hard law from soft law.

Daniel Thürer considers that soft law concerns commitments which are more than policy statements but less than hard law.[255] Commitments imply a notion of *voluntary compliance* to the instrument. The status of a political declaration is not always well defined and can lead to debates as was the case of the second Strategic Arms Limitations Treaty (SALT II) between the United States and the Soviet Union, of 1979. Even though the treaty had not been ratified, then President of the United States, Ronald Reagan, declared that 'the United States would voluntarily abide by SALT II as long as the Soviet Union did'.[256] Both countries *voluntarily complied* with the SALT II Treaty even though it was non-binding and non-enforceable as it was never ratified. The only reason they complied was that of their own will to do so. Fabien Terpan links *voluntary compliance* to soft *enforcement.* He gives the example of the General Agreement on Tariffs and Trade (GATT), of 1947, which was followed on a fully voluntary basis for many decades but where no action could be taken against a State that would not comply with the terms of the agreement.[257]

But on the other hand, voluntary compliance is also common for non-law, such as moral rules and rules of etiquette.[258] Rules of conduct can also be an example, as parties commit to abide by the rules in the absence of an enforcement mechanism. Even though there are no enforcement mechanisms there can be other types of moral enforcement pushing parties to follow a specific set of rules. The difference between soft law and hard law is the notion of '*voluntary*'. In hard law, the compliance is not voluntary, and the non-compliance is sanctioned while

253 Martha Finnemore and Stephen Toope, 'Alternative to "legislation": Richer views of law and politics' (2001) *Int Organ* 55 743, 748.

254 Beth A Simmons and Richard H Steinberg, *International Law and International Relations: An International Organization Reader* (Cambridge: Cambridge University Press 2007) 192.

255 Daniel Thürer (n227) 132.

256 Andrew Guzman and Timothy Meyer (n200) 173.

257 Fabien Terpan (n34) 73.

258 Gunther Siegmund Stent, *Paradoxes of Free Will* (Philadelphia, PA: American Philosophical Society 2002) 179–180.

in soft law parties abide by the rules because they want to. In the case of soft law and non-law the criterion seems to fail to distinguish between the two as in both cases the parties chose to obey freely.

Aim of the authors

If the *aim of the authors* is to have a non-binding soft law instrument, it usually will be. As indicated previously, in the case *French Republic v Commission of the European Communities*, the Court of Justice of the European Union (CJEU) declared that it is the intention of the parties that determines whether a soft law instrument is binding or not.[259] It is not always easy to determine what the intention of the authors was. In the case *The Netherlands v Council and Commission* of 1996,[260] the ECJ addressed an issue raised *a propos* the Code of Conduct adopted by the Council concerning public access to Council documents. The Netherlands argued that the Code of Conduct was merely a political instrument. The Court agreed, holding that the Code of Conduct was 'simply the expression of purely voluntary coordination', designed to prevent differences between the Council and the Commission on the public access to Council and Commission documents. Therefore, the court agrees that the Code of Conduct should not be annulled as it cannot have legal effects.

The aim of the authors when adopting a hard law instrument is clearly to be legally binding, which distinguishes it from soft law instruments that aim at being non-binding. The distinction between soft law and non-law according to this criterion can be a bit more difficult to draw as both can be aimed at being non-binding. The difference lays in the *will of the authors* to create a change. It is the creation of a goal that is reached through the implementation of the instrument that differentiates it from a purely informative (non-law) instrument, for example. The combination of the creation of this 'soft goal' and the voluntary compliance to reach the goal creates what Martha Finnemore and Stephen Toope, call 'a sense of obligation'.[261]

As mentioned when discussing the structure of Mobility Partnerships, the text of the Joint Declaration stipulates that 'the provisions of this joint declaration and its Annex are not designed to create legal rights or *obligations* under international law'.[262] The fact that parties decide to conclude a Mobility Partnership and to implement it, can be linked to the existence of a *soft obligation*. This *soft obligation* will then depend on the will of the parties to comply (*voluntary compliance* criteria).

259 Case C-327/91 *French Republic v Commission of the European Communities* [1994] ECR I-03641 para 42.
260 Case C–58/94 *The Netherlands v Council and Commission* [1996] ECR I–2169, paras 24, 27 and 38.
261 Martha Finnemore and Stephen Toope (n253) 748.
262 Council of the European Union, Joint declaration establishing a Mobility Partnership between the Kingdom of Morocco and the European Union and its Member States 6139/13 ADD 1 REV 1, Brussels, 12 April 2013, 1, 12; Council of the European Union, Joint Declaration on a Mobility Partnership between the European Union and the Republic of Cape Verde 9460/08 ADD2, Brussels, 21 May 2008, 1, 7.

The Commission has always presented Mobility Partnerships as *non-binding* political declarations.[263] To date, neither the Commission nor any State party have been forced to implement a project proposed in the Annex. According to officials from DG Home Affairs[264] as well as of the European External Action Service (EEAS),[265] it would not be possible or even suitable to legally *enforce* the implementation of Mobility Partnerships projects, since Mobility Partnerships are soft law instruments and would be inadmissible in front of a court. According to Carrera and Hernández I Sagrera, it seems that neither the ECJ nor Member States' courts are competent to control and *enforce* the implementation of Mobility Partnerships.[266] The provisions included at the end of the instrument withdraw the possibility of punishing 'breaches of commitments'.[267] However, if Mobility Partnerships are found to have legal effects the ECJ could be competent. It is the act of implementation that gives the starting point to an eventual legal or practical effect of the project. As long as the project is not implemented nothing happens, it is only a *non-binding*, declarative, proposition. Once a project is being implemented, through the actions taken for its implementation legal effects can occur. In this case, once a project has been implemented, and if there is a direct legal effect resulting from it, then the ECJ could be competent.

Arguably, there can still be *'soft' enforcement*,[268] such as political or financial pressure that can be put on the different parties. As stated by Anthony D'Amato, a consequence of the non-compliance with the Mobility Partnership, or the non-implementation of projects, could be reputational damages on the non-complying party.[269] If we take, for example, the case of a Member State that proposed a project opening legal migration possibilities for the third country but which, because of the start of the economic crisis, eventually abandoned the project, the 'reputational damage', if it exists, will be minimal compared to the burden of having to accept a certain number of immigrants in a unfavourable context. Financial pressure also do not seem to be efficient to push Member States to act in one way or the other. For example, the EU decided to allocate funding to projects proposed jointly by several countries[270] to enhance cooperation between different countries but most of the projects in the Annexes to the Joint Declarations are still bilateral. Financial pressures were not sufficient to convince Member States to cooperate. *'Soft' enforcement* applied to Member States is not working, but it could be more efficient when applied to the third country.

The main tool of *'soft' enforcement* with third countries lays in conditionality mechanisms. Conditionality is not a new tool used by the EU. Since the early 1990s, the EU uses the 'standard' conditionality in its relations with third

263 Commission of the European Communities (n51) 4.
264 Interview 3 (n135).
265 Interview 2 EEAS, Brussels (by phone), 15 October 2015.
266 Sergio Carrera and Raül Hernández I Sagrera (2011) (n2) 106.
267 Natasha Ward (n61) 146.
268 Fabien Terpan (n34) 74.
269 Anthony D'Amato (n244).
270 Interview 2 (n265).

countries.[271] In this case, the EU can use conditionality (even sometimes negative conditionality) to push third countries to follow and implement policies that are favourable to the EU and which often include the fight against irregular migration.[272] Sandra Lavenex and Nicole Wichmann argue that the negotiation of Mobility Partnerships is based on conditionality and the existence of effective incentives for the third country.[273] Carrera and Hernández I Sagrera add that conditionality puts a much higher pressure on the third country than on Member States' participation.[274] A new 'more for more' strategy was presented in 2011, based on three main components: institution building, greater involvement of citizens and civil society, and higher growth and sustainable and inclusive economic development.[275] The 'more for more' conditionality was included later in Mobility Partnerships, after the Arab Spring uprisings, as the EU realised that they would need to propose more positive incentives to third countries in order to increase cooperation on migration.[276] As this cooperation is important for the EU it is willing to pursue a more positive approach to conditionality.[277] The new 'more for more' conditionality strategy included financial and technical assistance, trade and mobility incentives.[278]

The criterion of *delegation* seems more appropriate in the case of Mobility Partnerships than *enforcement*. DG Home Affairs is coordinating the general implementation of the Mobility Partnerships. It is also in charge of keeping the partnership dynamic. The EU Delegation based in the third country works in close cooperation with the offices of DG Home Affairs in Brussels and with all the implementing partners in the field. DG Home Affairs makes the link between the third country and the Member States. I argue that in case of disputes or failure to implement projects the officials of DG Home Affairs will arguably be in charge to find solutions or to find ways to incentivise Member States to be more active.

Mobility Partnerships' Joint Declarations are meant to be a 'living document', which means that they change and therefore cannot be *precise*. Parties join Mobility Partnerships on a voluntary basis and therefore arguably propose initiatives that they consider of interest. It is to be expected that a country that chooses to participate will commit to it. Moreover, the flexibility of the tool allows countries

271 Standard conditionality refers to aid conditionality. See: Elena Fierro, *European Union's Approach to Human Rights Conditionality in Practice* (The Hague, The Netherlands: Nijhoff 2003) 94–95; Katharina Tomasevski, *Between Sanctions and Elections: Aid Donors and their Human Rights Performance* (London: Pinter 1997) 9–10.

272 Rosa Balfour, 'EU Conditionality after the Arab Spring' (2012) European Institute of the Mediterranean; European Commission (n264) 15.

273 Sandra Lavenex and Nicole Wichmann (n240) 93.

274 Sergio Carrera and Raül Hernández I Sagrera (2009) (n2) 2.

275 Macarena Nuño, 'Migration Policies of the European Union with its Mediterranean Partners: Need for greater mobility', Study, Directorate-General for External Policies of the Union, Directorate B, European Parliament PE 457.131 (2014) 1, 15.

276 Rosa Balfour (n272) 21.

277 Ibid 22.

278 Ibid 21.

to adjust their participation to their policy priorities. Most Mobility Partnerships have led to the implementation of projects which can be seen as additional proof of voluntary compliance as no enforcement mechanism exists. In the case of the Mobility Partnerships with Cape Verde and with Morocco, projects have been implemented and new projects proposed after their conclusion. The fact that all parties continue to work towards achieving at least some of the goals set in the Joint Declarations over a time span of several years is arguably proof of their commitment and of their *voluntary compliance* to the Mobility Partnership. The *aim of the authors* to have a soft law instrument is clear and the analysis of the content of the Joint Declarations goes in this direction. There is no doubt that the intention of the parties leans in favour of a *non-binding* instrument. The analysis of the wording of the Joint Declarations, the mention that 'the provisions of this joint declaration and its Annex are not designed to create legal rights or *obligations* under international law' clearly demonstrates that point.

Mobility Partnerships are *non-binding*, in accordance to the *aim of the authors*, so they do not create *obligations* for the parties to the agreement and are therefore not *enforceable*. Even without being *enforceable*, we can argue that DG Home plays a role in *delegation*. The parties decided voluntarily to conclude a Mobility Partnership presumably because the objectives of the instrument coincided with their policy orientations. Parties are also *voluntarily complying* with the instrument and, although no action can be taken against a State, or the EU, unwilling or incapable of complying, the fact is that projects are being implemented and new initiatives proposed. Cape Verde and Moldova, the pilot Partnerships, illustrate this *voluntary compliance* since 2008.

1.4.3 The legal and policy relevance of Mobility Partnerships

Many authors distinguish between legally binding instruments and instruments susceptible to produce legal effects. As noted by Linda Senden, soft law instruments can potentially have legal effects.[279] This means that an instrument does not need to be legally binding in order to produce legal effects. Snyder also argues that legal effects are not linked to the fact that an instrument is legally binding.[280] Filippa Chatzistavrou made the distinction between the non-legally binding criteria and the possible effects of soft law.[281] The recognition of the potential legal effects of soft law is not new, since already in 1971, the ECJ held, in *ERTA*, that instruments that are not legally binding can still have legally binding force or legal effects.[282]

Legal effects usually entail the ability to develop rights and obligations.[283] Snyder proposed a complete list of the legal effects that soft law instruments may

279 Linda AJ Senden (n212) 23.

280 Francis Snyder, 'Interinstitutional Agreements: Forms and Constitutional Limitations' 453 in Gerd Winter (ed.), *Sources and Categories of European Union Law: A Comparative and Reform Perspective* (Baden-Baden, Germany: Nomos 1996) 461–463.

281 Filippa Chatzistavrou (n208) 7.

282 Case 22/70 *ERTA* [1971] ECR 263.

283 Trevor C Hartley (n21).

have.[284] According to this list, soft law can be used in and outside of a court of law. In a court of law, soft law can either interpret hard law (its most common function), be used in litigation, provide bases for judicial review or be itself the object of judicial review and be annulled. A soft law instrument can be annulled if it was concluded to replace a law and was intended to have legal effects. In the Case *France v Commission*, of 1990,[285] the ECJ ruled that soft law instruments that create new obligations lack a legal basis and are therefore to be annulled. The Commission, for its part, acknowledged the 'Guidance document' on Article 6(4) of Directive 92/43/EEC, of May 1992 ('Habitats Directive') that legal action may be taken against a non-binding instrument (such as an opinion) in case of non-conformity with EU law.[286] Moreover, soft law instruments can also have legal effects outside of a court. They can, for example, provide the normative framework for future hard law negotiations, bring legal certainty to existing hard law and influence rights and obligations of third parties to an agreement.

It has also been argued that soft law instruments can have effects on policy or 'practical effects', which are extra-legal. Snyder defines soft law as: 'rules of conduct which, in principle, have no legally binding force but which nevertheless may have practical effects'.[287] According to Linda Senden, soft law instruments are '[r]ules of conduct that are laid down in instruments which have not been attributed legally binding force as such, but nevertheless may have certain – indirect – legal effects, and that are aimed at and may produce practical effects'.[288] Several other authors also recognise the potential practical effects of soft law.[289] For example, it has been argued that the OMC can have effects on social policy.[290] Another area where soft law instruments can have practical effects is, according to Snyder, the area of European integration.[291] In this book, I am discussing the legal and policy relevance of Mobility Partnerships. This includes the development of new laws, new policies as well as changes in official discourses, behaviours and implementation of existing laws.

Legal and policy relevance is the terminology adopted in this book. The term *relevance* implies some 'reasonable connection' with something. In the Oxford dictionary, relevance is defined as '[t]he quality or state of being closely connected or appropriate'. According to the Cambridge dictionary, relevance is 'the degree to which something is related or useful to what is happening or being talked about'. In this book I am discussing to what extend the implementation of Mobility Partnership projects are linked to the legal and policy developments

284 Francis Snyder (n280) 463.
285 Case C-366/88 *France v Commission* [1990] ECR I 03571.
286 Guidance document on Article 6(4) of the "Habitats Directive" 92/43/EEC, January 2007, 1, 24.
287 Francis Snyder (n227) 198.
288 Linda AJ Senden (n212) 23.
289 Ulrika Mörth (n571) 4; Gustaaf Borchardt and Karel Wellens (n227) 285.
290 David Trubek and Louise Trubek, 'Hard and Soft Law in the Construction of Social Europe: The Role of the Open Method of Co-ordination' (2005) 11(3) *ELJ* 343, 343.
291 Francis Snyder (n227) 198.

occurring in a third country. Legal relevance includes potential legal effects of Mobility Partnerships, but also some practical effects. Practical effects can in other cases be equated to policy relevance. There could be policy relevance if Mobility Partnerships are used by the third country as a tool to support a domestic political agenda.

According to Oana Andrea Stefan, practical effects 'were generally linked in the literature with the transformations that soft law may generate in the behaviour and practices of the Member States ranging from policy changes to subtler changes at the level of discourse, understanding and policy principles'.[292] This type of practical relevance is comprised under policy relevance. Practical effects can also include the way the law is being implemented and in this case, it is included under legal relevance. The term legal relevance is often related to the notion of evidence in the American system, but this is not the understanding that we have of the notion of *legal relevance* here.[293] The term *legal relevance* has previously been used in relation to soft law. Fabien Terpan for example, uses the expression '*legal relevance*' in order to distinguish soft law from hard law or no law at all.[294] The understanding of Fabien Terpan of the notion of legal relevance is narrower than the one that we have of the term in this book. According to Fabien Terpan, legal relevance equals direct legal effects that soft law can have when used in court. Our definition of *legal relevance* includes such direct legal effects but is broader than that.

Despite its non-binding nature, several authors have observed that Mobility Partnerships can have concrete legal implications especially regarding visa facilitation and readmission.[295] The logic behind this is that Mobility Partnerships often combine interests from both the EU (e.g.: an effective readmission policy of third countries) and third countries (e.g.: access for its nationals to the territory of the EU through visa facilitation). These could be considered as direct intended effects. The projects designed to achieve these specific goals are the exception. The vast majority of projects has potential indirect effects as they do not directly aim at creating hard law or a specific policy but may lead to its creation indirectly. Despite the absence of enforcement mechanisms of these partnerships, their *quid pro quo* nature may ensure sufficient political will on the part of the partner third country to implement the required legal changes in its domestic legal orders.

As previously noted, the parties to the Mobility Partnerships did not aim at creating rights and obligations. Even though Mobility Partnerships are not expected to create rights, their implementation can have direct/indirect legal and policy relevance with repercussions for the way in which migrants are granted

292 Oana Andrea Stefan (n38) 879, 881.

293 Rosemary Pattenden, 'The Discretionary Exclusion of Relevant Evidence in English Civil Proceedings' (1996) 1 *Int'l J Evidence & Proof* 361; John Woods and Dov Gabbay, 'Relevance in the Law: A Logical Perspective' 261 in Dov Gabbay and others (eds), *Approaches to Legal Rationality* (Dordrecht, Germany: Springer 2010).

294 Fabien Terpan (n34) 71.

295 Sergio Carrera and others, 'Labour Immigration Policy in the EU: A renewed Agenda for Europe 2020' (2011) Policy Brief No 240, CEPS 1, 6.

rights and/or can exercise their rights. Because the Annex to the Joint Declarations is a living document, Mobility Partnerships change over time as well as their consequences. Legal and policy relevance can be consequences of Mobility Partnerships. Hussein Kassim and Patrick Le Galès argue that not only the consequences can change but also the power structure between the different parties.[296] They add that the 'adoption of instruments is likely to produce indirect unintended consequences'.[297] Sarah Wolff adds that migration policy instruments 'do not always respond to the original intended effect and can escape the objectives assigned to them'.[298] Even though Mobility Partnerships are not designed to create rights and obligations, due to their evolving structure, they can become relevant. The negotiation of Mobility Partnerships means that political priorities are translated into projects, to which resources are allocated and which aim at creating results.

The *external effects* relate to legal effects on the legal orders of partner third countries.[299] The *external effects* of EU law have been discussed from different perspectives. A first example is 'territorial extension' where the EU tries to impose EU law on activities that are happening abroad.[300] Second, Anu Bradford discusses the normative power of the EU at the global level, also called 'The Brussels Effect'.[301] Third, third countries can voluntary decide to adopt EU's institutional model.[302] But on the contrary, the EU can also actively try to impose its norms to third countries.[303] Sandra Lavenex has also observed the existence of external effects for Eastern Countries related to European integration.[304] The enlargement had direct consequences for these countries, since it required reforms to their border regime, for example. When looking at the external effects of Mobility Partnerships I look at the effects these instruments have on the policy or legal framework of the third country party to the agreement. This is a critical issue as it touches directly on the sovereignty of a third country. What I discuss is whether Mobility Partnerships can be relevant for the development of the legal framework of a third country through the implementation of the projects listed in the Annex to the Joint Declarations.

Sandra Lavenex and Emek Uçarer use the term 'externalities' when referring to effects of EU policies on third countries.[305] They argue that these external effects

296 Hussein Kassim and Patrick Le Galès, 'Exploring Governance in a Multi-Level Polity: A Policy Instruments Approach' (2010) 33(1) *West Eur Politics* 1, 8.
297 Ibid 13.
298 Sarah Wolff, 'The Politics of Negotiating EU Readmission Agreements: Insights from Morocco and Turkey' (2014) 16 *EJML* 69, 94.
299 Bart Van Vooren (n2) 181.
300 Joanne Scott, 'Extraterritoriality and Territorial Extension in EU Law' (2013) 62(1) *Am J Comp Law* 87.
301 Anu Bradford, 'The Brussels Effect' (2012) 107(1) *Northwest University Law Rev* 1.
302 Anja Jetschke and Philomena Murray, 'Diffusing Regional Integration: the EU and Southeast Asia' (2012) 35(1) *West Eur Politics* 174.
303 Tobias Lenz, 'Spurred Emulation: The EU and Regional Integration in Mercosur and SADC' (2012) 35(1) *West Eur Politics* 155.
304 Sandra Lavenex (n209) 89.
305 Sandra Lavenex and Emek Uçarer, *Migration and the Externalities of European Integration* (Lanham, MD: Lexington Books 2003) 8.

can result from EU intended policy transfer or be the unintended result of policy diffusion or policy learning. The effects can be intended or unintended results of the common asylum and migration policies, particularly the result of stricter border controls or the fight against irregular migrants, which are bound to lead to changes in migration routes and/or the rise in the number of migrants and asylum seekers who settle in third countries.[306] According to Sandra Lavenex and Emek Uçarer, the effects of EU policies on third countries can happen voluntarily, through opportune conditionality, or under pressure from the EU through inopportune conditionality. External effects can result from firm action from the EU and the Member States to implement their migration policy in the third country. The authors note, that, although in some cases third countries are put under pressure to adapt to EU policies, this does not mean that such adaptation is always opposite to the domestic priorities of the third country.[307] When applying these distinctions to Mobility Partnerships we can consider that there can be a 'differentiated relevance' of Mobility Partnerships. Differentiated relevance means that in some cases legal and policy changes can be imposed by the EU but in other cases the EU can support them according to the will of the third country. The level of influence of the EU in the legal and policy developments as well as in the content of the new legal acts or policies can be differentiated depending on external factors.

Sandra Lavenex and Emek Uçarer underline conditionality as a main factor influencing the existence of external effects.[308] Sandra Lavenex and Frank Schimmelfennig add that three factors can lead to external effects of EU migration policy: 'institutions, power, and domestic structure'.[309] 'Institutions' relates to the fact that the EU gained in competences over migration issues, 'power' includes issues of conditionality and geopolitics and 'domestic structures' includes the administrative capacity of a third country. They add that unintended external effects can be explained by factors such as the promotion of economic development, education and frequent contacts between the EU, Member States and a third country.[310] Several other factors have been observed in the literature which can potentially influence the externalisation of EU immigration policy. Christina Boswell identifies three factors: the potential to meet migration goals, the institutional structures and the electoral pressures.[311] Jean-Pierre Cassarino argues that cooperation with third countries on migration issues[312] can depend on four

306 Ibid.

307 Ibid 11.

308 Sandra Lavenex and Emek Uçarer, 'The External Dimension of Europeanization: The Case of Immigration Policies' (2004) 39(4) *Cooperation and Conflict* 417, 424–425.

309 Sandra Lavenex and Frank Schimmelfennig, 'EU Rules Beyond EU Borders: Theorizing External Governance in European Politics' (2009) 16(6) *J Eur Public Policy* 791, 792.

310 Ibid 891–892.

311 Christina Boswell, 'The "External Dimension" of EU Immigration and Asylum Policy' (2003) 79(3) *International Affairs* 619, 620.

312 Jean-Pierre Cassarino takes the case of readmission agreements.

factors, which are often combined: 'geographic proximity', 'the level of migration salience' (which relates to the postcolonial ties between an EU Member State and a third country), 'incentives and conditionality' and 'the positions of relative power certain non-EU states' have.[313] This last factor relates to the power of negotiation of a third country linked to its geopolitical importance for the EU.

Stefan Brocza and Katharina Paulhart argue that it is impossible to solely link developments in the third country to the implementation of the Mobility Partnership and that 'surrounding factors' can influence these developments.[314] However, they do not give details on what these 'surrounding factors' could be. Meng-Hsuan Chou presents the contextual factors that have led to the decision to conclude Mobility Partnerships.[315] The first factor underlined by Meng-Hsuan Chou is also the institutional factor, presented by Sandra Lavenex and Frank Schimmelfennig, but she puts it in parallel with the interests of Member States particularly on legal migration issues. The second factor is linked to the need to propose incentives to third countries in exchange of their cooperation in the readmission of irregular migration. This can be achieved through conditionality. Daniel Wunderlich argues that implementation dynamics, in the field of EU external migration policy, are related to the understanding of a problem and the way it can be influenced by other organisations, called 'distributional factors', the political context and organisational factors including administrative capacity.[316] Daniel Wunderlich adds that the organisational factor is the predominant one in influencing the implementation dynamics.[317] Natasja Reslow gives a list of factors potentially influencing the implementation of Mobility Partnerships.[318] These factors are the following: tractability of the problem, nature of change required, clarity of policy objectives, financial and organisational resources for implementation, relationship between implementing agencies, disposition of implementing officials and the implementation context.[319]

We can see that several factors can be combined either because they overlap or because different denominations refer to similar notions. This is the case for example of conditionality and power of negotiation, or, for example, 'migration salience' and frequent contacts between the EU, Member States and a third country, which can be included under the state of relations between Member States and a third country. In this book the focus will be put on the three factors considered as being the most influential. These three factors are the state of relations between third countries and EU Member States, the power of negotiation and the administrative capacity of third countries.

313 Jean-Pierre Cassarino, 'A Reappraisal of the EU's Expending Readmission System' (2014) 49(4) *The International Spectator* 130, 135.
314 Stefan Brocza and Katharina Paulhart (n113) 4.
315 Meng-Hsuan Chou (n76).
316 Daniel Wunderlich, 'The Limits of External Governance: Implementing EU External Migration Policy' (2012) 19(9) *JEPP* 1414.
317 Ibid 1419.
318 Natasja Reslow (n136) 122.
319 Ibid.

State of relations between third countries and EU Member States

Several of EU Member States are former colonial empires that keep privileged relations with their former colonies, through cultural, political and economic cooperation. It is often argued in the literature that the cooperation between the EU and third countries which are former colonies is strongly influenced by the existence of postcolonial ties that they have with specific Member States.[320] Meng-Hsuan Chou and Marie Gibert argue that postcolonial ties are the key of entry for third countries to the EU policy discussions, increasing the likelihood of third countries being in line with the specific Member State's objectives.[321] To a considerable extent, the relations between the EU and Africa were built on these postcolonial ties between its Member States and their former African colonies. The existence of historical relations with individual Member States can impede the adoption of agreements at the EU level if these EU agreements are not favourable to the existing, postcolonial, bilateral relations. This can be explained by the fact that Member States have different interests linked to their historical past. For example, Meng-Hsuan Chou and Marie Gibert wonder if the unsuccessful conclusion of the Mobility Partnership with Senegal could be related to the reluctance of France to conclude the partnership.[322] Senegal, a former French colony, had a close relationship with France at the time of the negotiation of the Mobility Partnership. Not only was it France's largest recipient of development aid and its third major trade partner in West Africa[323] but they also have good diplomatic relations and the French Embassy in Dakar is one of the largest in the world.

Additionally, Agnieszka Weinar argues that, before the launch of the GAM, the EU had not started discussions with Africa on migration issues, as this was undertaken 'by a few Member States, mostly with colonial past'.[324] The negotiations in the framework of the GAM suggest that cooperation with Africa is mostly of interest to former colonial powers and the Mediterranean Member States,[325] and that EU's cooperation on migration issues is impeded by its 'weak position' towards third countries that prefer negotiating through existing bilateral relations with the Member States and particularly with their former colonial powers.[326] Meng-Hsuan Chou and Marie Gibert concur with the claim that third countries

320 Marie Gibert, 'The New European Security Architecture: An Example of "Messy Multilateralism"?' 179 in Tony Chafer and Gordon Cumming (eds), *From Rivalry to Partnership? New Approaches to the Challenges of Africa* (Aldershot, UK: Ashgate 2011); James Mayall, 'The Shadow of Empire: The EU and the Former Colonial World' 292 in Christopher Hill and Michael Smith (eds), *International Relations and the European Union* (Oxford: Oxford University Press 2005).

321 Meng-Hsuan Chou and Marie Gibert (n49) 415.

322 Ibid 415.

323 'France/Africa: Remaking an Old Relationship' (2009) *Africa Confidential* 50(18).

324 Agnieszka Weinar, 'Improving EU and US Immigration Systems' Capacity for Responding to Global Challenges: Learning from experiences', EU–US Immigration Systems 2011/02, Robert Schuman Centre for Advanced Studies, San Domenico di Fiesole (FI): European University Institute, 2011 1, 5.

325 Ibid 6.

326 Ibid 14.

prefer discussing migration issues at the bilateral level rather than the EU level.[327] However, they put forth the argument that bilateral cooperation is not always conducted between a Member State and a former colony; bilateral cooperation can exist outside of bilateral ties.[328] James Hampshire argues that it is the multiplicity of Member States' interests on migration issues rather than postcolonial ties that gives the EU a difficult position in cooperating with third countries on these questions.[329]

As it has been pointed out in the literature, countries that have recently gained their independence from colonial powers have comparable migration models.[330] Heinz Fassmann and Rainer Munz argue that migration is influenced by 'cultural and political affinities rooted in history'.[331] Due to a shared cultural and linguistic background as well as administrative, education and trade systems built on the same model, special links exist between the former colonies and the former colonial powers, which make migration flows particularly likely between them.[332] The enduring relevance of postcolonial ties has been questioned in the literature. Simona Vezzoli argues that time can affect the relevance of postcolonial ties.[333] She believes that when the former colony goes through reforms such as the change of the national language, for example,[334] it can lead to looser ties. The former colony can then decide to have closer links with another country which can also impact the strength of postcolonial ties.[335] Geographical location also explains a strong interest of Southern European countries for Northern Africa and the Mediterranean region.[336]

The concept of 'migration salience' characterises postcolonial relations between a Member State and a third country where a consequent group of immigrants reside in the territory of the former colonial power and where movements of

327 Meng-Hsuan Chou and Marie Gibert (n49) 418.
328 Ibid 419.
329 James Hampshire, 'Speaking With One Voice? The European Union's Global Approach to Migration and Mobility and the Limits of International Migration Cooperation' (2016) 42(4) *J Ethn Migr Stud* 571, 576.
330 Heinz Fassmann and Rainer Munz, 'Patterns and Trends of International Migration in Western Europe' (1992) 18(3) *Popul Dev Rev* 457; Marc Hooghe and others, 'Migration to European Countries: A Structural Explanation of Patterns, 1980–2004' (2008) 42(2) *Int Migr Rev* 476; Douglas S Massey and others, *Worlds in Motion: Understanding International Migration at the End of the Millennium* (Oxford: Clarendon Press 1998).
331 Fassmann and Munz (n330) 464.
332 Douglas S Massey and others, 'Theories of International Migration: A Review and Appraisal' (1993) *Popul Dev Rev* 431, 447–448
333 Simona Vezzoli, 'The role of the state in international migration: Exploring the transition from colony to independence' (2014) IMI Working Papers Series (102) 1, 13.
334 For example, in Morocco the official language now is Arabic and not French anymore.
335 Simona Vezzoli (n333) 13.
336 James Hampshire (n329) 576; Jean-Pierre Cassarino, 'Dealing with Unbalanced Reciprocities: Cooperation on Readmission and Implications' 1 In Jean-Pierre Cassarino (ed.), *Unbalanced Reciprocities: Cooperation on Readmission in the Euro-Mediterranean Area* (Washington, DC: Middle East Institute 2010) 14.

people between the former colony and the Member State are frequent.[337] This is the case of France and Morocco as well as Portugal and Cape Verde. Jean-Pierre Cassarino argues that 'migration salience' can hinder the cooperation between a Member State and its former colony on migration issues.[338] Cassarino argues more specifically that the conclusion of readmission agreements can be hindered by 'migration salience' and illustrates his point as follows: France has signed several readmission agreements with Latin America, but Spain was not able to conclude readmission agreements with this part of the world.[339]

We can distinguish four different patterns in which postcolonial ties could influence the conclusion and implementation of Mobility Partnerships. In the first case, if the former colonial power is interested in the conclusion of a Mobility Partnership, it is likely that the third country will follow its will and conclude the partnership. On the other hand, if the former colonial power is not in favour of the conclusion of the Mobility Partnership the negotiations have high chances to fail. The other patterns are related to the proposition of projects in the framework of the Mobility Partnership and its implementation. We saw that usually bilateral relation between Member States and a third country is favoured over the relation between the EU and the third country. This would mean that most of the projects proposed will be bilateral Member State-third country projects rather than EU-third country or joint projects. The third pattern is that bilateral relations are not always preferred by countries with postcolonial ties therefore former colonies could prefer concluding agreements with Member States with which they do not have postcolonial ties. This can have an impact on which country will be the most active in proposing and implementing Mobility Partnerships projects. The last pattern was that postcolonial ties could impede the conclusion of bilateral agreements.

The last point to underline concerning the influence of the *state of relations between third countries and EU Member States* is that postcolonial ties have strongly influenced the political system of their former colonies.[340] Joy Asongazoh Alemazung argues that the influence of some European States (and the West in general) on the political system of their former colonies led to a form of 'dependence in political processes' from the former colony towards the former colonial power.[341] This means that not only can postcolonial ties influence the level of administrative capacity of a third country but also influence policies that are being developed and implemented in these countries. This aspect of the factor of the *State of relations between third countries and EU Member States* can be combined with the factor of the *level of administrative capacity* because Member States, and particularly former

337 Jean-Pierre Cassarino (n336) 15.

338 Ibid.

339 Ibid 17–18.

340 Joy Asongazoh Alemazung, 'Post-Colonial Colonialism: An Analysis of International Factors and Actors Marring African Socio-Economic and Political Development' (2010) *JPAS* 3(10) 62; Rollin F Tusalem, 'The Colonial Foundations of State Fragility and Failure' (2016) 48(4) *Polity* 445.

341 Joy Asongazoh Alemazung (n340) 64.

colonial powers, can influence the content of new laws and policies through development aid funding but also through the intervention of national expert to support these developments.[342] We will see at the end of this section, when presenting the *administrative capacity* factor, that more the former colony is dependent on the influence of a Member State higher the risk of legal transplant exists.

Power of negotiation

It may be said that there are two opposite scenarios for the position of third countries vis-à-vis the EU: either the third country has a high geopolitical importance for the EU's migration policy, which gives it a strong negotiating position, or it has low geopolitical importance placing it in a weak negotiating position.[343] The question raised is that of knowing when is a third country considered to have geopolitical importance for the EU? For over a decade, the EU has adopted the practice of externalising some of its migration control to neighbouring third countries to fight the entry of irregular migrants in its territory, converting these third countries into EU's 'gate-keepers'.[344] The externalisation of migration control is not a new phenomenon. Sandra Lavenex argues that the 'external dimension' of EU asylum and immigration policies has always existed involving non-European countries to 'share the burden of migration control'.[345] Being a 'gate-keeper' means that a third country on the other side of an EU border is able to prevent migrants from entering the EU irregularly, which gives it a high geopolitical importance for the EU. Michael Teitelbaum observed since several decades that third countries can use migration as a threat in their negotiations.[346] Kelly Greenhill builds on Teitelbaum's work and argues that countries may use the argument of outflows of migration (real or threatened) 'as a foreign policy tool, to induce (or prevent) changes in political behaviour and/or extract side-payments from the target(s)'.[347] On the other hand, if a third country has low migration fluxes towards the EU or is not located on a major migration route, it will have low geopolitical importance for the EU. This third country will therefore have a low level of negotiation power with the EU. It should be noted that the power of negotiation is not static and depend on the geopolitical situation at a specific moment. This means that, as the Mobility Partnership and particularly the Annex

342 Jean-Claude Berthelemy, 'Bilateral donors' interest vs. recipients' development motives in aid allocation: Do all donors behave the same?' (2005) Cahiers de la Maison des Sciences Economiques 1; Sarah Wolff, *The Mediterranean Dimension of the European Union's Internal Security* (London: Palgrave Macmillan 2012); Sarah Wolff (n298) 69.

343 Frank R Pfetsch, 'Power in International Negotiations: Symmetry and Asymmetry' (2011/2) *Négociations* 16, 39.

344 Sandra Lavenex (n209) 94.

345 Ibid 335.

346 Michael S Teitelbaum, 'Immigration, Refugees, and Foreign Policy' (1984) 38(3) *Int Organ* 429.

347 Kelly M Greenhill, 'Strategic Engineered Migration as a Weapon of War' (2008) 10 (1) *Civil Wars* 6, 8–10

to the Joint Declaration is a living document, new projects can be proposed, and their implementation can be influenced according to the geopolitical importance and power of negotiation of a third country at a specific moment in time.

It may be assumed that, with a third country with low level of negotiation power, the Mobility Partnership will be mainly used as a tool by the EU and the Member States to impose their interests on the third country which may only 'take it or leave it'.[348] Reslow highlights the 'take it or leave it' approach taken in the cases of Moldova, Cape Verde and Senegal, where the same Mobility Partnership text was unilaterally proposed by the EU to these third countries with little room for negotiation.[349] If the third country agrees to conclude a Mobility Partnership under these terms, the content of the Mobility Partnership will presumably be mainly influenced by the EU and the Member States. One can envisage that the power (in)balance would stay the same during the implementation of the Mobility Partnership, so long as the EU's interest in the third country in question remains the same. In this case, the projects that would be implemented would also be largely influenced by the EU and the Member States, including projects having a relevance for the development of the legal framework of the partner third country. It is not excluded that the power dynamics evolves, as these dynamics are influenced by several external factors (e.g. political priorities or economic situation).

Conditionality is a key concept of Mobility Partnerships. Frank Schimmelfennig and Ulrich Sedelmeier note that the use of conditionality by the EU in its relations with third countries is a way to disseminate its norms and stimulate third countries to adopt new laws or different behaviour on specific issues.[350] Political conditionality is defined by Karen Smith as 'perceived benefits for another state (such as aid, [trade concessions, cooperation agreements, political contacts, or international organisation membership]), to the fulfilment of conditions relating to the protection of human rights and the advancement of democratic principles'.[351] Smith adds that, to be efficient, conditionality should not be contradictory in the many (and overlapping) instruments used by the EU in its migration policy with third countries.[352] Attaching strings to financial assistance and aid was primarily done by international financial institutions in the 1980s. By the 1990s, donors, including the EU, had adopted the practice of binding financial assistance and aid to political conditions, as they thought that an effective use of aid required the rule of law and the administrative capacity to implement it.[353] Judith Kelley defines conditionality as the

348 Natasja Reslow (n106) 395.
349 Ibid.
350 Frank Schimmelfennig and Ulrich Sedelmeier, 'Governance by Conditionality: EU Rule Transfer to the Candidate Countries of Central and Eastern Europe' (2004) 11 (4) *JEPP* 661, 661.
351 Karen E Smith, 'The Use of Political Conditionality in the EU's Relations with Third Countries: How Effective?' (1998) 3 *European Foreign Affairs Review* 253, 256.
352 Ibid 254.
353 Rosa Balfour (n272) 15.

'existence of incentives'.[354] Conditionality can be positive or negative. Positive conditionality rewards the compliance of third countries with given goals by, for example, increasing funding whereas negative conditionality is designed to 'punish' third countries by denying them access to funding that they used to receive. Positive conditionality is understood in the literature as the fact that conditionality can enhance wilful compliance and mechanisms of 'reinforcement by reward'.[355] On the contrary, negative conditionality is seen as a mean of coercion.[356] The use of negative conditionality is not always well accepted. For example, in 1992, Morocco was sanctioned for its human rights abuses in Western Sahara and with political prisoners.[357] Consequently, EU's budget for Morocco was frozen, which was strongly contested by Spain and other EU Member States.[358] This response by Spain and other Member States has been used to show that applying 'negative' conditionality can have a detrimental outcome on relations with third countries as well as on EU governments that have strong ties with them.[359]

Conditionality used to be related mainly to democratic progress in third countries.[360] In the Southern Mediterranean region, the EU collaborated for a long time with undemocratic regimes, on areas such as the fight against terrorism, the fight against irregular migration, and peace and stability in the region, without much talk of conditionality.[361] Quite to the contrary, the EU gave economic incentives to these regimes.[362] After the Arab Spring, political cooperation between the EU and southern Mediterranean countries gained significant political appeal and conditionality was redefined.[363] The power of conditionality has been

354 Judith Kelley, 'New Wine in Old Wineskins: Promoting Political Reforms through the New European Neighbourhood Policy' (2006) 44(1) *JCMS* 29, 36.
355 Frank Schimmelfennig, Stefan Engert and Heiko Knobel, 'Costs, Commitment and Compliance: The Impact of EU Democratic Conditionality in Latvia, Slovakia and Turkey' (2003) 41(3) *JCMS* 495.
356 Frank Dobbin, Beth Simmons and Geoffrey Garrett, 'The Global Diffusion of Public Policies: Social Construction, Coercion, Competition, or Learning?' (2007) 33 *Annu Rev Sociol* 449.
357 Elena Baracani, 'The European Neighbourhood Policy and Political Conditionality: Double Standards in EU Democracy Promotion?' 133 in Thierry Balzacq (ed.), *The External Dimension of EU Justice and Home Affairs Governance, Neighbours, Security* (Basingstoke, UK: Palgrave Macmillan 2009) 137–138.
358 Ibid 138.
359 Said Haddadi, 'Two Cheers for Whom? The European Union and Democratization in Morocco' (2002) 9 *Democratization* 149, 161.
360 Sandra Lavenex and Frank Schimmelfennig (n309); Frank Schimmelfennig, Stefan Engert and Heiko Knobel (n679), Aurelia Dercaci, 'European Neighbourhood Policy: New Models of External Governance' 287 in Beatriz Pérez de las Heras (ed.), *Democratic Legitimacy in the European Union and Global Governance: Building a European Demos* (Cham, Switzerland: Springer 2016).
361 Sandra Lavenex and Frank Schimmelfennig (n309) 899; Assem Dandashly, 'The EU Response to Regime Change in the Wake of the Arab Revolt: Differential Implementation' (2014) 37(1) *J Eur Integr* 37, 38.
362 Assem Dandashly (n362) 38.
363 Ibid.

questioned in the literature. Several authors argue that, since southern Mediterranean countries have no possibility of accessing EU membership, the EU lacks a strong enough incentive to offer.[364] Even if southern Mediterranean countries are aware that they cannot gain access to the EU, they still try to bargain with the EU on other issues of interest, such as increased mobility, funding, political support or a closer relation status with the EU. In practice, the application of conditionality by the EU has been limited regarding southern Mediterranean countries.[365] This can be explained by the importance of migration control in the region as well as, other strategic and security priorities which make it difficult for the EU to adopt a strong position towards countries with which strategic cooperation is needed.[366]

The new 'more for more' conditionality includes financial and technical assistance, trade and mobility incentives.[367] It is interesting to note that in practice the Mobility Partnership can be used as a tool to materialise conditionality.[368] Mobility Partnerships are presented by the EU as a way to enhance mobility for third country nationals, so they include mobility incentives, but they also draw financial means for specific projects and many capacity building initiatives which are financial and technical incentives.[369] For example, the SPRING programme (Support for the Partnership, Reforms and Inclusive Growth) can finance specific projects included in a Mobility Partnership aiming at supporting concrete reforms in the third country.[370] Another incentive offered to third countries under the 'more for more' approach is the Deep and Comprehensive Free Trade Agreement (DCFTA). The DCFTA will be proposed only to countries that comply with EU's democracy standards.[371]

It is generally agreed in the literature that Mobility Partnerships are one-sided and put more pressure on the third country than on participating Member States.[372] However, for the Governments of third countries, cooperating with the EU can also be a source of political leverage. Third countries may strategically exploit what they can offer the EU in terms of the objectives of the EU's external

364 Rosa Balfour (n272) 19; Rachel Epstein and Ulrich Sedelmeier, 'Beyond Conditionality: International Institutions in Postcommunist Europe After Enlargement' (2008) 15(6) *JEPP* 795, 803; Tanja A Börzel and Bidzina Lebanidze, '"The Transformative Power of Europe" Beyond Enlargement: The EU's Performance in Promoting Democracy in its Neighbourhood' (2017) 33(1) *East European Politics* 17, 20; Vera van Hüllen, *EU Democracy Promotion and the Arab Spring: International Cooperation and Authoritarianism: Governance and Limited Statehood* (Basingstoke, UK: Palgrave Macmillan 2015).

365 Rosa Balfour (n272) 16.

366 Jean-Pierre Cassarino, 'Informalising Readmission Agreements in the EU Neighbourhood' (2007) 42(2) *The International Spectator* 179, 191–192.

367 Rosa Balfour (n272) 21.

368 Ibid 22.

369 Ibid 21–22.

370 Ibid 21.

371 Ibid 21.

372 Sergio Carrera and Raül Hernández I Sagrera (n2); Sergio Carrera and Raül Hernández I Sagrera (n2); Agnieszka Weinar (n121); Mohammed Limam and Raffaella Del Sarto (n114).

migration policy, such as the conclusion of an EU Readmission Agreement (EURA). Since 1999, the EU has strived to conclude EURAs with third countries including the obligation to readmit third country nationals. The conclusion of these agreements has subsequently been a political priority for the EU.[373] The conclusion of a Mobility Partnership suggests the willingness on the part of the partner third country to negotiate a EURA, even though there is no obligation to conclude one. Mobility Partnerships can be seen as tools to provide leverage to the EU for the negotiations of EURAs with third countries by proposing a whole set of initiatives. Given that the EU prioritises the control of migration, third countries which cooperate with this control agenda gain a more strategic position to negotiate their own conditions. In concrete terms, the negotiation of a readmission agreement can be a strong bargaining chip for a third country and allows it to negotiate a broader spectrum of positive incentives through the Mobility Partnership. Such a situation where the third country takes over the bargaining initiative and demands financial and political support in return for cooperation with the EU can be seen as 'reversed conditionality'.[374] Cassarino illustrates his argument with the refusal of Morocco, as far as 2017, to sign an EURA if the EU does not conclude further EURAs with other countries in Africa.[375] This power can be used by the third country as a bargaining chip to gain more leverage in negotiations. The hypothesis follows that the Mobility Partnership is used not only by the EU but also by the partner third countries to achieve their objectives. In this configuration, the third country can also influence the content of the Mobility Partnership. For example, the third country can push for the creation and implementation of specific projects benefitting its own interests. Projects related to the development of the partner third country's domestic legal framework will probably be influenced not only by the EU and/or its Member States, but also directly by the partner third country. The use of 'reversed conditionality' thus provides third countries with a possibility to put forth their own interests and the ability to counterbalance the disadvantages linked to their cooperation with the EU leading to more dynamic relations between the EU and a third country than that which is often pictured. Certainly, the increased reliance of the EU on third countries to fight irregular migration and to cooperate on border control has a price. The introduction of the 'more for more' conditionality, together with the increased interdependence between the EU and the partner third countries on border management and the fight against irregular migration, have shifted power relations. Third countries are gaining a strategic position giving them the possibility to impose their own conditions to the EU and the Member States. Syrian neighbouring countries are using migration as a bargaining chip in their relations with the EU since the outbreak of the migration crisis (Turkey being a blatant

373 Florian Trauner and Imke Kruse, 'EC Visa Facilitation and Readmission Agreements: Implementing a New EU Security Approach in the Neighbourhood' (2008) CEPS Working Document No 290.

374 Jean-Pierre Cassarino (n366) 192; Fanny Tittel-Mosser (n115).

375 Jean-Pierre Cassarino (n366) 192.

example).[376] Zeynep Özler argues that Turkey was using 'reversed conditionality' in its negotiation of a EURA with the EU affirming that they would only conclude it if the EU would offer them visa liberation in exchange.[377] Additionally, a report by the Advisory Committee on Migration Affairs shows that 'reversed conditionality' is the main reason countries of origin do not cooperate on forced return.[378]

The power of negotiation of a third country is not only related to its importance for the EU, but also to the state of its relations with the EU Member States. As seen previously, Member States have different interests, sometimes linked to their historical past, such as strong bilateral relations with former colonies.[379] A third country which is strongly dependent on a Member State (e.g.: a former colonial power) has higher risks of being influenced by it in its legal and policy developments. The same reasoning supports this argument than the 'take it or leave it' approach taken by the EU in terms of proposition and implementation of projects. When presenting the *state of relations between third countries and EU Member States* factor we saw that former colonies are usually likely to be in line with specific Member State's objectives. When a third country has a power of negotiation towards the EU but is also dependent on a specific Member State the implementation of the Mobility Partnership can be influenced by both factors at the same time. These factors can be conflicting and depending on the situation one can be more influential than the other. This could mean that in some cases a Member State refuses to implement projects that the third country, former colony, pushes forth because it goes against its own interests, but the EU could support the initiative because the third country has the power to convince the EU to do so.

Administrative capacity

There is no commonly accepted definition of administrative capacity and it is often assumed that measuring it is extremely complex,[380] but, for the purposes of this study, it suffices to say that administrative capacity refers to the capacity of a state to define and implement policies and to legislate and enforce the law. Administrative capacity can comprise human and financial resources, the possibility to provide training and capacity building to staff, the awareness of a specific issue (migration), the existence of a legislative framework and the effective application of laws. Jonathan Miller argues that developing countries are usually lacking

376 Zeynep Özler, 'Breaking the Vicious Circle in EU-Turkey Relations: Visa Negotiations' (2012) 11(1) *TPQ* 121.

377 Ibid 128.

378 ACVZ, 'The strategic country approach to migration, advisory report Addressed to the Minister for Foreign Trade and Development Cooperation and the State Secretary of Security and Justice' (2015) 1, 25–26.

379 Sarah Wolff (n342) 16; James Hampshire (n329) 576.

380 Helen J Addison, 'Is Administrative Capacity a Useful Concept? Review of the Application, Meaning and Observation of Administrative Capacity in Political Science Literature' (2009) LSE Research Paper 1, 4.

administrative capacity.[381] Anna Triandafyllidou doubts the capacity of third countries to implement simultaneously legal migration and border control policies if they have low administrative capacity and argues that Mobility Partnerships should have a strong capacity building component.[382] The notion of administrative capacity is directly linked to capacity building. Again, the term 'capacity building' does not have a unanimous definition.[383] Peter May argues that capacity building is a tool facilitating policy implementation.[384] Certainly, it can be argued that the advancement of the functioning of a country's institutions and bureaucracy leads to a more efficient implementation of policies and that it is in the interest of the EU to fund capacity building projects, since a third country with low administrative capacity can be difficult to cooperate with (as it will not be able to effectively implement agreements, for example).

Capacity building can be provided to third countries by development aid. It is common that aid programmes are assisting both with drafting legislation and with the development of administrative capacity and African countries are among the main beneficiaries of such aid programmes. This is, for example, the case of the MIgration EU eXpertise (MIEUX) facility, funded by the European Commission and implemented by the International Centre for Migration Policy Development (ICMPD).[385] It facilitates capacity building and peer-to-peer knowledge sharing. The main goal of this initiative is to strengthen 'the migration governance capacities of governments in Africa, Asia, the Middle East, and Latin America by mobilising experts from EU Member States and other countries'. It is widespread practice in aid programmes that foreign experts assist the governments and parliaments of the beneficiaries. These foreign experts can, consciously or not, replicate laws or policies that are in force in their country of origin when providing capacity building in a third country. According to Iann Manners, EU norms can be transferred to third countries through aid and technical assistance, or 'transference'.[386] He also argues that 'overt diffusion' arise from 'the physical presence of the EU in third states', such as the EU Delegation and Member States' embassies.[387] Third countries' governments can increasingly become open to such

381 Jonathan Miller, 'A Typology of Legal Transplants: Using Sociology, Legal History and Argentine Examples to Explain the Transplants Process' (2003) 51(4) *Am J Comp L* 839, 857.

382 Anna Triandafyllidou (n12) 11.

383 See, for example, the definition given by the United Nations: United Nations Economic and Social Council, Definition of basic concepts and terminologies in governance and public administration E/C.16/2006/4, New York, 27–31 March 2006, 7–8; Or the definition given by the OECD, OECD, 'The Challenge of Capacity Development: Working Towards Good Practice' (2006) OECD Papers, Vol. 6/1, 1, 44.

384 Peter May, 'Policy Design and Implementation' 223 in B Guy Peters and Jon Pierre (eds), *Handbook of Public Administration* (London: Sage 2003).

385 For more information see: https://www.icmpd.org/our-work/capacity-building/multi-thematic-programmes/mieux-iii (accessed 18 January 2018).

386 Iann Manners, 'Normative Power Europe: A contradiction in Terms?' (2002) 40(2) *JCMS* 235, 245.

387 Ibid 245.

influence as they become used to working with foreign advisors or because of strong relations with the Member States that provided them with 'legislative support'. This factor interplays with the *state relations* factor, as often, for linguistic reasons, the foreign experts originate from the former colonial powers in Europe. This situation can open the ground for legal transplants or policy transplant.

Alan Watson coined the concept of legal transplants and defined it as 'the moving of a rule or a system of law from one country to another, or from one people to another'.[388] He explains the occurrence of legal transplants by the fact that they are cost-saving as it 'saves time and effort' to the receiving society or by the 'prestige' of the foreign model that gives legitimacy and legal authority to the transplanted law.[389] Jonathan Miller points out that third countries lacking financial or human resources can be interested in adopting laws based on pre-existing laws.[390] Moreover, according to Rodolfo Sacco, strong societies are inclined to impose and disseminate their own values and institutions to weaker societies.[391] Similarly, Linda Hantrais discussed the possibility to 'transplant' policies[392] and several authors examined the capacity of the EU in framing migration and asylum policies in third countries.[393]

Several situations in which 'transplant policies' can occur have been selected in the literature (besides those mentioned earlier in the text such as overt diffusion) as they might apply to the case of Mobility Partnerships. Iann Manners suggests that the EU can diffuse its norms to third countries by different means. For example, it can be through *contagion*, which is unintended. In this case, the EU does not really decide to transfer its norms, but third countries adopt them because they seem efficient or a 'model'. It can also be through the strategic communication about new policies. The *procedural* diffusion can be the consequence of the institutionalisation of a relationship through for example cooperation agreements. Mobility Partnerships aiming at institutionalising dialogue and cooperation between the EU and third countries can subsequently also be subject to procedural diffusion.[394] Whether these are situations leading to policy transfer in the implementation of Mobility Partnerships with Morocco and Cape Verde will be discussed further in the book.

388 Alan Watson, *Legal Transplants: An Approach in Comparative Law* (Edinburgh: Scottish Academic Press 1974) 21.

389 Ibid; Alan Watson, 'Aspects of Reception of Law' (1996) 44 *Am J Comp L* 335.

390 Jonathan Miller (n381) 845–846.

391 Rodolfo Sacco, 'Legal Formants: A Dynamic Approach to Comparative Law (Installment II of II)' (1991) 39 *Am J Comp L* 343, 398.

392 Linda Hantrais, *International Comparative Research: Theory, Methods and Practice* (New York: Palgrave Macmillan 2009) 45.

393 Sergo Mananashvili, 'The Diffusion of the EU Asylum Acquis in the Eastern Neighbourhood: A Test for the EU's Normative Power' (2015) 20(2) *EFAR* 187, 187; Laure Delcour, 'The EU: Shaping Migration Patterns in Its Neighbourhood and Beyond' 261 in Dimitri Kochenov and Fabian Amtenbrink (eds), *The European Union's Shaping of the International Legal Order* (Cambridge: Cambridge University Press 2013).

394 Iann Manners (n386) 244.

1.5 Conclusion

This chapter gave an overview of the Mobility Partnership tool first exposing its genesis and the way it has been presented and portrayed by the EU. It then provided more details into its structure, content and monitoring mechanisms. Mobility Partnerships were inaugurated in 2007 by the EU Commission and presented as the most innovative and sophisticated tool of the GAM. Mobility Partnerships are non-binding instruments concluded between the EU, interested Member States and a third country. They are Joint Declarations in which the objectives of the Mobility Partnership are set following the objectives of the GAM/GAMM. Additionally, Mobility Partnerships are composed of an Annex, which is a list of projects aiming at implementing the Mobility Partnership. This Annex is a living document and projects can be added and deleted through time. The number of projects and the number of Member States participating in a Mobility Partnership varies. The fact that Mobility Partnerships are non-binding means that the parties do not have the obligation to implement the proposed projects. A monitoring mechanism in the form of a scoreboard exists to follow the implementation of each Mobility Partnership. Apart from the Mobility Partnership with Moldova, these scoreboards are not public and their content and the assiduity in their updating depends widely from one partnership to the other. It is also interesting to note that despite the high interest the EU seems to have for the Mobility Partnership tool, no thorough evaluation of their implementation has officially been conducted since 2009.

An assessment of the advantages to conclude non-binding instruments has been conducted and three main factors have been highlighted. First, non-binding instruments offer a safe way to deal with uncertainty as they are flexible, which means that these instruments can be adapted to changes in policy priorities and circumstances. In the EU context, flexibility is an important feature and becomes increasingly so as the EU grows, and the legislative process becomes more burdensome. Second, non-binding instruments are a 'tool of compromise'. It is easier to negotiate a non-binding agreement than a legally binding one. Third, non-binding instruments allow fast agreements and shorten the adoption process which is one of the main reasons why the Commission prefers this type of instruments. It also helps to circumvent long and difficult national ratification procedures, which can lower sovereignty costs. This raises the question of competence and the application of the principle of subsidiarity.

Additionally, the legal nature of Mobility Partnerships has been scrutinised. Mobility Partnerships have been widely considered as soft law in the literature, but several questions remain concerning the type of instrument Mobility Partnerships are and how they fit in the EU legal architecture. The suggestion resulting from our analysis is that Mobility Partnerships are non-traditional EU instruments, which are non-binding but may, however, have legal relevance. In the case of Mobility Partnerships having legal relevance, the ECJ could be competent on Mobility Partnership related issues. This contradicts the view that Mobility Partnerships escape juridical control. Mobility Partnerships might escape democratic and juridical control, but they do not escape financial accountability

Mobility Partnerships are non-binding soft law instruments, but they can be relevant for the development of the legal and policy framework of the third country party of the partnership. The relevance can take different forms, it can be direct or indirect. Direct implies that the Mobility Partnership aims directly at concluding hard law. It also means that the development is a clear objective of the Mobility Partnership that one or more party wanted to achieve. This is the case of the conclusion of Readmission Agreements or Visa Facilitation Agreements. The relevance can be indirect which means that the legal or policy framework of a third country are developed through the implementation of Mobility Partnership projects not directly aiming at modifying the law or policy. It also means that the legal and policy developments can be a side effect of the implementation of a project or the result of changes in policy priorities that were not foreseen.

Three main factors can influence the relevance of Mobility Partnerships. These factors are the state of relations between third countries and EU Member States, the power of negotiation of a third country and its administrative capacity. These three factors can facilitate or impede the relevance of Mobility Partnerships on the legal and policy frameworks of third countries by favouring or not the proposition and implementation of legally or policy relevant projects. They can also influence the content of the new laws and policies adopted in the third country. The EU influence could take several forms including legal transplant and policy transfer.

2 EU Mobility Partnerships with Cape Verde and Morocco

Context of adoption, content and stage of implementation

The Mobility Partnership with Cape Verde was concluded in 2008, whereas Morocco's Mobility Partnership was concluded in 2013, five years later, in a context of crisis that required a political shift of position from the EU. Cape Verde is a small country with limited migration flows towards Europe, whereas Morocco has significantly more emigration towards Europe and plays a more strategic position as an entry point towards Europe. However, some similarities exist between both cases, such as the role of the former colonial power. France and Portugal play a prominent role in the selection of the third country but also in the proposition of projects shaping the content of the Mobility Partnerships and determining their implementation. Moreover, this chapter explores the relation between the Mobility Partnership tool and the broader EU policy related to migration, notably the implementation of the GAM and GAMM. The Mobility Partnership is the instrument of predilection for the EU to implement the principles of the GAM/ GAMM, therefore it substantially influences the structure of the partnerships. Finally, this chapter provides an overview of the implementation of both Mobility Partnerships including distinct stages of implementation: *in preparation*, *ongoing*, *concluded* and *deleted/not impleme nted*. Projects are also divided in three different typologies: *pre-existent*, *concomitant* and *new*.

2.1 Context of adoption of the Mobility Partnerships with Cape Verde and Morocco

In order for a third country to be selected to conclude a Mobility Partnership it has to comply with criteria set by the Commission. The Communication on Circular Migration and Mobility Partnerships between the European Union and Third Countries indicates a non-exhaustive list of criteria.[1] The main criteria are the geographical balance between the South and East of Europe, the willingness to cooperate on irregular migration and border control, the engagement to negotiate a readmission agreement and the weight of migration flows from the

1 Commission of the European Communities, on Circular Migration and Mobility Partnerships between the European Union and Third Countries COM(2007) 248 final, Brussels, 16 May 2007, 1.

third country to Europe. I argue that it is not mandatory to fulfil all criteria as Cape Verde was not a country with an important migration flow towards Europe. Moreover, Morocco is known for not willing to commit to a readmission agreement including third country nationals. In addition to the criteria mentioned, the Commission also advises to take into account broader economic, political and security factors.[2] In practice, Member States substantially influence the choice of the third country to which a Mobility Partnership is proposed.[3] The main reason why the Commission has to accept Member States' preferences lays in the nature of Mobility Partnerships itself; the Member States are free to participate or not. In order to have enough Member States participating in a Mobility Partnership and proposing and implementing projects, the Commission has to give priority to Member States' preferences.[4] Carrera and Hernández I Sagrera argue that national migration policies are at the heart of Mobility Partnerships.[5] In other words, a Member State would agree to participate only if it furthers its national policy.

Potential initiatives enhancing mobility towards Europe through Mobility Partnerships would not affect EU Member States' sovereignty in this regard as they have the last word when it comes to project implementation.

2.1.1 The conclusion of the Mobility Partnership with Cape Verde

The relation between the EU and Cape Verde is uncommon compared to usual relations between the EU and African countries.[6] Cape Verde was uninhabited when it was discovered by Portugal in 1462 and was a Portuguese colony for over 500 years, until 1975. During the colonial period, Cape Verde already had a singular position compared to other African colonies. Cape Verdeans worked as part of the Portuguese administration in other colonies, such as Guinea-Bissau and Angola, giving Cape Verdeans a special status in the colonial structure. Cape Verde is also a mixed society with most of its population being of mixed African and European origins. After its independence Cape Verde was totally reliant on foreign aid.[7] Peter Meyns explains that 'the new leaders of Cape Verde faced the dual challenges of 'viability' and 'vulnerability', common to island countries. Structurally unable to achieve self-sufficiency in food production and with only limited export potential, Cape Verde needed donor support to survive'.[8] Cape Verde has struggled with its lack of resources since its independence and has

2 European Commission, on the Global Approach to Migration and Mobility, COM (2011) 743 final, Brussels, 18 November 2011, 1, 10.

3 Natasja Reslow, 'Deciding on EU External Migration Policy: The Member States and the Mobility Partnerships' [2012] *JEI* 34(3) 223, 230.

4 Interview 29 DG Home Affairs, Brussels, 26 October 2016.

5 Sergio Carrera and Raül Hernández I Sagrera, 'The externalisation of the EU's labour immigration policy: Towards mobility or insecurity partnerships?' (2009) CEPS Working Document 321 1, 31.

6 Jairzinho Lopes Pereira, 'Theorizing the EU Conditionality Policy and Its Application in West African Countries: The Case of Cape Verde' [2014] *ESJ* Special Edition 389, 401.

7 Armelle Enders, *Histoire de l'Afrique lusophone* (Paris: Chandeigen 2013) 133.

8 Peter Meyns, 'Cape Verde: An African Exception' [2002] *JoD* 13(3) 153, 157.

understood since early on that having close relations with the major aid donor, the EU, could be beneficial.[9] EU's financial support (even if not the only provider) has been a key influence for the improvement of the poverty level and the consolidation of democratic institutions.[10]

Since 2005, Portugal and Cape Verde have been working together in order to help the archipelago build even closer ties with the EU.[11] As a result from their colonial past, both countries have strong bilateral ties and Cape Verde was prompted to go beyond the Cotonou Agreement in its cooperation with the EU.[12] In March 2005, Mário Soares, a former President of the Portuguese Republic, Diogo Freitas do Amaral, at the time Portugal's Foreign Minister, and Adriano Moreira, a former Portuguese Minister of the Overseas Territories, supported Cape Verde's candidacy to become an EU Member State.[13] Cape Verdean authorities did however not submit an official membership application. The idea of Cape Verde becoming an EU Member State has also never been formally rejected.

Chou and Gibert argue that pre-existing postcolonial ties are determinant factors in the cooperation between the EU and third countries and regions.[14] It is usually agreed that EU Member States keep strong relationships with former colonies as illustrated by the relationship between Cape Verde and Portugal. Chou and Gibert believe that third countries and a Member State that have postcolonial ties will tend to adopt a common position when negotiating with the EU as they will favour the existence of the postcolonial link versus the relationship with the EU. This means that third countries would only agree to conclude a Mobility Partnership if the former colonial power is favourable to it. It could also mean that the former colonial power will be more involved than the EU in the proposition and implementation of projects. This is particularly true when the Mobility Partnership has little or no 'added value' in comparison to the pre-existing cooperation with the former colony.[15]

In January 2007, a task force aiming at creating a Special Partnership for Cape Verde was created. In the second semester of 2007, the Council was presided by Portuguese Prime Minister José Socrates and the Commission was chaired by José Manuel Durão Barroso, a former Portuguese Prime Minister. Both officials wanted the EU to focus more on Africa and were sensitive to the aspirations of Cape-Verdeans having a closer status with the EU. The perfect configuration for

9 Jairzinho Lopes Pereira (n6) 390.

10 Ibid.

11 Alena Vysotskaya Guedes Vieira and Laura C Ferreira-Pereira, 'The European Union-Cape Verde Special Partnership: The Role of Portugal' [2009] *PJIA* 42(1) 42, 44.

12 Natasja Reslow, 'The Role of Third Countries in EU Migration Policy: The Mobility Partnership' [2012] *EJML* 393, 400.

13 Jairzinho Lopes Pereira (n6) 391; Petition urging EU membership for Cape Verde launched in Portugal, available at: https://web.archive.org/web/20050623165034/http://www.eubusiness.com/External_Relations/050317090821.tnkf9k7j (accessed 24 November 2017).

14 Meng-Hsuan Chou and Marie V Gibert, 'The EU-Senegal Mobility Partnership: From Launch to Suspension and Negotiation Failure' [2012] *JCER* 8(4), 408, 414–415.

15 Ibid 415.

the conclusion of the Special Partnership with Cape Verde was in place.[16] In December 2007, the EU and Cape Verde concluded a Special Partnership.[17] Hitherto, the cooperation on migration issues between Cape Verde and the EU was essentially conducted by Portugal alone.[18] The Special Partnership has been described as a means for the EU to diminish alleged security threats coming from West Africa, specifically drug trafficking, terrorist activities and irregular migration.[19]

The Special Partnership is based on six pillars: good governance; security and stability; regional integration; the convergence of technology and standards policies in the areas covered by the action plan; knowledge-based society; and the fight against poverty.[20] The Special Partnership encompasses the issues of immigrants' integration and the management of migration flows under the pillars of good governance and security and stability, but there is no pillar that specifically focuses on migration. The focus on migration and mobility is done through the Mobility Partnership.[21] The Special Partnership and the Mobility Partnership are connected. Even though the Mobility Partnership has some degree of autonomy, it is not independent of the Special Partnership.[22] According to a Cape Verdean official, the existence of the Special Partnership shaped the content of the Mobility Partnership.[23] The Council Presidency saw in the conclusion of this Mobility Partnership a way to 'improve the political profile of Cape Verde'.[24]

It was in the favourable climate of the negotiation of the Special Partnership that discussions about the Mobility Partnership started. Spain and Portugal were enthusiastic supporters of Cape Verde being chosen as a pilot country for the conclusion of a Mobility Partnership. Both countries have significant economic interests in the country. Portugal and Spain were Cape Verde's main trade partners at the time of the negotiations, and still are today. In 2007, Spain (44.2%) and Portugal (21.7%) were Cape Verde's main exports partners and part of its top three main imports partners (Portugal 41.1%, the Netherlands 10.6% and Spain 6.5%).[25] Moreover, a fisheries agreement[26] was concluded between the European

16 Alena Vysotskaya Guedes Vieira and Laura C Ferreira-Pereira (n11) 42, 46.
17 Commission of the European Communities, on the Future of Relations between the European Union and the Republic of Cape Verde, COM(2007) 641 final, Brussels, 24 October 2007.
18 Sergio Carrera and Raül Hernández I Sagrera (n5) 21–22.
19 Jairzinho Lopes Pereira (n6) 397.
20 Commission of the European Communities (n1) 4–6.
21 Interview 36, MIREX, Praia, 23 February 2016.
22 Commission of the European Communities (n1) 4–6.
23 Interview 36 (n21).
24 Alena Vysotskaya Guedes Vieira and Laura C Ferreira-Pereira (n11) 48.
25 Cape Verde Business Mission Fact Sheets, available at: http://www.conscv.nl/images/documentos/Cape_Verde_Business_Mission_Fact_Sheet_NABC.pdf (accessed 27 November 2017).
26 Acordo entre a Comunidade Económica Europeia e a República de Cabo Verde relativo à pesca ao largo de Cabo Verde – Protocolo que fixa as possibilidades de pesca e a compensação financeira previstas no Acordo entre a Comunidade Económica Europeia e o Governo da República de Cabo Verde relativo à pesca ao largo de Cabo Verde OJ L 212, 9.8.1990.

Economic Community (EEC) and Cape Verde in 1990 allowing Portugal, Spain and France to fish in the waters of Cape Verde.

Portugal strongly supported the conclusion of the Mobility Partnership with Cape Verde leading multiple meetings with different EU Member States, to raise awareness on the case of Cape Verde in order to promote the Special Partnership as well as the Mobility Partnership linked to it.[27] The Cape Verdean ambassador in Brussels was responsible for the negotiations of the Mobility Partnership. Cape Verde was also proactive in its attempts to be selected as a pilot country for the Mobility Partnership. The Cape Verdean ambassador in Lisbon approached Portuguese officials and the Cape Verdean ambassador in Brussels discussed a potential Mobility Partnership with the Permanent Representation of Luxembourg.[28] The Cape Verdean government did however not submit a formal written expression of interest to the Commission or Council.[29]

EU officials based in Brussels and Praia agree on the fact that Cape Verde had been chosen as a pilot country due to its willingness to cooperate and its good relations with the EU, therefore preventing the risks of failure. Moreover, it is a small country with a manageable migration flow, it is isolated, it is a stable country, democratic, and culturally close to the EU due to its colonial past.[30] It had all the 'ingredients' to be a successful partnership and a 'quick win'. Jairzinho Lopes Pereira argues that '[t]he EU has Cape Verde in high regard because the country is an example of stability and good governance and makes good use of the European funds'.[31] Due to its high level of governance the Commission hopes that Cape Verde can be a model for other African, Caribbean and Pacific (ACP) countries to follow. Cape Verde can be seen as a success story of decolonisation in Africa. It is a stable and democratic country and has been included by the United Nations in the group of middle-income countries, in 2007.[32] Moreover, Cape Verde was considered as being the 'best student' in the region because of its existing cooperation on migration and security issues which played a significant role in being chosen as a Mobility Partnership beneficiary.[33] Migration was not the primary reason to conclude the Mobility Partnership but rather the motivation of Cape Verde to cooperate on security issues such as the fight against transnational organised crime.

27 Alena Vysotskaya Guedes Vieira and Laura C Ferreira-Pereira (n11) 47.

28 Natasja Reslow, *Partnering for Mobility? Three-level Games in EU External Migration Policy* (Maastricht, The Netherlands: Datawyse/Universitaire Pers Maastricht 2013) 191.

29 European Commission, on Mobility Partnerships as a Tool of the Global Approach to Migration SEC(2009) 1240 final, Brussels, 18 September 2009, 1, 3.

30 Interview 29 (n4); Interview 32 ICMPD, Brussels, 28 October 2016; Interview 39 EU Delegation, Praia, 25 February 2016.

31 Jairzinho Lopes Pereira (n6) 390.

32 Committee for Development Policy Expert Group Meeting, Review of the list of Least Developed Countries, Monitoring the progress of graduated countries: Cape Verde, New York, 16–17 January 2011, 1, 1.

33 Interview 36 (n21).

The reasons for Member States to participate in the Mobility Partnership were various. In 2005, there were 53,008 Cape Verdeans in Portugal; 18,180 in France; 11,532 in the Netherlands; 3,243 in Spain; and 1,234 in Luxembourg.[34] These are the main destinations for Cape Verdean migrants towards Europe.[35] These are also the countries that participate in the Mobility Partnership with Cape Verde. The flux towards the other Member States being so insignificant or even inexistent, they had no reason to participate in the Mobility Partnership. Moreover, in the case of Spain, Portugal and France, trade and the fisheries agreement also played a role as it increased the interests of these countries in collaborating with Cape Verde. In addition, Portugal has strong bilateral ties with Cape Verde due to their postcolonial ties. But the fact that Cape Verde became a middle-income country in 2007 also played a role. Indeed, leaving the group of least developed countries meant higher economic pressures on the country. The country lost the possibility to access the EU market without quotas and will now have to pay taxes on the products they sell in the EU.[36] Cape Verde being economically dependent on the EU had to find a new way to access funding. Moreover, this new classification led to the loss of aid funding from several Member States. The fact that Cape Verde became a middle-income country was a reason for the Netherlands to participate in the Mobility Partnership. Indeed, as a result of Cape Verde entering the category of middle-income countries, it ceased to be a priority of the Dutch national aid programme.[37] That meant funding cuts for development projects in Cape Verde by the Netherlands. The Netherlands saw the Mobility Partnership as a new possibility to keep development cooperation programmes with Cape Verde going, allowing for the allocation of funding for Mobility Partnerships projects that could no longer be funded directly through their national aid programme. The Netherlands would join the Mobility Partnership at a later stage, as at first they did not consider the Mobility Partnership with Cape Verde sufficiently relevant, even though they were the third recipient country of Cape Verdean immigrants in Europe at the time.[38]

In December 2007, in parallel to the conclusion of the Special Partnership, the EU Council for Justice and Home Affairs adopted the Decision to start a dialogue on Mobility Partnership with Cape Verde.[39] Following the adoption of this decision, the Commission approached Cape Verdean officials. However, Cape Verdean officials, after some success in being chosen as a pilot country, were less able

34 United Nations, DESA, 'Population Division: International migrant stock 2005', available at: http://www.un.org/en/development/desa/population/migration/data/estimates2/estimates15.shtml (accessed 26 October 2016).

35 The United States being the first country of destination of Cape Verdean migrants.

36 Ministério dos Negocios Estrangeiros, *Balanço da Presidência Portuguesa do Conselho da Uniao Europeia*, 1 July–31 December 2007, 1, 150.

37 Ibid 234.

38 Natasja Reslow (n3) 232.

39 Council of the European Union, Draft Council Conclusions on Mobility Partnerships and Circular Migration in the Framework of the Global Approach to Migration 16283/07 Brussels, 7 December 2007.

to negotiate the text of the Mobility Partnership. Meng-Hsuan Chou[40] argues that third countries have no authority over the content of EU migration policy. According to the Commission's communication, Cape Verde had clear aspirations when it came to the content of the Mobility Partnership reckoning that the main concerns of the Cape Verdean government were security and mobility.[41] Interviews with Cape Verdean officials stressed however some of their shortcomings in the negotiations. Several respondents underlined the fact that the officials on the Cape Verdean side participating in the negotiations on the content of the Mobility Partnership were not sufficiently prepared and did not adequately assess their needs and priorities.[42] Their lack of preparation and clear expectations put them in a position where they could not have negotiated the content in a suitable way. One official declared that it is the Cape Verdeans' fault for not being prepared.[43] Several officials also underlined the inexperience of Cape Verdean officials in these types of negotiations and the fact that EU officials were well prepared and used to the negotiation process.[44] It seems that there was no power balance and Cape Verdean authorities did not have much choice but to accept the content proposed by the EU. Additionally, Lisa Akesson discusses the fact that Cape Verde was dependent on the EU funding received under the Special Partnership and as such did not have much room to object to the conclusion of the Mobility Partnership as both partnerships went hand in hand.[45]

At the time of the negotiations, Cape Verdean officials saw in the Mobility Partnership an opportunity to enhance the mobility perspectives of Cape Verdean citizens. Cape Verde is a country that highly depends on remittances from its nationals abroad.[46] With more possibilities to legally travel and work abroad, more Cape Verdeans could be sending remittances, a positive for the national economy. It should also be considered that at the time of the conclusion of this pilot Mobility Partnership the economic crisis had not yet hit the European economy and several labour mobility schemes were envisaged.[47] It is likely that the inclusion

40 Meng-Hsuan Chou, 'EU and the migration-development nexus: What prospects for EU-wide policies?' (2006) Working paper 37 Oxford: Centre on Migration, Policy and Society.

41 Commission of the European Communities (n1) 3.

42 Interview 33, Direção Geral das Comunidades, Praia, 23 February 2016; Interview 45, Ex-Secretário de Estado dos Negócios Estrangeiros/Former Ambassador, Praia, 16 November 2016.

43 Interview 33 (n42).

44 Interviews 33 and 45 (n42).

45 Lisa Akesson, 'Under the Cover of Partnership' [2011] *NAI Annual Report* 16, 16.

46 Jørgen Carling and Lisa Akesson, 'Mobility at the Heart of a Nation: Patterns and Meanings of Cape Verdean Migration' [2009] *Int Migr* 47(3) 123; IOM, Migração em Cabo Verde: Perfil Nacional (2009).

47 For example, between France and Cape Verde a bilateral agreement has been concluded in November 2008 opening the French labour market for Cape Verdeans working in specific types of positions. Accord entre le gouvernement de la République française et le gouvernement de la république du Cap Vert relatif à la gestion concertée des flux migratoires et au développement solidaire 20080297, 24 November 2008.

of Cape Verde in the Macaronesia combined with the talks envisaging the discussions about Cape Verde becoming an EU Member State, may have misled Cape Verdean authorities.[48] Moreover, at an early stage of the negotiation of the Mobility Partnership, the idea of granting a visa exemption status to Cape Verde was presented, but because of the start of economic and migration crises in Europe, it did not gain further traction. As Reslow puts it, Mobility Partnerships are 'being implemented in unfavourable circumstances, as these socio-economic conditions are not conducive to the creation of new channels of immigration from non-EU countries'.[49]

The Mobility Partnership between Cape Verde, the European Community and Spain, France, Luxembourg and Portugal, was concluded on 21 May 2008.[50] Cape Verde was the first pilot Mobility Partnership to be concluded in parallel with the Mobility Partnership with Moldova. Cape Verde is the only country outside of the EU neighbourhood that benefitted of a Mobility Partnership instead of a Common Agenda for Migration and Mobility (CAMM).

2.1.2 The conclusion of the Mobility Partnership with Morocco

Since its independence, immigration from Morocco has always been mainly directed towards Europe. The conclusion of various labour migration agreements with European countries accentuated this trend.[51] The large Moroccan diaspora in Europe plays a key role in the relations between the EU and Morocco.[52] Morocco, since early on, has chosen to have a close relationship with the EU.[53] The Moroccan candidacy to become an EU Member State presented in 1987 illustrates this point. Morocco's candidacy was rejected by the Council which argued that Morocco is not a European country.[54] Moreover, Morocco is a reliable partner in the area of border control to fight against irregular migration flows toward Europe.[55] Morocco works closely with Spain in order to secure the border

48 World Markets Analysis, Government to Request EU Membership for Cape Verde, 9 May 2005; Interviews 33 (n42) and 36 (n21).

49 Natasja Reslow, 'EU "Mobility" Partnerships: And Initial Assessment of Implementation Dynamics' [2015] *PaG* 3(2) 117, 125.

50 Council of the European Union, Joint Declaration on a Mobility Partnership between the European Union and the Republic of Cape Verde (2008) 9460/08 ADD 2.

51 Myriam Cherti and Michael Collyer, 'Immigration and Pensé e d'Etat: Moroccan Migration Policy Changes as Transformation of "Geopolitical Culture"' [2015] *The Journal of North African Studies* 20(4) 590, 600; Hein de Haas, 'Migration, Remittances and Regional Development in Southern Morocco' [2006] *Geoforum* 37 565; Mohamed Khachani, 'La Migration Circulaire: Cas du Maroc' (2008) CARIM Analytic and Synthetic Notes 2008/07.

52 Michael Collyer, and others, 'Migration and Development: The Euro–Moroccan Experience' [2009] *J Ethn Migr Stud* 35(10) 1555.

53 Berramdane Abdelkaleq, 'Le Maroc et l'Europe, un destin commun' 39 in *Annuaire de l'Afrique du Nord 1990, vol. XXIX* (Paris: CNRS Éditions 1992).

54 Herman Lelieveldt, Sebastiaan Princen, *The Politics of the European Union* (Cambridge: Cambridge University Press 2015) 284.

55 Paula García Andrade and Iván Martin, 'EU cooperation with third countries in the field of migration Study for the LIBE Committee' (2015) 1, 95.

between both countries. Additionally, between 2006 and 2008, Morocco and Spain implemented a project on the management of seasonal Moroccan migration workers going to Spain. The project aimed to prevent irregular migration by creating legal migration channels for temporary workers.[56] Morocco is considered by the EU as the 'good student' in the region, which is why it has been granted an 'advanced status' in 2008.[57] With the 'advanced status', Morocco can beneficiate from favourable policies related to maritime transport and better access to EU funding.[58] Economically, Morocco is heavily dependent on the EU.[59] The EU is the main market for Morocco to sell its goods and the tourism industry in Morocco is also dependent on European tourists. However, from the European perspective, Morocco is also an important trade partner and over half of Moroccan importations are coming from the EU. Under the Association Agreement concluded between the EU and Morocco (since 2000) a Free Trade Area (FTA)[60] liberalising two-way trade in goods was established. An agreement on trade in agricultural, agro-food and fisheries products[61] was added to the FTA later on. Furthermore, remittances are almost exclusively being sent from European countries. For Morocco, remittances constitute a major source of additional income for families of the diaspora. Morocco is the third largest recipient of remittance in the Middle East and North Africa (MENA) region, estimated by the World Bank at over USD 6.5 billion in 2012, which accounts for almost 7.5% of Morocco's GDP.[62] The need for financial support from the EU can explain why Morocco is eager to keep its position as 'the best student' in the Southern Mediterranean area and its distinct status within the EU.[63] Between 2007 and 2010 the EU spent EUR 67.6 million in budget support to Morocco in order to strengthen its border control, turning Morocco into a 'gate-keeper'.[64] Being a gate-keeper means that a

56 Commission of the European Communities (n1) 19.

57 Abdelwahab Biad, 'La construction du Maghreb au défi du partenariat euro-méditerranéen de l'Union européenne' in *L'Année du Maghreb* [online], Vol. IX (2013), 21 October 2013, available at: http://anneemaghreb.revues.org/1866 (accessed 23 November 2017).

58 Ibid.

59 Ibid.

60 European Union, Euro-Mediterranean Agreement Establishing an Association between the European Communities and their Member States, of the one part, and the Kingdom of Morocco, of the other part OJ L70/2 18.3.2000.

61 Council Decision of 2 December 2010 on the signature of the Agreement in the form of an Exchange of Letters between the European Union and the Kingdom of Morocco concerning Reciprocal Liberalisation Measures on Agricultural Products, Processed Agricultural Products, Fish and Fishery Products, the replacement of Protocols 1, 2 and 3 and their Annexes and Amendments to the Euro-Mediterranean Agreement establishing an Association between the European Communities and their Member States, of the one part, and the Kingdom of Morocco, of the other part 2012/496/EU OJ L 241, 7.9.2012.

62 World Bank (2013) *Migration and Development Brief 21*, Washington, DC: The World Bank.

63 Interview 29 (n4).

64 Paula García Andrade and Iván Martin (n55) 95.

third country on the other side of an EU border would prevent migrants from entering the EU irregularly.

The number of Moroccans residing abroad in 2012 is 2.8 million out of which 87% live in Europe.[65] The top European countries of emigration for Moroccans are France (31%), Spain (25%), Italy (12%), Belgium (7%), the Netherlands (5%), Germany (3%) and the UK (1%). All these countries are part of the Mobility Partnership with Morocco in addition to Portugal and Sweden. Migration fluxes are among one of the reasons as to why Morocco has decided to cooperate on a Mobility Partnership, but the cases of Sweden and Portugal hint to the fact that there are other factors. Indeed, several other reasons can explain why Member States have decided to participate in the Mobility Partnership with Morocco. One of them is that Morocco has strong bilateral ties to Spain and France; it also has postcolonial ties to both. Spain and France are well-known examples of Member States pushing forth their own national priorities at the EU level.[66] An EU official declared that Spain and France exploited the Mobility Partnership to promote and implement their own national policies.[67] Both have a long history with Morocco and firmly established interests in the country. They also share main concerns; the fight against irregular migration and internal security threats. It is interesting to see that the main countries pushing for the Mobility Partnership with Morocco were Spain, Portugal and Belgium.[68] Spain is not a surprise as it has strong bilateral ties with Morocco and is the recipient of the second largest population of Moroccans in Europe after France.[69] Moreover, having a shared border with Morocco, Spain is willing to have a good cooperation with Morocco. Furthermore, Moroccans are the first group of non-European immigrants in Belgium, also explaining its strong interest in participating in the Mobility Partnership. More surprisingly, Portugal, with only 1,736 Moroccans[70] in its territory, was a major supporter of the Partnership. EU officials explained that this Portuguese support was due to the fact that Portuguese migration policy goes hand in hand with the Spanish migration policy.[71] The participation of Sweden is somewhat unexpected as migration flows from Morocco to Sweden are not high. Sweden has only had limited trade exchanges with Morocco, no postcolonial ties and is geographically far away.

With the Arab Spring uprisings in Southern Mediterranean countries in 2011, the EU had to adapt its migration policy to consider the increasing migration

65 Françoise de Bel-Air, 'Migration Profile: Morocco' (2016) MPI Policy Brief, May 2016, 1, 3.
66 Sarah Wolff, 'The Politics of Negotiating the EU Readmission Agreements: Insights from Morocco and Turkey' [2014] *EJML* 69, 93.
67 Interview 29 (n4).
68 Interviews 29 (n4); Interview 28, DG Home Affairs, Brussels, 20 October 2016.
69 In 2010, France had 856,493 Moroccan immigrants; Spain had 763,735; Belgium had 81,535; and Portugal had 1,736. See United Nations (n34).
70 Serviço de Estrangeiros e Fronteiras, Relatório de Imigração, Fronteiras e Asilo 2014, 1, 52–53.
71 Interviews 28 (n68) and 29 (n4).

flows coming from the region as well as the potential security threats that could arise from the political unrest. The EU needed to find a quick solution in order to guarantee stability in its neighbouring countries. As an answer, the EU launched the dialogue for migration, mobility and security with the southern Mediterranean countries in 2011.[72] The end goal of this dialogue was the conclusion of Mobility Partnerships with Southern Mediterranean countries. The Commission proposed to start dialogues with Tunisia, Morocco and Egypt.[73] According to EU officials in Brussels, Tunisia was the first country of choice for the conclusion of a Mobility Partnership. The reason being that it was politically important for the EU to show that they were supporting a democratic regime in Tunisia as they sought to avoid an analogous situation to the one in Libya following the fall of Muammar Gaddafi.[74]

The degradation of the political situation in Tunisia made the EU further reconsider Morocco. In 2011, the February 20 Movement[75] called for the drafting of a new Constitution and better representation of the people.[76] In response, the King declared that 'comprehensive constitutional reforms' would take place[77] and a new Constitution was adopted in July 2011. In the meantime, structural changes were made, such as the creation of an economic and social committee and the National Council for Human Rights – *Conseil National des Droits de l'Homme* (CNDH). These different measures taken by the Moroccan government and the King were received positively by the EU.[78] An EU official affirmed that with the Arab Spring the way of thinking about EU-Moroccan relations started to change and the EU (along with the Member States) had to give a strong signal to Morocco.[79] Nonetheless, EU support came at a price. The condition was for Morocco to put its promises into practice or it would lose the EU's financial and political support.[80]

72 European Commission, on a Dialogue for Migration, Mobility and Security with the Southern Mediterranean Countries COM(2011) 292 final, Brussels, 24 May 2011.
73 Ibid 1, 12.
74 Interview 29 (n4).
75 The February 20 Movement was organising the protests in Morocco in 2011–2012.
76 Mounia Bennani-Chraïbi and Mohamed Jeghllaly, 'La dynamique protestataire du Mouvement du 20 février à Casablanca' [2012] *RFSP* 62(5) 867, available at: https://www.cairn.info/revue-francaise-de-science-politique-2012-5-page-867.htm (accessed 10 September 2017).
77 Annonce des réformes constitutionnelles: Texte intégral du discours adressé par SM le Roi à la Nation, available at: http://www.maroc.ma/fr/discours-royaux/annonce-des-r%C3%A9formes-constitutionnelles-texte-int%C3%A9gral du discours adress%C3%A9-par-sm-le (accessed 10 September 2017).
78 Ibid.
79 Interview 29 (n4).
80 European Commission, Joint statement by EU High Representative Catherine Ashton and Commissioner Štefan Füle on Morocco's Future Constitutional Reform, MEMO/11/155, Brussels, 10 March 2011; Mohamed Limam and Raffaella A Del Sarto, 'Periphery under pressure: Morocco, Tunisia and the European Union's Mobility Partnership on migration' [2015] EUI Working Paper RSCAS 2015/75 1, 11.

The Member States that concluded the Mobility Partnership with Morocco on 3 June 2013[81] were Belgium, France, Germany, Italy, the Netherlands, Portugal, Spain, Sweden and the United Kingdom. With the strengthening of the border, and strong border cooperation between Morocco and Spain, migration flows were already being better contained from Morocco and the conclusion of the Mobility Partnership was perceived to be 'like a cherry on the top of the cake'.[82]

According to Mohamed Limam and Raffaella Del Sarto, the EU took advantage of the vulnerability of Morocco following the Arab uprising.[83] They argue that the EU concealed its genuine interests behind a supposedly reshaped policy aiming at supporting democracy in the region.[84] They saw the unrest in Morocco as the reason 'a largely uneven Mobility Partnership' was concluded.[85] According to Sergio Carrera and others, Southern Mediterranean countries, including Morocco, perceive the Mobility Partnership as a 'strong insecurity- and control-oriented approach while allowing only restricted, temporary, and highly selective forms of immigration into the Union'.[86] However, the argument that the Mobility Partnership with Morocco is unbalanced in the favour of the EU can be debated. Van Criekinge argues that certain third countries are increasingly able to reposition their dialogue with the EU to more closely reflect their own interests[87] and Morocco seems to be one of these countries. The Mobility Partnership with Morocco is often perceived as a turning point in the way negotiations are conducted. EU officials declared that unlike Eastern European countries that tend to accept 'in block' everything proposed by the EU, this was not the case with Southern countries.[88] The pivotal reason appears to be that Eastern European countries have the prospect of joining the EU while countries in the South do not.

According to officials from the EU Delegation but also from Morocco and several Member States, the Mobility Partnership with Morocco was negotiated in depth with Morocco requesting that Member States delete some of the proposed initiatives because they were not in Morocco's interest.[89] This is interesting

81 Joint Declaration establishing a Mobility Partnership between the Kingdom of Morocco and the European Union and its Member States 6139/13 ADD 1 REV 3, Brussels, 3 June 2013.
82 Interview 29 (n4).
83 Mohamed Limam and Raffaella A Del Sarto (n80) 1, 1.
84 Ibid.
85 Ibid 3.
86 Sergio Carrera, Leonhard den Hertog and Joanna Parkin, 'EU Migration Policy in the Wake of the Arab Spring: What prospects for EU-Southern Mediterranean Relations?' (2012) MEDPRO Technical Report 15, 1, 14.
87 Tine Van Criekinge, 'The EU-Africa migration partnership: A case study of the EU's migration dialogue with Ghana and Senegal' in *EUI Migration Working Group*, March 2010, European University Institute, Florence, Italy.
88 Interview 28 (n68).
89 Interview 17, Spanish Embassy, Rabat, 22 January 2016; Interview 7, EU Delegation, Rabat, 13 January 2016; Interview 10, Expertise France, Rabat, 15 January 2016;

because it shows that Morocco had some leverage that countries concluding prior Mobility Partnerships did not have. This leverage could be the recognition by Morocco to negotiate a readmission agreement with the EU including third country nationals. Indeed, one of the preconditions to conclude a Mobility Partnership is the commitment of the third country to negotiate a readmission agreement. It is without surprise that Sergio Carrera and others argue that this topic was the main bone of contention between the EU and Morocco.[90] For the EU, the conclusion of the partnership was giving new leverage to the negotiation of a readmission agreement. The position of Morocco is however not novel in its relations with the EU. As early as 1999, Morocco rejected an Action Plan proposed by the EU requesting the conclusion of a readmission agreement including nationals of other third countries.[91] At the time Moroccan officials already criticised the EU for imposing this Action Plan without prior concertation with Moroccan authorities and used the EU's interest for cooperation on irregular migration to increase their own geopolitical influence.[92] Since 2000, the Commission has had a mandate from the Council to negotiate a readmission agreement with Morocco, but the negotiations never came to a successful conclusion. By concluding a Mobility Partnership with Morocco, the EU revitalised the negotiations that had been stalled since 2010.[93] An EU official emphasised that the EU realised that they needed a more balanced approach in order to give the readmission agreement a chance to succeed. On the other hand, Member States did not want to give any positive incentive as long as Morocco had not accepted to resume the negotiations of the readmission agreement, while inversely, Morocco did not want to accept a restart to the negotiations as long as no positive incentives were given by the Member States.[94] The Mobility Partnership provided the EU and member States with the opportunity to give the negotiations of the readmission agreement a more balanced perspective.[95]

2.2 Content of the Mobility Partnerships with Cape Verde and Morocco

The Mobility Partnership with Cape Verde is composed of an Annex including 31[96] projects. The Mobility Partnership with Morocco includes 105 projects,

Interview 13, Moroccan Ministry of Labour, Rabat, 19 January 2016; Interview 14, GiZ, Rabat, 20 January 2016.

90 Sergio Carrera, Leonhard den Hertog and Joanna Parking 1, 14 (n86).

91 Council of the European Union, Action Plan for Morocco 11426/99 LIMITE JAI 75 AG 30, Brussels, 30 September 1999, 1, 15.

92 Katharina Natter, 'The Formation of Morocco's Policy Towards Irregular Migration (2000–2007): Political Rationale and Policy Processes' [2013] *Int Migr* 52(5) 15, 18.

93 Sarah Wolff (n66) 77.

94 Interview 29 (n4).

95 Ibid.

96 In the Annex there are 29 projects listed but two projects have been divided into several projects. This is the case of the project in Annex. (Project 1) Proposal by the Kingdom of Spain to launch, for the benefit of Cape Verde, a schools/workshops programme aimed at facilitating the integration of apprentices, particularly through

which is over three times the size of the Mobility Partnership with Cape Verde. The Annex for Morocco provides clear information, for example, the identity of the Ministry in charge (in the Member States) of the proposed projects. This information is not included in the Annex in the case of Cape Verde.

2.2.1 The structure of the Mobility Partnerships

The Mobility Partnerships with Cape Verde and Morocco follow similar structures. First, they comprise a list of objectives based on the four pillars of the GAMM. Second, their Annexes list the different projects proposed by the EU, Member States and the third country. If the list of objectives is similar in both Mobility Partnerships, the list of projects in the Annex is not, as we will see in detail throughout this chapter. It is not surprising that the phrasing of the objectives shows the influence of the dominant political discourse at the time of the conclusion of the respective Mobility Partnership. Under each objective directly linked to the different pillars of the GAM/GAMM, each Mobility Partnership identifies a set of topics. The topics in the case of Morocco are more numerous than those for Cape Verde (37 for Morocco and only 13 for Cape Verde).

First, the list of topics in the case of Morocco is much longer and more detailed than in the case of Cape Verde. We can notice that all topics introduced in the Mobility Partnership with Cape Verde are also included in the Mobility

training actions tailored to the Cape Verdean labour market, to meet labour needs identified by that country. Other interested Member States and the European Community could join the programme if they so wished. The Kingdom of Spain also proposes to support the development of business initiatives by women (Project 2). It is also the case of: (Project 1) Proposal by Cape Verde and the participating Member States to foster cooperation and partnerships between their hospital and research institutions, particularly with a view to strengthening the capacities of the Cape Verdean institutions, reducing the effects of the lack of qualified staff in the field of health in Cape Verde and encouraging exchanges of staff. In this context, a proposal by the Kingdom of Spain to launch a programme to strengthen the capacities of the Cape Verdean national health system (Project 2), and a proposal by the Portuguese Republic to support the Cape Verdean national health system in the fields of haemodialysis and oncology (Project 3). Finally, one project was divided into two in the annex but is analysed as one: Proposal by the French Republic to develop, within the framework of a bilateral agreement on concerted management of migratory flows, a co-development programme for the benefit of Cape Verde under which Cape Verdean migrants legally established in France and French citizens of Cape Verdean origin could contribute, through transfers of money, skills or other resources, to the development of Cape Verde and carry on economic activities there on the basis of experience already acquired in other countries. The programme would have five parts:

- Promoting the reduction of the cost of money transfers;
- Promoting productive investment;
- Mobilising the skills of elites within the diaspora;
- Support for local development projects;
- Support for young people's initiatives.

Partnership with Morocco with the exception of the conclusion of a working agreement with FRONTEX. Similar topics are, for example, 'visa facilitation for short-stay visa', 'voluntary return and reintegration of returning migrants' or 'information on the risks of irregular immigration and human trafficking'. The Moroccan list of topics includes issues related to asylum, which is a topic that was not included in the Mobility Partnership with Cape Verde at the time of its conclusion, as it only became the fourth pillar of the GAMM in 2011. The fact that the list of topics from the Cape Verdean Mobility Partnership can be found almost entirely in the Mobility Partnership with Morocco could suggests that both partnerships were built following the same set of priorities, the GAM/GAMM. This argument could support the claim that they are not really being negotiated by all parties but rather 'imposed' via a general model applied to all. However, this argument has limitations. Topics are directly linked to the pillars of the GAMM (GAM in the case of Cape Verde) that Mobility Partnerships aim at implementing. The fact that the Mobility Partnership with Morocco includes topics related to asylum, and the one with Cape Verde does not, illustrates this point. It is therefore not surprising that topics following the main objectives of the GAM(M) are quite similar across Mobility Partnership declarations. This arguably does not mean that the partnership has not been negotiated. The projects proposed in the Annex and later on in the scoreboard are the ones being negotiated and tailored to the specific country concluding the Mobility Partnership. On this question, I will first observe the distribution by GAM(M) pillars of projects proposed in both Mobility Partnerships and then I will discuss their implementation.

2.2.2 The distribution of projects by GAM(M) pillars

The first pillar of the GAMM[97] covers mobility, legal migration and integration. The objective corresponding to this pillar in the Mobility Partnership with Cape Verde puts forwards 'circular and temporary migration' as the main way to achieve legal migration. At the time of the conclusion of the Mobility Partnership with Cape Verde, circular migration was a popular topic and had a positive connotation as it was considered as an effective way to manage labour migration. In the Mobility Partnership with Morocco, the term circular migration is missing even though the idea of managing 'the movement of persons for short periods' remained. At the time of the conclusion of the Mobility Partnership with Morocco, circular migration had already been widely criticised. As seen in Chapter 1, the argument according to which circular migration is beneficial for sending countries or migrants has been contested in the literature. The prevailing view seems to be that circular migration rather reinforced the power of receiving countries to fight against irregular migration and did not propose different options for legal migration from the pre-existing bilateral agreements.[98] In the case of the

97 European Commission (n2).

98 Sandra Lavenex, 'Multilayered Migration Governance: The Partnership Approach in the EU and Beyond, Regional Governance of Migration and Socio-Political Rights – Institutions, Actors and Processes' 14–15 January 2013, Geneva, Switzerland 1, 12.

Mobility Partnership with Morocco, the emphasis was put on the capacity of absorption of 'the labour market of the signatories'. The Mobility Partnership with Morocco was concluded after the economic crisis that struck the EU, resulting in Member States' labour markets being more constrained.

The second pillar of the GAMM encompasses '[p]reventing and reducing irregular migration and trafficking in human beings'. Both Mobility Partnerships make a direct reference to 'the promotion of an effective readmission and return policy' stressing their will to negotiate in the future on a readmission agreement. This is interesting in the case of Morocco, as the country is notoriously reluctant to conclude such an agreement. The clear mention of the effective readmission policy shows the crucial importance readmission agreements take in the Mobility Partnerships. In the case of Cape Verde, the conclusion of a readmission agreement was also foreseen in the Mobility Partnership, but Article 13 of the Cotonou Agreement already foresees a readmission obligation. This can be seen as an overlap between Article 13 of the Cotonou Agreement and the Mobility Partnership project. However, there are two main reasons to include a separate readmission agreement in the Mobility Partnership with Cape Verde. The first one is that Article 13 only includes the readmission of citizens of the country that is bound by the agreement, whereas the readmission agreement included in the Mobility Partnership includes migrants that only crossed the third country concluding the agreement but that are not citizens of this country. The second reason lays in the poor operational implementation of Article 13 which is not enforceable.[99] Additionally, Article 13 foresees the negotiation of bilateral readmission agreements including nationals of third countries other than the one concluding the agreement. By all means, the conclusion of the readmission agreement between the EU and Cape Verde is legally relevant for Cape Verde.

The third pillar, '[p]romoting international protection and enhancing the external dimension of asylum policy', is only included in the Mobility Partnership with Morocco because at the time of the conclusion of the Mobility Partnership with Cape Verde only the GAM existed, comprising three pillars. The pillar on international protection was added when the GAM evolved into a more strategic approach to migration management in 2011; the Global Approach to Migration and Mobility (GAMM).[100] Finally, the fourth pillar encompasses 'maximising the development impact of migration and mobility, migrant rights and the empowerment of migrants'. In the case of Cape Verde, migration and development did not take the significant role one would expect. Especially from a country that is highly dependent on its diaspora and counts a higher number of nationals abroad than living in the country itself. Relegating migration and development to a second role can be explained by the fact that the priorities of the EU and Member States are security oriented, favouring the fight against irregular migration. According to an interview with a Cape Verdean official, the hope among Cape Verdeans is that

99 European Commission, Evaluation of the Cotonou Partnership Agreement SWD (2016) 250 final, Brussels, 15 July 2016, 1, 41.

100 European Commission (n2).

migration and development becomes the new priority of the second phase of implementation of the Mobility Partnership.[101] The Mobility Partnership with Moldova is a good illustration. At first, the Mobility Partnership with Moldova was dedicated to the fight against irregular migration. But, with the conclusion of the first wave of projects, the focus shifted towards migration and development.[102] In the case of Morocco, the idea that migration and development can be an added value for Europe is raised. Developing the regions predominantly sending migrants towards Europe by supporting the development of the labour market in the third country is considered as a way to mitigate the immigration fluxes. This idea is now at the centre of the new Migration Partnership Framework (MPF) (2016). One of the long-term measures of the MPF is to 'address the root causes of irregular migration and force displacement by supporting partner countries in their political, social and economic development'.[103]

Under the first pillar, Cape Verde has 14 projects, almost half of the total number of projects proposed. This is in line with Cape Verdeans' interests in favouring the mobility of its people and creating new channels of legal labour migration. In fact, 11 out of the 14 projects are related to 'employment, management and facilitation of legal migration and integration'. These projects aim at meeting the following two aspirations: to develop better legal migration opportunities for Cape Verdeans and to inform potential migrants of possibilities and risks related to migration. A major project called '*Centro de Apoio ao Migrante no Pais do Origem*'[104] (Centre for Migrant Support in the Country of Origin: CAMPO) has been proposed by Portugal and aims at providing information to prospective migrants about possibilities to work in the participating Member States, the risks of irregular migration and assistance to Cape Verdeans willing to return to Cape Verde. Additionally, it is interesting to note that Portugal and France have proposed to promote the admission of distinct groups of workers under particular legal schemes. In the case of Portugal, one project consists of 'the signing of a new Protocol on migration [extending] the scope of the Protocol on temporary migration of Cape Verdean workers to work in Portugal'.[105] France proposes to conclude a bilateral agreement on concerted management of migratory flows with Cape Verde including opening up the French labour market for specific

101 Interview 36 (n21).
102 Interview 32 (n30).
103 European Commission, 'Fact sheet: Migration Partnership Framework A New Approach To Better Manage Migration', available at: https://eeas.europa.eu/sites/eeas/files/factsheet_ec_format_migration_partnership_framework_update_2.pdf (accessed 28 November 2017).
104 For more information, see: http://www.instituto-camoes.pt/activity/o-que-fazemos/cooperacao/cooperacao-na-pratica/projetos-historico/14856-campo-centro-de-apoio-ao-migrante-no-pais-de-origem (accessed 26 November 2017).
105 Council of the European Union, Joint Declaration on a Mobility Partnership between the European Union and the Republic of Cape Verde 9460/08 ADD2, Brussels, 21 May 2008. The project is included in the Annex to the Mobility Partnership with Cape Verde; Serviço de Estrangeiros e Fronteiras, 'Temporary and Circular Migration in Portugal: Facts, Policies and Strategies', European Migration Network 2010, 1, 23.

activities.[106] Both projects have potential legal relevance, as will be discussed below. An additional project having potential legal relevance concerns the negotiation of a visa facilitation agreement[107] for the issuance of short-stay visas. In parallel, Portugal proposes the creation of a Common Visa Application Centre in Praia[108] to facilitate Cape Verdeans' visa process. Finally, a specific project is proposed in order to help Cape Verde identify its needs and develop adequate migration policies.[109]

The Mobility Partnership with Morocco accounts for only 15 projects under the first pillar, out of 105. Similarly, to the Mobility Partnership with Cape Verde, a project proposed by the EU relates to the negotiation of a visa facilitation agreement. This project was proposed hand in hand with the negotiation of the readmission agreement. It is the first time that the EU proposed a visa facilitation agreement with a Southern Mediterranean country.[110] It is interesting to see that projects that aim to inform about legal and irregular migration are not only directed to prospective migrants but also to Moroccan civil servants. Italy proposed a project aimed at training Moroccan civil servants to better manage migration flows to Italy. This training could influence Moroccan civil servants' behaviours and their interactions with migrants, resulting in potential political effects. A striking fact is that most of the information initiatives proposed to prospective migrants aim at showing the risks of irregular immigration and therefore trying to deter Moroccans to immigrate irregularly. Finally, the most notable point is that no project aims at developing new legal migration opportunities towards Europe unlike in the Mobility Partnership with Cape Verde. Most of the proposed initiatives are capacity building and information projects.

The Annex to the Joint Declaration with Morocco has a particularity. The list of projects in the Annex is divided into two parts: new projects as of 25 March 2013 and projects in progress as of 25 March 2013. This means that a whole list of projects pre-existing the conclusion of the Mobility Partnership have been added in the Annex. The reason is political. The negotiation of the Mobility Partnership was difficult, and the EU wanted to show successful initiatives already being implemented by the Member States in Morocco to give the impression of a balanced partnership.[111] The list of pre-existing projects included under the first pillar is an interesting illustration. Indeed, 20 pre-existing projects aiming at facilitating mobility and legal migration have been listed; more than the number of

106 Accord France – Cap-Vert relatif à la gestion concertée des flux migratoires et au développement solidaire signé à Paris, 24 November 2008.

107 Agreement between the European Union and the Republic of Cape Verde on facilitating the issue of short-stay visas to citizens of the Republic of Cape Verde and of the European Union OJ L 282, 24.10.2013.

108 For more information, see: https://www.eurovisaccv.eu (accessed 26 November 2017).

109 For more information, see: https://publications.iom.int/books/migracao-em-cabo-verde-perfil-nacional-2009 (accessed 28 November 2017).

110 Sarah Wolff (n66) 72.

111 Interviews 28 (n68) and 32 (n30).

new projects under the same pillar. Most of these projects are proposed either by France or Spain, showing their strong former bilateral cooperation on migration matters. These projects touch upon the easier access to short-stay visas for Moroccans travelling to France and Spain. In the case of France, the French Minister of the Interior, Manuel Valls, declared that the French government was thinking about a scheme to ease the access for Moroccans to short-term visas[112] preceding the conclusion of the Mobility Partnership. Projects also deal with the information about legal migration through web portals such as 'Make it in Germany'[113] or 'The EU immigration portal'.[114] However, it is important to note that these platforms are not directed only towards Moroccans but at everyone willing to immigrate to Germany or other EU Member States. Similarly, France lists a project aiming at authorising Moroccan citizens who studied in France to stay a year in France in order to find their first job. However, in practice, this possibility is open to all non-EU citizens (excluding exceptional cases such as Algerians) and not only to Moroccans.[115] Proposing general projects in the Annex adds to the feeling that it is a catch-all document aimed at convincing Morocco to collaborate, but it does not, in fact, provide much added value.

Under the second pillar, the EU and Member States aim at involving Morocco and Cape Verde in the cooperation on border management, the fight against irregular migration and trafficking in human beings (people-smuggling). This includes the improvement of the security of travel documents, identity documents and residence permits. The Mobility Partnership with Cape Verde includes 10 projects under this pillar and the Mobility Partnership with Morocco 38 (11 are pre-existing). The idea of better border management and document security was already a priority for Cape Verde in the Special Partnership and was transposed to the Mobility Partnership. A project proposed[116] in the Annex relates to the effective implementation by Cape Verde of the United Nations Convention against Transnational Organised Crimes and its Protocols on smuggling of migrants and trafficking in persons as well as its obligations to rescue at sea. The implementation of this Convention is relevant for Cape Verde as authorities will have at the least to modify their practices in this field and might also have to modify their legal framework in order to support the effective implementation of the Convention. Additionally, the project aiming at concluding an operational arrangement between Cape Verde and FRONTEX on border management will have a direct

112 Jeune Afrique, 'Manuel Valls à Rabat: La France souhaite faciliter l'obtention de visas pour les Marocains' (2012), available at: http://www.jeuneafrique.com/175018/politique/manuel-valls-rabat-la-france-souhaite-faciliter-l-obtention-de-visas-pour-les-marocains (accessed 17 October 2016).

113 For more information, see: http://www.make-it-in-germany.com/en (accessed 28 November 2017).

114 For more information, see: http://ec.europa.eu/immigration (accessed 28 November 2017).

115 Code de l'entrée et du séjour des étrangers et du droit d'asile: articles L311–10 à L311–12.

116 There is no information in the Annex or scoreboard about who proposed this project.

influence on the behaviour of authorities and modify the effective border management practices in the country. These are key initiatives that have the potential to deeply reshape Cape Verde's border management policy. A parallel project proposed by FRONTEX and Cape Verde is a good illustration of the potential impact of the operational agreement on the Cape Verdean National Police's work, including the securitisation of travel documents. Moreover, Portugal, Spain and France proposed the implementation of several training sessions designed for Cape Verdean authorities on border management and document controls as well as maritime security. On this last issue, Spain is also proposing to extend the Seahorse Atlantic Network project, which has included Cape Verde, Senegal and Mauritania since 2006. In 2007, the Seahorse Atlantic Network included three more countries, Morocco, Gambia and Guinea Bissau. It is a framework of regional cooperation aimed at preventing irregular migration and cross-border crime by establishing regional networks which cooperate and share information.[117]

In the case of Morocco, three projects under the second pillar are related to the negotiation and conclusion of the readmission agreement showing the importance of this issue in the Mobility Partnership. Similarly, to Cape Verde, the conclusion of a working agreement with FRONTEX[118] is also proposed in two different projects but Morocco never concluded such an agreement.[119] A significant initiative proposed by the Netherlands aims at providing guidance on the formulation of a legal framework on irregular immigration and human trafficking. Two other projects are related to the support for the Moroccan legal framework on human trafficking issues only.[120] These three projects are intended to be directly legally relevant for Morocco. Finally, four of the projects cover the issue of voluntary return including for migrant children. It should be noted that the vast majority of projects aim at implementing training courses or capacity building initiatives for Moroccan officials on questions of border control, fraudulent documentation or the fight against irregular migration. It is interesting to note that over two third of the projects proposed under this pillar regarding Morocco are new. This might be explained by the fact that for the purpose of negotiations with Morocco, it was not in the interest of the EU to concentrate on the fight against irregular migration but rather on mobility

117 Maribel Casas-Cortes, Sebastian Cobarrubias and John Pickles, '"Good Neighbours Make Good Fences": Seahorse Operations, Border Externalization and Extra-territoriality' [2016] *Eur Urban Reg Stud* 23(3) 231; For more information about the Seahorse and the Seahorse Atlantic Network projects, see: http://51.255.195.60//En/En/image.php?id=125 (accessed 26 November 2017).

118 As noted earlier, the conclusion of a working agreement with FRONTEX was not a topic in the Joint Declaration with Morocco. This does not mean that such a working agreement cannot be proposed as a project in the Annex.

119 For more information about working agreements/arrangements with FRONTEX, see: https://frontex.europa.eu/about-frontex/key-documents/?category=working-arrangements-with-non-eu-countries (accessed 28 November 2017).

120 One of the projects listed is a MIEUX project. For more information, see: https://www.mieux-initiative.eu/en/actions/178-morocco-trafficking-in-human-beings (Accessed 28 November 2017).

perspectives. The pre-existing projects include initiatives about the cooperation between Moroccan and Member States' authorities in airports (three projects), four projects on return and reintegration including unaccompanied children and two projects preventing the irregular immigration of unaccompanied children. The remaining projects propose training courses and capacity building for Moroccan authorities on the fight against irregular migration and human trafficking.

The third pillar comprises the projects on migration and development. In the case of Cape Verde only five projects have been proposed under this category. This is surprising seeing how important remittances are for the development of Cape Verde[121] and the fact that a larger number of Cape Verdeans live outside of Cape Verde than in the country. This might be attributed to the lack of negotiation leverage on the Cape Verdean side and a 'take it or leave it' approach taken by the EU.[122] The projects included under this pillar comprise a circular migration initiative proposed by Portugal and a project proposed by France. The purpose of the latter project was to enhance the possibilities of transfer of competences and money from the Cape Verdean diaspora living in France towards their country of origin. Out of the four projects proposed, one is a Cape Verdean proposal to enhance cooperation with Portuguese and Spanish hospitals in order to strengthen the Cape Verdean health system.

Table 2.1 Distribution of projects in Annex by pillars and countries

	Cape Verde	***Morocco***	
	Number of projects	*Number of concomitant projects*	*Number of pre-existing projects*
Mobility, legal migration and integration	14	15	20
Border management, the fight against irregular migration and trafficking in human beings	10	27	11
Migration and development	5	7	13
International protection	2	6	0
Horizontal initiatives*	–	5	1
Total	31	60	45

* Horizontal initiatives are not directly linked to a pillar of the GAMM.

Note: This table shows the distribution of the projects in the Annexes of the Joint Declarations with Cape Verde and Morocco according to the four pillars of the GAMM. For example, in the Mobility Partnership with Morocco 27 projects related to border management, the fight against irregular migration and trafficking in human beings have been included in the Annex. These projects were not pre-existent on the 25 March 2013.

121 André Corsino Tolentino, Carlos Manuem Rocha and Nancy Curado Tolentino, 'A importancia e o impacto das remessas dos immigrates em Portugal no desenvolvimento de Cabo Verde', Observatório Da Imigração, April 2008.

122 Natasja Reslow (n12) 395.

In the case of Morocco, it is also clear that 'migration and development' is not a key priority as only 7 new projects out of 105 are part of this category. Interestingly, 13 pre-existing projects[123] have been included under migration and development, suggesting, as previously argued, that the EU wanted to use positive initiatives as bargaining chips to conclude the Mobility Partnership with Morocco and provide a sufficiently balanced package in order for Morocco to re-open the readmission agreement negotiations. The bulk of the projects under this pillar focuses on ways for Moroccans abroad to participate in the development of their country of origin financially or through their expertise. To favour migration and development financially, projects aiming at developing businesses and productive investments are proposed. In addition, projects aiming at the transfer of competencies are suggested including an interesting initiative that aims at using the competencies of the Moroccan community abroad to plan and implement the national development policy. This last project could have particular relevance for Morocco. Finally, Italy proposes technical training courses for migrants and potential migrants in order to develop specifically needed working skills. Pre-existing projects cover similar initiatives such as transfer of competencies through, for example, temporary return schemes or by offering facilitated procedures and training for migrants willing to start a business in the country of origin or wishing to invest. Most of the projects were proposed by the Member States and were part of their national bilateral activities in the field of migration and development. Similarly, the EU supports business and job creation in Morocco through a broader project directed at the whole of the Maghreb. Even though this project is not country specific, it is added in the Annex to the Joint Declaration with Morocco. The EU also included former funded initiatives aimed at developing the main regions of origin of migrants in order to provide new economic opportunities to young people, therefore limiting their migration towards Europe. An initiative also aimed at supporting Moroccan migrants' organisations in Germany, in their work assisting the development of Morocco. Germany also proposed a project aiming at facilitating circular migration, by allowing Moroccans to leave Germany for two years without losing their permanent residence permits. Finally, three return and reintegration projects are included under migration and development even though they are generally directed at fighting irregular migration. In practice, these projects are aimed at unsuccessful asylum seekers, irregular migrants, victims of trafficking or other vulnerable groups.

In the case of Cape Verde, the Mobility Partnership was still concluded under the GAM, and therefore asylum was not included in the topics in the declaration. However, interestingly, the Mobility Partnership comprises two projects on asylum and immigration. Both projects can be legally relevant for Cape Verde. The first project proposes the ratification and implementation by Cape Verde of the 1951 United Nations Convention on the Status of Refugees and its Protocol from 1967. The second project relates to the establishment of an asylum system in Cape Verde with the assistance of Portugal. Both these projects would have direct

123 The list of projects can be found in the Annex to the Mobility Partnership.

effects on the situation of asylum seekers in Cape Verde if implemented. The Mobility Partnership with Morocco includes six projects on international protection. Several of the projects proposed can have legal relevance for Morocco. These projects include support in the drafting of legislation in the fields of 'immigration, residency law, international protection and asylum', as well as the development of a national asylum system and legal framework. The projects directly aim at the development of new laws and policies which means that the legal framework and (it is to be expected) the practices of authorities would be modified following the implementation of these projects. It is interesting to underline these initiatives as they have the potential to really modify the situation in the country. The remaining projects cover training courses on asylum issues. It is also noticeable that no pre-existing projects on this issue have been included in the Mobility Partnership.

Finally, in the Annex to the Joint Declaration with Morocco, there are some 'horizontal initiatives'. Horizontal initiatives are projects that cover more than one pillar of the GAMM. There is one pre-existing project which enters this category which relates to the support by the EU of a Joint European Master's in International Migration and Social Cohesion.[124] Five new initiatives have been proposed in the Annex. Interestingly, one of these new projects aims at reproducing a project proposed in the Mobility Partnership with Cape Verde. The project relates to the development of a data collection centre on migration issues that would help set priorities in migration policies. This project can have policy relevance for Morocco. Additionally, under these horizontal initiatives, the EU proposes 'possible courses of action' or broader initiatives that could potentially be of interest to Morocco and fully open to negotiation. The latter cannot really be considered as projects because of their wide and open scope. The next section covers some projects added to the Mobility Partnership later on based on these 'possible courses of action'.

2.3 The stage of implementation of the Mobility Partnerships with Cape Verde and Morocco

Over ten years have passed since the conclusion of the Mobility Partnership with Cape Verde and six years in the case of Morocco. In this section, I will discuss the implementation of the Mobility Partnerships with Morocco and Cape Verde and analyse the evolution of their content since their conclusion.

2.3.1 The analysis of the scoreboards

The analysis of the implementation of the Mobility Partnerships is based on the scoreboards. Scoreboards are Excel documents listing the projects related to Mobility Partnerships and their stage of implementation. Other information can be included, depending on the level of detail provided, such as the timeframe of the project, the actor in charge of its implementation or the amount and origin of

124 For more information, see: http://www.misoco.org (accessed 12 December 2017).

its funding. The first scoreboard for Morocco used in this analysis has been provided by Directorate General Migration and Home Affairs (DG Home), the EU Delegation in Morocco and the German Interior Ministry in September 2015.[125] The first scoreboard for Cape Verde used in this analysis dates from September 2014 and was provided by DG Home.[126] At the time, it was relatively difficult to access information for several reasons. First, there seemed to be little coordination between the different Ministries in a given Member State. Several Ministries did not have a global picture of all initiatives proposed and implemented by their country.[127] Scoreboards were not available to the public and were not easy to obtain. Moreover, the information presented in the scoreboards was not consistent. For example, in the case of Morocco, three different scoreboards were obtained but the content of these scoreboards was not exactly the same. Some projects were included in one scoreboard but not in the other, while some scoreboards were more detailed than others. In the case of Cape Verde, the scoreboard is merely a list of projects with little additional information, even on their stage of implementation. However, the scoreboards for Morocco are more detailed and included information about the time frame of the projects, the implementing organisation and the organisation in charge of the project, in some cases also including the budget allocated. Finally, information available on the websites of different actors involved in the implementation of projects has also been considered. It should be noted that in order to create an overview of the implementation of the Mobility Partnerships a set of information has been compiled that goes further than the information available in the scoreboard itself, in order to provide the most accurate picture possible. These results, therefore, need to be interpreted with caution. This has been done, to mitigate some problems regarding the updating of the scoreboards, as a project can be indicated as being in the course of implementation when it has already been concluded, for example.

Another problem lies in the fact that there is no unanimous acceptance of what projects should be included in the scoreboard because there is no clear definition of what a 'Mobility Partnership project' is. There are three different approaches to the use of the scoreboard and the projects that should figure in it.[128] The first approach, according to the EU Delegation in Morocco, is that all projects created after the signature of the Mobility Partnership and funded by EU funds should be included in the scoreboard.[129] The EU official argues that Mobility Partnerships are framework agreements with the third country and that new projects exist because this cooperation framework exists. It is because the Mobility Partnership exists that Morocco became an even higher priority country and that an increased amount of funds was unlocked in order to implement the new projects, which are therefore linked to the Mobility Partnership. However, this understanding is

125 The last version of the scoreboard for Morocco is from 2017.

126 The last version of the scoreboard for Cape Verde is from 2016.

127 Observation made during emails exchanges with German and French officials from different ministries.

128 Interview 32 (n30).

129 Interview 7 (n89).

already problematic as such because the scoreboard also includes projects that have been concluded prior to the conclusion of the Mobility Partnership and, according to the Member States, some new projects would have existed anyway.[130] According to an interviewee, at first, the Annex was considered as a political tool and aimed at promoting existing projects in the framework of the negotiations with Morocco, but now the scoreboard is a coordination and cooperation tool. According to EU officials, the objective is to keep the coherence of the action and to avoid reproducing projects.[131] Therefore, many pre-existing projects were included in the Annex to the Joint Declaration with Morocco. It also explains why some projects were deleted from the scoreboard if they were not destined to be implemented further. In the case of Cape Verde, the EU Delegation takes a different line of thinking and does not seem to believe that the scoreboard should gather all bilateral activities implemented in Cape Verde.[132] Some Member States agree with the definition of the Moroccan EU Delegation and consider the Mobility Partnership as the framework for cooperation, but this view is not accepted by all. The second approach is the one adopted by the Member States with strong bilateral ties with the third country according to which all bilateral projects should not be included in the scoreboard. Member States with strong bilateral ties with the third country, such as Spain and France with Morocco, prefer to give visibility to their bilateral cooperation rather than including projects in the scoreboards.[133] According to a respondent in Brussels, these countries disregard the Mobility Partnership as a tool of cooperation.[134] Third, third countries sometimes include in the scoreboard projects linked to migration even though they are not EU related and are financed by other donors, such as the UN. I consider that all projects included in the Annex and/or the scoreboard, projects that have been deleted and new projects added at a later stage are Mobility Partnership projects.

Before proceeding to examine the implementation of the Mobility Partnerships, it is important to determine what implementation means. The projects that are defined as *implemented* refer to those in which foreseen activities have already been fully or partially executed. It includes ongoing projects and projects that are already completed. The term implementation is understood in its *stricto sensu* meaning. It is also through the implementation, the first concrete action, that potential legal or policy relevance occurs. This differs from the idea that the implementation includes everything that comes after the conclusion of the Mobility Partnership itself, including the negotiation of new projects to be included in the scoreboard at a later stage. Therefore, concrete activities need to be undertaken for a project to be defined as *implemented*. In this section, the various stages

130 Interview 8 French Embassy, Rabat, 14 January 2016; Interviews 14 (n89) and 17 (n89).

131 Interview 2, EEAS, Brussels (by phone), 15 October 2015; Interview 3, DG Home Affairs, Brussels, 18 November 2015.

132 Interview 39 (n30).

133 Interviews 32 (n30), 17 (n89) and 8 (n131).

134 Interview 32(n30).

of implementation of the projects are identified. This analysis catalogues projects in the following categories according to their stage of implementation: *concluded*, *ongoing*, *in preparation* and *deleted/not implemented*. The categorisation depends on the stage mentioned in the scoreboard but can be different if other sources of information indicate that the project has reached another stage ('other sources of information' are: interviews, projects documents or email exchanges).

The scale of both Mobility Partnerships is different. Not only because of the number of Member States signatories but because of the number of projects proposed. In the Annex to the Joint Declaration with Cape Verde, there are 31 projects compared to 105 for Morocco. The list of the projects covered by the Mobility Partnership of Cape Verde has evolved subsequently and the scoreboard from September 2014 counts 43 projects. The 2014 scoreboard for Cape Verde was difficult to decipher. Little information was provided and only few details about the country in charge of the projects' implementation or the timeframe were given. The projects are either *concluded* or *ongoing*, but no information is given on projects that are still *in preparation* or even on those not being considered as relevant anymore. The lack of clarity and information of the document does not favour exchanges of information between the different signatory countries. In 2016 a new scoreboard was published, including only one new project on border management. On the other hand, the scoreboard of the Mobility Partnership with Morocco is much more detailed. This suggests a stronger interest in the implementation of the Mobility Partnership. An official from DG Home pointed out that there is a good dialogue between all parties to this Mobility Partnership including Morocco.[135] However, in 2016 during the fieldwork in Morocco, the relations between Morocco and the EU were tense following the Court of Justice of the European Union ruling of 2015[136] annulling a Council Decision on trade liberalisation between Morocco and the EU including goods issued from the Western Sahara territory. Morocco suspended its diplomatic relations with the EU following the ruling. After a year the diplomatic relations resumed, and a new scoreboard was published including six new projects. These projects are linked to the implementation of the National Strategy on Immigration and Asylum, the improvement of migration governance, the support to enhance migrants and refuges access to rights and the fight against racism. Additionally, a project focuses on South–South cooperation between Morocco, Senegal, Ivory Coast and Mali underlining the need for diaspora engagement and labour mobility between these countries. Another new project aims at supporting circular migration and training of young people between Italy, Morocco and Tunisia. Half of these projects have been implemented and three others are in preparation.

135 Interview 28 (n68).

136 CJEU, Judgement of the General Court, Case T-512/12, *Front Polisario v Council*, 10.12.2015.

2.3.2 The role of the different actors

The implementation of the Mobility Partnerships includes a wide variety of actors at various levels. In this section, a brief overview of these actors will be given introducing the relationship between the actors and the different funding possibilities linked to specific actors. However, by no means does this section give a complete overview of the funding landscape. Such an overview has been completed in the past.[137]

Daniel Wunderlich underlines that implementation of EU external migration policy depends on third countries,[138] therefore their role has to be considered in order to grasp a complete understanding of the implementation process. The main actors are local authorities in the third country, international organisations acting as implementation organisations, such as the International Organisation for Migration (IOM), the United Nations High Commissioner for Refugees (UNHCR) or the International Centre for Migration Policy Development (ICMPD) and EU Member State development agencies such as the *Gesellschaft für Internationale Zusammenarbeit* (GIZ) for Germany, Expertise France for France or LuxDev for Luxembourg. The detailed information provided by one of the scoreboards for Morocco was helpful in having a good idea of who was in charge of which project. However, in the case of Cape Verde, this exercise has been arduous due to the scarce information provided by the scoreboard.

In Cape Verde and Morocco, the main organisations that implement projects are ICMPD and IOM. ICMPD implements projects under the MIEUX programme in both countries. MIEUX is a facility funded by the European Commission and implemented by the ICMPD.[139] It aims at facilitating capacity building and peer-to-peer knowledge sharing. The activities are designed between the third country and the ICMPD. Of course, it is also in the interest of the EU, as the ICMPD follows the global agenda for change and the GAMM on behalf of the EU itself.[140] If the project proposed by the third country is not following the priorities of the EU, it will not be funded. In both cases MIEUX projects aimed at supporting the national strategies for immigration that were being developed at the national level, as well as the development of new laws related to these strategies. Additionally, the IOM is implementing several projects in both countries mainly relating to the creation of a migration profile and the voluntary return of migrants. However, other types of projects have also been implemented by the organisation. In Cape Verde, 'DIAS de Cabo Verde' was a project that ran from 2008 to 2010.[141] It was created and administered by IOM, with funding from the

137 Leonhard den Hertog, 'Money Talks: Mapping the Funding for EU External Migration Policy', CEPS Paper in Liberty & Security in Europe, No 95/November 2016.

138 Daniel Wunderlich, 'Implementing EU External Migration Policy: Security-driven by Default?' [2013] *Comp Eur Politics* 11(4) 406, 409.

139 For more information, see: https://www.mieux-initiative.eu/en (accessed 28 November 2017).

140 Interview 31 ICMPD, Brussels, 27 October 2016.

141 Serviço de Estrangeiros e Fronteiras (n105) 23.

EU and the Portuguese development cooperation. It promoted and reinforced the ties between members of the diaspora and the public and private sectors, both in Cape Verde and Europe, and contributed to the strengthening of transnational linkages of the Cape Verdean diaspora in Portugal, Italy and the Netherlands. In Morocco, the IOM implemented a project called 'E-BOSLA' aiming at favouring the integration of Moroccan migrants towards Italy, by providing pre-departure language courses and information about Italy.[142]

Member States have a key role in the implementation of Mobility Partnerships. First, they are the ones which propose most of the projects to be implemented. As we can see in the Annexes and the scoreboards, the vast majority of projects are bilateral initiatives. Member States have to secure funding for the projects that they want to implement. Some funding is national, but most of the projects are funded through EU funding. In the Annex to the Joint Declaration with Cape Verde, out of 31 projects, 20 have been proposed bilaterally by either Portugal (8 projects), Spain (6 projects), France or Luxembourg (3 projects each). Three projects are joint initiatives between several Member States and six projects have been proposed by the European Commission and two by FRONTEX. Without surprise, the Member State proposing the largest number of projects is Portugal, with which Cape Verde has strong postcolonial ties and which strongly supported the Cape Verdean candidacy. Three projects are also proposed by Cape Verde in Partnership with the EU and FRONTEX. The Annex of the Joint Declaration with Morocco is slightly different. Even though 66 projects are bilateral initiatives proposed by the Member States and only 39 are proposed by the EU or jointly with a Member State, a large disparity between Member States exists. It might be surprising that the country which proposed the largest number of projects was the Netherlands (with 16 projects) as this is not a country having strong historical ties with Morocco. This might be explained by the fact that the Netherlands did not have existing bilateral corridors to propose these projects and that countries with strong bilateral ties were reluctant to include all of their projects with Morocco in the Annex.[143] Yet, we can see that the country that proposed the largest number of pre-existing projects was France (8 projects). This can be explained by the fact that France has a long-standing cooperation with Morocco. Lastly, it is noticeable that Sweden, Portugal and the United Kingdom did not propose any pre-existing project and proposed few projects in general. Again, the link could be made with the lack of previous ties with the third country.

Finally, at the EU level, several Directories General are playing important political, coordination and financial roles. DG Home is coordinating the general implementation of the Mobility Partnerships. DG Home is in charge of guaranteeing the effective implementation of projects by monitoring the implementation of the Mobility Partnerships, updating and gathering of the scoreboards.[144] DG

142 For more information, see: http://www.italy.iom.int/en/news/il-programma-e-bosla-avviato-lunedi-scorso-roma (accessed 28 November 2017).

143 Interviews 8 (n131) and 17 (n89).

144 Interview 3 (n132).

Home is also in charge of keeping the partnership dynamic. The EU Delegation based in the third country works in close cooperation with the offices of DG Home in Brussels and with all the implementing partners in the field. DG Home makes the link between the third country and the Member States. The Directorate-General for International Cooperation and Development (DG Devco) coordinates development-related projects. According to the Annexes and scoreboards, these projects are proposed and implemented by the EU. Several funding instruments are available such as the Migration and Asylum thematic programme. Moreover, the Development and Cooperation Instrument can fund projects outside of the EU related to development issues. Projects from the Mobility Partnerships that are related to migration and development can be funded by this instrument. For example, the scoreboard with Morocco includes projects that are under the coordination of DG Devco and financed by the migration and asylum thematic programme that is implemented by the Organisation for Economic Co-operation and Development (OECD) or the United Nations Development Programme (UNDP). Finally, the Directorate-General for Neighbourhood and Enlargement Negotiations (DG NEAR) plays a more political and financial role than the two previously described Directorates-Generals. DG NEAR does not coordinate individual initiatives but works closely with the European External Action Service (EEAS). DG NEAR is in charge of the implementation of the financial aid for the Maghreb, which includes Morocco (but not Cape Verde). The EEAS has a political role that DG NEAR supports financially. They also link between the EEAS and the other General Directories and the EU Delegations. Additionally, DG NEAR is drafting the orientations for the European Neighbourhood Policy that are negotiated with third countries, such as Morocco. Their role is much broader than the Mobility Partnership itself, but through funding and policy orientation it impacts implementation and creation of new projects. Finally, other agencies such as FRONTEX, the European Asylum Support Office (EASO) or the European Training Foundation (ETF) are also proposing and implementing specific projects.[145]

2.3.3 Overview of implemented projects

Not all projects included in the Annex to the Joint Declarations with Cape Verde and Morocco were subsequently found in the scoreboards. For Cape Verde, this is the case of three projects. The first project relates to a proposal by Portugal to develop a bilateral cooperation instrument between the Portuguese Institute for Employment and Vocational Training (IEFP) and its Cape Verdean counterpart, with the aim of simplifying and boosting the efficiency of worker migration procedures. This project was implemented bilaterally and struck out of the scoreboard. Simultaneously, while implementing the Mobility Partnership, a bilateral cooperation instrument was signed between the Portuguese IEFP and its counterpart in Cape Verde, with a view to simplifying and reinforcing the efficacy of the procedures for labour migration.

145 Ibid.

Second, Luxembourg proposed to offer a twinning project between partner universities. In February 2009, the Universities of Luxembourg and Cape Verde signed a Framework Agreement setting the basis for cooperation between both universities.[146] The agreement was valid for a period of five years but has not been renewed. Third, Spain proposed to reinforce the capacity of the Ministry of Defence in respect to new information and communication technologies. It was not possible to ascertain further details concerning this project. In 2008, Spain and Cape Verde concluded an agreement for joint Maritime surveillance. However, limited information is available to conclude that these two initiatives are linked.

In the case of Morocco, 12 projects proposed in the Annex were no longer in the scoreboard. Several reasons have been put forth by the different partners. One project aimed at supporting the Joint Master in International Migration and Social Cohesion, but in January 2014 its Erasmus+ funding was not renewed, which marked the end of the project.[147] This project was not included in the scoreboard. One project proposed by France, relating to police capacity building on issues such as human trafficking and false identification documents, is still ongoing but was no longer included in the scoreboard. When enquiring about it, a French official answered that it might just have been forgotten.[148] This illustrates the problem linked to the updating of the scoreboard. Generally, partners are required to update all information on short notice, before a meeting through emails exchanges as there is no real organ in charge of monitoring Mobility Partnership projects. The level of details and precision varies with the amount of time available to complete this task.[149] A project proposed by the Netherlands is still ongoing but not included as such in the scoreboard, as it is now linked to the voluntary return and reintegration project implemented by IOM.[150] Finally, a Spanish official indicated that the projects proposed in the Annex by Spain were not being implemented if they were not included in the joint *Sharaka* project.[151] Some projects have been included in the joint initiative and others have been mostly excluded from the scoreboard. This does however not mean that the projects have not been implemented. One project on irregular migrant children was implemented as a bilateral activity. This illustrates the fact that Spain prefers not to include all their bilateral activity with Morocco in the scoreboard in order to have some visibility on key initiatives.[152]

Out of these 12 projects, 5 have been cancelled. An EU official declared that the fact that these cancelled projects are no longer mentioned anymore in the

146 European Migration Network, National Contact Point Luxembourg, Circular and Temporary Migration, September 2011, 1, 94.

147 For more information, see: http://www.misoco.org/about-misoco/about-misoco.html (accessed 28 November 2017).

148 Interview 8 (n131).

149 Interview 7 (n89).

150 For more information, see: https://www.iom.int/assisted-voluntary-return-and-reintegration (accessed 29 November 2017).

151 For more information, see: http://www.sharaka.ma (accessed 29 November 2017).

152 Interview 17 (n89).

scoreboard is a problem, as it results in a loss of memory on the evolution of the Mobility Partnership.[153] For now, no tool exists which keeps all the information centralised, thus making it difficult to conduct an evaluation of the implementation. A project proposed by the ETF has also been cancelled. This project was not aimed directly at Morocco and had already been implemented in Moldova and Georgia however it did not seem sufficiently relevant for Morocco. Portugal also cancelled a project that they proposed. According to a Portuguese official interviewed in Rabat, no projects proposed by Portugal have been implemented so far.[154] He added that the cooperation between Portugal and Morocco is good but not of prime importance, which can explain the lack of action. The lack of available funding on the Portuguese side is another explanation. The latter official made a further remark that Portugal concluded the Mobility Partnership with Morocco for political reasons, rather than, for the concrete implementation of projects. This is in line with the argument in which Portugal's migration policy goes hand in hand with the Spanish migration policy. As the Mobility Partnership with Morocco is of high importance for Spain, Portugal supported its conclusion. Moreover, he suggested that the project proposals were not received with enthusiasm by Morocco. The Portuguese representative argued that if Morocco decided to take the initiative, the projects could be implemented at a bilateral level. The Netherlands also cancelled two projects. According to a Dutch official, the activities that were proposed by the Immigration and Naturalisation Service (INS) in the framework of the Mobility Partnership have not yet started. As of the time of writing, it is not clear when exactly the implementation will take place, due to matters of finance. The INS is in regular contact with the Ministry of Security and Justice of the Netherlands and with the EU, regarding funding possibilities and the timing of the activities mentioned. Most of the cancelled and not implemented projects are the result of a lack of funding from the Member States. Nonetheless, when looking at the content of the mentioned projects, there is some evidence that the projects may have affected the content of the two main joint projects included in the Mobility Partnership at a later stage. Namely, the *Sharaka* project and the project '*promouvoir l'integration des Migrants au Maroc*' (Promoting the integration of migrants in Morocco).[155]

A surprising finding is the transformation of four general initiatives proposed by the EU in major joint Mobility Partnership projects. The initiatives are aimed at supporting the implementation of the Mobility Partnership itself, as well as developments in Moroccan policy. The first project aims at fighting human trafficking and included activities relating to the elaboration of the legal framework, the training of Moroccan officials and information campaigns for the sensitisation of public opinion and the protection of victims. The second project supports the

153 Interview 3 (n132).
154 Interview 11, Portuguese Embassy, Rabats, 18 January 2016.
155 For more information, see: http://www.migration4development.org/fr/content/lancement-projet-%C2%AB-promouvoir-l%E2%80%99int%C3%A9gration-migrants-maroc-%C2%BB-cadre-partenariat-mobilit%C3%A9-ue-m (accessed 29 November 2017).

implementation in Morocco of a national asylum system and its related legal framework. The third project comprises a set of possible axes of intervention to be discussed with Moroccan authorities, such as the support to the implementation of the Mobility Partnership and support to the implementation of a migration policy. Finally, the objective of the fourth project is to reinforce the capacities of the National Agency for the Promotion of Employment and Skills (*Agence Nationale pour la Promotion de l'Emploi et des Competences* (ANAPEC)), the Moroccan employment agency, to enhance employment possibility in Morocco. The first three propositions by the EU have been translated into a key project, introduced into the Mobility Partnership in 2015 and benefiting from EUR 10 million[156] in EU funding: 'Promoting integration of migrants in Morocco'. It aims to support the implementation of the National Strategy for Immigration and Asylum (NSIA)[157] adopted in 2014. The strategy covers several aspects such as access to health care, the right to legal housing and the fight against human trafficking. Another initiative financed by the project 'Promoting integration of migrants in Morocco', is included as a new initiative in the scoreboard and was started in 2014. It aims at drafting a strategy for the reception and integration of refugees, asylum seekers and their families, directly relating to the NSIA.

Finally, in the Annex to the Joint Declaration with Morocco, the EU suggested several 'possible axes of intervention to be identified in collaboration with the Moroccan government', which became three out of the four pillars of the *Sharaka* project:[158] capacity building of the ANAPEC in the field of labour migration, the creation of a migratory profile of Moroccans living abroad and the mobilisation of their competences and migration and development. In the framework of this third pillar, the EU offers a new project on financial education and money transfers. Concerning the last pillar, return and reintegration, the EU previously proposed two projects aiming at social and educative reintegration of Moroccans that have returned to Morocco and promoting the mobility of people and competencies. This shows the will for better and clearer communication between partners. It also illustrates the evolution of the working cooperation between all partners. It is an interesting case study for cooperation between different partners in the framework of the Moroccan Mobility Partnership. When proposing activities during the drafting of the Annexes to the Joint Declarations, Member States tend to propose bilateral initiatives that they either had already developed or were planning to develop. Through the *Sharaka* project, seven[159] Member States decided to collaborate on joint initiatives. The *Sharaka* project is one of the two projects that aims

156 Interview 28 (n68).

157 No official legal document is open to the public for now. For more information, see: http://www.marocainsdumonde.gov.ma/fr/le-minist%C3%A8re/affaires-de-la-migration/strat%C3%A9gie-nationale-dimmigration-et-dasile (accessed 29 November 2017).

158 For more information, see: http://www.expertisefrance.fr/fre/Domaines-d-activite/Gouvernance-et-Droits-humains/Migrations-projet-SHARAKA-au-Maroc (accessed 29 November 2017).

159 Germany, Belgium, Spain, France, Italy, the Netherlands and Sweden.

at supporting the Mobility Partnership.[160] According to an EU official, it also aims at showing Morocco that the Member States are working to avoid overlapping projects.[161] This project is a way to reward the conclusion of the Mobility Partnership as it foresees ways for Moroccans to access the EU labour market.[162] In practice and as of the time of writing this aspect of the project has still not been launched. This initiative had a considerable effect on the reshaping of proposed projects. For instance, the Italian Ministry of Labour and social policies decided to delete the projects that they proposed at the time of the conclusion of the Mobility Partnership.[163] This was due to the fact that they were not considered by Morocco as responding sufficiently to their needs and therefore were not included in the *Sharaka* project. Out of three projects, two appear as deleted in the scoreboard and one as concluded because Italy realised previous activities in 2013, 2014 and in January 2015. Moreover, the Ministry of Labour and Social Policy proposed a new bilateral project which was implemented from February to August 2015, relating to circular migration for young workers in fields such as tourism and agriculture. Spain is also an important partner in the *Sharaka* project; the Ministry of Employment and Social Security[164] decided not to implement their proposed initiatives as bilateral projects but to propose them all through *Sharaka*. Out of six projects, four have been included in *Sharaka*. In the scoreboard, the other two initiatives are still defined as being in preparation, showing that Spain has not abandoned the idea of implementing these projects bilaterally. The only project proposed by Sweden has been included in *Sharaka*. France is an interesting case as it proposed to delete four projects in order for the scoreboard to reflect as satisfactorily as possible the initiatives that are effectively implemented through the Mobility Partnership. This includes two initiatives that have not been accepted as being part of *Sharaka* concerning students' residency permits and an information programme on the French labour market.

Moreover, when analysing the scoreboard, we can see that several key projects have been implemented satisfactorily. In Cape Verde, a Common Visa Application Centre has been running since 2010, processing approximately 9,000[165] visa applications a year. In addition, different bilateral initiatives related to labour migration are ongoing. Two of the main initiatives were the CAMPO project[166] and the project Diaspora for Development of Cape Verde (DIAS de Cabo Verde),[167] which have already been concluded. These two projects aimed at

160 Interview 3 (n132).

161 Ibid.

162 Ibid.

163 Informal email exchanges with the Italian Ministry of Labour, May 2015.

164 Informal email exchanges with the Spanish Ministry of Employment and Social Security, May 2015.

165 Information available in the Scoreboard.

166 For more information about this project, see: http://www.campo.com.cv (accessed on 12 December 2017).

167 For more information, see: https://gfmd.org/pfp/ppd/3 (accessed on 12 December 2017).

promoting legal mobility between Cape Verde and Europe, circular labour migration and return and reintegration of migrant workers. Once the initial CAMPO project ended it was incorporated into the Cape Verdean administration (in the Ministry of Communities) but it was discontinued in 2016. Finally, a visa facilitation agreement for short-term visas and a readmission agreement were concluded in October 2012 and April 2013, respectively, and both are currently in force. The negotiations of a readmission agreement have been taking place even though Cape Verde neither signed the Geneva Convention of 1951 on the status of refugees nor has the capacity to receive returned migrants. A proposed project related to the ratification by Cape Verde of the Geneva Convention has never been implemented and Cape Verde is still only part of the 1967 Protocol. They do not have the practical facilities, nor do they even have any clear idea of how to create such facilities.[168] The fact that Cape Verde is divided into different islands, with different airports, creates complex circumstances and would also require high financial means to replicate the same facilities on several islands.[169]

Projects that have been proposed after the conclusion of the Mobility Partnership with Cape Verde were directly answering the needs and interests of all parties. As mentioned during several interviews with EU and Cape Verdean officials, projects implemented in the framework of the Mobility Partnerships were used to identify specific needs for Cape Verde and to develop new projects aiming at addressing the recognised shortcomings.[170] As was in the case of the project 'Strengthening of Cabo Verde's Capacities in Migration Management', which supported the development of a policy to address irregular migration. This project is coordinated by Portugal but includes France, the Netherlands and Luxembourg.[171] It was also the case of a project implemented under the MIEUX Programme aiming at developing the National Migration Strategy and Action Plan in order to reduce irregular migration and improve legal mobility.[172] These projects have a high policy relevance for Cape Verde as they support the drafting and implementation of Cape Verde's new migration strategy. We will come across the same circumstances in the case of Morocco as follows. One initiative included in the scoreboard following the adoption of a Directive in 2014 on seasonal workers,[173] aimed at using the flexibilities offered by this Directive, in order to favour seasonal work and circular migration. Additionally, a short project on the theme of circular migration was proposed by Italy for implementation in 2015. However, this

168 Interview 38, IOM, Praia, 24 February 2016.

169 Ibid.

170 Interviews 33 (n42), 39 (n30) and 45 (n42).

171 The project is called 'Strengthening of Cabo Verde's Capacities in Migration Management'. For more information, see: https://ec.europa.eu/europeaid/case-studies/strengthening-cape-verdes-capacities-migration-management_en (accessed on 12 December 2017).

172 For more information about MIEUX, see: https://www.mieux-initiative.eu/en (accessed 12 December 2017).

173 Directive 2014/36/EU on the conditions of entry and stay of third-country nationals for the purpose of employment as seasonal workers, 26 February 2014, L 94/375.

was a bilateral initiative that was not solely directed towards Morocco. Another new initiative called '*Droit des migrants en action*',[174] aims at enhancing migrants' rights, however, it is not only directed towards Morocco. Finally, three *new* initiatives aim at directly supporting one or several pillars of the *Sharaka* project.

In each Mobility Partnership, projects are divided into topics. These topics are not always the same from one Mobility Partnership to the other and the categorisation can evolve between the Annex and the scoreboard. The policy context and priorities have an impact on the projects proposed and implemented. Table 2.2 shows the evolution of the distribution of projects by topics in the Annex to the Joint Declaration with Cape Verde and in the scoreboard.

We can see that even though the share of projects related to border management and irregular migration were plentiful in the Annex, it nonetheless increased over the years. On the other hand, the number of projects related to legal migration became less numerous and no direct reference to labour migration are further made. This could be seen as an argument supporting the existing assertion[175] that the Mobility Partnership is used by the EU as a migration management tool aiming at increasing the difficulty for third country nationals to accede to Europe.

In Cape Verde, the *new* projects that have already been implemented have been proposed in the areas of *legal migration*, *migration and development* and *horizontal issues*. Two of the horizontal projects consist in the development of the

Table 2.2 Evolution of the distribution of projects by topics for Cape Verde*

Topics	*Number of projects in the Annex*	*Number of projects in the Scoreboard*
Legal migration, integration, mobility and short stay visas	13	7
Links between migration and development, diasporas, money transfers	5	15
Asylum and immigration	2	2
Cooperation on border management, identity and travel documents, and the fights against irregular migration and trafficking in human beings	10	13
Monitoring and awareness of migration flows/horizontal initiatives	1	5
Total	31	42

* Based on the scoreboard for Cape Verde of 2016.

Note: This table shows the evolution of the distribution of projects by topics in the Annex to the Joint Declaration with Cape Verde and in the scoreboard. For example, projects related to legal migration and mobility went from 13 in the Annex to 7 in the scoreboard indicating a decrease in this type of projects.

174 For more information: http://www.ifrc.org/fr/introduction/migration/les-droits-des-migrants-en-action/about-the-project/ (accessed 29 November 2017).

175 Meng-Hsuan Chou, European Union migration strategy towards West Africa: the origin and outlook of "Mobility Partnerships" with Cape Verde and Senegal (2009) EUSA Working Paper 1, 20-22.

National Immigration Strategy and Action Plan and the drafting of the new Migration Framework Legislation. These projects illustrate the policy and legal relevance Mobility Partnerships can have. The increase in the number of projects under the topic *Migration and Development* can be linked to the adoption of the National Emigration Strategy for Development[176] in 2014, as it includes a significant migration and development component.[177] The National Emigration Strategy for Development includes projects that were previously falling under *employment*, such as the conclusion of bilateral working agreements, or a new project implemented by LuxDev aimed at the development of the labour market in Cape Verde.

Regarding Morocco, border management, irregular migration and human trafficking/smuggling are also a primary source for projects but unlike Cape Verde, mobility and legal migration is given more weight than migration and development. It is also interesting to note that the highest number of *pre-existing* projects for a category (20), was concentrated on mobility and legal migration. However, the highest number of *concomitant* projects (27) was centred on combatting irregular migration and border management. This illustrates the initiative of Member States to include in the Annex all positive initiatives that have already been implemented in Morocco to give more weight to their negotiations. As such, Member States benefit from a better negotiating position to impose more constraining projects, for instance, the conclusion of a much-criticised readmission agreement. The topic that has the best *ratio* of implementation is *Migration and Development* and particularly projects on the mobilisation of Moroccans' competencies. While the topic with the lowest implementation *ratio* pertains to *Mobility, legal immigration and integration*. The focus of these topics indicates policy orientations which are substantiated by the EU funding priorities for migration related issues.

Table 2.3 Evolution of the distribution of projects by topics for Morocco*

Topics	*Number of projects in the Annex*	*Number of projects in the Scoreboard*
Mobility, legal immigration and integration	35	44
Preventing and combatting irregular immigration, people-smuggling, border management	38	36
Migration and development	20	25
International protection	6	7
Horizontal Initiatives	6	10
Total	105	122

* Based on the scoreboard for Morocco of 2017.

Note: This table shows the evolution of the distribution of projects by topics in the Annex to the Joint Declaration with Morocco and in the scoreboard. For example, projects related to legal migration and mobility went from 35 in the Annex to 43 in the scoreboard indicating an increase in this type of projects.

176 Resolução do Conselho de Ministros n°33/2014 de 9 Janeiro (Estratégia Nacional de Emigração para o Desenvolvimento).

177 ICMPD and IOM, A Survey on Migration Policies in West Africa (2015) 1, 124.

Unlike the case of Cape Verde, the scoreboard for Morocco is very detailed and classifies projects under several *objectives* rather than general topics. The *objective* that includes the biggest number of new projects is *integration*, which belongs under the topic *mobility, legal immigration and integration*. This objective is not homogeneous and includes diverse types of projects related to migrants' rights, to asylum or also to business-related migration. The number of projects in the scoreboard does not exactly coincide with the actual number of projects as some projects are separated under different topics. Therefore, they seem to be slightly more numerous.

2.4 Conclusion

The aim of this chapter was to examine the Mobility Partnerships with Cape Verde and Morocco from their conclusion to their implementation. The analysis revealed that Mobility Partnerships are a complex tool that comprises many different actors, having separate roles and interests. I discerned that an imbrication of factors led to the choice of Cape Verde and Morocco as beneficiaries of the Mobility Partnerships and these factors highly differed in each case.

Taken together, these results suggest that EU Member States play a key role in the conclusion and implementation of Mobility Partnerships. First, EU Member States have the last say in the selection of the third country. Then, the vast majority of projects are bilateral activities proposed by EU Member States. These projects are the reflection of their own national interest. EU officials allow the inclusion of this type of projects because it is the condition for an effective implementation of the Mobility Partnerships. However, the conflict of interests between different Member States can lead to some implementation issues such as the overlapping of projects or the lack of will to cooperate.

3 Legal and policy developments in Morocco and Cape Verde

The aim of this chapter is to provide an overview of the legal and policy developments that have occurred in Morocco and Cape Verde since the conclusion of their respective Mobility Partnerships. The legal framework related to migration covers specific issues. First, the laws being presented are related to entry, stay and exit. The rights to entry and stay in a country can vary depending on the status and categories of people such as migrants, migrant workers, asylum seekers and refugees or victims of human trafficking. This chapter presents the legal frameworks not only from their purely administrative content but also from the perspective of migrants' rights. It also takes into consideration various groups that can have specific rights in a third country due to their particular historical and geographical proximity but also because of the existence of sub-regional organisations granting exceptional rights to their members. This is, for example, the case of the Economic Community of West African States (ECOWAS) Member States (Benin, Burkina Faso, Cape Verde, Ivory Coast, The Gambia, Ghana, Guinea, Guinea Bissau, Liberia, Mali, Niger, Nigeria, Senegal, Sierra Leone and Togo) or Portuguese-speaking African countries (Angola, Cape Verde, Guinea-Bissau, Mozambique, São Tomé and Príncipe and Equatorial Guinea).

3.1 Legal framework for migrants' rights in Morocco and Cape Verde before the conclusion of the Mobility Partnerships

This section presents the legal framework related to migration in Cape Verde and Morocco before the conclusion of the Mobility Partnerships. Accordingly, the legal framework for Cape Verde is presented as it existed in 2008, and the legal framework for Morocco is as it existed in 2013.

3.1.1 Entry, stay and exit rights

This section will be divided into three parts: immigration and emigration, asylum and human trafficking.

3.1.1.1 Immigration and emigration

Cape Verde Decree 6/97, of 5 May 1997,[1] regulated the legal status of foreigners and the rights and guarantees of the regime of entry, stay, expulsion and extradition. Decree 6/97 proposed to adapt and conform the text of the law in force[2] to the rules of international law, constitutional provisions and international conventions and agreements on foreigners binding on the State of Cape Verde.[3] One of the changes brought by the Decree 6/97 are the provisions introduced in Chapter I on general disposition. Article 2 introduces a definition of *extrangeiro* (foreigner) and *residente* (resident).

Decree 6/97 does not specifically mention the rights to family reunification of migrant workers who fall into the general conditions foreseen by the law. The entry of foreigners into national territory follows four different regimes: one for Cape Verdean nationals who are exempt from entry visas, one for visa-exempt entities, one for visa-exempt individuals and one for those who require an entry visa. Law 36/V/97, of 25 August 1997,[4] defines the special legal status enjoyed by foreigners originating from Portuguese-speaking countries (*Estatuto do Cidadão Lusófono*). In relation to the entry into Cape Verde, Portuguese-speaking citizens qualify for a multiple-entry and long-stay visa and may also be exempted from a visa by a decision of the Government.[5]

The criminalisation of irregular exit does not exist in Cape Verde. Freedom of movement was incorporated into the Cape Verdean Constitution by Article 50, entitled 'freedom of movement and emigration' and worded as follows: '[e]very citizen has the right to leave and enter freely into national territory, as well as to emigrate'. This provision takes up Article 13(2) of the Universal Declaration of Human Rights. Moreover, Article 64 of Decree 6/97 forbids the collective expulsion of foreigners, therefore, at least in theory, Cape Verde is abiding by the principle of *non-refoulement*. In practice this principle was not

1 Decreto-Legislativo 6/97 de 5 de Maio, que regula a situação jurídica do estrangeiro no território nacional, estabelecendo os direitos, garantias e deveres, o regime de entrada, permanência e saída, a expulsão e a extradiçao, bem como as taxas, as infracções e sanções B.O.C.V., I Série, n. 17.

2 In 1990, Decree-Law 93/III/90 of 27 October was adopted to regulate the legal situation of foreigners in the country and repeal Decrees 17/76, 46/76 and 47/76.

3 Ibid, preamble para 3.

4 Lei 36/V/97, de 25 de Agosto, que define o estatuto do cidadão lusófono B.O.C.V., I Série, n. 14.

5 Acordo sobre a Supressão de Vistos em Passaportes Diplomáticos, Especiais e de Serviço entre os Governos Membros dos Países de Língua Oficial Portuguesa (Maputo, 17 de Julho de 2000), Aprovado pelo Decreto 3/2001, de 30 de Julho, B.O.C.V, I Série, n. 23; Acordo sobre a Concessão de Vistos de Múltipla Entrada para Determinadas Categorias de Pessoas, Aprovado pelo Decreto 12/2003, de 22 de Dezembro, B.O.C.V, I Série; Acordo sobre a Concessão de Visto Temporário para Tratamento Médico a Cidadãos da Comunidade dos Países de Língua Portuguesa (Brasília, 30 de Julho de 2002), Aprovado pelo Decreto nº 15/2003, de 22 de Dezembro, B.O.C.V., I Série, n. 43.

always followed.[6] The fact that from 2006 to 2010 Cape Verde participated in the Seahorse project in cooperation with Mauritania, Senegal, Spain and FRONTEX (the European External Borders Agency) led to situations where boats of migrants were intercepted and returned to their ports of departure. This practice can be related to *refoulement* as migrants were not able to launch an asylum claim in Cape Verde, if they wanted to, and groups were sent back without considering individual cases. Cape Verdean officials were participating in the decision regarding the sending back of boats.[7] According to Decree 6/97, expulsion of foreigners towards countries where the foreigner can be persecuted for political, religious or opinion-related reasons, and in cases where punishments are considered as inhuman or degrading, is prohibited (Article 65). The deterrence of migrants' vessels can be seen as a breach of this provision, as the people who were returned without the chance to launch an asylum claim in Cape Verde could have been at risk of facing persecution for political, religious or opinion-related reasons.

The law also foresaw administrative and judicial expulsion (Articles 68 and 72). According to Article 36(2) of the Cape Verdean Constitution of 1999, 'a foreigner or stateless person who has been authorised to reside in the country or has applied for asylum can only be expelled by a judicial decision in accordance with the law'.[8] Additionally, Article 22(1) of the International Convention on the Protection of the Rights of All Migrant Workers and Members of Their Families (ICRMW) as well as Article 12 (5) of the African Charter on Human and Peoples' Rights forbid 'collective' or 'mass' expulsion of third country nationals. In Cape Verde, between 2003 and 2008, 852 individuals were expelled at an average of 146 persons per year.[9] The phenomenon in Cape Verde is clearly less intensive than in Morocco, as will be detailed later in this section. The ECOWAS region represents the significant and almost unique origin among the deportees.[10]

The Report of the Interministerial Commission for the Study and Proposition of the Bases of Immigration Policy pinpoints that the legal framework is acceptable for an efficient management of migration flows.[11] Acceptable does not mean flawless. There are contradictions and voids in the legislation as well as overlaps between Decree 6/97 and the Labor Code[12] (Article 280) in

6 Kees Wouters and Maarten Den Heijer, 'The Marine I Case: A Comment' (2010) 22 *IJRL* 1; Efthymios Papastavridis, 'Enforcement Jurisdiction in the Mediterranean Sea: Illicit Activities and the Rule of Law on the High Seas' (2010) 25 *IJMCL* 569; Guy S. Goodwin-Gill, 'The Right to Seek Asylum: Interception at Sea and the Principle of Non-Refoulement' (2011) 23(3) *IJRL* 443, 450.

7 Guy Goodwin-Gill (n6) 450.

8 Lei Constitucional 1/V/99. Revê a Constituição da República de Cabo Verde. Suplemento ao B.O. no 43, I Série, 23 November 1999.

9 IOM, 'Migração em Cabo Verde: Perfil Nacional' (2009) 1, 44.

10 IOM, 'Perfil Migratório de Cabo Verde' (2017 Draft) 1, 53.

11 EFG Consulting, 'Imigração em Cabo Verde: Subsídios para a Política Nacional de Imigração Relatório Final da Comissão Interministerial para Estudo e Proposição das Bases da Política de Imigração' (CIMI), Outubro 2010, 1, 53.

12 Decreto-Legislativo no 5/2007 Aprova o Codigo Laboral Cabo-verdiano B.O.C.V., I Série no 37, 16 de Outubro de 2007.

respect to the regularisation of migrants. This situation concerns migrants who exceed 90 days of stay without obtaining an authorisation of residence. The latter is problematic, because they need a work contract to have a residency permit and a residency permit to work, therefore they end up becoming irregular migrants as they are unable to regularise their situation. Moreover, the report also underlines the shortcomings in administrative capacity of the services involved (shortage of financial, human, technical and material resources) explaining, in part, the failures in supervision and control in the application of the law in force.[13]

It is important to note that, in 1982, within the framework of the ECOWAS, Cape Verde signed a Protocol of Free Movement of people and rights to residence and establishment.[14] Article 2 of the Protocol allows all citizens from the ECOWAS countries to enter and stay in another ECOWAS country, which has led to significant mobility within the region. According to the Protocol, citizens from the sub-region do not need an entry visa but must submit a request for a residency permit if they decide to remain in the country. Indeed, the Protocol does not provide for a right to permanent residence, which is regulated by national law.[15] Cape Verde has not ratified Additional Protocol A/SP.1/7/86[16] on the second phase (right of residence) of the Protocol of Free Movement. The Supplementary Protocol of 1986 regulates the right of citizens of the community to seek and perform paid work. In practice, Cape Verde has abolished the entry visa for 90-day stays but has not yet adopted the ECOWAS travel certificate[17] or the ECOWAS passport,[18] nor has it harmonised the immigration and emigration form for the ECOWAS Member States.[19] Since Cape Verde became a country of immigration, the authorities thought that maintaining the application of the Protocol on Free Movement of Persons would make it impossible to properly manage internal migratory flows, and it would risk an 'invasion of foreigners'.[20]

13 EFG Consulting (n11) 54.

14 Protocolo sobre a Livre Circulação de Pessoas, o Direito de Residência e de Estabelecimento, Aprovado pela Lei no 18/II/82, de 30 de Março, B.O.C.V., Suplemento, 7 de Maio de 1982.

15 José Pina-Delgado, 'O Cruzamento entre a Política Migratória Cabo-Verdiana para a Europa e a Política Migratória Cabo-Verdiana para a África Ocidental', 523 in Suzano Costa and Cristina Sarmento (eds), *Entre África e a Europa: Nação, Estado e Democracia em Cabo Verde* (Coimbra: Almedina 2013) 553.

16 Protocolo suplementar A/SP.1/7/86 sobre a segunda fase (direito de residência) do protocolo de Livre Circulação de Pessoas, Direito de Residência e Estabelecimento.

17 Decisão A/DEC.2/7/85 sobre o estabelecimento de um certificado de viagem para os Estados-Membros da CEDEAO.

18 Decisão C/DEC.1/5/2000, assinada em Abuja em 2000, sobre a adopção de um passaporte da CEDEAO.

19 Decisão C/DEC.3/12/92 sobre a introdução de um formulário harmonizado de emigração e imigração nos Estados-Membros da CEDEAO.

20 José Pina-Delgado (n15) 555.

Cape Verde concluded joint border control agreements and facilitation schemes for regular emigration with Portugal and Spain.[21] The agreement with Portugal allows Cape Verdeans to work in Portugal for a maximum of three years, on the condition that they have an employment contract.[22] These two agreements include a readmission clause for Cape Verdean nationals. Additionally, Cape Verde is part of the African, Caribbean and Pacific countries (ACP) and party to the Cotonou Agreement, which includes Article 13 stipulating a return and readmission obligation.[23] To overcome some of the gaps faced by the country's development challenges, Decree 3/2005, of 1 August,[24] amended Decree 6/97 in its Articles 30, 31, 54 and 12, to facilitate the entry of tourists, and the provisions of paragraph e of article 30(1) were revoked.

In Morocco, Law 02–03,[25] of 11 November 2003, regulates the entry and stay of foreigners as well as the exit of foreigners and nationals. It was adopted in a climate of fear following the terrorist attacks in Casablanca on 16 May 2003, which resulted in 41 people losing their lives. The Law was presented to the Parliament at the same time as Law 03–03 on anti-terrorism, which amalgamated migrants and terrorists.[26]

21 Tratado celebrado entre a República de Cabo Verde e a República Portuguesa no domínio da fiscalização conjunta de espaços marítimos sob a soberania ou jurisdição da República de Cabo Verde, assinado na cidade do Mindelo (Cabo Verde), no dia 16 de Setembro de 2006, Aprovado para ratificação pela Resolução 6/VII/2007, de 2 de Janeiro, B.O.C.V., I Série, n. 1, 2 de Janeiro de 2007; Protocolo entre a República de Cabo Verde e a República Portuguesa sobre a Emigração Temporária de Trabalhadores Cabo-Verdianos para a Prestação de Trabalho em Portugal (assinado na Praia, 18 de Fevereiro de 1997), Aprovado pelo Decreto n7/97, de 14 de Abril, B.O.C.V., I Série, n. 14; Acordo entre o Reino da Espanha e a República de Cabo Verde sobre a Vigilância Conjunta dos Espaços Marítimos sob Soberania ou Jurisdição de Cabo Verde, aprovado para ratificação pela Resolução 74/VII/2008, de 14 de Julho, B.O.C.V., I Série, n. 26, 14 de Julho de 2008; Acordo Quadro de Imigração entre a República de Cabo Verde e o Reino da Espanha (Madrid, 20 de Março de 2007), Aprovado pelo Decreto 9/2007, de 20 de Agosto, B.O.C.V, I Série, n. 31, 20 de Agosto de 2007; Acuerdo Marco de cooperación en materia de inmigración entre el Reino de España y la República de Cabo Verde, hecho «ad referendum» en Madrid el 20 de marzo de 2007 BOE 39 14 febrero 2008, 8028.

22 Protocol on Temporary Emigration of Cape Verdean Workers to Work in Portugal, concluded between Portugal and Cape Verde on 18 February 1997.

23 Partnership agreement 2000/483/EC between the members of the African, Caribbean and Pacific Group of States of the one part, and the European Community and its Member States, of the other part, signed in Cotonou on 23 June 2000.

24 Decreto-Legislativo 3/2005, de 1 de Agosto, que altera os artigos 30, 31, 54 e 112 do Decreto-Legislativo 6/97, de 5 de Maio, que regula a situação jurídica do estrangeiro no território nacional, incluindo o regime de entrada, permanência e saída.

25 Dahir no 1–03–196 du 16 ramadam 1424 (11 novembre 2003) portant promulgation de la loi n⊠ 02–03 relative à l'entrée et au séjour des étrangers au Royaume du Maroc, à l'émigration et à l'immigration irrégulières.

26 Abdelkrim Belguendouz, 'Immigration et émigration: la nouvelle loi marocaine' 11 in Driss El Yazami (ed.), *Un Siècle de migration Marocaines* (*Migrance* No 24 2005) 11; Abdeljabbar Arrach, 'The Moroccan new immigration policy and the constitutional protection of fundamental human rights of migrants', 6, available at: https://www.jus.uio.no/english/research/news-and-events/events/conferences/2014/wccl-cmdc/wccl/papers/ws6/w6-arrach.pdf (accessed 9 February 2018); GADEM, 'Rapport sur l'application au Maroc de la Convention internationale sur la protection des droits

The Law often has been criticised.[27] Abdelkrim Belguendouz, for example, condemns the exclusively security and repressive approach taken in Law 02–03.[28] Additionally, the Euro-Mediterranean Human Rights Network argues that Law 02–03 'led to a hardening of Morocco's migration policy and [is] partly responsible for exacerbating the country's xenophobic climate'.[29] Indeed, as Katharina Natter underlines it, before the adoption of Law 02–03, Moroccan authorities overlooked irregular migration and rejected the idea to address the issue politically.[30] The adoption of Law 02–03 constituted a drastic change in the way Morocco deals with irregular migration. Abdelkrim Belguendouz welcomes the new law as a much needed 'decolonisation' of the law.[31] The law replaced by Law 02–03 was from the Protectorate era and referred to outdated colonial institutions and even to the 'zone française de l'Empire chérifien' (French zone of the Sherifian Empire).[32] However, this 'decolonisation' is still only partial, and several authors, including Belguendouz, consider the law to be a by-product of European texts, especially French texts in the field of migration.[33] On the other hand, Katharina Natter argues that the decision of Morocco to adopt this new restrictive law was not in 'response to public demand' but

de tous les travailleurs migrants et des membres de leur famille', 2013, 1, 6. This report is a joint report written under the coordination of the GADEM. The following NGOs were involved in the joint report: Association lumière sur l'émigration clandestine au Maghreb (ALECMA), l'Association des ressortissants sénégalais au Maroc – 28 (ARESMA-28), Caminando Fronteras, Chabaka – Le réseau des associations du nord du Maroc pour le développement et la solidarité, le Collectif des communautés subsahariennes au Maroc (CCSM), le Conseil des migrants subsahariens au Maroc (CMSM), le Groupe antiraciste d'accompagnement et de défense des étrangers et migrants (GADEM), l'Organisation démocratique du travail – Travailleurs immigrés (ODT-IT) et Pateras de la vida.

27 Myriam Cherti and Michael Collyer, 'Immigration and Pensée d'Etat: Moroccan migration policy changes as transformation of "geopolitical culture"' (2015) 20(4) *The Journal of North African Studies* 590, 590–591.
28 Abdelkrim Belguendouz (n26) 13.
29 Euro-Mediterranean Human Rights Network, 'Analysis of the Mobility Partnership signed between the Kingdom of Morocco, the European Union and nine Member States on 7 June 2013', February 2014, 6.
30 Katharina Natter, 'The Formation of Morocco's Policy Towards Irregular Migration (2000–2007): Political Rationale and Policy Processes' (2014) 52(5) *Int Migr* 15, 16.
31 Abdelkrim Belguendouz (n26) 11–12.
32 See, for example: Dahir du 15 novembre 1934 (7 chaâbane 1353) réglementant l'immigration en zone française de l'Empire chérifien, signé le 17 novembre 1934 pour promulgation et mise à exécution par le commissaire résident général, Henri Ponsot.
33 Abdelkrim Belguendouz, *Le Maroc non africain, gendarme de l'Europe? Alerte au projet de loi no 02–03 relative à l'entrée et au séjour des étrangers au Maroc, à l'émigration et l'immigration irrégulière* (Salé: Imprimerie Beni Snassen 2003); Abdelkrim Belguendouz, 'Le Maroc et la migration irrégulière – une analyse sociopolitique (2009) CARIM – module socio-politique' 1, 38; Mehdi Lahlou, 'Le Maghreb dans son environnement régional et international: Un schéma migratoire reconfiguré, dans les faits et dans l'approche politique' (2011) Ifri-Programme Migrations, identités, citoyenneté, Paris; Mohamed Khachani, 'La migration irrégulière au Maroc: un état des lieux' 43 in Haut-Commissariat du Plan (ed.), *Les Cahiers du Plan* (2010) no 29.

because Morocco was interested in gaining more geopolitical power.[34] Even though there is an influence of the EU and its member states, such as France, in the development and content of the law, the agency of Morocco to act according to its own interests should not be overlooked. This argument still stands when looking at more recent developments.

Article 2 of Law 02–03 stipulates that people having a diplomatic status, subject to reciprocity, are not covered by the law. Diplomatic and consular relations are organised by the Vienna Conventions of 1961 and 1964.[35] Article 3 stipulates that any foreigner wishing to enter Morocco should have a valid passport or any other document recognised by Morocco as a valid travel document. Article 4 details the modalities of border control and specifies the conditions to refuse entry. Indent 1 states that during passport control additional information concerning reasons for the stay in Morocco and proof of sufficient means of subsistence can be required. Indent 2 stipulates that entry can be denied to any foreigner that could be a 'threat to the public order'. However, there is no definition in the law of what qualifies as such a threat, which can lead to arbitrary decisions.[36]

In the *Farouk Ben Mustafa Izzat Case* of 2005,[37] the 'threat to public order' is defined as something of 'effective danger', such as murder, drug trafficking or robbery with assault. This means that the danger must be sufficiently severe and real at the time when the decision is taken. Abdelkrim Belguendouz remarks that Law 02–03 is unbalanced due to an excessive use of the notion of 'threat to the public order' to justify many repressive provisions.[38] Articles 14 and 17 refer to 'threat to the public order' to deny a residency permit, and Article 21 refers to it to order a deportation. Articles 25 and 27 refer to the notion of 'threat to the public order' as a reason for expulsion. Article 40 sets the 'threat to public order' as a reason to cancel a visa. The 'threat to the public order' allows the deportation and expulsion of certain categories of people who are normally protected against it, such as pregnant woman and children.[39]

According to Article 5, there are two distinct types of residency permits: the *carte d'immatriculation* (registration card) and the *carte de residence* (residency card). Articles 6 to 18 establish the conditions to receive such cards and who can benefit from them. The registration card is given to foreigners that stay in Morocco for more than three months. There are three types of registration cards (Article 13): for visitors, for students and for working migrants. In the last case, specific employment must be mentioned on the card. It is noticeable that there is no possibility to obtain a registration card through 'family reunification' or 'long-term care'. However, Article 44(2) of the International Convention on the Protection of the Rights of All Migrant Workers and Members of Their Families

34 Katharina Natter (n30) 17.

35 Vienna Convention on Diplomatic Relations, 18 April 1961; Vienna Convention on Consular Relations, 24 April 1963.

36 GADEM (n26) 19.

37 Arrêt no 382 du 03 mars 2005, dossier No 81/03, affaire Farouk Ben Mustafa Izzat.

38 Abdelkrim Belguendouz (n26) 14.

39 GADEM (n26) 19.

(ICRMW)[40] imposes the possibility for family reunification for migrant workers. Morocco has ratified the ICRMW,[41] which grants special protection to migrant workers and their families. Law 02–03 is not in accordance with this provision.

The decree regulating the implementation of Law 02–03 was not adopted until seven years after the adoption of the law, on 1 April 2010.[42] The late adoption of the decree was a problem for the harmonised and efficient application of Law 02–03, as several articles refer to a regulatory decree for precisions. Another striking implementation problem in Article 19 regards the refusal of delivery or renewal of a residency permit. The article says that a residency permit can be withdrawn if the foreigner does not provide the documents and evidence foreseen in the regulatory decree. This means that, in the absence of such a regulatory decree, there are no clear rules regarding what documents or evidence are required for foreigners to be able to keep their residency permit, putting them in a precarious situation. In the absence of a regulatory decree determining the place in which the detention of irregular migrants should take place, Article 34 allows Moroccan authorities to detain foreigners in a place that is not regulated by the law before deporting them.[43] According to the Euro-Mediterranean Human Rights Network, Moroccan authorities are implementing these measures arbitrarily and without granting migrants and refugees their rights to an interpreter, lawyer and appeal.[44]

According to the Anti-Racist Group for the Support and Defence of Foreigners and Migrants [*Groupe Antiraciste de Défense et d'Accompagnement des Etrangers et Migrants* (GADEM)], foreigners that are not allowed to enter Morocco from the Casablanca Airport are not put in administrative custody, such as foreseen by Article 34, nor in waiting zones, foreseen by Article 38.[45] They are blocked in transit zones outside of any legal framework for undetermined periods, and they do not benefit from the protections of Articles 35, 36 and 38. According to Article 37, the transport company used to travel by the foreigner who is denied entry in Morocco should cover the costs of his return. In practice, the unsuccessful migrant must pay for these costs himself.[46]

The Decree of 1 April 2010 also corrected some discrepancies of Law 02–03. For example, as previously noted, it was not possible to obtain a registration card

40 International Convention on the Protection of the Rights of All Migrant Workers and Members of Their Families, Adopted by General Assembly resolution 45/158 of 18 December 1990.

41 UN General Assembly, International Convention on the Protection of the Rights of All Migrant Workers and Members of their Families, 18 December 1990, A/RES/45/158.

42 Décret no 2-09-607 du 15 rabii 1431 (1er avril 2010) pris pour l'application de la loi n° 02–03 relative à l'entrée et au séjour du Maroc, à l'émigration et l'immigration irrégulières.

43 Alecmo, CCSM, GADEM and Mission catholique de Nouadhibou, 'Situation des Migrants dans le Sud du Maroc: Mission d'observation conjointe,' September 2014, 1, 12–13.

44 Euro-Mediterranean Human Rights Network (n29) 7.

45 GADEM (n26) 53.

46 Ibid 68.

for family reunification or long-term care purposes. Articles 15 to 17 of Decree 2–09–607 now allow for these possibilities. However, the Decree now also requires foreigners to enter Morocco with a long-term visa. The category of long-term visa (family reunification, work, student, for example) has to remain the same as per the registration card. For instance, a foreigner will need a long-term visa that mentions 'family reunification' to apply for a registration card under family reunification. But a foreigner who entered Morocco with a visitor visa cannot ask for a registration card for family reunification. According to Nadia Khrouz, this procedure could toughen the conditions of entry and stay in Morocco.[47] Indeed, a report indicates that this condition is impossible to fulfil as Moroccan consulates in sub-Saharan countries refuse to deliver such visas.[48] Getting documents from the country of origin can be an obstacle in several cases besides family reunification. For example, migrants encounter problems when they have to provide certain documents, such as marriage certificates, birth certificates or criminal records. In practice, the process is exorbitant and complicated, and migrants rarely know the details about how to obtain them.[49] Additionally, Article 16 of the Decree of 1 April 2010 sets that, to benefit from family reunification, the foreigner must prove his family situation and have sufficient means of subsistence. In practice, the authorities require further conditions that are not required by law.[50] For example, in some cases a residency card was required instead of a registration card. In another example, it was forbidden for a woman to launch the process of family reunification for her husband under the argument that family reunification only works from a husband to his wife but not vice versa.

Nine years after the adoption of Law 02–03, and two years after the adoption of the Decree regulating the implementation of the said law, the Ministry of the Interior issued eight ministerial orders on 13 February 2012.[51] A ministerial order[52] was adopted that sets the exact list of documents that must be shown to Moroccan authorities to benefit from Article 17. Another ministerial order[53] was adopted setting the list of documents that must be joined to an application for the

47 Nadia Khrouz, 'De la respécification de la notion de transit' 1 in Nadia Khrouz and Nazarena Lanza (eds), *Migrants au Maroc: Cosmopolitisme, présence d'étrangers et transformations sociales* [en ligne] (Rabat: Centre Jacques-Berque, 2015) 103, 106.

48 Alecmo and others (n43) 9.

49 GADEM (n26) 92.

50 Ibid 129.

51 Arrêté no 498–12 fixant la forme et le contenu de l'imprimé de demande d'obtention des titres de séjour, Arrêté no 499–12 fixant la forme et le contenu du récépissé du dépôt de la demande d'obtention des titres de séjour, Arrêté no 500–12 relatif à l'autorisation exceptionnelle de séjour, Arrêté no 501–12 fixant les documents devant être joints à la demande d'obtention ou de renouvellement des titres de séjour, Arrêté no 502–12 relatif au document de circulation, Arrêté no 503–12 fixant les mentions de la carte d'immatriculation, Arrêté no 504–12 fixant les mentions de la carte de résidence. Arrêté no 505–12 fixant les documents devant être produits pour bénéficier des provisions de l'article 17 de la loi no 02–03 relative à l'entrée et au séjour des étrangers au Royaume du Maroc, à l'émigration et l'immigration irrégulières.

52 Arrêté du ministre de l'intérieur no 505–12.

53 Arrêté du ministre de l'intérieur no 501–12.

acquisition or renewal of a residency permit. These two ministerial orders added two new documents to be presented to the Moroccan authorities: a criminal record and a medical certificate.

Article 42 of Law 02–03 criminalises the irregular entry (or attempt to enter) and stay of migrants in Morocco, and Article 50 criminalises irregular exit from Morocco as well as entry into Moroccan territory outside of a port of entry. There is an overlap of both articles, which criminalise the entry into Moroccan territory outside of a port of entry. Irregular entry and exit include the use of falsified travel documents, the usurpation of identity, the non-presentation of travel documents through fraudulent manners or the entry/exit of the territory at locations other than an official port of entry/exit. What is striking is that Article 50 does not only apply to irregular foreigners but also to Moroccan nationals trying to leave the country irregularly. This is against Article 12(2) of the International Covenant on Civil and Political Rights (ICCPR) and Article 8 of the ICRMW, which state that everyone (or Migrant workers and members of their families) shall be free to leave any country, including their own. According to a Moroccan representative in France, one of the reasons for the criminalisation of the exit of Moroccan nationals could be that Morocco does not want to show that they cannot meet the needs of young people in terms of employment, for example.[54]

After the Arab Spring in 2011, Morocco started to shift its position towards sub-Saharan migrants, guaranteeing them new rights in the Preamble of the new Constitution of 2011. In the Preamble, Morocco commits itself to combat all types of discrimination, including discrimination based on colour, beliefs or regional origin. In the Constitution's Preamble, Morocco also underlines the pre-eminence of international conventions over national laws. This means that national laws cannot breach the ICCPR or the ICRMW, for example. In 2011, Morocco also created the National Council for Human Rights (*Conseil National des Droits de l'Homme* (CNDH)),[55] which replaced the National Human Rights Council (*Conseil Consultatif des Droits de l'Homme*). The CNDH aims at promoting and protecting human rights in Morocco. It has only a consultative power, and its recommendations have no binding effects for the Moroccan government.

The new Constitution[56] of Morocco of 2011, in theory, repealed the provisions of Law 02–03 criminalising irregular exit. Article 24 of the Constitution sets out to guarantee to all persons the right to leave the territory, re-enter and settle according to the law. The provisions of Law 02–03 have not yet been modified, however, and in practice criminalisation of irregular exit and re-entry of the territory is still valid. This concretely means that if a Moroccan citizen who leaves Morocco irregularly is sent back to Morocco, he can be sentenced to a fee or prison for irregular emigration. Moreover, Article 39 of Law 02–03 limits the

54 Interview 62 ATMF, Strasbourg, 2 June 2017.

55 Dahir no 1–11–19 du 1 mars 2011 en matière de protection et de promotion des droits de l'homme, publié au Bulletin Officiel no 5922 du 3 mars 2011.

56 Constitution du Maroc, 11 Juillet 2011, Bulletin officiel du Royaume du Maroc, Édition de traduction officielle, le 17 juin 2011, no 5952 bis, p. 1765 a 1794.

rights of migrants to leave Morocco. Migrants in irregular situations will need an authorisation of exit to leave Morocco; in some cases, an authorisation has to be given by the Moroccan authorities. If the migrant who wants to leave Morocco is in an irregular situation, he will have to pay a fee to the authorities. If the migrant in an irregular situation has not asked for this authorisation, he can be deported to the border with Algeria or be expulsed, fined or even jailed for irregular stay (Articles 43 and 44). If a migrant does not have a valid passport, he will have to ask for a laissez-passer at the consulate of his country of origin. In this case, it is the consulate that asks Moroccan authorities directly for the authorisation of exit. The Report of the UN Special Rapporteur on Torture, Juan Mendes, following his visit to Morocco in September 2012, recounts the increase of violence against migrants at Morocco's Northern border.[57] The report was particularly virulent against Moroccan practices towards migrants, describing practices of torture, sexual aggression, humiliation, and constant abuse conducted by Moroccan authorities. Doctors Without Borders (*Médecins Sans Frontières* (MSF)) underlined flagrant breaches by Morocco of its obligations relating to international conventions and its human rights abuses.[58] The report also highlighted disrespect for the principle of *non-refoulement* and practices of collective deportation. Law 02–03 has been strongly criticised, as it fails to grant sufficient protection for immigrants and refugees, criminalises emigration and is unjustly applied in practice.[59] Several officials and scholars called for the creation of a new legal framework for entry, stay and exit in Morocco, considering the increasing irregular migration flows from sub-Saharan Africa.[60]

Law 02–03 does not foresee collective expulsion, and Article 22(1) of the ICRMW forbids collective deportation for migrant workers and their families. Additionally, Article 12(5) of the African Charter on Human and Peoples' Rights states that 'mass expulsion' of third country nationals is forbidden. This means that all cases must be decided on an individual basis. However, the GADEM and other NGOs in Morocco reported various cases of collective deportation of migrants.[61] After the adoption of the Constitution, the situation towards sub-Saharan migrants even worsened. MSF published a report observing an increase in violence towards sub-Saharan migrants conducted by Moroccan and Spanish security forces in 2012, and expulsions to the border of refugees, children, pregnant woman and injured or sick people,[62] even though, according

57 Nations Unies, 'Rapport du Rapporteur spécial sur la torture et autres peines ou traitements cruels, inhumains ou dégradants sur sa mission au Maroc', 15–22 septembre 2012, A/HRC/22/53/Add.2, para. 24 1, 8.
58 Médecins Sans Frontières, 'Violences, vulnérabilité et migration: bloqués aux portes de l'Europe', 13 March 2013, available at: http://www.msf.fr/actualite/publications/violences-vulnerabilite-et-migration-bloques-aux-portes-europe (accessed 6 February 2016) 1, 16–21.
59 For example: GADEM (n26).
60 Conseil Consultatif des Droits de l'Homme, 'La Protection Des Refugies Au Maroc', Table ronde 14 février 2008, Rabat-Maroc, Série «Séminaires» 1, 14; Belguendouz (n26) 14.
61 GADEM (n26).
62 Médecins Sans Frontières (n58) 16–21.

to Article 29 of Law 02–03, expulsion and *refoulement* to the border are not allowed for most vulnerable people.

3.1.1.2 Asylum

The Cape Verdean Constitution of 1999 recognises the right to asylum in Article 38.[63] It outlines that foreign nationals or stateless persons persecuted for political reasons, or who are seriously threatened with persecution because of their activity in favour of national liberation, democracy or respect for human rights, have the right to asylum in Cape Verde. The Constitution foresees that the law defines the status of political refugee, which is done in Law 99/V/99.

Law 99/V/99, of 19 April,[64] foresees the legal status of refugees and asylum seekers in Cape Verde. However, the Cape Verdean asylum system is not operative because this law has not been regulated.[65] The only exception being Article 10 on the residency permit for humanitarian reasons. This permit is valid for a maximum period of six months and renewable only after analysing the evolution of the situation in the country of origin. It should be noted that Cape Verde is not part of the Geneva Convention. However, since the 1967 New York Protocol binds Cape Verde, it must, nevertheless, apply Articles 2 to 34 of the Convention. Law 99/V/99 defines a refugee as:

> [e]very person who, owing to well-founded fear of being persecuted for reasons of race, religion, nationality, membership of a particular social group or political opinion, is outside the country of his nationality and is unable or, owing to such fear, is unwilling to avail himself of the protection of that country, or who, not having a nationality and being outside the country of his former habitual residence as a result of such events, is unable or, owing to such fear, is unwilling to return to it. Or any person who, by virtue of an aggression, an external occupation, civil war, foreign domination or events which seriously disturb public order, in some or all of his country of origin or country of nationality, is obliged to leave their habitual residence to seek refuge in another country.

The Cape Verdean Asylum Law clarifies who has the right to apply for asylum but does not establish clear procedures for the application process itself. From the point of view of rights, the Asylum Law merely establishes that 'a refugee enjoys the rights and is subject to the duties of foreigners residing in Cape Verde' and recognises their 'right to have a title attesting their quality' (Article 8).

63 Lei Constitucional 1/V/99.

64 Lei 99/V/99, de 19 de Abril, Lei do Asilo, B.O.C.V., I Série, n. 12, 19 de Abril de 1999.

65 José Pina-Delgado, 'La regulación internacional de los flujos migratorios entre Cabo Verde y la Unión Europea (en especial hacia España)' (2011) 28 *Revista de derecho migratorio y extranjeria* 121, 135; Constança Urbano de Sousa and José Pina-Delgado, 'Estudo sobre o quadro legislativo da politica de Migração e Asilo na Republica de Cabo Verde' (2013) MIEUX/ICMPD 1, 29.

The problem lies in the fact that there are no clear procedures for applying for asylum in Cape Verde.[66] The reception of asylum seekers is provided for in Article 15 of the Law on Asylum and Law 106/V/99,[67] of August 2, establishing the legal regime for the reception of foreigners or stateless persons, for humanitarian or security reasons, in temporary accommodation centres. The total lack of implementation of this law is associated with the non-construction of centres foreseen by it.[68] Moreover, José Piña Delgado argues that the Cape Verdean asylum and maritime safety system is not properly implemented. He further argues that the country does not have the material conditions to exercise sovereignty rights in the maritime areas subject to its responsibility, thus hindering its efforts to combat practices that disproportionately put at risk the lives and physical integrity of persons.[69]

In the case of Morocco, it should be noted that, in accordance to the law and following the Convention Relating to the Status of Refugees,[70] Morocco directly grants a residency card to the foreigner who has been granted refugee status as well as his spouse and underage children (Law 02–03 Article 17(5)). There is no limit to the validity of the residency card. However, Article 17(5) is in contradiction with the Geneva Convention, as it conditions the acquisition of a residency card for refugees upon a regular entry in Morocco. The Geneva Convention sets that States 'shall not impose penalties, on account of [the] illegal entry or presence' of refugees (Article 31(1)). Penalty can be understood as any needless restriction to the full enjoyment of rights granted to refugees under the law. An example could be an arbitrary or discriminatory limitation of rights foreseen under international law.

Decree 2–57–1256, of 29 August 1957, sets the modalities of application of the Convention.[71] However, there is no specific legislation on asylum matters in Morocco. According to Article 1 of Decree 2–57–1256, the Office for Refugees and the Stateless [*Bureau des réfugiés et apatrides* (BRA)], under the authority of the Ministry of Foreign Affairs, ensures the judicial and administrative protection of those covered by the Convention. Article 2 adds that the BRA recognises the quality of refugee to those responding to the definitions of Article 1 of the Convention. However, in practice, the Decree remains empty as the BRA has not been operational since 2004 and does not receive any asylum requests. It is only the UNHCR that determines who is granted the status of refugee.[72] The law does not

66 José Pina-Delgado (n65) 135; Constança Urbano de Sousa and José Pina-Delgado (n65) 29.

67 Lei 106/V/99, de 2 de Agosto, Lei do Acolhimento por Razões Humanitárias ou de Segurança, B.O.C.V., I Série, n. 27, 2 de Agosto de 1999.

68 Constança Urbano de Sousa and José Pina-Delgado (n65) 29.

69 José Pina-Delgado (n65) 135.

70 UN General Assembly, Convention Relating to the Status of Refugees, 28 July 1951, United Nations, Treaty Series, vol. 189, 137.

71 Décret No. 2–57–1256 du 2 safar 1377 (29 août 1957) fixant les modalités d'application de la convention relative au statut des réfugiés signée à Genève le 28 juillet 1951, 6 September 1957.

72 Dahir 1–08–90 du 20 octobre 2008 portant promulgation de la loi 37–07 portant approbation, quant au principe, de la ratification du Royaume du Maroc de l'Accord de coopération fait à Genève le 20 juillet 2007 entre le gouvernement du Royaume du

foresee the granting of a residency card for refugees who are solely recognised by the UNHCR. One of the fundamental issues linked to the recognition of the status of refugee by the UNHCR, and not the BRA, is that refugees cannot access rights that are included in the Moroccan legislation.[73]

3.1.1.3 Human trafficking

Article 7 of the Additional Protocol to Prevent, Suppress and Punish Trafficking in Persons, Especially Women and Children, of which Cape Verde is a party, states that '[e]ach State Party shall consider adopting legislative or other appropriate measures that permit victims of trafficking in persons to remain in its territory, temporarily or permanently, in appropriate cases'. Decree 6/97 is silent on this matter, with no obligation or procedure for granting special treatment to victims of trafficking in human beings. Human trafficking was not specifically criminalised by the Cape Verdean Penal Code before the conclusion of the Mobility Partnership.[74]

Human trafficking issues only appeared in Moroccan law in 2007, when the Penal Code was amended. A law related to money laundering[75] introduced Article 574–2 of the Penal Code, which includes human trafficking and immigrants trafficking in its definition of money laundering (given in Article 574–1). Moreover, none of these notions are defined in the law, which makes it difficult, if not impossible, to sanction. In June 2013, the UN Special Rapporteur on trafficking underlined the insufficient recognition of human trafficking and the need for Moroccan authorities to enhance the protection offered to victims of human trafficking.[76] Following this visit, the Minister of the Interior announced that a new law on the trafficking of migrants and asylum seekers was in preparation.[77]

3.1.2 Access to socio-economic rights

Cape Verde and Morocco have ratified most of the international legal instruments for the protection of human rights. It should be noted that neither Cape Verde

Maroc et le Haut-commissariat des Nations-Unies pour les réfugiés, publié en français au Bulletin officiel no 5692 du 18 décembre 2008.

73 Conseil Consultatif des Droits de l'Homme (n60), 11.

74 Código Penal aprovado pelo Decreto Legislativo No 4/2003 de 18 de Novembro de 2003.

75 Dahir no 1–07–09 du 28 rabii I 1428 (17 avril 2007) portant promulgation de la loi no 43–05 relative à la lutte contre le blanchiment de capitaux.

76 United Nations Human Rights Office of the High Commissioner, 'Declaration by Joy Ngozi Ezeilo after her visit in Morocco', Rabat, 21 June 2013, available at: http://newsarchive.ohchr.org/EN/NewsEvents/Pages/DisplayNews.aspx?NewsID=13481&LangID=F (accessed 6 February 2017). A full report followed this visit: Nations Unies, Rapport de la Rapporteuse spéciale sur la traite des êtres humains, en particulier les femmes et les enfants, Joy Ngozi Ezeilo, 1 April 2014, A/HRC/26/37/Add.3.

77 Hassan Bentaleb, 'Un nouveau texte de loi contre les migrations irrégulières', *Liberation* 27 juin 2013, available at: http://www.libe.ma/Un-nouveau-texte-de-loi-contre-les-migrations-irregulieres_a39598.html (accessed 6 February 2016).

nor Morocco have ratified the 1954 and 1961 Conventions on Statelessness. The following table includes the main instruments:

Table 3.1 Main international legal instruments for the protection of human rights ratified by Morocco and Cape Verde

Instrument	*Adoption*	*Ratification*
International Covenant on Civil and Political Rights	Morocco: 1977 Cape Verde: N/A	Morocco: 1979 Cape Verde: 1993
International Covenant on Economic, Social and Cultural Rights	Morocco: 1977 Cape Verde: N/A	Morocco: 1979 Cape Verde: 1993
International Convention on the Elimination of All Forms of Racial Discrimination	Morocco:1967 Cape Verde: N/A	Morocco: 1970 Cape Verde: 1979
Convention on the Elimination of All Forms of Discrimination against Women	Morocco: NA Cape Verde: N/A	Morocco: 1993 Cape Verde: 1980
United Nations Convention against Torture and Other Cruel, Inhuman or Degrading Treatment or Punishment	Morocco: 1986 Cape Verde: N/A	Morocco: 1993 Cape Verde: 1992
Convention on the Rights of the Child	Morocco: 1990 Cape Verde: N/A	Morocco: 1993 Cape Verde: 1992
Convention on the Rights of Persons with Disabilities and the Optional Protocol	Morocco: 2007 Cape Verde: 2007	Morocco: 2009 Cape Verde 2011
International Convention for the Protection of All Persons against Enforced Disappearances	Morocco: 2007 Cape Verde: 2007	Morocco: 2013 Cape Verde: Not ratified
African Charter on Human and Peoples' Rights	Cape Verde: 1986	Cape Verde: 1987

Specifically, in the area of migration, Cape Verde and Morocco have ratified the following Conventions:

Table 3.2 International legal instruments in the area of migration ratified by Morocco and Cape Verde

Instrument	*Adoption*	*Ratification*
International Convention on the Protection of the Rights of All Migrant Workers and Members of Their Families	Morocco: 1991 Cape Verde: NA	Morocco: 1993 Cape Verde: 1997
The United Nations Convention against Transnational Organised Crime and the additional protocols*	Morocco: 2000 (Convention) Cape Verde: 2000 (Convention)	Morocco: 2002 (Convention) Cape Verde: 2004 (Convention)
Convention concerning Freedom of Association and Protection of the Right to Organise	N/A	Cape Verde: 1999
Convention concerning the Application of the Principles of the Right to Organise and to Bargain Collectively	N/A	Morocco: 1957 Cape Verde: 1979

Instrument	*Adoption*	*Ratification*
Convention concerning Forced or Compulsory Labour	N/A	Morocco: 1957 Cape Verde: 1979
Convention concerning the Abolition of Forced Labour	N/A	Morocco: 1966 Cape Verde: 1979
Equal Remuneration Convention	N/A	Morocco: 1979 Cape Verde: 1979
Convention concerning Discrimination in Respect of Employment and Occupation	N/A	Morocco: 1963 Cape Verde: 1979
Convention concerning Minimum Age for Admission to Employment	N/A	Morocco: 2000 Cape Verde: 2011
Convention concerning the Prohibition and Immediate Action for the Elimination of the Worst Forms of Child Labour	N/A	Morocco: 2001 Cape Verde: 2001
Multilateral cooperation agreement against child trafficking in West Africa	N/A	Cape Verde: 2006

* Morocco only accessed to the Protocol to Prevent, Suppress and Punish Trafficking in Persons, Especially Women and Children, supplementing the United Nations Convention against Transnational Organised Crime in 2011. Cape Verde signed this protocol in 2000 and ratified it in 2004. Morocco is not part of the Protocol against the Smuggling of Migrants by Land, Sea and Air, supplementing the United Nations Convention against Transnational Organised Crime, but Cape Verde signed it in 2000 and ratified it in 2004. Both Cape Verde (in 2004) and Morocco (in 2009) only access the Protocol against the Illicit Manufacturing of and Trafficking in Firearms, Their Parts and Components and Ammunition, supplementing the United Nations Convention against Transnational Organised Crime.

The International Covenant on Economic, Social and Cultural Rights (ICESCR)[78] grants rights including labour rights, the right to health, the right to education and the right to an adequate standard of living, which covers the right to decent housing.

Morocco was one of the first countries to ratify the ICRMW, on 21 June 1993. However, the Convention was only published in the *Bulletin Officiel* in February 2012, almost 20 years later.[79]

The ICRMW encourages countries that ratified it to respect the fundamental rights of all migrant workers. It also broadens equal treatment between all legally residing migrant workers and national workers. It guarantees equal chances and treatment in employment matters as well as on social security, union rights and cultural rights for migrant workers and the members of the family living in the country that ratified it. Morocco is in breach of the ICRMW[80] in several aspects.

78 UN General Assembly, International Covenant on Economic, Social and Cultural Rights, 16 December 1966, United Nations, Treaty Series, Vol. 993, 3.

79 Dahir no 1–93–517 du 2 août 2011 portant promulgation de la Convention internationale sur la protection des droits de tous les travailleurs migrants et des membres de leur famille, publié Bulletin Officiel no 6018 du 2 Février 2012.

80 International Convention on the Protection of the Rights of All Migrant Workers and Members of Their Families, Adopted by General Assembly resolution 45/158 of 18 December 1990.

First, the obligation of non-discrimination set out in Article 1 of the Convention is not respected as a clear discrimination towards sub-Saharan Africans is conducted. A report from the GADEM and several other organisations working on migrants' rights issues states that Europeans that are irregularly staying in Morocco are tolerated by Moroccan authorities, whereas sub-Saharan Africans are victims of repeated roundups and police checks based on skin colour.[81] The 'hunt for foreigners'[82] leads sub-Saharan migrants to hide. When they hide, they cannot access public services such as education, health or justice.[83] Migrants' representatives in Morocco argue that it is difficult to find accommodation.[84] In Cape Verde, such practices are not heard of. Even though some cases of discrimination are present, according to migrants' representatives in Cape Verde,[85] the scale is not at all equivalent to the situation in Morocco.

Morocco adopted a new Constitution in 2011, consecrating economic, social and cultural rights for all. Article 161 of the Constitution establishes the National Human Rights Council (CNDH). In collaboration with the government and civil society, the CNDH has been monitoring human rights in Morocco and has played an important role in the development of the new national migration policy. Furthermore, the new Constitution's recognition of the primacy of international conventions over national law led to the reformation of the penal code, including new provisions criminalising human trafficking. However, Article 70 expressly states that the citizenship and status of foreigners, the relations of work and social security and access to healthcare are of the domain of the law only. The new Constitution does not bring direct changes on these issues.

Finally, it should be noted that the recognition of certain categories of human rights is gradual, dependent on economic and financial resources and, therefore, subject to compression stemming from the limited budgetary conditions of countries such as Cape Verde and Morocco. This is the case with the right to education, health, social security or housing. This idea is grounded on Article 2(1) of the ICESCR. Article 2(3) of the same convention allows developing countries to differentiate between citizens and foreigners in their enjoyment of economic, social and cultural rights.

81 GADEM (n26) 9–10.

82 Migreurop, Press release, 'In Morocco, the hunt for foreigners kills, and while this is going on, the EU negotiates and keeps quiet', 2 August 2013, available at: http://www.migreurop.org/article2272.html?lang=fr (accessed 8 March 2017).

83 GADEM (n26) 12.

84 Interview 21, CCSM, Rabat, 15 April 2016; Interview 22, FASED, Rabat, 19 April 2016; Interview 23, CNDH, Rabat, 21 April 2016; Interview 24, Red Chabaka, Tanger, 22 April 2016; Interview, 26, CEI, Rabat, 25 April 2016.

85 Interview 44, Associação dos Filhos e Amigos para o Desenvolvimento Integrado da Região de Bafatá, Praia, 16 November 2016; Interview 47, Associação dos Estudantes e investigados Guineenses, Praia, 17 November 2016; Interview 51, Association des senegalais, Boa Vista, 29 November 2016; Interview 53, Associação Esperança Africana, Praia, 2 December 2016.

3.1.2.1 Employment and social security

Articles 6 and 7 of the ICESCR recognise the rights to work and to freely choose employment as well as the rights to fair and equal remuneration for equal work and safe working conditions. Article 24 of the ICRMW underlines the right to treatment no less favourable than that of nationals in regard to pay and working conditions. Additionally, Article 15 of the African Charter on Human and Peoples' Rights stipulates that '[e]very individual shall have the right to work under equitable and satisfactory conditions, and shall receive equal pay for equal work'.

In Cape Verde, the applicable regime regulating access to the labour market for migrant workers is to be found in the Labour Code of 2007, still in force, which requires that migrant workers submit an authorisation, in the form of a visa, to be allowed to work (Article 283). Article 280 stipulates that only migrants residing regularly in the country may work. However, in practice, this is not applied.[86] The problem with this provision is that it conflicts with Decree 6/97, which requires a labour contract in order to have a residency permit. Moreover, many migrants speak of the difficulty of obtaining and presenting the required documents as per implementation decree 11/99 of 9 August 1999.[87] The consequence is that often contracts are either nonexistent or do not comply with the visa obligation required in the Labour Code. An observation of the working relations of migrant workers shows that illegality and impunity are generalised.[88] Most migrant workers do not have a written contract or a visa from the *Direção-Geral do Trabalho* (DGT), the General Directory for Labour. This situation favours the disrespect of migrant workers' fundamental rights by the employers.[89] An interministerial report adds that there is an apparent lack of knowledge, a lack of means and inattention within the institutions responsible for the management and monitoring of labour relations. Moreover, the application of relevant national laws (Labour Code and Decree-Law 6/97) and international conventions signed and ratified by Cape Verde are accentuating immigrants' vulnerability.[90]

In Cape Verde there is no regime of national preference. The Labor Code prohibits discrimination in access to employment, and the Penal Code contains provisions criminalising this type of discrimination. Article 15–2 grants equal rights to migrant workers vis-à-vis national workers. Only a few government positions are for Cape Verdean nationals only. This is in accordance with Article 24(2) of the Constitution of 1999, which stipulates that foreigners and stateless persons may carry out predominantly technical public functions, under the terms of the law. The national labour law does not define specific provisions on the employment situation for ECOWAS citizens, thus applying the common regime for immigrants. Furthermore, Article 10 of Law 36/V/97 gives any foreigner domiciled in Cape Verde who is a citizen of a Portuguese-speaking country the right to access any private economic or

86 Constança Urbano de Sousa and José Pina-Delgado (n65) 13.
87 EFG Consulting (n11) 53–54.
88 Ibid 53.
89 Ibid.
90 Ibid 66.

professional activity, on the same basis as a national. Article 24(3) of the Constitution of 1999 stipulates that citizens of Portuguese-speaking countries may be granted more rights than foreigners and stateless persons, except for access to bodies that exercise sovereign power, service in the Armed Forces and diplomatic careers. Moreover, access to vocational training is free, subject to age, and accessible to irregular migrants.[91] Cape Verde is complying with the provisions of Article 43 of the Convention on migrant workers, giving them the right to equality of access to employment, vocational guidance and vocational training.

In Morocco, The Labour Code (adopted by Law 65–99)[92] regulates the conditions of foreigner workers (Articles 516 to 519), including access to labour for foreigners requiring a working visa. Article 516 requires that every employer who wants to recruit a foreign employee must receive an authorisation from the Moroccan authorities. It is the system of 'national preference'. However, this obligation does not apply to citizens from Senegal, Algeria and Tunisia, who can directly apply for a registration card with the 'labour' mention if they can prove the existence of a labour contract within three months of their entry in Morocco. An establishment agreement has been concluded with each of these three countries giving their nationals the same rights as Moroccan citizens in terms of employment.[93] Similarly, the spouse and underage children of a French citizen holding a residency card and working visa are exempted from this obligation.[94] The Annex to the Decree of 9 February 2005 by the Ministry of Labour and Vocational Training exempts some other categories of workers.[95] It should be noted that refugees and asylum seekers are not exempt from the obligation, which means the majority of them will not be able to access work through the legal process as they do not possess the necessary documents to launch it.[96] Moreover, migrants (regular or not) have no access to the services provided by the ANAPEC and, therefore, cannot benefit from professional training, for example, which is only provided to Moroccan citizens.

91 Constança Urbano de Sousa and José Pina-Delgado (n65) 35.

92 Dahir no 1–03–194 du 11 septembre 2003 portant promulgation de la loi no 65–99 relative au code du travail, publié au Bulletin officiel no 5210 du 6 mai 2004.

93 Convention d'établissement entre le Royaume du Maroc et la République du Sénégal signée à Dakar le 27 mars 1964 et ratifiée par le décret royal no 108–65 du 17 chaabane 1385 (11 décembre 1965), publiée au Bulletin officiel no 2773 du 22 décembre 1965; Convention d'établissement entre le Maroc et la Tunisie, signée à Tunis le 9 décembre 1964 et ratifiée par le décret royal no 208–66 du 14 safar 1386 (3 juin 1966), publiée au Bulletin officiel no 2808 du 24 août 1966; Convention d'établissement entre le Maroc et l'Algérie, signée le 15 mars 1963 et ratifiée par le dahir no 1–69–114 du 26 moharrem 1389 (14 avril 1969), publiée au Bulletin officiel no 2945 bis du 15 avril 1969.

94 Dahir no 1–95–227 du 2 août 2011 portant publication de l'Accord en matière de séjour et de l'emploi fait à Rabat le 9 octobre 1987 entre le Royaume du Maroc et la République française, publié en français au Bulletin officiel no 6080 du 6 septembre 2012.

95 Arrêté du Département de l'Emploi no 05.350 du 29 Di El Hijja 1425 (09 février 2005) et son annexe no 1395.05 du 22 Chaoual 1426 (25 novembre 2005).

96 Clair Escoffier, *Droits Economiques et Sociaux des Migrants et des Réfugiés dans la Région Euromed: Accès aux Soins de Santé et au Marché du Travail* (Copenhagen: Euro-Mediterranean Human Rights Network 2008) 100, 102.

3.1.2.2 Education

Articles 13 and 15 of the ICESCR state the right to quality education and training that fully respects people's cultural identity. Additionally, Article 30 of the ICRMW guarantees the right to access to education to the children of all migrant workers. Lastly, Article 17 of the African Charter on Human and Peoples' Rights recognises the right to education for all.

Cape Verde has guaranteed the right to education (in the case of children) of foreigners in an irregular situation. The Basic Law of the Educational System[97] guarantees free universal education for up to eight years. Law 6/97 recognises the right to education to foreigners legally residing in Cape Verde in its Article 9. In some cases, children who do not speak Portuguese or those who are handicapped may be unable to access school. However, officials from the National Commission on Human Rights (Comissão Nacional de Direitos Humanos(CNDH)) in Praia perceive the issue to be more a matter of the lack of means and adapted structures rather than a denial of access to rights.[98]

In accordance with Moroccan law, all migrant children, even if their status is irregular, have the right to attend school in a public or private institution. In practice, access to education is not a problem for migrants in a regular situation as they generally have the required supporting documents, such as a birth certificate, proof of residence, the parents' proof of employment and an attestation of schooling or certificate of equivalence if the child already attended school in another country. The same documents are required for Moroccan children. However, migrants in an irregular situation generally do not have the required supporting documents, which makes it difficult to register their children at schools.[99] These marginalised children are supported by NGOs, but Myriam Cherti and Michael Collyer appropriately argue that the Moroccan government has to tackle this issue in order to avoid having a growing group of 'permanently disenfranchised sub-Saharan Moroccans'.[100]

A huge obstacle in accessing school for migrants' children, however, is the fact that proficiency in Arabic is a precondition to registration in public schools. Moreover, Morocco has not put into place any courses in Arabic to help migrant children integrate into the public scholar system.[101] Furthermore, a child whose parents are not Muslim will still have to follow religious classes in public school, as it is part of the national curriculum. In primary school, religious classes represent the highest hourly amount. This is not in conformity with Article 18(4) of the ICCPR, which foresees that the State has to respect the parents' right to choose 'the religious and moral education of their children in conformity with their own convictions'. This is an issue for many families that do not want their children to follow these classes. Their only choice would be to register their children in a private school, but if they do not have the means to pay for it, they may decide not to send their children to

97 Lei 103/III/90 de 29 de Dezembro, Lei de Bases do sistema educativo.
98 Interview 42, CNDH, Praia, 26 February 2016.
99 Myriam Cherti and Michael Collyer (n27) 596.
100 Ibid.
101 GADEM (n26) 103.

school at all. Finally, the GADEM also underlines the lack of protection for migrant children against racism at school.[102]

3.1.2.3 Health

Article 12(1) of the ICESCR states that everyone has the right to the enjoyment of the highest attainable standard of physical and mental health. Additionally, Article 28 of the ICRMW recognises:

> the right to receive any medical care that is urgently required for the preservation of their life or the avoidance of irreparable harm to their health on the basis of equality of treatment with nationals of the State concerned. Such emergency medical care shall not be refused to them by reason of any irregularity with regard to stay or employment.

Article 43 adds that:

> migrant workers shall enjoy equality of treatment with nationals of the State of employment in relation to access to social and health services, provided that the requirements for participation in the respective schemes are met.

Article 45 grants the same right to the members of the family of the migrant worker. Besides, the African Charter on Human and Peoples' Rights recognises that State Parties to the present Charter shall take the necessary measures to protect the health of their people and ensure that they receive medical attention when they are sick (Article 16(2)).

In Cape Verde, Article 70(1) of the Constitution recognises universal access to health. Everyone is entitled access to healthcare regardless of their financial situation or status, even if they are in an irregular situation. In theory, healthcare is guaranteed.[103] In practice, access to healthcare is difficult, but mostly because the system is underdeveloped and lacks funding. According to Cape Verdean migrants' representatives in Portugal, Cape Verde lacks the financial means to have a more efficient health system, it lacks infrastructures and access to health is more or less difficult depending on the specific island. Inhabitants of isolated islands, such as Brava and Santo Antão, have extremely scarce access to health infrastructures or even drugs.[104] A migrant representative from Guinea Bissau also argues that there is discrimination in the access to health, not on the basis of origins, but on the basis of wealth.[105] This practice is in contradiction with Article 70(1) of the Cape Verdean Constitution.

102 Ibid 90; Alecmo and others (n43).

103 Comissão Nacional para os Direitos Humanos e a Cidadania e o PNUD, I Relatório Nacional De Direitos Humanos (Praia 2010) 62.

104 Interview 51 (n86); Interview 66, Associação Girassol Solidario, Lisbon, 4 November 2017; Interview 68 Associação dos Antigos Alunos do Ensino Secundario de Cabo Verde, Lisbon, 4 November 2017.

105 Interview 43 Associação dos Guineenses Residentes em Cabo Verde, Praia, 14 November 2011.

Social health protection in Morocco is based on a system of basic healthcare coverage leaning on two pillars: 1) a compulsory, basic health coverage for students, workers and retired people, and 2) a medical-assistance scheme, the *Régime d'assistance médicale* (RAMED), for the poorest. Law 65–00 of the code of basic healthcare coverage defines beneficiaries in general terms and does not make any distinction of citizenship or administrative situation.[106] The law includes all workers, Moroccans or migrants. Law 02–03 does also not exclude migrant workers from basic healthcare. This means that migrant workers in a regular or irregular situation should all benefit from basic healthcare, either under the compulsory basic health coverage or under the RAMED depending on their situation. But in practice migrants are excluded from the RAMED. According to the report of the GADEM, a representative of the National Health Insurance Agency confirmed that the RAMED only concerns Moroccan citizens.[107] In practice, access to healthcare for migrant workers and the poorest migrants became more difficult since the generalisation of the RAMED in 2012. It was possible for migrants to access hospitals by showing a *certificat d'indigence* (certificate of indigence) and a declaration of need before the generalisation of the RAMED, but now it is requested that all patients present a beneficiary card, which excludes *de facto* irregular migrants from accessing hospitals. Hicham El Moussaoui is critical of the RAMED in general and sees it as a quick response to the Arab Spring without real political or financial support, which explains the dysfunction of the system as a whole.[108]

3.1.2.4 Housing

Article 11 of the ICESCR recognises the right of everyone to an adequate standard of living for themselves and their family, including adequate food, clothing and housing, and to the continuous improvement of living conditions. Article 43 of the ICRMW recognises the right to equal access to housing.

Article 72 of the Constitution of Cape Verde recognises the right to housing. However, it should be noted that in Cape Verde a housing policy that fully meets the needs of the population is not yet a reality.[109] The case of the '*Barracas*' (slums) in Boa Vista is an extreme example of the lack of access to decent housing. Irregular migrants started to gather in illegal housing on the outskirts

106 Loi no 65–00 portant code de la couverture médicale de base, publiée au Bulletin officiel no 5058 du 21 novembre 2002. This law has been completed by Dahir no 1–14–141 du 25 chaoual 1435 (22 août 2014) portant promulgation de la loi no 120–13 modifiant et complétant la loi no 65–00 portant Code de la couverture médicale de base, publié au Bulletin Officiel no 6292 du 18 Septembre 2014

107 GADEM (n26) 76.

108 Hicham El Moussaoui, 'Maroc – Carte RAMED: couverture médicale gratuite ou chèque en bois?' *Libre Afrique*, 8 February 2016, available at: http://www.libreafrique.org/ElMoussaoui-RAMED-maroc-080216 (accessed 22 March 2017).

109 UN Habitat, Conferência das Nações Unidas sobre a Habitação e o Desenvolvimento Urbano Habitat III Relatório de Cabo Verde 1, 37.

of the main city of the island, Sal-Rei.[110] According to some migrants' representatives, the '*Barracas*' were built because locals did not want to rent their properties to immigrants from other African countries.[111] With the increase of tourism on the island, more and more immigrants came to work and went to live in the '*Barracas*'. An official of the Town Hall of Boa Vista and migrants' representatives living in the '*Barracas*' revealed that the '*Barracas*' were not connected to the electricity, water or sewage services provided by the city. Even though poor Cape Verdeans also live there, the situation has remained in a state of limbo for over a decade.[112]

In Morocco, Article 52 of Law 02–03 establishes a '*délit de solidarité*' (a 'crime of solidarity'), which punishes anyone who helps an irregular migrant to enter or leave the territory. Some landlords use it as an excuse in order not to deliver a proof of residency to sub-Saharan migrants.[113] Without a residency document, it is difficult for the migrant in an irregular situation to access to basic rights. In some cases, landlords openly do not rent apartments to sub-Saharan migrants.[114] For example, in Casablanca in 2013, landlords put out posters forbidding renting apartments to 'Africans' in several buildings known to be the residences of many sub-Saharan students.[115] The right to housing does not exist in Moroccan law.[116] Morocco is a country where family members usually take care of those in need, which is called 'family solidarity'. Until recently, homelessness was a marginal phenomenon.

3.2 Legal framework for migrants' rights in Morocco and Cape Verde after the conclusion of the Mobility Partnership

This section will discuss the legal changes that occurred in the respective legal systems after the conclusion of the Mobility Partnership with Cape Verde in 2008 and Morocco in 2013. The first section introduces major policy changes in both countries related to the legal developments.

110 Interview 49, Câmara Municipal, Boa Vista, 25 November 2016; Interview 50, Plataforma das Communidades Africanas Residentes em Cabo Verde, Boa Vista, 29 November 2016; Interview 51 (n86).

111 Interviews 50 (n111) and 51 (n86).

112 Interviews 49 (n111) 50 (n111) 51 (n86).

113 GADEM (n26) 14.

114 Ibid 13.

115 'A Casablanca, des propriétaires tentent d'interdire la location aux Africains', France24, 18 July 2013, available at: http://observers.france24.com/fr/20130718-casablanca-proprietaires-interdire-location-africains-discrimination-raciale (accessed 10 March 2017).

116 CNDH, 'Secteur De L'habitat Et Le Droit Au Logement', available at: http://www.cndh.org.ma/fr/bulletin-d-information/secteur-de-lhabitat-et-le-droit-au-logement (accessed 12 September 2017); CCDH – PNUD, 'Le droit au développement au Maroc. Entre Pacte International relatif aux Droits Economiques, Sociaux et Culturels et Objectifs du Millénaire pour le Développement', juillet 2010, 1, 6.

3.2.1 Overview of the national strategies on immigration and emigration

On 28 June 2013, different Moroccan associations (ALECMA, GADEM, FMAS and AMDH) launched a campaign to raise public awareness of the resurgence of violence against migrants at Morocco's Northern border, which led to several deaths.[117] In July 2013, the CNDH, the Interministerial Delegation for Human Rights (*Délégation Interministérielle aux Droits de l'Homme* – DIDH) and IOM in Rabat published a critical paper on the state of migrants' rights in Morocco.[118] On 30 July, a migrant died at the hospital in Nador after being pushed out of a moving bus by a policeman during a collective expulsion operation.[119] During this period, there was a strong international mobilisation on the issue of the mistreatment of Sub-Saharan migrants in Morocco, which was relayed by several reports from civil society and international organisations as well as through documentaries.[120] Morocco was accused of severe breaches of human rights and migrant mistreatment. In response, the CNDH published a report putting forth measures to improve the situation of refugees and asylum seekers, the treatment of irregular migrants and the fight against human trafficking.[121] The conclusions of this report were presented to the King Mohammed VI, on 9 September 2013, and the next day the King announced a series of 'High Orientations'. On September 17, the government created four sub-commissions: 1) on the regularisation of irregular migrants; 2) on asylum; 3) on the development of the legal framework in relation to immigration, asylum and human trafficking; and 4) on regional and international cooperation on migration issues. In October, the Ministry for Moroccan Residents Abroad and Migration Affairs (*Ministère chargé des MRE et des affaires de la Migration* (MCMREAM))[122] was created as the first national institution addressing immigration issues. The MCMREAM is officially in charge of the coordination, planification, implementation and evaluation of the new immigration policy. On 6 November, the King called for a new global policy on immigration and asylum and recognised Morocco, for the first time,

117 GADEM (n26) 22.

118 Délégation interministérielle aux droits de l'Homme, Conseil national des droits de l'Homme, Bureau de l'Organisation Internationale pour les Migrations, argumentaire du séminaire régional 'Gouvernance des migrations et droits de l'Homme', Rabat, 15 juillet 2013.

119 GADEM (n26) 22.

120 For example: Sara Creta, 'Number 9 – Stop violence at the borders!', available at: https://www.youtube.com/watch?v=w67k5MkUEWQ (accessed 6 February 2016). Movie realised from images recorded on 16 March 2013 by Sara Creta, who was accompanying the association ALECMA in one of its missions, with the support of the GADEM, following an 11 March 2013 massive attempt to cross the border between Morocco and Spain.

121 CNDH, 'Foreigners and Human Rights in Morocco for a Radically New Asylum and Migration Policy' (2013) Rabat 1, 8–11.

122 The MCMREAM is the new name of the pre-existing Ministry for Moroccan Residents Abroad following the addition of the new migration component to the Ministry in 2013.

as a country of immigration and declared that there was a need to review the migration and asylum policy.[123]

The first step following the King's announcement of a series of 'High Orientations' in September was the reopening of the Office of Refugees and Stateless Persons (*Bureau des Réfugiés et des Apatrides* (BRA)) on 25 September 2013. Direct results of this new policy included the regularisation of asylum seekers in November 2013, the launch of the regularisation campaign held from January to December 2014 and a second regularisation campaign held December 2016 to December 2017. It is in the framework of the new policy that the National Strategy for Immigration and Asylum (NSIA) was launched in December 2014. This strategy is to be supported by three new laws on migration, human trafficking and asylum. Law 27–14 on human trafficking has already been adopted. Bill 26–14 on asylum is ready, but since December 2015 its discussion in Parliament has been postponed.[124] With regard to the revision of the Immigration Act, a draft bill has been finalised that takes into account all the comments and proposals of the ministerial departments concerned. The Bill 95–14 'On Migration' was transmitted to the General Secretariat of the Government on 4 July 2016, but it has not been adopted yet.[125] The NSIA has been divided into 27 specific objectives and 81 actions, which have been defined in eleven programmes.[126] A significant component of the NSIA is the integration of newly regularised migrants and refugees. The component includes measures concerning access to the labour market, the basic health system and education, and it is directly linked to the legal developments discussed in the following sections. It is the first time that a country in the region has launched such an immigration and asylum policy and strategy.

In Cape Verde, before the launch of the National Immigration Policy (NIP) in 2012,[127] there were nearly no policies related to migrants' integration, and the few initiatives launched by different institutions involved lacked consistency.[128] The National Immigration Strategy (NIS) was tasked with translating the objectives and principles of the NIP. The approval of the NIP and the NIS were considerable steps forward from the previous absence of a policy on the matter and provided political

123 'Discours de SM Le Roi À L'occasion Du 38ème Anniversaire de La Marche Verte', Maroc.ma, available at: http://www.maroc.ma/fr/discours-royaux/discours-de-sm-le-roi-loccasion-du-38eme-anniversaire-de-la-marche-verte (accessed 25 July 2016).

124 A new bill on the right of asylum and the conditions for its granting, Bill 66–17, has been ready since 2017 to start the process of legislative adoption according to MCMREAM, Politique Nationale d'Immigration et d'Asile, Rapport 2018. It was not possible to access this document.

125 A new bill on migration, Bill 72–17, was introduced in 2017 according to ibid. It was not possible to access this document.

126 MCMREAM, Stratégie Nationale d'Immigration et d'Asile, 2014, available at: http://www.marocainsdumonde.gov.ma/fr/le-minist%C3%A8re/affaires-de-la-migration/strat%C3%A9gie-nationale-dimmigration-et-dasile (accessed 13 August 2016).

127 UCI, 'Plano de Acção 2013–2016 da Estratégia Nacional de Imigração' (2013).

128 UCI/OFII, 'Estudio Diagnostico: Identificação das necessidades dos imigrantes no processo de integração social em Cabo Verde' (2014) 29.

guidance on the various aspects of immigration. Both the Government's 2011–2016 programme[129] and the Poverty Strategy and Growth and Poverty Reduction Paper for the period 2012–2016[130] explicitly mention the immigration dimension as an axis of government action.

The main strands of the strategy are data and research; dialogue, solidarity and partnership; investment and economic activity; and migrants' integration and coherent national policies on migration[131] that impact several areas of migration law and shape Cape Verdean policy towards immigration and emigration. The first strategic axis of the NIS provides for the legal development of matters such as the asylum of foreign citizens, trafficking in persons and illicit trafficking of immigrants.[132] The primary areas impacted by the implementation of the NIS focus on increasing immigration control and improving the protection of migrants' rights, including migrant workers and victims of trafficking.[133] The NIS explicitly mentions that it is expected to reinforce and sustain cooperation between agencies and regional cooperation with the aim to better fight irregular immigration.[134] In addition to the NIS, and through Decree-Law 19/2011 of 28 February 2011, the Immigration Coordination Unit (*Unidade de Coordenação da Imigração* (UCI)) was created as a coordination and integration tool for immigration policies and other policies associated with the entry, stay and exit of foreigners from the national territory. In October 2014, by Decree-Law 57/2014 of 24 October 2014, the Directorate-General of Immigration (DGI) was created to replace the UCI. The DGI is a central mechanism for coordinating, integrating, monitoring, regulating and evaluating immigration policies. The NIP and NIS were the starting point for practical intervention in the management of immigration, and the actions to be taken were included in an action plan for 2013–2016.[135]

It is important to understand the causality between the Mobility Partnerships and the national immigration strategies as well as the sequential order of developments. In the case of Morocco, the Mobility Partnership was concluded first. Shortly after, the King launched a series of new policies on immigration and asylum, which were later materialised under the NSIA. Even though, according to an official of the EU Delegation in Morocco, the EU had been pushing in this direction for several years,[136] it was globally accepted by all the interviewees that the Mobility Partnership did not influence the new policy orientations. The launch of the NSIA seemingly implies a complete reversal of the position of Morocco

129 República de Cabo Verde, Governo de Cabo Verde, Programa do Governo para A VIII Legislatura 2011–2016 (2011).
130 Governo de Cabo Verde, Estratégia de Crescimento e de Redução da Pobreza III 2012–2016 (2012).
131 UCI/OFII (n129) 30.
132 DGI, Balanço e Avaliação da Implementação do Plano de Acção da ENI de 2013 a 2015 (2016) 1, 45.
133 ICMPD and IOM, 'A Survey on Migration Policies in West Africa' (2015) 1, 119–120.
134 UCI (n128) 29.
135 Ibid.
136 Interview 6 EU Delegation, Rabat, 13 January 2016.

during the negotiations of the Mobility Partnership. The understanding that the EU takes a reactive position, by supporting its implementation *a posteriori*, rather than a proactive role, is shared both by the EU and Moroccan officials and academics.[137]

In the case of Cape Verde, the situation is different, and the EU clearly took a more *proactive* approach. The development of the NIS is the fruit of distinct phases in which the EU had been involved since the conclusion of the Mobility Partnership. A representative of the Direção Geral das Comunidades argued that at the time of the conclusion of the Mobility Partnership, Cape Verdean migration policy was nonexistent.[138] From March to April 2009, the Netherlands conducted a 'needs assessment in order to chart Cape Verde's problems and needs in relation to asylum and migration'.[139] This corresponds to the first diagnostic report leading to the NIP. Then, in 2010, another report was presented containing proposals for the NIP. The ICMPD implemented a project under the MIEUX facility aimed at 'developing the Cape Verdean national comprehensive migration policies with a view to reducing irregular migration and maximizing migration benefits'.[140] With this project, the NIS and Action Plan were developed. Finally, in 2014, a joint study conducted by Portugal, France, Luxembourg and the Netherlands was completed to identify immigrants' needs for integration.[141] The approval of the NIP and NIS was a turning point in the management of immigration in Cape Verde. In fact, these two instruments created political, strategic and action targets for the numerous services and actors involved.[142]

3.2.2 *Entry, exit and re-entry rights*

This section will be divided into three parts: immigration and emigration, asylum and human trafficking.

3.2.2.1 *Immigration and Emigration*

In Cape Verde, on 6 November 2014, a new law, Law 66/VIII/2014,[143] on entry, stay, exit and expulsion of foreigners and their legal status was adopted,

137 Interview 5, AMERM, University Mohammed V, Rabat, 12 January 2016; Interview 6 (n137); Interview 7, EU Delegation, Rabat, 13 January 2016; Interview 13 Moroccan Ministry of Labour, Rabat, 19 January 2016; Interview 16, MCMREAM, Rabat, 21 January 2016; Interview 17, Spanish Embassy, Rabat, 22 January 2016.

138 Interview 33 Direção Geral das Communidades, Praia, 23 February 2016.

139 This example, as well as the following one used in this section, are taken from the scoreboard of Cape Verde and Morocco from July 2017.

140 Source: https://www.mieux-initiative.eu/en/actions/155-cabo-verde-policy-development (accessed 8 March 2020).

141 UCI (n128).

142 Ibid 10.

143 Lei no 66/VIII/2014 de 17 de Julho (Define o regime jurídico de entrada, permanência, saída e expulsão de estrangeiros do território caboverdiano, bem como a sua

replacing Law 6/97.[144] Decree-law 2/2015 clarifies the rules of the Law's implementation.[145] A MIEUX project was implemented in 2012–2013 aimed at reviewing and developing the national migration legal framework. This MIEUX project is part of the Mobility Partnership with Cape Verde. In the project, experts (one Portuguese and one Cape Verdean) reviewed the current legislative framework and assessed its consistency with the NIS and other instruments. In the second part of the report, the two experts gave an overview of European legal standards and experience on legal and irregular migration, asylum and human trafficking. They provided support, coordinated the legislative proposal drafting process, and prepared and reviewed a final proposal for the main legislation to replace Law 6/97 as well as all related legislative documents. In other words, the project lead to the development of Law 66/VIII/2014 on entry, stay and expulsion of foreigners, considering the best practices of relevant legislation in the EU.

Law 66/VIII/2014 is applied to everyone who enters and wants to stay in Cape Verde (Articles 3 and 4). It does not cover refugees (who are covered by the asylum law) or diplomats and their families. During the preparation of the New Legislative Framework for Immigration and Asylum, organised in partnership with the European Union (through the MIEUX project cited above), Marisa Morais, the Cape Verdean Minister of Internal Affairs (*Ministra da Administração Interna*) stressed that it was not a simple revision of the legislation, it was the drafting and approval of a 'totally new' legal framework. It covers not only the issue of entry and exit, but also issues of permanence, the legal status of immigrants, and administrative and judicial expulsion. It can be noted that the current legal regime is similar to that of Portugal. Law 66/VIII/2014 is influenced by Portuguese Law 23/2007.[146] Moreover, the Council of Ministers in Cape Verde approved, in May 2017, the decree amending the law, which will initiate the process of exemption of visas for the citizens of the European Union.[147] The visa waiver for European citizens entered into force on 1 January 2019. This measure was taken in

situação jurídica) BO IS no 43 de 17 de Julho de 2014; Law 80/VIII/2015 aterates Articles 29, 47, 52, 89, 97 and 103 of Law 66/VIII/2014 of 17 of July, which defines the legal status of entry, stay, exit and expulsion of foreigners from the Cape Verdean territory, according to their legal status BO IS no 2 de 7 de Janeiro de 2015.

144 Decreto-Legislativo no 6/97 de 5 de Maio (regula a situação jurídica do estrangeiro no território nacional, estabelecendo os direitos, garantias e deveres, o regime de entrada, permanência e saída, a expulsão e a extradição, bem como as taxas, as infracções e sanções) B.O.C.V., I Série, n. 17.

145 Decreto-Lei no 2/2015 (Regulamenta o regime jurídico de entrada, permanência, saída e expulsão de estrangeiros do território caboverdiano, aprovado pela Lei nº 66/VIII/2014 de 17 de Julho) BO IS no 1 de 6 de Janeiro 2015.

146 Lei 23/2007 sobre o regime juridico de entrada, permanência, saide e asfastamento de estrangeiros do territorio nacional, Diário da República, 1.a série, no 127, 4 de Julho de 2007.

147 'Isenção de vistos aos cidadãos da União Europeia e Reino Unido vai ser discutida na sessão parlamentar de Junho 18 May 2017', *Inforpress*, available at: http://www.inforpress.publ.cv/isencao-de-vistos-aos-cidadaos-da-uniao-europeia-e-reino-unido-vai-ser-discutida-na-sessao-parlamentar-de-junho/ (accessed 6 December 2017).

order to increase tourism to Cape Verde.[148] In relation to foreigners entering Cape Verde, there is no existing computerised, common database of visas, either from the diplomatic representatives abroad or national authorities in Cape Verde. The fact that the procedure for issuing and managing residency permits is not yet computerised means that it is not yet possible to know precisely how many foreigners are residing regularly in Cape Verde and for what purpose.[149]

The entry into force of Law 66/VIII/2014 substantially improved the legal framework regarding the entry, stay, exit and expulsion of foreigners from Cape Verdean territory. Indeed, there are positive changes vis-à-vis the previous legislative framework. The first is the introduction of administrative deadlines for the issuance of visas and authorisation of residency permits. But all ambiguity has not been eliminated.[150] There are still complaints from the immigrant population about the slowness of the proceedings, as well as the irregular and relatively opaque ways the procedures are applied.[151] Only one Senegalese migrant representative thought that the new law made the process easier.[152] The procedure to renew residency documents requires more documents, and the price of the procedure is higher, leading to many people not renewing their papers.[153] A migrant representative from Sierra Leone underlines an interesting fact. Since the renewal of the residency permit is more difficult, more foreigners are asking for Cape Verdean citizenship because it 'makes their stay easier'.[154] Increasing the difficulty of renewing residency permits, arguably with the idea of deterring immigrants from staying in Cape Verde, seems to have the unintended consequence of immigrants asking for citizenship instead. This does not mean that asking for citizenship is an effortless process, but it can be seen as a better solution than annually having to repeat the burdensome process of renewing the residency document.

According to migrants' representatives in Cape Verde, foreigners' major barriers to obtaining a residency permit are related to obtaining criminal records in the country of origin, the absence of a work contract because employers generally do not sign contracts, or the absence of a rent contract either because they sometimes live in illegal housing or in situations in where their landlords do not intend to declare rental income.[155] A representative of the *Câmara Municipal* (Town Hall)

148 'Cabo Verde: Isenção de vistos para a UE', *Observador*, 05 May 2017, available at: http://observador.pt/2017/05/05/cabo-verde-isencao-de-vistos-para-a-ue/ (accessed 7 December 2017).

149 IOM (n10) 11.

150 DGI (n153) 67.

151 Interviews 43 (n106) and 44 (n86); Interview 46, Associação dos Serraleoneses Residentes em Cabo Verde, Praia, 17 November 2016; Interview 48, Associação de Guineenses, Boa Vista, 24 November 2016; Interviews 49 (n111), 51 (n86) and 53 (n86); Interview 54, Association des senegalais, Praia, 2 December 2016.

152 Interview 52, Associação dos Emigrantes Senegaleses Residentes em Cabo Verde, Praia, 2 December 2016.

153 Interviews 43 (n106), 44 (n86), 46 (n151), 47 (n86), 48 (n151), Interviews 49 (n111), 50 (n111), 51 (n86) and 54 (n151).

154 Interview 46 (n151).

155 Interviews 44 (n86), 46 (n151) and 47 (n86).

in Boa Vista said that a special document is accepted by the authorities, which is a declaration of housing that migrants living in the '*Barracas*' can use when registering or renewing their documents.[156] As these '*Barracas*' are illegal, it would be impossible to prove that migrants live there. She adds that the processes take longer because they are far from Praia, and communication is difficult between the immigrants in Boa Vista and the authorities in Praia. However, a migrant representative living in the '*Barracas*' pointed out that the special document was no longer recognised by the border authorities, making it impossible for immigrants staying in this area to regularise their situation.[157]

According to migrants' representatives, the main reason for refusal of entry is a lack of sufficient means of subsistence; more rarely entry is refused in cases of the absence of passports or presentation of false documents.[158] Given that most foreigners denied entry to Cape Verde are citizens of an ECOWAS Member State, it can be concluded that the country is not entirely complying with the Protocol of Free Movement of Persons and Goods in ECOWAS. Law 66/VIII/2014 had consequences on the application of the ECOWAS Protocol of Free Movement. Law 66/VIII/2014 requires the presentation of a passport and proof of sufficient financial means, which to some extent interferes with ECOWAS citizens' freedom of movement.[159] As noted previously in this section, the conditions of entry into the Cape Verdean territory were inspired by Portuguese law, which can explain why the provisions are in contradiction with the provisions of the ECOWAS Treaty (which Portugal is not part of). A visa, travel documents and proof of sufficient means of subsistence are required (Article 6 of Law 66/VIII/2014 and Articles 10 and 11 of Law 23/2007). If a citizen of an ECOWAS country cannot prove sufficient financial means, he will be denied entry into Cape Verde even though, according to the Free Movement Protocol, he should be able to enter and stay in Cape Verde for a period of up to 90 days. Moreover, requesting a passport for all entries is contrary to the clause of the Free Movement Protocol that provides an ECOWAS citizen the right to enter Cape Verde with only a national identity card. The different contradictions between Cape Verdean laws and the ECOWAS Protocol of Free Movement have been raised on several occasions. The most recent example being the criticism of the President of the ECOWAS Parliament about entry and stay of Senegalese nationals in Cape Verde.[160]

156 Interview 49 (n111).

157 Interview 51 (n86).

158 Interviews 50 (n111), 51 (n86) and 54 (n151).

159 Article 4 of the Free Movement Protocol: Notwithstanding the provisions of Article 3 above, Member States have the right to refuse entry into their territories to any citizen of the Community entering the category of immigrants ineligible under their laws and regulations.

160 'Governo está a estudar situação dos senegaleses em Cabo Verde', *Expresso das Ilhas*, 13 May 2017, available at: http://www.expressodasilhas.sapo.cv/politica/item/53189-governo-esta-a-estudar-situacao-dos-senegaleses-em-cabo-verde (accessed 7 December 2017).

These criticisms are in line with several stories gathered from immigrants in Cape Verde, which underline the non-respect of the Free Movement protocol and the obligation for ECOWAS citizens to prove their sufficient means of living, a return ticket and a passport (instead of an ECOWAS recognised ID).[161] In some cases, it has been argued by migrants' representatives that the ECOWAS is letting Cape Verde infringe the Free Movement Protocol because it is a small country that cannot economically provide for a large population of immigrants.[162] The Minister of Foreign Affairs, Luís Filipe Tavares answered the criticisms of the President of the ECOWAS Parliament by guaranteeing that Cape Verde is applying the Free Movement Protocol, but also agreeing that the country is facing some problems in its implementation, in particular, with the delivery of residency permits by the Immigration and Borders Services.[163]

Moreover, Cape Verde concluded a joint border control agreement with the European External Borders Agency (FRONTEX)[164] to prevent irregular immigrants from entering by sea in the territory of the European Union.[165] The joint border control agreement with FRONTEX gives Cape Verdean border authorities better means to effectively apply Law 66/VIII/2014 by developing border procedures, training border guards, sharing best practices and introducing technical equipment to support border guards' work.[166] These developments can be related to the implementation of the Mobility Partnership. Indeed, a project aimed at implementing the 'FRONTEX Common Core Curriculum for Border Guard basic training' and another initiative led to the conclusion of a working agreement between FRONTEX and Cape Verde.

Furthermore, Cape Verde is part of the African, Caribbean and Pacific countries (ACP) and party to the Cotonou Agreement, which includes Article 13 stipulating a return and readmission obligation (of nationals only).[167] Moreover, France and Cape Verde concluded a facilitation scheme for regular migration shortly after the conclusion of the Mobility Partnership, which also includes a readmission clause of nationals only (Article 4). A project included in the Annex to the Joint Declaration foresees the conclusion of a 'bilateral agreement on concerted management of migratory flows'. Besides the readmission clause, the agreement with France includes simplified access to 40

161 Interviews 50 (n111), 51 (n86), 52 (n152) and 54 (n151).

162 Interviews 52 (n152) and 54 (n151).

163 *Expresso das Ilhas* (n160).

164 Acordo de Trabalho estabelecendo uma Cooperação Internacional entre a FRONTEX e a Polícia Nacional de Cabo Verde, 2011.

165 Sergio Carrera, 'The EU Border Management Strategy: Frontex and the Challenge of Irregular Migration to the Canary Islands', CEPS Working Document 261 (2007); Ruben Anderson, 'Frontex y la creación de la frontera euroafricana: golpeando la valla ilusoria' (2011) (9)28 *Revista de Derecho Migratorio y Extranjería* 177.

166 Statewatch, 'Frontex: cooperation with non-EU states', Briefing (March 2017) 1, 18.

167 Partnership agreement 2000/483/EC between the members of the African, Caribbean and Pacific Group of States of the one part, and the European Community and its Member States, of the other part, signed in Cotonou on 23 June 2000.

designated professions, police cooperation, the reintegration of migrants returning to Cape Verde and co-development with the diaspora in France.[168] This provision was already foreseen in the Annex to the Joint Declaration.[169] Only around 700 Cape Verdeans each year receive a residency permit, most of them for family reunification.[170] Labour migration is low between Cape Verde and France, with approximately 100 people per year between 2004 and 2008.[171] Nathalie Kotok argues that following the ratification of this agreement, Cape Verde obtained many more residency permits for its nationals than previously.[172] She does not give numbers, however, to illustrate her argument. When looking at the numbers of the French Ministry of Interior for 2014, it seems that Kotlok's claim should be taken with precaution. The number of residency permits for family reasons seems to have increased to 784 in 2014, although only 41 Cape Verdeans received work permits and 19 were admitted to pursue their studies.[173] This agreement does not seem to have led to better access to the French labour market for Cape Verdean citizens. Additionally, Luxembourg concluded an agreement on circular migration with Cape Verde in October 2015.[174] The agreement should simplify mobility and enhance temporary circular labour migration. It also aims at fighting irregular immigration and facilitating the reintegration of migrants into their countries of origin.[175] The Annex to the Joint Declaration already foresaw the introduction of 'an initiative on temporary circular migration with Cape Verde'.

168 Décret no 2011–403 du 14 avril 2011 portant publication de l'accord entre le Gouvernement de la République française et le Gouvernement de la République du Cap-Vert relatif à la gestion concertée des flux migratoires et au développement solidaire (ensemble trois annexes), signé à Paris le 24 novembre 2008.

169 Project 1: 'Proposal by the French Republic to open a certain number of professional activities to Cape Verdean migrants and no longer to maintain objections based on the employment situation in the sectors concerned […]'. Project 2: 'Proposal by the French Republic to develop, within the framework of a bilateral agreement on concerted management of migratory flows, a co-development programme for the benefit of Cape Verde under which Cape Verdean migrants legally established in France […]'.

170 Nathalie Kotlok, 'Le 'développement solidaire'. Une politique migratoire au service du développement des pays africains?' (2010) *Hommes et migrations* 268, 275–276.

171 Ibid.

172 Ibid 276.

173 Ministère de l'Intérieur, 'L'admission au séjour: Les titres de séjour (statistiques)', available at: https://www.immigration.interieur.gouv.fr/Immigration/L-admission-au-sejour-Les-titres-de-sejour-statistiques (accessed 7 December 2017).

174 '7e réunion de dialogue politique entre le Cabo Verde et l'UE au niveau ministériel et signature d'un accord bilatéral entre le Luxembourg et le Cabo Verde en matière de Migration', Press release, *Gouvernement.lu*, 14 October 2015, available at: http://www.gouvernement.lu/5329991/13-dialogue-politique (accessed 9 February 2018).

175 European Migration Network, '2016 Annual Report on Migration and Asylum 25th April 2017 Final Version' 1, 58.

Cape Verde concluded a visa facilitation agreement for short term visas in October 2012[176] and an EU Readmission Agreement in April 2013,[177] and both entered into force simultaneously. Both agreements work in parallel, and no visa facilitation agreement is concluded without the conclusion of an EURA. It is the first time that an African country concluded a visa facilitation agreement. The visa facilitation agreement does not apply to everyone (Article 4). There is a visa exemption for diplomats, and there is visa facilitation for specific categories of people, which allows for longer visas and multiple-entry visas for those who meet the criteria and who have already been in good standing with the visas received previously. For example, simplified conditions for the issue of multiple-entry visas valid for five years are foreseen for members of governments or permanent members of official delegations, or valid for one year for scientists, journalists and students. The acquisition of a visa also became cheaper (Article 5). According to a Portuguese official in Cape Verde, the visa rules set in the agreement are, in fact, the rules of the bilateral agreement with Portugal.[178]

The EURA and visa facilitation agreement are clearly the result of the Mobility Partnership. One of the preconditions to conclude a Mobility Partnership is the commitment of the third country to negotiate an EURA. The negotiations of a readmission agreement took place even though Cape Verde did not possess the logistical capacity to receive returned migrants. According to an IOM official in Cape Verde, the country does not have the facilities, and the government does not seem to have a clear idea on how to create such facilities.[179] She adds that, the fact that Cape Verde is divided into different islands, with different airports, creates complex circumstances and would require high financial means to replicate the same facilities everywhere.[180] Following the conclusion of the Visa Facilitation and Readmission Agreements, the National Committee on the management of the Visa Facilitation Agreement and the National Committee on Readmission have been created.[181] According to a Portuguese and an IOM official in Cape Verde, so far, there has not been any case of readmission registered since the entry into force of the EURA.[182] However, with the conclusion of the EURA, Cape Verde is committing itself to working on strengthening the

176 Resolução 106/VIII/2014 de 23 de Maio, aprova, para ratificacçao, o Acordo de Cooperação entre a União Europeia e a Republica de Cabo Verde sobre a Facilitação da Emissão de Vistos de Curta Duração para cidadãos da Republica de Cabo Verde e da União Europeia, BO SI 35 de 23 de Maio.

177 Resolução 107/VIII/2014, de 23 de Maio, aprova, para ratificação, o Acordo entre a União Europeia e a Republica de Cabo Verde relativo à Readmissão de Pessoas que Residem sem Autorização, BO SI 35 de 23 de Maio.

178 Interview 34, Centro Comum de Vistos/ Portuguese Consulate, Praia, 23 February 2016.

179 Interview 38, IOM, Praia, 24 February 2016.

180 Ibid.

181 Resolução 70/2015, Constitui o Comité Nacional de Gestão de Acordo de Facilitação de Vistos BO SI 47 de 7 de Agosto de 2015; Resolução 71/2015, Constitui o Comité Nacional de Readmissão BO SI 47 de 7 de Agosto de 2015.

182 Interviews 34 (n178) and 38 (n179).

control of irregular immigration towards Europe.[183] Consequently, since the adoption of the EURA in 2012, Cape Verde has tried renegotiating the ECOWAS Protocol and implementing it in a more 'flexible' way.[184]

In addition, to achieve some of its objectives related to the management of migratory flows with the European Union, maintaining the sub-regional scheme of regional integration can be detrimental. Even if there is no obligation to receive foreigners with a right of entry, the fact that Cape Verde could be used as a stopover point due to facilitated circulation into Cape Verde under the ECOWAS Protocol provides a sufficient basis for creating some problems, according to José Pina-Delgado.[185] Indeed, the ECOWAS region is considered the main reserve of immigrants from all of Africa.[186] Even though the Visa Facilitation Agreement does only apply to certain categories of citizen, according to a migrant representative and the official of the *Câmara Municipal* of Boa Vista, it can be used as an easier and safer way to reach Europe by ECOWAS citizens[187] after they succeed in acquiring Cape Verdean nationality. The Cape Verdean authorities are planning to revise the ECOWAS protocols, including entry regulations, arguing that the specific situation of the country (an island State) justifies the possibility of the country deviating to a certain extent from the principle of free movement among the States of ECOWAS.

There are several studies that point to the high number of irregular immigrants residing in Cape Verde. It is believed that the majority enter regularly into the country, but they extend their residence in the archipelago beyond the legal deadlines. The report by the ICMPD pointed to 14,373 immigrants in Cape Verde in 2010.[188] That same year, the Interministerial Commission for the Study and Proposition of the Bases of the Immigration Policy's (*Comissão Interministerial para o Estudo e Proposição das Bases da Política de Imigração* (CIMI)) report estimated that more than half of the foreigners residing in Cape Verde were in an irregular situation, corresponding to approximately 8,373 people.[189] At present, according to the DGI study, the Directorate of Aliens and Borders of the National Police (*Direcção de Estrangeiros e Fronteiras* (DEF)) estimates that the

183 Odair Varela, 'Readmitidos e/ou Repatriados? Uma Re-leitura do Acordo de Readmissão de Cabo Verde com a União Europeia' 61–72 in Iolanda Évora (ed.), *Diaspora Cabo-Verdiana: Temas em Debate* (2016) Centro de Estudos sobre Africa, Asia e America Latina, available at: https://issuu.com/comunicacao_cesa/docs/livro_diaspora-cabo-verde_final (accessed 16 April 2017) 69.

184 Ibid; 'Cabo Verde defende aplicação flexível dos protocolos de livre circulação na CEDEAO', *RadioTelevisão Caboverdiana*, 21 May 2012, available at: http://rtc.cv/index.php?paginas=21&id_cod=4221 (accessed 16 April 2017); Odaïr Santos 'A livre circulação de pessoas e bens na CEDEAO está em debate em Cabo Verde', *RFI Português*, 24 May 2010, available at: http://pt.rfi.fr/africa/20100524-livre-circulacao-de-pessoas-e-bens-na-cedeao-esta-em-debate-em-cabo-verde (accessed 16 April 2017).

185 José Pina-Delgado (n15) 552–553.

186 EFG Consulting (n11) 42.

187 Interviews 49 (n111) and 52 (n152).

188 Constança Urbano de Sousa and José Pina-Delgado (n65) 12.

189 EFG Consulting (n11).

number of these cases is about 6,000.[190] The decline in the number of undocumented migrants can be attributed to three main factors: a) more effective action by the DEF in terms of border management; b) the promulgation in 2014 of the new legal regime for entry, stay, exit and expulsion of foreigners from the Cape Verdean territory; and c) the subsequent extraordinary regularisation process that took place between January and April 2015. According to data provided by DEF, 1,524 applications for regularisation were received, of which 616 were accepted, giving rise to the issuance of the respective residency permits.[191]

In Morocco, Bill 95–14 on migration aimed at revoking Law 02–03 on migration. In September 2013, the CNDH published a report, 'Foreigners and Human Rights in Morocco', paving the way for the preparation of draft laws on immigration, asylum and trafficking in human beings. The CNDH's main recommendations for the Bill 95–14 responded to the criticisms made in a joint report by the GADEM and other major NGOs representing sub-Saharan migrants.[192] The CNDH underlined the need to guarantee migrants (including irregular migrants) effective access to justice, security against exploitative employers, freedom from all forms of violence and easier access to the registration of births and deaths.[193] The new Bill 72–17 on migration (replacing Bill 95–14), was reviewed by the General Secretariat of the Government, and comments were sent to the MCMREAM in June 2018. The process of finalisation was launched on 25 September 2018, and several consultation meetings were scheduled to develop the final version of the bill and begin the process of legislative adoption. No information on the content of the new bill was available at the time of writing.

Regarding the EURA with Morocco, there was only one negotiating session in January 2015. Morocco has refused to sign an EURA since 2006 due to a refusal by the EU to conclude further EURAs with other countries in Africa. Morocco is known for its reluctance to conclude an EURA with the EU.[194] Mobility Partnerships can be seen as tools to provide leverage to the negotiations of EURAs with third countries. They can propose a full set of initiatives, including migration and development and legal migration possibilities, to counterbalance the burden of an EURA including third country nationals. It is the first time that the EU proposed a visa facilitation agreement to a Southern Mediterranean country,[195] going hand in hand with the conclusion of the EURA. However, for several reasons, such as, for example, Morocco's position with sub-Saharan Africa, it is unlikely

190 DGI (n153).

191 Ibid.

192 GADEM (n26).

193 CNDH, Conclusions et recommendations du rapport: 'Etrangers et droits de l'Homme au Maroc: pour une politique d'asile et d'immigration radicalement nouvelle' (2013) 5–6.

194 Sergio Carrera and others, 'EU-Morocco Cooperation on Readmission, Borders and Protection: A Model to Follow?' (2016) CEPS Papers in Liberty and Security in Europe 1, 5–7; Sarah Wolff, 'The Politics of Negotiating EU Readmission Agreements: Insights from Morocco and Turkey' (2014) 16 *EJML* 69.

195 Sarah Wolff (n194) 72.

for Morocco to sign it as is. Having good relations with Africa is a new priority for Morocco,[196] which wants, according to officials from Expertise France and the Council of Europe in Rabat, to be a major interlocutor on African issues and strengthen its economic relations with the African continent.[197] This is in line with Morocco's 'Politique Africaine'.[198] According to a Moroccan scholar and an official of the EU Delegation in Rabat, improving relations with African countries of origin was one of the main reasons for the adoption of the NSIA in the first place.[199]

3.2.2.2 Asylum

Cape Verdean Law 66/VIII/2014 is more specific about the status of refugees than Law 6/97. Article 13(4) specifies who is competent to deliver a travel document to refugees, and Article 15 introduces the single travel document for refugees. However, the absence of comprehensive and consistent asylum and refugee integration policies have not been filled to date.[200] The idea of cooperation for the revision of the asylum system in Cape Verde has been included in the Mobility Partnership, which could be an opportunity to improve the country's response in this field. A project has been proposed to develop an asylum system, but to date this has not been translated into legal developments. As a result of the MIEUX project, discussed above, a new law on asylum was proposed at the same time as Law 66/VIII/2014, but it has not been adopted.[201]

Since UNHCR has no established presence in the country, asylum seekers seeking protection and assistance are referred by the International Organisation for Migration to the UNHCR regional representation for West Africa in Dakar, Senegal, which is responsible for the determination of refugee status. In fact, there are few asylum applications made in Cape Verde (UNHCR reported only two cases in total in 2011 and 2012), but the definite number of asylum seekers is unknown, as there are no efficient procedures to register and process asylum claims.[202] Because Cape Verdean Law forbids expulsion of foreigners towards countries where the foreigner can be persecuted (Article 75(1) Law 66/VIII/2014), the UNHCR is authorised by Cape Verde to evaluate the asylum claims. Additionally, the law on migration provides against the collective expulsion of

196 Ayah Aman, 'Why Morocco Really Wants Back in the African Union', 27 July 2016, available at: http://www.al-monitor.com/pulse/originals/2016/07/morocco-join-african-union-western-sahara-dispute-egypt.html (accessed 13 August 2016).

197 Interview 10, Expertise France, Rabat, 15 January 2016; Interview 12, Council of Europe, Rabat, 19 January 2016.

198 Royal Institute for Strategic Studies, 'La Politique Africaine du Maroc', 26 Octobre 2015.

199 Interviews 5 (n138) and 6 (n82)

200 Comissão Nacional para os Direitos Humanos e a Cidadania e o PNUD (n104) 50.

201 Interview 38 (n179); Interview 40, Institute of Social and Legal Sciences of Cape Verde, Praia, 26 February 2016; Interview 42 (n99).

202 US Department of State, Bureau of Democracy, Human Rights, And Labor, 'Country Reports on Human Rights Practices, Cape Verde Report 2012', 19 April 2013, available at: https://www.state.gov/j/drl/rls/hrrpt/2012/af/204100.htm (accessed 8 December 2017); IOM (n10) 35.

foreign nationals (article 74), in accordance with international law, and complies with the international principle of *non-refoulement*.

Following the discourse of the King Mohamed VI,[203] Morocco reopened the BRA on 25 September 2013. Since then, the BRA has been validating individuals who have been granted refugee status by the Office of the United Nations High Commissioner for Refugees (UNHCR). This has important consequences for asylum seekers, as being recognised by the Moroccan government as refugees gives them access to a residency permit. A residency permit allows refugees to legally work in Morocco as well as allows access to public services and legal housing. The Euro-Mediterranean Human Rights Network adds that several difficulties are stopping refugees from applying for asylum with the UNHCR in Morocco, such as the fact that asylum seekers who are refused entry to Morocco at an airport are not able to apply for asylum.[204] Indeed, the only place an asylum claim can be launched is at the UNHCR office in Rabat.[205] A Mobility Partnership project concerns support for drafting a strategy for the reception and integration of refugees. In the framework of this project, the ICMPD works with the CNDH and the MCMREAM to map of the integration of refugees and create a refugee profile.

Bill 26–14 on asylum was ready to be examined by the Governing Council and begin its legislative adoption process, but since December 2015, its discussion in Parliament has been postponed. The reason for this rescheduling, according to a UNHCR official, is a disagreement between the different ministries on the content of the law.[206] A new bill, Bill 66–17 on the right of asylum and the conditions for its granting, has been ready since 2017. The Ministry in charge of Migration Affairs submitted the draft to the General Secretariat of the Government, which submitted it to the Council in September 2018. The Bill still has not been adopted.

Bill 26–14 included the creation of a national authority for refugees, the 'Moroccan office in charge of refugee affairs' (*bureau marocain chargé des affaires des réfugiés*) (Article 35). This office was meant to be under the authority of the Ministry of Foreign Affairs, and it aimed at replacing the BRA (Article 37). However, in December 2018, the BRA resumed delivering refugee cards after being suspended since March 2017.[207] Bill 66–17 still foresees the creation of the Moroccan office in charge of the refugee affairs.[208]

203 Discours de SM Le Roi À L'occasion Du 38ème Anniversaire de La Marche Verte (n124).
204 Euro-Mediterranean Human Rights Network (n29) 12.
205 UNHCR, Rapport de fin d'année 2016 (2017) 1, 4.
206 Interview 9, UNHCR, Rabat, 15 January 2016.
207 Zaïnab Aboulfaraj and Mehdi Mahmoud, 'Les réfugiés peuvent à nouveau obtenir des titres de séjour au Maroc', *Telquel*, 12 December 2018, available at: https://telquel.ma/2018/12/12/les-refugies-peuvent-a-nouveau-obtenir-des-titres-de-sejour-au-maroc_1621607/?utm_source=tq&utm_medium=normal_post (accessed 13 October 2019).
208 MCMREAM (n125) 1, 93.

3.2.2.3 Human trafficking

A project aimed at supporting Cape Verde in the implementation of the Palermo Convention and its Protocols related to human trafficking. It was translated into the legal framework through the development of new provisions in the revised Penal Code and the new Law 66/VIII/2014. The change brought by Law 66/VIII/2014, in Cape Verde, is the introduction of mechanisms to protect victims of human trafficking with the possibility of granting them residency permits. In June 2015, a new Penal Code was adopted to address this issue.[209] The Government argued for criminalisation, invoking international standards and commitments. The Parliament responded to the arguments and authorised the government to legislate accordingly. Law 94/VIII/2015 Articles 3–2(3) and 3–3(12) gave the government authorisation to include the crime of human trafficking in the new Penal Code. The new immigration law of 2014 also included a specific provision on human trafficking (absent in the previous act). Subsection IV regulates the granting of residency permits for victims of human trafficking. Article 58 recognises a right of residence for trafficking victims, even if they entered the country irregularly and do not fulfil the legal requirements for a residency permit. Additionally, Article 58–6 guarantees victims with insufficient means of subsistence with minimal means as well as access to urgent medical care. Article 97–3 provides that employers who hire victims of human trafficking can face imprisonment. Because of the recent introduction of this crime in the Cape Verdean legal system, official data on trafficking in persons are still residual, which does not allow for sizing or characterising the phenomenon. There are no records prior to December 2015, and, as of this date, information is provided by the Attorney General's Office. It should be noted that there are still no convicted traffickers and no identified child victims of trafficking.[210]

Pursuant to its 2013 National Strategy, Morocco adopted a law specifically dealing with human trafficking.[211] Law 27–14 on human trafficking influenced the modification of the new Penal Code adopted in June 2016. Indeed, it added a new section specifically on human trafficking in the Penal Code, introducing 14 new articles. Before its adoption, the CNDH issued a series of recommendations on the Bill. One of the recommendation was regarding the wording of the definition of human trafficking. The definition proposed by the CNDH has been included in Article 448.1 of the Penal Code. The same Article also defines the notion of exploitation in accordance to the suggestions of the CNDH. Still in accordance with the CNDH report, cases that involve minors are more severely punished (Article 448.10). However, all the recommendations have not been considered. For example, concerning Article 1 of Law 27–14, the CNDH recommended adding a first indent to define specific terms related to human

209 Decreto-legislativo no 4/2015 (Altera o Código Penal, aprovado pelo Decreto-legislativo no 4/2003, de 18 de novembro) BO I Série no 69 11 de Novembro de 2015.

210 IOM (n10).

211 Dahir no 1–16–127 du 21 kaada 1437 (25 août 2016) portant promulgation de la loi no 27–14 relative à la lutte contre la traite des êtres humains.

trafficking, such as vulnerability, slavery or secondary victimisation of the victims.[212] Secondary victimisation does not result directly from a criminal act, but from the way the authorities or individuals react to the victim. Law 27–14 does not define terms related to human trafficking, contrary to what was proposed by the CNDH and foreseen in a Model Law created by the United Nations Office on Drugs and Crime.[213]

In 2016, the CNDH issued a critical opinion on the content of Law 27–14 and criticised provisions foreseen in Article 448.1, which required the victim of human trafficking to prove that they were trafficked against their own will. The CNDH proposed to include a statement saying that the consent of the victim is irrelevant in the case of offenses constituting trafficking.[214] Article 448.14 also puts the victim of human trafficking in the position of having to prove they were trafficked against their will and under the existence of a threat.[215] These provisions put the victim of human trafficking in a vulnerable position, as victims could be considered guilty of criminal activities until they can prove the lack of will and the existence of a threat. The CNDH argues that victims of human trafficking should be exempted from criminal charges for prostitution, irregular immigration or other infractions related to the trafficking.[216] This suggestion seems fair, as victims should be considered as such and be protected, rather than prosecuted, which adds to already existing suffering. Moreover, the CNDH rightly indicates that Article 448.2 does not allow an individualisation of criminal charges according to the importance of the infraction committed. The term '*quiconque*' (whoever), does not consider the offender's personality or the consequences of the gravity of the offense. A clearer formulation of Article 448.2 should be proposed where a specific infraction and the related charges are stated. Next, the proposition by the CNDH to delete the second indent of Article 448.7 has also not been taken into consideration, and it does not reflect the fact that people other than the ones included in the Law can be threatened.[217] We agree with this proposal, because witnesses of human trafficking, other than direct relatives, can also be threatened. For human trafficking offenses to be exposed, witnesses play an important role, and they should feel sufficiently protected to expose such crimes, in a broader scope than what is currently foreseen by Article 446.7. The CNDH also advised the inclusion of an article that would provide social security protection to victims working in the sector of traditional handicrafts,[218] but it has not been added to the law. Additionally, the CNDH encouraged the attribution of residency documents to victims of human trafficking awaiting trial and allowances for victims to benefit from the basic healthcare system (RAMED).[219] Besides the project '*Promouvoir*

212 CNDH, 'Avis du Conseil national des droits de l'Homme sur le projet de loi no 27.14 relatif à la lutte contre la traite des personnes', Rabat (2016) 1, 6.
213 Ibid; CNDH (n193) 6.
214 CNDH (n212) 7.
215 Ibid 9.
216 Ibid.
217 Ibid 8.
218 Ibid 9–10.
219 Ibid 11–12.

l'intégration des Migrants au Maroc', which supports the drafting of the new law on human trafficking, a MIEUX project on human trafficking was included in the Mobility Partnership, however it has been interrupted since 2014. According to an ICMPD official, the aim of the project was to support the drafting of a Protocol on human trafficking, but the new law on human trafficking had to be adopted first.[220] The project has never been implemented due to a change in priorities in Morocco.

Finally, it should be noted that discussions on the law on human trafficking started in Morocco before the launch of the NSIA and conclusion of the Mobility Partnership. The Council of Europe[221] was involved in discussions since 2012. Moreover, ICMPD launched a MIEUX project in May 2013 (before the conclusion of the Mobility Partnership and NIP/NSIA), aiming at supporting the Moroccan authorities in elaborating a new protocol on the identification of and provision of assistance to victims of human trafficking, and designing guidelines for field implementation.[222] The Mobility Partnership projects aiming at supporting the implementation of the NSIA and the development of the new law on human trafficking are proposed and implemented a posteriori and support financially and technically the drafting and later the implementation of the law.

3.2.3 Access to socio-economic rights and citizenship

3.2.3.1 Employment and social security

Law 66/VIII/2014 introduces the imposition of fines on anyone who irregularly employs a foreigner who has not been granted a residency permit or who authorises the pursuit of a subordinate professional activity. The Labour Code was modified in 2010 and 2016,[223] but the provisions about migrant workers have yet not been amended. It should be noted that the precariousness of the labour market is a reality in Cape Verde for foreigners and for Cape Verdeans. Both nationals and foreigners work mainly without any employment contracts. Indeed, informal work is one of the central features of the labour market in Cape Verde. About 70% of foreigners are without a work contract, and the percentage is even greater among women.[224] According to several migrants' representatives, the main work-related issue is the absence of labour contracts.[225] Moreover, a provision that was aimed at protecting migrant workers had unintended effects. According

220 Interview 18, ICMPD, Brussels, 13 May 2016.

221 Interview 4, Council of Europe, Strasbourg, 21 December 2015; Interview 12 (n197).

222 More information about this project is available at: https://www.icmpd.org/our-work/capacity-building/multi-thematic-programmes/mieux-iii/middle-east-north-africa/#c7410 (accessed 22 December 2017).

223 Decreto-Legislativo no 5/2010 (Altera o Codigo Laboral) BO I Série no 22 de Junho de 2010; Decreto-Regulamentar no 1/2016 (Altera o Codigo Laboral) BO I Série no 6.

224 IOM (n10) 29.

225 Interviews 43 (n106), 44 (n86) and 47 (n86).

to several migrants' representatives in Cape Verde, it is now more difficult to find a job if you are an irregular migrant, particularly in the tourist industry. The new measure is seen as a way to fight irregular migration rather than to protect migrant workers' rights.[226]

Since 2015, the process to access the labour market for foreigners (not regularised immigrants) has been eased in Morocco for some high-level profiles and specific positions, as well as for the renewal of an authorisation for the same position with the same employer.[227] In such cases, the vacancy does not have to be published in the newspapers, and the authorisation can be given in 48 hours. Additionally, since 2015, regularised migrants may also work legally without requiring a prior attestation from the ANAPEC, and they have access to education and training programmes offered by the ANAPEC.[228] One of the goal of the *Sharaka* project is to support the ANAPEC in the integration of regularised migrants into the Moroccan labour market. However, in practice, some migrant representatives are still arguing that access to labour for sub-Saharan migrants is blocked, and that only a few are employed through the ANAPEC process.[229] Two representatives of an organisation working to support immigrants' rights in Morocco added that it is impossible for a sub-Saharan migrant in Tangier to find legal employment because of racism and discrimination.[230] Some respondents, however, noted slow improvement in the matter[231] and, mainly, underlined the new possibility for sub-Saharan migrants to benefit from vocational training as an important step forward.[232] Other major changes have been made, such as the extension to non-Moroccans of laws relating to the exercise of certain regulated professions. It is important to note that all of the changes in access to labour in Morocco are related to the implementation of the NSIA, which is supported by the Mobility Partnership.

3.2.3.2 Education

In Cape Verde, the Decree-Law 2/2010, of 7 May 2010, refers to the conditions of free education.[233] There are no records or data regarding situations of discrimination in access to education based on gender, age, colour or religious

226 Interview 44 (n86), 46 (n151), 47 (n86), 48 (n151) and 51 (n86).

227 Note conjointe (Intérieur-Emploi-Industrie-DGSN-ANAPEC-AMDI) relative à la mise en place d'une procédure spécifique d'octroi de titre de séjour pour les investisseurs étrangers et compétences rares (septembre 2015).

228 Ministère de l'Emploi et des Affaire Sociales, 'Stratégie Nationale pour l'Emploi, Comité de pilotage de la SNE du 24 février 2015' 1, 62.

229 Interviews 21 (n85) and 26 (n85).

230 Interview 24 (n85).

231 Interview 20, CEI, Rabat, 15 April 2016; Interview 22 (n85); Interview 27, Collectif des travailleurs migrants au maroc, Rabat, 25 April 2016.

232 Interviews 21 (n85) and 22 (n85).

233 Decreto-Legislativo 2/2010, de 7 de Maio, Bases do sistema educativo, B.O.C.V., I Série no 17 de 7 de Maio de 2010, supplemento. Repealing tacitly Lei 103/III/90, de 29 de Dezembro, na redacção dada pela Lei 113/V/99, de 18 de Outubro.

denomination. The major problems that now arise relate to the issue of fairness and real equality of opportunity, not in universal and compulsory education, but at the levels of pre-school, secondary and higher education.[234] Concerning the observance of the right to education, it is particularly important to note that in some public education establishments, the composition of classes is interwoven with the interests of parents and teachers, and that the distribution of pupils per class aligns to socio-economic criteria, in flagrant violation of the Constitution of the Republic and of the Basic Law of the Educational System. In that regard, Article 4(1) of Decree 2/2010 states that Cape Verde progressively promotes equal access for all citizens to varying degrees of education and equal opportunities in school success. In addition, in its article 6, it is determined that the educational system is addressed to all individuals regardless of age, sex, socioeconomic, intellectual or cultural level, religious belief or philosophical conviction. For the unanimity of migrant's representatives, there is no issue for migrants' children to access education and go to school, even if they are in an irregular situation. The CNDH also provides alphabetisation classes with the support of the DGI.[235] The NIS foresees the improvement of the educational system in order to favour the integration of immigrants.[236]

In Morocco, a new Circular 13–487[237] of the Ministry of National Education and Vocational Training, of 9 October 2013, authorises immigrant and refugee children to access public and private schools and non-formal education ('second chance school') regardless of their administrative situation. Moreover, the registration has been simplified. A campaign aiming at registering children to attend school benefited 30,174 children in the year 2014–2015.[238] New programmes are being implemented aiming at promoting cultural diversity and the learning of Moroccan languages and cultures to allow migrants to communicate and understand the habits and values of Moroccan society. There were 100 beneficiaries of non-formal education in 2013–2014, which increased to 362 in 2015–2016, and 688 migrant children benefited from courses of Moroccan languages and cultures.[239] Except the migrant representative based in Tangier, all recognised a vast improvement in the access to education, even for children in an irregular situation.[240] The project '*Promouvoir l'intégration des Migrants au Maroc*' provides EUR 3 million to provide migrant children access to public formal or non-formal education.

234 Comissão Nacional para os Direitos Humanos e a Cidadania e o PNUD (n104) 66.
235 Interview 35, DGI, Praia, 23 February 2016; Interview 42 (n99).
236 EFG Consulting (n11) 55.
237 La circulaire no 13–487 du Ministère de l'Éducation Nationale et de la Formation Professionnelle du 9 Octobre 2013.
238 MCMREAM, 'Politique nationale d'immigration et d'asile: 2013–2016', Septembre 2016, 1, 33.
239 Ibid 37.
240 Interview 25, APIMA, Rabat, 23 April 2016; Interviews 27, Collectif des travailleurs migrants au Maroc, Rabat, 25 April 2016; Interviews 22 (n85), 23 (n85), 24 (n85) and 26 (n85).

3.2.3.3 Health

In Morocco, access to the RAMED now depends on the access to the regularisation process, which is only open during specific periods.[241] Refugees have benefited from access to the RAMED since 2015.[242] Most respondents underlined that the RAMED is still not applied to immigrants, as the paperwork must be fully filled out in Arabic, which represents another barrier to immigrants who try to make requests in order to access it.[243] However, two respondents argue that access to healthcare is easier since the regularisation period, even though they cannot access the RAMED, and they no longer fear being arrested and deported.[244] They add that because of the fear of the police, many irregular migrants were not going to a hospital and, therefore, totally lacked access to health. The project '*Promouvoir l'intégration des Migrants au Maroc*' provides EUR 3 million to provide regularised migrants access to the RAMED.

No specific developments occurred in Cape Verde in relation to health. According to migrants' representatives and a former Cape Verdean government official, access to health can be a problem because of a lack of money, mainly because medicine costs are not reimbursed, and there is a lack of specialists.[245] The NIS foresees the improvement of the health system in order to favour the integration of immigrants.[246]

3.2.3.4 Housing

Migrants with low incomes and refugees are now included in social housing programmes in Morocco and can benefit from housing loans more easily.[247] The Moroccan budget for 2015 foresees migrants benefiting from social housing and housing of low property value. The aim of this action is to provide immigrants and refugees with access to property within the framework of the social housing programmes subsidised by the State. It amends the conditions of access defined in the legislation governing social housing to allow immigrants who meet defined criteria (duration of residence, level of income, professional status) to be eligible for the acquisition of social housing under the same conditions as Moroccans. Moreover, 26 partnerships have been concluded with associations, and a framework agreement has been concluded with the Red Crescent, which includes housing issues. Housing is an area that

241 Myriam Cherti and Michael Collyer (n27) 595.

242 MCMREAM, 'Politique nationale d'immigration et d'asile' (n238) 74.

243 Interviews 21 (n85) 22 (n85), 23 (n85); Interview 25, APIMA (n241) Interview 26 (n85).

244 Interviews 20 (n231) and 25 (n240).

245 Interviews 43 (n106) and 44 (n86); Interview 45, Ex-Secretário de Estado dos Negócios Estrangeiros/Former Ambassador, Praia, 16 November 2016; Interviews 46 (n151), 47 (n86), 52 (n152).

246 EFG Consulting (n11) 55.

247 Dahir no 1–14–195 du 1er rabii I 1436 (24 décembre 2014) portant promulgation de la loi de finances 100–14 pour l'année budgétaire 2015, publié au Bulletin Officiel n.6320 bis du 2 rabii I 1436 (25 décembre 2014), Article 247.

did not see much improvement, according to migrants' representatives. According to two migrants' representatives, there are still issues regarding obtaining renting contracts.[248] Moreover, the rent required from migrants is higher than that asked from Moroccans for the same place, and racism and discrimination are still high.[249]

No specific developments occurred in Cape Verde in relation to housing. Regular migrants have access to social housing programmes.[250] It was noted by migrants' representatives and the official of the *Câmara* Municipal in Boa Vista, however, that it is much easier to find 'decent' housing in Praia than on other islands, with Boa Vista being the worst-case scenario for immigrants (regular or not) and even Cape Verdeans coming from other islands.[251] The lack of financial means is the reason that came out of an interview with a migrants' representative when discussing the issue of access to housing.[252] The NIS foresees the improvement of the housing system in order to favour the integration of immigrants.[253]

3.2.3.5 Regularisation of irregular migrants and access to citizenship

The fifth axis of the NIS provides for the updating of the nationality law. The strategy refers to the national interest in allowing foreigners residing in Cape Verde, under certain conditions, to become nationals of the country.[254] In the period under analysis, a draft proposal for the nationality law was developed, which, after being discussed and approved by the Council of Ministers, ended up being rejected in the national parliament. There has been no further progress since then.

In 2010, Cape Verde opted for a gradual approach to the process of regularisation of irregular immigrants, initially choosing the citizens of a single country and

> [t]aking into account the reasons of a historical, linguistic and cultural nature and aware of the positive contribution that immigrants in general and Guineans, in particular, have been giving in all sectors of the labor market in the country, the Government has decided to take, on an experimental basis, the process of special legalization in favor of the citizens of Guinea-Bissau.[255]

In 2015, Decree-Law 1/2015[256] on the extraordinary regularisation of irregular migrants was adopted. Following the adoption of this law, irregular migrants who

248 Interviews 23 (n101), 26 (n101).
249 Ibid.
250 UCI/OFII (n129) 37.
251 Interviews 44 (n86), 49 (n111), 52 (n152) and 54 (n151).
252 Interview 54 (n151).
253 EFG Consulting (n11) 55.
254 UCI (n128) 46–47.
255 Decreto Lei 13/2010, de 26 de Abril (Estabelece um processo especial de regularização dos cidadãos originários da Guiné-Bissau que se encontrem no território cabo-verdiano sem autorização legal de permanência), B.O.C.V., I Série, n. 16, 26 de Abril de 2010.
256 Decreto-Lei 1/2015 Estabelece as disposições necessárias á regularização extraordinária de cidadãos estrangeiros que se encontrem em situação irregular no território nacional BO IS n. 1 de 6 de Janeiro de 2015.

had entered Cape Verde before 17 November 2011, and who were in an irregular situation, had 90 days to apply for a residency permit. Several migrants criticised the difficulty of the regularisation process, saying that many migrants were not able to regularise due to a lack of access to the necessary documents.[257] However, it should be noted that it is largely agreed that even though foreigners are in an irregular situation, irregularity is not a reason for expulsion. Migrants' representatives argue that the only situation when an irregular migrant was deported was when he was convicted of a crime.[258]

In Morocco, the regularisation of asylum seekers in November 2013, as well as the launch of the regularisation campaign held from January to December 2014, were direct consequences of the migration policy. Following its launch, a regularisation campaign for migrants was introduced. The categories of migrants affected by the regularisation procedure were set in a Circular of 16 December 2013:[259] foreigners married to a Moroccan citizen, foreigners married to a foreigner in a regular situation, the children of the above-mentioned couples, migrant workers able to prove the existence of their work contract, foreigners living in Morocco for at least five years and foreigners with serious diseases. Several issues have been highlighted in relation to the documents necessary to prove one's situation. A report from the GADEM and FIDH highlights that, in some cases, the requirements were higher than Law 02–03 itself. For example, two years of cohabitation were required from married couples, whereas the law did not require any minimum period of living jointly to deliver a residency permit.[260] By the end of the regularisation period in December 2014, 23,096 out of 27,649 migrants had been regularised,[261] and 643 out of 2,937 asylum seekers had been granted refugee cards by the UNHCR.[262] Based on the statistics provided, by 2 August 2016, 5,471 refugees and asylum-seekers were registered with the UNHCR representative. The number of refugees recognised by the BRA on the recommendation of the ad hoc commission reached 687 of various nationalities.[263]

A second regularisation period for migrants based on the same criteria as the first regularisation period was launched by the King on 15 December 2016 and ended December 2017. Over 20,000 migrants, out of the 28,400 who applied, have been regularised.[264] It should be noted that the existence of these regularisation periods does not mean the end of the arrest and detention of irregular migrants. The FIDH and GADEM give the example of a large campaign of arrest

257 Interviews 43 (n106), 48 (n151), 49 (n111), 50 (n111) and 51 (n86).
258 Interviews 42 (n99) 44 (n86), 46 (n151) and 50 (n135).
259 Circulaire conjointe du Ministre de l'Intérieur et du Ministre Chargé des Marocains Résidant à l'Étranger et des Affaires de la Migration no 8303 du 16 décembre 2013 régissant l'opération exceptionnelle de régularisation de la situation de séjour des étrangers.
260 FIDH and GADEM, 'Maroc: entre rafles et régularisations. Bilan d'une politique migratoire indécise' (2012) 19.
261 MCMREAM (n125) 1,78.
262 UNHCR, 'Morocco Factsheet', 1 April 2015.
263 MCMREAM, 'Politique nationale d'immigration et d'asile' (n238) 112–113.
264 Ibid.

in the northern forest of Gourougou, known for its large population of irregular sub-Saharan migrants, which occurred shortly after the end of the regularisation period.[265] It seems that this new campaign of regularisation aims at keeping Morocco's good image following the massive deportation of sub-Saharan migrants that occurred in Algeria 11–12 December 2016.[266] Finally, it should be noted that the Moroccan Citizenship Code has remained unmodified since the regularisation periods, making it almost impossible for regularised migrants to be granted citizenship.

3.3 Conclusion

The legal and practical frameworks related to migration can be broad and do not only comprise migration law *per se*. The findings of this research provide insights for the analysis of the relevance of the Mobility Partnerships on the development of legal frameworks in Morocco and Cape Verde. By looking at a before and after 'picture' of the legal frameworks of both countries, this chapter highlighted the different legal developments that occurred since the conclusion of the Mobility Partnerships in 2008 in Cape Verde and 2013 in Morocco. In the cases of Morocco and Cape Verde, the Mobility Partnerships clearly influenced the development of laws related to the entry and stay of foreigners, human trafficking and asylum.

In Cape Verde, a MIEUX project included in the Mobility Partnership led to the development of Law 66/VIII/2014 on the entry, stay and expulsion of foreigners. The same project led to the drafting of a new law on Asylum, but the law was not adopted. Another change brought by Law 66/VIII/2014 in Cape Verde, was the introduction of mechanisms to protect victims of human trafficking, with the possibility of granting residency permits to the victims. Another project aimed at supporting Cape Verde in the implementation of the Palermo Convention and its Protocols related to human trafficking. It has been translated into the legal framework through the development of new provisions in the revised Penal Code and the new Law 66/VIII/2014. Moreover, a joint border control agreement with FRONTEX was concluded, giving the Cape Verdean border authorities better means to effectively apply Law 66/VIII/2014 by developing border procedures, training border guards, sharing best practices and introducing technical equipment to support border guards' work. The conclusion of such an agreement was foreseen by two projects in the Annex to the Joint Declaration. Additionally, France and Cape Verde concluded a 'bilateral agreement on concerted

265 FIDH and GADEM (n263) 20.

266 Christophe Sidiguitiebe, 'Campagne de régularisation des migrants: ce qu'il faut savoir', *Telquel.ma*, 13 December 2016, available at: http://telquel.ma/2016/12/13/campagne-regularisation-migrants-ce-quil-faut-savoir_1527188 (accessed 8 February 2017); 'Une nouvelle opération de régularisation de migrants au Maroc', *h24info.ma*, 13 December 2016, available at: http://www.h24info.ma/maroc/une-nouvelle-operation-de-regularisation-de-migrants-au-maroc/49045 (accessed 8 February 2017).

management of migratory flows', the conclusion of which was proposed in a Mobility Partnership project. Additionally, Luxembourg concluded an agreement on circular migration with Cape Verde in October 2015. The Annex to the Joint Declaration already foresaw the introduction of 'an initiative on temporary circular migration with Cape Verde'. Furthermore, the conclusion by Cape Verde of an EURA and a visa facilitation agreement were clearly results of the Mobility Partnership, as one of the preconditions to conclude a Mobility Partnership was the commitment of the third country to negotiate an EURA.

The scoreboard of the Mobility Partnership with Morocco foresees several projects aimed at supporting Morocco in the development of new laws on immigration, asylum and human trafficking. The conclusion of the Law on Human Trafficking is a consequence of these projects. The project '*Promouvoir l'intégration des Migrants au Maroc*' is a key initiative that supports the development and implementation of the NSIA and supports the development of the three new laws. This project, as well as several others, aims at supporting 'the strengthening of the Moroccan legislative and institutional framework for asylum'.[267]

Both Mobility Partnerships have also influenced the implementation of National Strategies in relation to the integration of immigrants and the provision of further rights to migrants in Cape Verde and Morocco. Both National Strategies on Immigration (and asylum in the case of Morocco) foresee the development of new laws on human trafficking, asylum and migration. These two strategies also include measures to favour the integration of immigrants by opening regularisation periods and striving to enhance access to a set of rights, including rights to healthcare, education and better access the labour market.

In the case of Morocco, the EU acted *a posteriori*, supporting Morocco's existing national priorities through various projects, the main ones being '*Promouvoir l'intégration des Migrants au Maroc*' and '*Sharaka*'. It is important to note that all of the changes related to access to labour, education, health and housing in Morocco are associated with the implementation of the NSIA, which is supported by the Mobility Partnership. In the opposite case of Cape Verde, the EU has had a *proactive* role, heavily influencing the development of the legal and policy frameworks in a more asymmetrical way through several projects included in the scoreboard. In Cape Verde, the development of the NIP and NIS are the fruits of distinct phases in which the EU was involved since the conclusion of the Mobility Partnership. A first diagnostic report conducted by the Netherlands lead to the NIP. Then the ICMPD implemented a MIEUX project developing the NIS and Action Plan. Concerning migrants' access to rights, the NIS foresees improvement of the education, health and housing systems in order to favour the integration of immigrants. It is interesting to note here that it is the national systems that are being improved, as regular migrants benefit from the same rights as Cape Verdean citizens. We believe that when the law does not differentiate

267 Source: 'Joint Declaration establishing a Mobility Partnership between the Kingdom of Morocco and the European Union and its Member States' 6139/13 ADD 1 REV 1, Brussels, 12 April 2013.

between immigrants and nationals for the access to rights, it can show a higher level of integration than a country implementing differentiated laws for nationals and immigrants.

The NIS and NSIA also led to several policy changes that influenced refugees' access to rights. This is the case, for example, in the regularisation periods and the reopening of the BRA in Morocco, which started to deliver refugee cards granting refugees access to rights related to their status. Another Mobility Partnership project also concerns support for the drafting of a strategy for the reception and integration of refugees. In the framework of this project, the ICMPD works with the CNDH and the MCMREAM in the mapping of the integration of refugees and the creation of a refugee profile.

Moreover, through this analysis, the question of the relevance of the legal changes for migrants' rights can also be answered. By looking at the evolution of the legal framework, we can analyse whether an immigrant has access to more rights within new legal developments, or whether his situation is worsening. We can see, in the case of Morocco, that the rights granted to migrants improved in several areas, such as the access to labour, education and housing, but rights related to health diminished. It is also interesting to note that, in the case of Cape Verde, some laws are also restricting the rights of migrants, such as the new law on entry, stay and exit, which makes it more difficult for a migrant to regularise his situation. In both countries the situation of refugees and victims of human trafficking improved, as they now have access to a specific status.

4 Contextualisation of the legal and policy developments in Morocco and Cape Verde

Recently, researchers have shown an increased interest in the consequences of the implementation of Mobility Partnerships. This chapter provides a detailed overview of the complexity and interaction of various factors and actors. Identifying the relevance of Mobility Partnerships is difficult, and therefore we should contextualise it. The chapter aims at providing a comprehensive picture of how the implementation of Mobility Partnerships projects can lead to legal and policy developments.

Key aspects of the analysis regarding the importance of the relations between third countries and EU Member States are the role played by bilateral negotiations in the Mobility Partnership and the added value of projects proposed bilaterally by one Member State in the framework of the Mobility Partnership. The importance of postcolonial ties is assessed in the first section, and Member States' cooperation preferences are also considered as they can explain behaviours when participating in a Mobility Partnership.

Subsequently, I explain why the concepts of negotiation power and conditionality are central to analysing the relevance of the Mobility Partnership. First, the 'standard' conditionality used by the EU Commission in its relations with third countries is described, which shows that the Commission can use conditionality (sometimes even negative conditionality) to push third countries to follow and implement policies that are favourable to the Commission and that often include the fight against irregular migration. Then the 'more for more' conditionality included in Mobility Partnerships is discussed, as the Commission realised that it needed to propose more positive incentives to third countries in order to increase cooperation on migration after the Arab Spring uprisings. Finally, 'reversed conditionality' is discussed. 'Reversed conditionality' can be used by third countries that have gained an important level of negotiating power because they are of key geopolitical importance for the Commission in terms of migration control.

Finally, in the last section I discuss how the administrative capacity of the third country is instrumental in our understanding of the relevance of Mobility Partnerships, mainly in the development of the content of new policies and laws through Mobility Partnership projects. This last section shows how development aid and capacity building can influence the legal and policy developments in Morocco and Cape Verde, As well as how the level of administrative capacity may be detrimental to effective implementation of the developed instruments or other EU priorities, such as border control.

4.1 State of relations between third countries and EU Member States

In this section, I discuss the extent to which strong bilateral relations or pre-existing postcolonial ties between the EU Member States and Morocco or Cape Verde influenced the relevance of the concluded Mobility Partnerships.

4.1.1 Influence of the relation between Member States and the third country on the conclusion and negotiation of the content of Mobility Partnerships

Member States conduct a substantial volume of their external policy goals through EU instruments and cooperation.[1] This does not, however, imply that they give up on national priorities or preferential relationships with specific third countries. Accordingly, Carrera and Hernandez i Sagrera argue that national migration policies are at the heart of Mobility Partnerships.[2] This argument has been confirmed by several interviewees on the Member States' and third countries' sides.[3] In other words, a Member State agrees to participate only if it furthers its national policy.

It is important to understand that without a solid commitment of the Member States partaking in Mobility Partnerships (not only those with postcolonial ties, but all Member States that are a part of a Mobility Partnership), the Partnerships will not be successful as no projects would be proposed or implemented. The main reason why the Commission must accept Member States' preferences when it comes to the conclusion, negotiation and implementation of Mobility Partnerships lies in the nature of Mobility Partnerships themselves. Member States are free to participate or not participate, and their inaction cannot be sanctioned. In order to have enough Member States participating in a Mobility Partnership, proposing and implementing projects, the Commission must give priority to Member States' preferences as put forth by an official of DG Home Affairs.[4] A reason for this is the fact that the Member States must secure funding for the projects that they want to implement or at least participate in the funding of multilateral activities. Another official from DG Home Affairs underlined that Mobility Partnerships do not have a specific financial envelope.[5] Meng-Hsuan Chou and Marie Gibert believe that

1 Natasja Reslow, 'EU "Mobility" Partnerships: An initial Assessment of Implementation Dynamics' (2015) 3(2) *Politics and Governance* 117, 123.
2 Sergio Carrera and Raul Hernández i Sagrera, 'The Externalisation of the EU's Labour Immigration Policy: Towards Mobility or Insecurity Partnerships?' (2009) CEPS Working Document 321/October 1, 31.
3 Interview 8, French Embassy, Rabat, 14 January 2016; Interview 10, Expertise France, Rabat, 15 January 2016; Interview 13, Moroccan Ministry of Labour, Rabat, 19 January 2016; Interview 14, GiZ, Rabat, 20 January 2016; Interview 16, MCMREAM, Rabat, 21 January 2016; Interview 17, Spanish Embassy, Rabat, 22 January 2016.
4 Interview 29, DG Home Affairs, Brussels, 26 October 2016.
5 Interview 3, DG Home Affairs, Brussels, 18 November 2015.

third countries and Member States with postcolonial ties will tend to adopt a common position when negotiating with the EU, and they will favour the existence of the postcolonial link versus the relationship with the EU.[6] This means that third countries will usually only agree to conclude a Mobility Partnership if the former colonial power is favourable to it. Both Portugal and France were in favour of the conclusion of the Mobility Partnership with their respective colonies, even though the degree of support provided by each former colonial power was not the same.

According to a Moroccan academic, bilateral relations between France and Morocco resulting from postcolonial ties play an important role.[7] Spanish officials pointed out that Spain also has had a long history of cooperation with Morocco on migration issues, notably with their common border in Ceuta and Melilla, and that Spain had a strong interest in the conclusion of the Mobility Partnership.[8] Both France and Spain have long histories with Morocco and firmly established interests within the country. According to a Moroccan migrant in France, France no longer plays a key role in Morocco's relations with the EU, and links with Spain are much stronger now.[9] France and Spain also share main concerns: the fight against irregular migration and internal security threats. Rather than the pre-existing cooperation between France or Spain and Morocco, national interests can explain the different approaches taken by these two countries. Spanish officials saw the Mobility Partnership as a way to attract increased funding from the EU for their bilateral cooperation with Morocco.[10] An EU official explained that Member States that have concluded a Mobility Partnership have prior access to EU funding for projects implemented with the third country in question,[11] even those bilateral projects that would have implemented anyway.

The vast majority of projects are bilateral activities proposed by EU Member States. Bilateral ties are more important than what is proposed in the Mobility Partnerships, according to a Moroccan official.[12] These projects reflect their own national interests. EU officials allow the inclusion of these types of projects because they are conditions for an effective implementation of the Mobility Partnerships. An EU official declared that Spain and France exploited the Mobility Partnership with Morocco to promote and implement their own national policies.[13] Member States with strong bilateral ties with the third country play a prominent role in the proposition of projects shaping the content of the Mobility Partnerships. In the case of Cape Verde, Portugal, with whom it has postcolonial ties, proposed the largest number of projects. A Cape Verdean official and academic believes that postcolonial

6 Meng-Hsuan Chou and Marie Gibert, 'The EU-Senegal mobility partnership: From launch to suspension and negotiation failure' (2012) 8(4) *JCER* 408.
7 Interview 5, AMERM, University Mohammed V, Rabat, 12 January 2016.
8 Interview 17 (n3).
9 Interview 61, Calima, Strasbourg, 1 June 2017.
10 Interview 17 (n3).
11 Interview 3 (n5).
12 Interview 13 (n3).
13 Interview 29 (n4).

ties favour cooperation because sensitivities between countries are closer.[14] The case of Morocco is different because the Netherlands, which has no postcolonial ties with Morocco, proposed the largest number of projects. The difference between Cape Verde and Morocco could be explained by the fact that decolonisation happened earlier in Morocco than in Cape Verde. Time can affect the relevance of post-colonial ties.[15] It can also be explained by the preference of Spain and France towards bilateral relations rather than cooperation in the framework of the Mobility Partnership. Representatives of both countries admitted to not including all of their bilateral activities in the scoreboard as they wanted their activities to be seen as projects of bilateral national cooperation, rather than projects linked to the Mobility Partnership, which could undermine national 'prestige'.[16] However, the country that proposed the largest number of pre-existing projects in the Annex to the Joint Declaration establishing a Mobility Partnership with Morocco was France, underlining the longstanding cooperation between both countries.

I argue that not only do Member States want to keep control of Mobility Partnerships by proposing overwhelmingly bilateral projects, they also do not want to lose any existing special dynamics with third countries to the EU's influence. Accordingly, Parkes argues that the Member States 'wrangle' among themselves to guarantee that third countries with which they have a strong relationship are treated with favouritism.[17] The interests of Member States, however, are not limited to those with pre-existing historical ties. Cape Verde, for example, cooperates bilaterally with EU Member States on migration issues, primarily with Portugal, but also closely with Spain and France, with which it does not share historical ties.

4.1.2 Bilateral cooperation vs. cooperation in the framework of the Mobility Partnership: is there an added value?

A Mobility Partnership is generally presented as an 'umbrella', centralising the various bilateral and multilateral projects that are being implemented in a third country (on migration issues). According to French, Spanish and Belgian officials, as well as an ICMPD representative from Brussels, the majority of projects being proposed and implemented are bilateral initiatives that, in most cases, would have existed without the Mobility Partnership.[18] We saw that in many cases the projects proposed and implemented were not new, and the Member States simply reshaped pre-existing initiatives. I argue that if the only way for the Member States to agree to commit to Mobility Partnerships is by including bilateral activities that would

14 Interview 40, Institute of Social and Legal Sciences of Cape Verde, Praia, 26 February 2016.

15 Simona Vezzoli, 'The role of the state in international migration: Exploring the transition from colony to independence' (2014) IMI Working Papers Series 102, 1, 13.

16 Interviews 8 and 17 (n3).

17 Roderick Parkes, 'EU mobility partnerships: A model of policy coordination?' (2009) 11(4) *EJML* 327, 343.

18 Interviews 8 and 17 (n3); Interview 18, ICMPD, Brussels, 13 May 2016; Interview 19, Belgian Embassy, Rabat, 12 April 2016.

have existed anyway or already ongoing activities, then Mobility Partnerships bring no added value to the proposals made to third countries. EU officials prefer cooperative projects among several Member States over bilateral initiatives because they can be of added value. To push for its preference, the funding allocated to Mobility Partnerships projects was partially conditional on the collaboration between member states, and the funding of joint projects was given priority. The analysis of the different scoreboards shows that the financial incentives proposed to the Member States were not sufficient to alter their preference for bilateral activities.

Agnieszka Weinar argues that added value projects could be proposed by two actors: a group of Member States or by the EU.[19] Several important new projects were proposed by the EU or jointly by the Member States. The '*Sharaka*' project is an example of cooperation between different partners in order to avoid overlapping activities. Through the '*Sharaka*' project, seven Member States[20] decided to collaborate on joint initiatives. This 'umbrella' project revolves around four different axes: migration and development, mobilisation of Moroccans living in Europe, capacity building of the ANAPEC (the Moroccan employment agency) to integrate migrants in the labour market in Morocco, placement of Moroccans in the labour market abroad and return and reintegration.

When looking at specific topics of projects that could have an added value in the framework of Mobility Partnership, I highlight legal migration and the conclusion of an EU Readmission Agreement (EURA). Legal migration was presented as one of the novelties of the Mobility Partnership. Agnieszka Weinar argues that a Member State modifying its legal order to open new legal migration channels would be a 'clear value added of a Mobility Partnership'.[21] However, in practice, few projects were implemented which aimed at developing legal migration channels for third country nationals. Quite the opposite, I found that the topic with the lowest implementation *ratio* pertains to *Mobility, legal immigration and integration.* The negotiations of the first Mobility Partnerships, including the one with Cape Verde, were influenced by the idea of a triple win approach using circular migration. Mobility Partnerships were seen as a tool favouring circular migration and, therefore, enhancing legal migration options for third country nationals in the limits and (temporary) conditions set by the Member States. In the Mobility Partnership with Cape Verde, projects were included favouring the implementation of circular migration schemes with France, Portugal and Luxembourg. Labour migration agreements were concluded with both Portugal and France. In 1997, Portugal concluded an agreement with Cape Verde on Temporary

19 Agnieszka Weinar, 'Improving EU and US Immigration Systems' Capacity for Responding to Global Challenges: Learning from Experiences', EU-US Immigration Systems 2011/02, Robert Schuman Center for Advanced Studies, San Dominico di Fiesole (FI)/European University Institute (2011) 5.

20 Germany, Belgium, Spain, France, Italy, the Netherlands and Sweden.

21 Agnieszka Weinar, 'Mobility Partnerships – what impact do they have on legal migration and mobility?', available at: http://www.migrationpolicycenter.eu/publication/mobility-partnerships-what-impact-do-they-have-on-legal-migration-and-mobility (accessed 25 August 2017).

Emigration of Cape Verdean Workers to Work in Portugal.[22] A Mobility Partnership project aimed

> to continue to promote the admission of certain categories of Cape Verdean workers, particularly on a temporary basis and with a focus on circular migration, through the signing of a new protocol on migration questions with the government of Cape Verde extending the scope of the Protocol on the temporary migration of Cape Verdean workers to work in Portugal, signed by the two parties on 18 February 1997.[23]

In addition, France concluded a new bilateral agreement with Cape Verde several months after the conclusion of the Mobility Partnership. Luxembourg also concluded an agreement on circular migration with Cape Verde in October 2015.[24] The agreement should simplify mobility and enhance temporary circular labour migration. It also aims at fighting irregular immigration and facilitating the reintegration of migrants into their countries of origin.[25] The Annex to the Joint Declaration already foresaw the introduction of 'an initiative on temporary circular migration with Cape Verde'.

However, even though the agreements with Portugal and France are signed and ratified by both parties, it remains dubious whether Cape Verdeans have benefitted from this scheme due to the economic crisis in Europe as well as the lack of information provided by the Cape Verdean authorities. The labour migration scheme with France concluded on 24 November 2008 is included in the 'Agreement on the joint management of migratory flows concluded between France and Cape Verde'.[26] According to Cape Verdean migrants living in France, the Cape Verdean population does not know this scheme exists, and they are not aware of anyone who has benefitted from it.[27] The scheme with Portugal has not been

22 Protocolo entre a República de Cabo Verde e a República Portuguesa sobre a Emigração Temporária de Trabalhadores Cabo-Verdianos para a Prestação de Trabalho em Portugal (assinado na Praia, 18 de Fevereiro de 1997), Aprovado pelo Decreto n7/97, de 14 de Abril, B.O.C.V., I Série, n. 14.

23 Council of the European Union, 'Joint Declaration on a Mobility Partnership between the European Union and the Republic of Cape Verde' (9460/08 ADD2), Brussels, 21 May 2008.

24 '7e réunion de dialogue politique entre le Cabo Verde et l'UE au niveau ministériel et signature d'un accord bilatéral entre le Luxembourg et le Cabo Verde en matière de migration', *Gouvernement.lu*, Press release, 14 October 2015, available at: http://www.gouvernement.lu/5329991/13-dialogue-politique (accessed 9 February 2018).

25 European Migration Network, '2016 Annual Report on Migration and Asylum 25th April 2017 – Final Version' 1, 58.

26 Décret no 2011–403 du 14 avril 2011 portant publication de l'accord entre le Gouvernement de la République française et le Gouvernement de la République du Cap-Vert relatif à la gestion concertée des flux migratoires et au développement solidaire (ensemble trois annexes), signé à Paris le 24 novembre 2008.

27 Interviews 56, Association Cap – Vert Amiens, Amiens, 19 December 2016 (1); Interview 57, Association Cap – Vert Amiens, Amiens, 19 December 2016 (2); Interview 59, Section des femmes du Secteur France du Parti africain pour l'indépendance du Cap Vert (PAICV), Paris, 20 December 2016.

utilised much either, partially because of the trouble of securing employment contracts, but also owing to an absence of information about the scheme.[28] Similar projects do not exist in the Mobility Partnership with Morocco as, at the time of conclusion, circular migration was considered an inadequate option, and no other concrete legal migration options were proposed in place of these schemes.

The economic crisis that struck Europe starting in 2008 had a negative impact on the implementation of Mobility Partnerships in terms of legal migration opportunities. Natasja Reslow has noted that Mobility Partnerships are being implemented in 'un-favourable circumstances' resulting in the absence of creation of legal migration opportunities for third country nationals.[29] A representative from the German development agency (GIZ) commented towards this respect, arguing that the question of legal migration and mobility is always pushed to the side. According to this representative, Germany often made proposals to DG Home and DG Devco to implement labour migration projects, but they were rejected because EU officials from these DGs believe that legal migration had to be dealt with at the European level rather than through bilateral agreements with Germany.[30] When Member States made their immigration policies more restrictive and focused on the fight against irregular migration and return,[31] it was startling that a Member State was willing to open its labour market while not being supported by the EU, even though it would help materialise the main (official) goal of Mobility Partnerships: legal migration. Moreover, a Moroccan official added that during the negotiations of the Mobility Partnership, the questions of opening the EU labour market to Moroccans and the portability of social rights were crucial.[32] Though, on the Moroccan side, some incoherence on the issue of legal migration can also be found. For example, the project e-bosla was stopped even though it favoured access to the Italian labour market for Moroccans. IOM officials declared that the project did not lead to the conclusion of a protocol of understanding with Italy because Morocco was unwilling to continue to train Moroccan migrants to learn Italian when they were leaving Morocco.[33]

For Cape Verde, the crisis had an even more severe toll, as the visa exemption first put forth during the negotiation of the Mobility Partnership, was replaced in the official Joint Declaration by the term 'visa facilitation'. During the talks concerning the conclusion of the Mobility Partnership with Cape Verde, the idea of

28 Jorgen Carling, 'Migration in the age of involuntary immobility: Theoretical reflections and Cape Verdean experiences, Journal of Ethnic and Migration Studies' (2002) 28(1) 5, 28; Interview 37, CAMPO, Praia, 24 February 2016.

29 Natasja Reslow (n1) 125.

30 Interview 14 (n3).

31 IOM, 'Migration and the economic crisis in the European Union: Implications for policy' (2010), available at: http://www.labourmigration.eu/research/report/12-migration-and-the-economic-crisis-implications-for-policy-in-the-european-union (accessed 28 August 2017); Christiane Kuptsch, 'The Economic Crisis and Labour Migration Policy in European Countries' (2012) 37(1–2) *Comparative Population Studies* 15.

32 Interview 13 (n3).

33 Interview 15, IOM, Rabat, 20 January 2016.

granting visa exemption to Cape Verde was put forth. The Portuguese official in charge of the visa facilitation center argued that the center would exist until full visa exemption was into place 'in 5 or 10 years'.[34] Whereas an official of the EU Delegation in Praia declared that visa exemption for Cape Verdeans was not in question and probably would not be so for a long-time, due to the economic and 'migrant' crisis currently occurring in Europe.[35]

As not all Member States are part of a Mobility Partnership, the legal migration schemes can only be bilateral. All Member States would have to agree to such schemes for them to be effective at the EU level. Indeed, Member States independently decide on the total number of migrants that can be admitted into the country to search for work (Article 79(5)). Therefore, legal migration schemes are proposed bilaterally. The analysis of the implementation of Mobility Partnerships showed that countries that proposed such schemes did not all have strong bilateral or postcolonial ties with the third country (e.g., France and Cape Verde). The conclusion of the scheme between France and Cape Verde can be seen as an added value of the Mobility Partnership.

Moreover, Weinar argues that 'to give the [Mobility Partnerships] more value added, the legal migration and mobility should go beyond bilateral relations.[36] Participating Member States should think about multilateral initiatives, which bring a real EU dividend'.[37] Several joint projects have been implemented satisfactorily under the legal mobility header. The first project led to the creation of a Common Visa Application Center, which has been running since 2010 and has processed approximately 9,000[38] visa applications a year. This project is seen as an important success by the representatives of the EU Delegation in Cape Verde and the Portuguese representative in charge of the Common Visa Application Center.[39] It is characterised by the aforementioned officials as an initiative facilitating the mobility of Cape Verdeans. The Common Visa Application Center has been used since 2013 to process visas in the framework of the visa facilitation agreement. The main initiative implemented in the framework of the Mobility Partnership in relation to legal migration was the conclusion of a visa facilitation agreement[40] between Cape Verde and the EU in 2013 in parallel with the conclusion of a readmission agreement. Even though visa facilitation is only aimed at a small section of the Cape Verdean population, a representative of the EU Delegation in Praia as well as a Cape Verdean official see the initiative as positive and

34 Interview 34, Centro Comum de Vistos/Portuguese Consulate, Praia, 23 February 2016.
35 Interview 39, EU Delegation, Praia, 25 February 2016
36 Agnieszka Weinar (n21).
37 Ibid.
38 This example as well as the following ones used in this section are taken from the scoreboards of Cape Verde and Morocco of July 2017.
39 Interviews 34 (n33) and 39 (n34).
40 Agreement between the European Union and the Republic of Cape Verde on facilitating the issue of short-stay visas to citizens of the Republic of Cape Verde and of the European Union OJ L 282, 24.10.2013.

efficiently enhancing mobility.[41] According to the Portuguese official in charge of it, the Common Visa Application Center is the fruit of the Mobility Partnership.[42] It should be noted that even though it started as a joint initiative between Portugal, Belgium and Luxembourg, since 2014 Portugal is the only Member State to finance the center (without EU funding), even though it now manages visa applications for 14 countries. Thanks to the creation of the Common Visa Application Center, it is considerably easier for Cape Verdeans, who fulfill the conditions for visa facilitation, to request or be granted a visa. One official of the Ministry of Foreign Affairs pointed out that before the existence of this center, Cape Verdeans had to travel to Dakar to apply for a visa.[43]

A second example of a project considered a 'success story' is the CAMPO (Center for Migrant Support at the Country of Origin) project. The project aimed to support legal migration and fight irregular migration of Cape Verdeans towards Portugal and Spain. The Portuguese and Spanish governments and IOM first implemented the project, but it has since been incorporated in the Cape Verdean institutions formed as part of the *Ministério das Comunidades*. Following the elections of 2016, the project was suspended. According to a Cape Verdean official working on the CAMPO project, in practice the activities proposed were mostly focused on providing information about departure, such as facts about destination countries, information on weather conditions, appropriate clothing to wear in a specific country and existing study-abroad opportunities.[44] However, they did not intervene to support Cape Verdeans in finding employment abroad as legal migration was outside of their power. The same official indicated that without the conclusion of a bilateral agreement with a Member State, it would not be possible for Cape Verdeans to find jobs, and even in cases where such an agreement did exist, like with Portugal, only a few Cape Verdeans could benefit from it.[45] Without the Member States engaging themselves through labour agreements, the project remains inoperative as it cannot support the access of Cape Verdeans to Member States' labour markets. Moreover, Cape Verdean representatives added that few people inquired about migration at CAMPO, because the vast majority were migrating on a tourist visa with the intent of overstaying irregularly in Europe.[46] In this case, they could not ask the support of CAMPO without raising the suspicions of the authorities. Those requiring assistance from CAMPO had already managed to secure a work contract abroad. Finally, the information provided to returnees included possibilities for studying or finding a job in Cape Verde, which was a positive development. However, it was sometimes considered insufficient, according to the official involved in the CAMPO project, as usually no concrete opportunities could be offered to returnees due to a lack of existing prospects.[47]

41 Interview 39 (n34); Interview 36, MIREX, Praia, 23 February 2016.
42 Interview 34 (n33).
43 Interview 36 (n40).
44 Interview 37 (n27).
45 Ibid.
46 Interview 37 (n27); Interview 49, Camara Municipal, Boa Vista, 25 November 2016.
47 Interview 37 (n27).

Concerning the conclusion of EU Readmission Agreements, the added value compared to existing bilateral readmission agreements seemed to be the inclusion of a third country national (TCN) clause, which the Member States were not able to negotiate at the bilateral level.[48] However, the conclusion of an EURA would only have a real added value if it was implemented, which is not always the case (i.e., Morocco and Spain).[49] If there is no way to enforce the implementation of the EURA, the third country could be willing to conclude it, even though it has no intention to implement it, as the cost of concluding the agreement is low. According to a migrant representative from Guinea Bissau, Cape Verde's immigration policy is more 'permissible' because Cape Verde itself has a large diaspora.[50] Having this large diaspora gives Cape Verde a better understanding of the difficulties linked to the integration of migrants, but also the burden that readmission can sometimes put on the third country. The migrant representative from Guinea Bissau argues that the existence of this large Cape Verdean diaspora also leads Cape Verde to be reluctant to apply the readmission agreement to third country nationals.[51] Therefore, the conclusion of such an EURA would not create real added value. Carrera et al. argue, however, that an EURA should not be seen as a goal within itself.[52] Indeed, taking into account the example of Cape Verde, the conclusion of the EURA was considered a way to 'dynamise the special relationship with the European Union'.[53] Even though the conclusion of an EURA can be seen as a burden for Cape Verde, the Cape Verdean government believes that any additional cooperation with the EU is beneficial for the country, as the basis of Cape Verdean's external relations is its good relationship with the EU. This case exemplifies Carrera et al.'s argument, as it suggests that EURAs can be seen as a way to contribute to strong relations, rather than only a readmission agreement which disadvantages the third countries concluding them. The use of Mobility Partnerships as frameworks for discussion and cooperation can already be seen as an added value as such. They not only push the parties to discuss issues related to the Mobility Partnership during the different meetings aimed at monitoring and evaluating progress, according to an IOM official in Rabat, an official of DG NEAR and a former Cape Verdean Ambassador, Mobility Partnerships send strong political signals.[54] An official from DG NEAR added that moving points forwards on an agenda is already important

48 Sergio Carrera and others, 'EU-Morocco Cooperation on Readmission, Borders and Protection: A Model to Follow?' CEPS civil liberties 87/January 2016, 1, 5.

49 Lorenzo Gabrielli, 'Corridor Report on Spain: The case of Ecuadorian and Moroccan immigrants' (2015) Interact Research Report 2015/15, 1, 14.

50 Interview 43, Associação dos Guineenses Residentes em Cabo Verde, Praia, 14 November 2011.

51 Ibid.

52 Sergio Carrera and others (n47) 13.

53 República de Cabo Verde, 'Programa do Governo, IX legislature' (2016), retrieved June 15, 2017, available at: http://www.governo.cv/images/Programa_do_Governo_da_IX_Legislatura_2016-2021.pdf (accessed 11 February 2018) 1, 31.

54 Interviews 30, DG Near, Brussels, 27 October 2016 and 15 (n32); Interview 45, Ex-Secretário de Estado dos Negócios Estrangeiros/Former Ambassador, Praia, 16 November 2016

for the Commission.[55] A former high representative from Cape Verde declared that even though Mobility Partnerships are not balanced agreements, they are used to create a perspective of equality and possibilities. He added that the Mobility Partnership is a 'permanent publicity' tool that creates a favourable diplomatic atmosphere, although, in reality, only the bilateral relations are important.[56]

A point that has yet not been presented is the added value Mobility Partnerships can have if they lead to developments in third countries' legal frameworks. If these developments would not have occurred without the existence of the Mobility Partnership, then there is a clear added value. Even though a direct correlation can be difficult to make between the Mobility Partnership and potential legal developments, I will seek to draw some causal links in the next section. If potential connections between the implementation of the Mobility Partnership and legal developments in Morocco and Cape Verde can be identified, they can be considered an added value of the Mobility Partnership, even if the Partnership is only indirectly relevant.

4.1.3 Influence on the policy and legal developments

It has been observed in the literature and presented in an interview that the EU is primarily driven by the Member States, mainly under the conditions of the strongest Member States.[57] The literature as well as an interview with a Cape Verdean scholar point out that the EU's migration policy is dictated by a maximum of five Member States, including France and Germany, but excluding southern European countries, such as Portugal.[58] Therefore, it can be argued that the strongest Member States are making the decisions for European asylum and migration policies. When I speak about the EU's aims and goals, it should not be forgotten that the Member States are behind them. As I discussed earlier, Member States play a prominent role in proposing projects and shaping the content of the Mobility Partnerships to their own interests. They propose projects either bilaterally or jointly. However, this does not mean that cooperation on migration issues at the EU level should be dismissed. Member States do face difficulties in

55 Interview 30 (n53).

56 Interview 45 (n53).

57 Rosa Balfour and Kristi Raik, *The European External Action Service and National Diplomacies* (2013) EPC Issue Paper, no. 73; Patrick Müller, 'EU Foreign Policy: No Major Breakthrough Despite Multiple Crises' (2016) 38(3) *JEI* 359; Sarah Wolff, 'The Politics of Negotiating the EU Readmission Agreements: Insights from Morocco and Turkey' (2014) *EJML* 69, 93; Natasja Reslow, 'Deciding on EU External Migration Policy: The Member States and the Mobility Partnerships' (2012) 34(3) *JEI* 223; Interview 40 (n14).

58 Stefan Lehne, 'The Big Three in EU Foreign Policy' (2012) Carnegie Europe, available at: http://carnegieeurope.eu/2012/07/05/big-three-in-eu-foreign-policy-pub-48759 (accessed 27 December 2017); Stewart M. Patrick, 'The EU's Migration Crisis: When Solidarity and Sovereignty Collide' (2015) Council on Foreign Relations, available at: https://www.cfr.org/blog/eus-migration-crisis-when-solidarity-and-sovereignty-collide (accessed 27 December 2017); Interview 40 (n14).

the implementation of their national migration policies.[59] Third countries are becoming less willing to cooperate with the Member States, as too little is given to third countries in exchange for their support in the fight against irregular migration.[60] The EU and the Member States both share common goals; they want to avoid irregular immigrants and asylum seekers from reaching their territories. Even though bilateral cooperation between Member States and third countries is key, Member States sometimes need to propose incentives that consider third countries' interests. Such incentives include mobility facilitation and migration and development projects. The Mobility Partnership gives a framework for the Member States to offer higher incentives to third countries than those offered at the bilateral level (e.g., better access to funding or EU visa facilitation). This does not weaken the relation between Member States and third countries, nor the position of Member States within the EU on migration issues; rather, it offers a larger variety of tools to be exploited.

The first interest Member States share with the EU lies in the conclusion of an EURA with Morocco, which includes third country nationals who are not Moroccan nationals. Member States are playing a prominent role in the negotiations. Morocco has rejected such an agreement for almost two decades.[61] Mobility Partnerships can be seen as a tool to provide leverage to the negotiations of EURAs with third countries. They can be used to propose a full set of initiatives, including migration and development and legal migration possibilities, to counterbalance the burden of an EURA that includes third country nationals. An EU official emphasised that the EU realised that they needed a more balanced approach to allow the EURA a chance to work. Member States did not want to give any positive incentives if Morocco had not accepted to resume the negotiation of the EURA. While inversely, Morocco did not want to restart the negotiations if no positive incentives were given from the Member States.[62] The Mobility Partnerships provided the EU and Member States the opportunity to give the EURA negotiations a more balanced perspective, as negotiations of the EURAs and visa facilitation agreements go hand-in-hand in the Mobility Partnership. It is the first time that the EU proposed a visa facilitation agreement with a Southern Mediterranean country,[63] in parallel with the conclusion of the EURA. The proposal of a visa facilitation agreement with Morocco is deemed to be 'revolutionary' according to an official from the EU Delegation in Rabat.[64] However, Member

59 Steffen Angenendt, 'EU Mobility Partnerships: The "most innovative and sophisticated tool" of European Migration Policy?', (2014) migration strategy group policy brief 1, 5

60 Ibid.

61 Sergio Carrera, Leonhard den Hertog and Joanna Parkin, 'EU Migration Policy in the Wake of the Arab Spring: What Prospects for EU-Southern Mediterranean Relations?' (2012) MEDPRO Technical Report 15, 1, 14.

62 Interview 29 (n4).

63 Sarah Wolff, *The Mediterranean Dimension of the European Union's International Security* (Houndmills, Basingstoke, UK: Palgrave Macmillan 2012) 72.

64 Interview 6, EU Delegation, Rabat, 13 January 2016.

States also concluded bilateral readmission agreements with Morocco, outside (and even before) the Mobility Partnership. These bilateral readmission agreements usually did not include a TCN clause, which made them easier to conclude.[65] A Belgian representative declares that they are frustrated because negotiations are not moving forward for an EURA, which explains the fact that there are more and more contacts between the Member States and Morocco to negotiate bilaterally.[66] For example, Belgium concluded a Memorandum of Understanding (MoU) on irregular migration with Morocco to facilitate their readmission.

Additionally, France discussed bilateral visa facilitation with Morocco in 2012.[67] These discussions did not go further, as the Mobility Partnership was concluded a year later and included a visa facilitation agreement. In this case, the interests of Member States can conflict with EU's interests and impede the conclusion of agreements at the EU level. If visa facilitation agreements are concluded with the Member States, bilaterally offering an EU visa facilitation agreement can lose its value for third countries and make the 'negotiation package' for a readmission agreement less attractive. I can also argue that, in this case, the conclusion of the Mobility Partnership would lead to a less favourable perspective in terms of mobility. As the EU visa facilitation agreement is linked to the EURA, it would be highly unlikely for Morocco to conclude such an agreement. Whereas, concluding a visa facilitation agreement with France would have been more likely. This argument is supported by a Moroccan academic and an EU official, both who believe that the EURA will not be concluded through the Mobility Partnership,[68] as no negotiations on the EURA have taken place since January 2015.[69]

A key aspect of the Moroccan NSIA is the regularisation of immigrants and the improvement of their access to work and basic rights, such as minimum healthcare, access to the labour market and education. This was an unintended consequence of the implementation of the Mobility Partnership, as the NSIA was launched only after the conclusion of the Mobility Partnership.[70] The relevance of the Mobility Partnership in legal and political developments in relation to the NSIA is, therefore, unintended and a combination of direct and indirect relevance. Mobility Partnerships are directly relevant when the new projects proposed clearly aim at supporting the drafting of a new law. They are indirectly relevant when projects support the general implementation of the NSIA with the policy or legal changes being 'side effects' of the implementation. The relevance is more direct in

65 The readmission agreement concluded in 1992 between Morocco and Spain included a TCN clause, but readmissions have only been applied on a case-by-case basis by Morocco.

66 Interview 19 (n18).

67 *Jeune Afrique*, 'Maroc-Espagne, une relation qui s'intensifie', 3 October 2012, available at: http://www.jeuneafrique.com/174027/politique/maroc-espagne-une-relation-qui-s-intensifie (accessed 4 January 2018).

68 Interviews 5 (n7) and 6 (n63).

69 Interview 6 (n63).

70 Fanny Tittel-Mosser, 'The Unintended Legal and Policy Relevance of EU Mobility Partnerships: A Comparative Implementation Analysis of Morocco and Cape Verde' (2018) 20(3) *EJML* 314–337.

the case of Cape Verde. Through the projects proposed, Member States also can lead to the development of policies and laws in the third country. For example, the Mobility Partnership with Cape Verde included several diagnosis studies to help the local administration develop their inexistent immigration policies and legal frameworks. From March to April 2009, the Netherlands conducted a 'needs assessment in order to chart Cape Verde's problems and needs in relation to asylum and migration',[71] which corresponds to the first diagnosis report leading to the National Immigration Policy.

Strong bilateral ties, mainly postcolonial ties, are one of the factors influencing the content of Mobility Partnerships and, therefore, the projects being proposed and implemented. This means that, by proposing and implementing relevant projects, they can influence whether Mobility Partnerships are politically or legally relevant for the third country. This factor is not necessary, however, for the Mobility Partnerships to be legally and policy relevant. Even though postcolonial ties still play a significant role in relations with both third countries, we can see that other Member States can also take an influential role. For example, the Netherlands, which has no postcolonial ties with Cape Verde, implemented an important policy relevant project setting the foundation of Cape Verdean's immigration policy. We will see that the Member States can impact the way Mobility Partnerships are relevant by influencing the content of legal changes, for example, by providing development aid and capacity building. I argue that this influence can be mitigated by a third country's level of power of negotiation, as is discussed in the following section.

4.2 Power of negotiation

According to a Moroccan academic, everything is related to the interests of the parties and their powers of negotiation.[72] Moreover, although the EU is seen as the main negotiator in the Mobility Partnership, the Member States also have strong negotiation power. For a third country to be a partner, there must be an interest on both sides and a geopolitical and geostrategic equilibrium.[73] In this section, we will see how the distinct types of conditionality can affect the development and implementation of Mobility Partnerships, and how the power of negotiation can influence the way conditionality is being used.

4.2.1 The use of 'classical' conditionality by the EU towards Morocco and Cape Verde

Conditionality refers to the relations between political demands and diverse types of incentives, such as economic, technical or political enticements. For conditionality

71 Council of the European Union, Joint Declaration on a Mobility Partnership between the European Union and the Republic of Cape Verde (9460/08 ADD2), Brussels, 21 May 2008.

72 Interview 5 (n7).

73 Interview 13 (n3).

to work, it must be sufficiently attractive to the third country, while negative conditionality has to be credible. Historically, conditionality was linked to the improvement of the rule of law and democracy in third countries, but since the development of the EU's external migration policy, conditionality is also used to push third countries to cooperate on migration issues. Chou defines conditionality on migration matters as the use of 'development aid or related incentives in exchange for third countries' cooperation in achieving EU migration objectives, such as the tackling of irregular migration.'[74] Conditionality and the instrumentalisation of development aid support the EU's migration policy goals. In order to say that conditionality is effective, policy changes have to occur that would not have happened without the pressure made by the donor.[75] The EU and Member States increasingly use development aid to support their geopolitical interests, including the fight against irregular migration. Meanwhile, third countries' goals to fight irregular migration have become a condition for benefitting not only from EU development aid, but also technical assistance and equipment.[76] Though, at the Member States level, the approach towards conditionality differs. Portugal, for example, usually does not make use of conditionality, and its bilateral aid programmes focus mainly on its former colonies, disregarding their levels of democracy or promotion of human rights.[77] Hence, Portugal was not in favour of the EU's conditionality approach, but endorsed it because the country did not want to 'stay out'.[78]

Different tools are utilised in order to implement conditionality, and Mobility Partnerships are one of them. According to Natasja Reslow and Maarten Vink, Mobility Partnerships are used to 'compensate third countries for their cooperation'.[79] They are presented as 'packages', including potential legal migration opportunities and migration and development projects. When Mobility Partnerships are proposed and discussed, the emphasis is put on these aspects rather than on strengthening borders or fighting against irregular migration. When analysing the projects proposed, as well as the surrounding political discourse, it seems that Mobility Partnerships are not much more than a pleasant way to present an old policy orientation: the fight against irregular migration. When jointly analysing the different Commission Communications, which introduced the Mobility

74 Meng-Hsuan Chou, 'EU and the Migration-Development Nexus: What Prospects for EU-Wide Policies?' (2006) Center on Migration, Policy and Society, University of Oxford, Working Paper 37.

75 Georg Sorensen, *Political Conditionality* (Routledge 2013) 68.

76 Mohamed Limam and Raffaella A. Del Sarto, 'Periphery under Pressure: Morocco, Tunisia and the European Union's Mobility Partnership on Migration' RSCAS 2015/75 Robert Schuman Center for Advanced Studies Borderlands Project 1, 7.

77 António Raimundo, 'Mapping the Agency of a Small, Former Colonial Power: Portugal and EU Political Conditionality in Sub-Saharan Africa' (2014) 15(4) *Perspectives on European Politics and Society* 589, 591.

78 Ibid 599.

79 Natasja Reslow and Maarten Vink, 'Three-Level Games in EU External Migration Policy: Negotiating Mobility Partnerships in West Africa' (2015) 53(4) *JCMS* 857, 863.

Partnership tool between 2007 and 2009, and the actual content of the Mobility Partnerships, it can be argued that the main reason for including positive incentives was to ensure the cooperation of third countries in situations where conditionality might not have been sufficiently efficient. Being evolving instruments, in order to keep a satisfying level of incentives for the third country, Mobility Partnerships would have to include, in the long run, projects not solely focused on the fight against irregular migration. Therefore, according to the EU Delegation in Morocco, projects that would have been implemented anyway by the Member States should be included in the scoreboard.[80] According to an IOM representative, it is in the interest of the EU to add all projects in the scoreboard.[81] It is interesting to see that the EU Delegation in Cape Verde[82] does not take the same approach, as it does not hold the view that bilateral projects should be included in the Mobility Partnership in each case. This might mean that, at the time of the interviews (2016), the continuity of the Mobility Partnership with Cape Verde was no longer a priority. I can say that the EU's priorities have been met, because all security-related projects have been implemented. According to a Portuguese official, the efficiency of the Cape Verdean border control improved[83] as the border officers benefited from capacity-building training, such as requesting foreigners to present biometric passports and updating the law on migration in order to have a clear and uniform procedure to follow when letting foreigners into the territory. Moreover, the strengthening of the border control capacity also helped the fight against irregular migration and human trafficking. According to a Senegalese migrants' representative in Cape Verde, cases of irregular migration and human trafficking have entirely stopped since the implementation of the Mobility Partnership, because it became too difficult to organise irregular embarkations, and it became 'bad for business'.[84] Moreover, Cape Verde included new articles in the Penal Code in order to criminalise human trafficking. The Mobility Partnership with Cape Verde was legally and politically relevant for Cape Verde, including the implementation of projects related to capacity building and support of border guards as well as support for the development of Cape Verde's legal framework.

When looking at the scoreboard, the main projects proposed in the framework of the Mobility Partnerships ended by 2014, and only one new project on border control has been included in the scoreboard in 2015.[85] 2014 is also the date the EURA entered into force between the EU and Cape Verde. According to a Portuguese official, the conclusion of a Readmission Agreement and a Visa Facilitation Agreement were at the heart of the Mobility Partnership with Cape Verde.[86]

80 Interview 6 (n63); Interview 7, EU Delegation, Rabat, 13 January 2016
81 Interview 15 (n32).
82 Ibid.
83 Interview 34 (n33).
84 Interview 54, Association des Senegalais, Praia, 2 December 2016.
85 Except the Common Visa Application Center and the CAMPO project. The latter was included in the Cape Verdean Ministerio das Comunidades and was shut down in 2016.
86 Interview 34 (n33).

Now that they are concluded, evidence suggests that the Mobility Partnership is dying. Other factors also show the lack of interest on behalf of some Member States towards Cape Verde. This is the case of France. Until 2014, France was particularly active in the framework of the Mobility Partnership and implemented the largest joint project of the Partnership, '*Renforcement des Capacités du Cap-Vert dans la Gestion des Migrations*'. After the conclusion of the project, France did not implement any other initiatives, nor did it propose any new projects. During the fieldwork conducted in Cape Verde in 2016, the size of the French Embassy was drastically reduced, and no interview was granted because, according to an official from the French Embassy in Cape Verde contacted via phone, 'France is not having any project in the framework of the Mobility Partnership anymore' and will not propose new ones in the future.

On the Cape Verdean side, the Mobility Partnership is also considered to be dead by the Cape Verdean official who worked on the CAMPO project.[87] While the representative of the Cape Verdean Foreign Affairs Ministry had a more positive perspective and hoped that, after the implementation of the security-oriented projects pushed by the EU, a new phase including more migration and development initiatives could start.[88] At the time of writing (October 2019), this new phase still has not materialised (and it probably never will), even though an EU official explained that no one wants to see a Mobility Partnership die, and therefore the Member States will always be pushed to propose and fund new initiatives.[89] An EU official said that, in the case of Mobility Partnerships that do not work well or ones that lost the interest of Member States after some years (like Cape Verde), meetings are organised by DG Home in order to keep the parties included in the process. He adds that Mobility Partnerships are used to show that the parties will continue to work in the long term, and that they should normally be consistent and not show any separate phases.[90] However, Cape Verde, as well as Moldova, show otherwise. In both cases, I identified a first phase focused on the fight against irregular migration and border control, and a second phase trying to focus on migration and development issues, with varying degrees of success. The separate phases do not seem to affect the Mobility Partnership with Morocco in the same way, but this could be due to the fact that cooperation on irregular migration was already well established with Morocco before the conclusion of the Mobility Partnership. The EU official points out that, even though the Member States have political obligations to propose and implement projects, and the EU can put some pressure on them to do so, Mobility Partnerships do not guarantee rights for third country nationals.[91] The EU has little ability to put pressure on the Member States, which are the central actors of the Mobility Partnerships. Financial incentives are not conclusive, as we saw regarding the preferred funding offered to

87 Interview 37 (n27).
88 Interview 36 (n40).
89 Interview 3 (n5).
90 Ibid.
91 Ibid.

the Member States that proposed cooperative projects. Moreover, as the breach of political obligations cannot be sanctioned, Mobility Partnerships' success depends greatly on the will of the parties to comply.

An assumption is that, when a third country has a low level of negotiation power, a Mobility Partnership is mainly used as a tool by the EU and the Member States to impose their interests upon the third country, which may either 'take it or leave it'.[92] Reslow highlights the 'take it or leave it' approach taken in the cases of Moldova, Cape Verde and Senegal, where the same Mobility Partnership text was unilaterally proposed by the EU to the third countries with little room for negotiation.[93] If the third country decides to conclude a Mobility Partnership in this configuration, its content will presumably be mainly influenced by the EU and the Member States. One can envisage that the power structure would stay the same during the implementation of the Mobility Partnership as long as the EU's interest in the third country in question remains the same. In this case, the implemented projects would also largely be influenced by the EU and the Member States, including projects having a relevance for the development of the legal framework of the third country. Cape Verde was considered the 'best student' in the region because of its existing cooperation on migration and security issues, which played a significant role in Cape Verde becoming a 'pilot' Mobility Partnership.[94] The Mobility Partnership included in the Special Partnership between the EU and Cape Verde is considered by Meng-Hsuan Chou and Marie Gibert as a symbolic instrument corroborating the will of Cape Verde to have closer ties with the EU.[95] Additionally, Cape Verde is a small country of half a million inhabitants, which is located 3,000 km away from European land borders. Migration flows from Cape Verde are not a big threat for Europe, as Cape Verde is not located on a major migration route towards Europe. In 2015, there were 108,721 Cape Verdeans in Europe, most of them located in Portugal (57,636), France (22,292) and the Netherlands (11,997), and the numbers have changed minimally since the conclusion of the Mobility Partnership.[96] Furthermore, Cape Verde is highly dependent on foreign, and particularly European, development aid and trade relations. For all of these reasons, I argue that Cape Verde has a low level of negotiation power with the EU.

I argue that countries with low negotiating power are more influenced in the development of their legal and policy frameworks than countries with high powers

92 Fanny Tittel-Mosser, 'Mobility Partnerships: A tool for the externalization of EU migration policy? A comparative study of Morocco and Cape Verde' 238 in Sergio Carrera, Juan Santos Vara and Tineke Strik, *Constitutionalising the External Dimensions of EU Migration Policies in Times of Crisis. Legality, Rule of Law and Fundamental Rights Reconsidered* (Cheltenham, UK: Edward Elgar 2019)

93 Natasja Reslow, 'The Role of Third Countries in EU Migration Policy: The Mobility Partnerships' (2012) 14(4) *EJML* 393, 395.

94 Sergio Carrera and Raul Hernández i Sagrera (n2) 21.

95 Meng-Hsuan Chou and Marie Gibert (n6) 418.

96 United Nations, DESA, 'Population Division: International Migrant Stock 2005 and 2015', available at: http://www.un.org/en/development/desa/population/migration/data/estimates2/estimates15.shtml (accessed 26 October 2016).

of negotiation. I do not speak here about influence on the content of new laws or policies; in the next section, we will see that this type of influence is related to administrative capacity. What I am discussing here is influence on the creation of a new law or policy, as such; for example, influence on the decision to launch a new strategy on immigration or replace an existing law on migration with a new law (but not influence on the content of the new strategy or law). In the case of Cape Verde, the development of the NIP and NIS were clearly influenced by the EU and the Member States at each step of the process. Related laws on migration and human trafficking are also clearly influenced by the EU and the Member States. Moreover, the high dependence of Cape Verde upon the EU also played a decisive role in its decision to sign the EURA.[97]

The Mobility Partnership with Cape Verde included several diagnostic studies to help the local administration develop the immigration policy and legal framework. As we have seen previously, from March to April 2009, the Netherlands conducted a 'needs assessment in order to chart Cape Verde's problems and needs in relation to asylum and migration'.[98] This corresponds to the first diagnosis report leading to the National Immigration Policy.[99] Then, the ICMPD implemented a project under the MIEUX facility aimed at 'developing the Cape Verdean national comprehensive migration policies with a view to reducing irregular migration and maximizing migration benefits'.[100] With this project, the NIS and Action Plan were developed. Experts from the Cape Verdean, Dutch, Finnish and French national administrations were involved.[101] An ICMPD representative adds that the initiative of the Strategy comes from Cape Verde with the support of specialists.[102] A second MIEUX project was implemented to review and develop the national immigration legal framework. In this project, law academics from Cape Verde and Portugal reviewed the current legislative framework and assessed its consistency with the NIS and other instruments. They provided support, coordinated the legislative proposal drafting process and prepared and reviewed a final proposal for the main legislation to replace Law 6/97 and all related legislative documents. In other words, the project led to the development of Law 66/VIII/2014. Another project aimed at supporting Cape Verde in the implementation of the Palermo Convention and its Protocols related to human trafficking. It was translated into the legal framework through the development of new provisions in the revised Penal Code and the new Law 66/VIII/2014.

97 Linde-Kee van Stokkum, 'More Mobility for Development!: Policy Coherence for Development in Practice: Making the EU Mobility Partnership a Tool for Development in Cape Verde' (2015) Foundation Max van der Stoel 47.

98 Council of the European Union, Joint Declaration on a Mobility Partnership between the European Union and the Republic of Cape Verde (9460/08 ADD2), Brussels, 21 May 2008.

99 Fanny Tittel-Mosser (n69).

100 See: https://www.mieux-initiative.eu/en/actions/155-cabo-verde-policy-development

101 ICMPD, available at: https://www.icmpd.org/our-work/capacity-building/multi-thematic-programmes/mieux-iii/sub-saharan-africa/#c7363 (accessed 28 December 2017).

102 Interview 32, ICMPD, Brussels, 28 October 2016.

Before the Arab Spring, Morocco already enjoyed an ever-increasing amount of financial support from the EU in exchange for the implementation of a restrictive migration policy and cooperation on its shared border with the EU. The EU rewarded Morocco's 'gatekeeper' position and disregarded its human rights violations towards sub-Saharan migrants and the need to improve its democratic system (e.g., lack of independent judiciary, blurred separation of powers).[103] Morocco's cooperation in the fight against irregular migration was more valued than its respect of human rights and democracy. It should not be dismissed, however, that Morocco had its own interests in cooperating with the EU on the fight against irregular migration, and they might not have been only financial. According to a DG Home official, as a result of the Arab Spring, thinking about EU-Moroccan relations started to shift, and the EU and the Member States had to give a strong signal showing their support of the Moroccan regime.[104] Closer cooperation through the conclusion of the Mobility Partnership embodied such a sign. Nonetheless, EU support came at a price. The condition was for Morocco to put its promises to deepen its democracy through political reforms into practice, or else it would lose the EU's financial and political support.[105] We will see in the next section that the attempt to impose conditionality on Morocco was not successful.

Since the Arab Spring, cooperation on migration management with Mediterranean countries, including Morocco, changed. Mohamed Limam and Raffaella Del Sarto argue that the EU increased its pressure on Morocco (and other southern Mediterranean countries) and used the unstable situation to put in place policies following the EU's own interests.[106] This argument can be contested, because it does not seem that the EU has the capacity to increase pressure on a country that plays a strategic role in its migration management. Morocco has been considered by the EU as a 'gatekeeper' for over a decade, as the EU has externalised its migration control to neighbouring third countries. Moreover, the population of Moroccans in Europe is important. In 2015, there were 2,507,560 Moroccans in Europe, mainly in France (926,466), Spain (699,800) and Italy (425,238). Until 2008, the relations between the EU and Morocco were chiefly focused on irregular migration. An EU official pointed out that the pressure of irregular migration put the negotiation of the readmission agreement with Morocco at the center of the relations.[107] With the Arab Spring uprisings in Southern Mediterranean countries in 2011, the EU had to adapt its migration policy by considering increasing migration flows coming from the region as well as potential security threats that could arise from the political unrest. As an answer, the EU launched a

103 Mohamed Limam and Raffaella A. Del Sarto (n74) 8.
104 Interview 29 (n5).
105 European Commission, 'Joint statement by EU High Representative Catherine Ashton and Commissioner Štefan Füle on Morocco's Future Constitutional Reform', MEMO/11/155, Brussels, 10 March 2011; Mohammed Limam and Raffaelle Del Sarto (n82) 11.
106 Mohamed Limam and Raffaella A. Del Sarto (n74) 1.
107 Interview 29 (n4).

dialogue for migration, mobility and security with the southern Mediterranean countries in 2011. The end goal of this dialogue was the conclusion of Mobility Partnerships with Southern Mediterranean countries. For the first time, a Mobility Partnership was negotiated with the third country in order to create a 'balanced' proposal. Several officials, from Morocco, Member States and the EU Commission agreed that the Mobility Partnership with Morocco was negotiated in depth,[108] showing that Morocco had some leverage, which prior countries concluding Mobility Partnerships did not have. An EU official declared that the Annex to the Joint Declaration was not negotiated with Morocco and was only proposed by the Commission and the Member States, but this particular Annex was rejected by Morocco, which led to a fully renegotiated document (the first scoreboard) to which projects related to the NSIA were added and projects that were not in Morocco's interests were deleted.[109] Certainly, due to its strategic geopolitical position, Morocco has a high negotiation power with the EU.

4.2.2 The 'more for more' approach

The difference regarding conditionality linked to the Arab Spring uprising was the inclusion of a 'more for more' approach. The Communication on a Partnership for Democracy and Shared Prosperity of 2011 stated the justification behind this move, emphasising that a 'radically changing political landscape in the Southern Mediterranean requires a change in the EU's approach to the region'.[110] Two subsequent EU Communications further clarified the 'more for more' approach.[111] With the 'more for more' approach, the third country must show its willingness to cooperate with the EU on its migration objectives in order to get EU's support tailored to its needs.[112] This new conditionality approach can partially explain the supportive role taken by the EU in the case of the Mobility Partnership with Morocco and, particularly, the development and implementation of Morocco's NSIA.

It is crucial to understand the causality between the Mobility Partnership and the NSIA, as well as the sequential order of developments.[113] The Mobility Partnership was concluded first. Shortly after, the Moroccan King launched a series of new policies on immigration and asylum, which would later be materialised under the NSIA. Most of the officials interviewed agreed that the NSIA was first related to Morocco's political strategy and the will of the King.[114] This does not dismiss

108 Interviews 6 (n63), 13 (n3), 14 (n3), 17 (n3), 7 (n78); Interview 9, UNHCR, Rabat, 15 January 2016; Interview 28, DG Home Affairs, Brussels, 20 October 2016.
109 Interview 7 (n78).
110 European Commission, 'A Partnership for Democracy and Shared Prosperity with the Southern Mediterranean' COM(2011) 200 final Brussels, 8 March 2011, 3.
111 European Commission, 'A New Response to a Changing Neighbourhood' COM (2011) 303, Brussels, 25 May 2011; European Commission, 'Delivering on a new European Neighbourhood Policy' JOIN(2012) 14 final Brussels, 15 May 2012.
112 European Commission (n107) 3.
113 Fanny Tittel-Mosser (n69) 333.
114 Interviews 5 (n7), 6 (n63), 7 (n78), 9 (n104), 13 (n3), 14 (n3) and 16 (n3).

the EU's influence, through the implementation of the Mobility Partnership, on the development of the NSIA.[115] One Moroccan official added that because officials and experts drafting the different reports studied mostly in Europe, they shared European values and ways of thinking, and, therefore, the EU had an indirect influence.[116] According to a Moroccan official, the Mobility Partnership supports the King's will by substantiating it through the development of new laws.[117] According to the same representative, the EU has to act in financial and technical support. Even though an official from the EU Delegation in Morocco argues that the EU had pushed for this direction for several years,[118] EU officials argue that the launch of the strategy was a surprise.[119] According to an official from the Council of Europe, the issue of human trafficking, for example, was not a priority of Morocco in 2012–2013, but it gained considerably in importance and was included in the NSIA.[120] One EU official adds that during the negotiation of the Mobility Partnership, the reference to the Geneva Convention was a problem, because Morocco did not agree on its provisions in relation to migrants' rights or asylum rights.[121] Moreover, according to an EU official, even though Morocco disregarded the work of civil society organisations, it was their work of bringing forth and vocalising Moroccan authorities' mistreatments and abuses of the rights of sub-Saharan migrants that pushed the King to take measures to improve Morocco's image towards the EU and Africa. The pressure of the civil society compelled the King to act and was one of the factors leading to the launch of the immigration policy and, later, the NSIA.[122]

The launch of the NSIA seemingly implies a complete reversal of Morocco's position Morocco during the negotiations of the Mobility Partnership.[123] According to an EU official, had they known about the NSIA at the time of negotiating the declaration, the joint declaration would have been drafted in a different way.[124] The strategy covers several aspects, such as access to healthcare, the right to legal housing and the fight against human trafficking. Another initiative financed by the project '*Promoting integration of migrants in Morocco*', was included as a new project in the scoreboard and started in 2014. It aimed at drafting a strategy for the reception and integration of refugees, asylum seekers and their families, which directly related to the NSIA. The understanding that the EU takes a reactive position by supporting the NSIA's implementation *a posteriori*, rather than a proactive role, is shared by the EU and Moroccan interviewees,

115 Interviews 5 (n7), 9 (n104) and 13 (n4).
116 Interview 13 (n4).
117 Interview 13 (n4)
118 Interview 6 (n63).
119 Interviews 6 (n63) and 7 (n78).
120 Interview 4, Council of Europe, Strasbourg, 21 December 2015.
121 Interview 7 (n78).
122 Ibid.
123 Fanny Tittel-Mosser, 'Reversed Conditionality in EU External Migration Policy: The Case of Morocco' (2018) 14(4) *JCER* 349, 356.
124 Interview 7 (n78).

officials and academics.[125] Morocco set its policy orientations and indicated its needs to effectively implement the NSIA. This is in line with Mohamed Berriane, Hein de Haas and Katharina Natter's argument that Morocco's officials 'play an active role in shaping the country's migration policy', taking into account its own interests and needs in terms of immigration policy and geopolitical positioning.[126] I concur with Berriane, de Haas and Natter and argue that Morocco's agency is often overlooked, with the country being inaccurately portrayed as a 'passive recipient' of EU migration policy.[127]

As seen previously, the Mobility Partnership is a flexible instrument, and the Annex and scoreboard are living documents. The Annex was reviewed following the launch of the NSIA. Four new projects were added to the Mobility Partnership directly supporting the implementation of the NSIA. Moreover, one pre-existing project on human trafficking now supports the NSIA. These projects are in accordance with Moroccan needs. They were first proposed to Morocco by the EU and the Member States, considering Morocco's new policy orientations. Then, an EU official declared that they were discussed with Morocco, which accepted them.[128] In the case of Morocco, the new laws supported by the Mobility Partnership are part of the NSIA and are in line with the policy and strategy put forth by the King.

The Moroccan NSIA is based on the adoption of three laws on migration, asylum and human trafficking. Only the law on human trafficking has been adopted so far. Two MIEUX projects are included in the Mobility Partnership, and they aim at strengthening the capacities of the Moroccan authorities in the implementation of the NSIA. The first project concerns support for the drafting of a strategy for the reception and integration of refugees. The ICMPD works with the CNDH and the MCMREAM in mapping the integration of refugees and the creation of a refugee profile. Experts from the Belgian, Portuguese and Dutch national administrations are involved in this project, as well as representatives from NGOs.[129] The second MIEUX project on human trafficking has been interrupted since 2014, according to a source from the Council of Europe.[130] The aim of the second project is to support the drafting of a Protocol on human trafficking, but the new law on human trafficking had to be adopted first, according to an ICMPD staff member.[131] French and Belgian experts were involved in the project.[132] It has finally never been

125 Interviews 5 (n7), 6 (n69), 7 (n78), 13 (n3), 16 (n3) and 17 (n3).

126 Mohamed Berriane, Hein de Haas and Katharina Natter, 'Introduction: Revisiting Moroccan Migrations' (2015) 20(4) *The Journal of North African Studies* 503, 517.

127 Ibid.

128 Interview 7 (n78).

129 ICMPD, available at: https://www.icmpd.org/our-work/capacity-building/multi-thematic-programmes/mieux-iii/middle-east-north-africa/#c7410 (accessed 28 December 2017).

130 Interview 4 (116).

131 Interview 18 (n17).

132 ICMPD, available at: https://www.icmpd.org/our-work/capacity-building/multi-thematic-programmes/mieux-iii/middle-east-north-africa/#c7410 (accessed 28 December 2017).

implemented as Morocco lost interest in it. The project '*Promoting the integration of migrants in Morocco*' is key and has clear policy relevance for immigrants and refugees in Morocco, as it aims to support the MCMREAM with the implementation of the NSIA. Additionally, the '*Sharaka*' project influenced the lifting of the authorisation requirements for accessing the labour market for migrant workers.

According to the EU Commission, 'those that go further and faster with reforms will be able to count on greater support from the EU. Support will be reallocated or refocused for those who stall or retrench on agreed reform plans'.[133] According to this logic, if the EU supported the implementation of the NSIA, it is because it fulfilled its expectations. According to a Moroccan official, it seems that the EU is only primarily interested by the NSIA, not questions of labour and mobility.[134] The SPRING programme unlocked EUR 10 million, specifically for one new project to support the implementation of the strategy. It appears that there are three main benefits for the EU in the development and implementation of the NSIA. First, the EU wants to avoid irregular immigrants or asylum seekers from reaching the EU's territory. To achieve this goal, the EU uses its policy of externalisation of immigrants and refugees' reception. For over a decade, the EU has externalised some of its migration control to neighbouring third countries to fight the entry of irregular migrants in its territory, converting neighbours into the EU's 'gatekeepers'.[135] The implementation of the Regional Protection Programme (RPP), in line with the European strategy of externalising refugees' reception, aims at involving third countries in the procedure of asylum seeker reception.[136] As noted by Lavenex and Wichmann, the RPP is a manner for the EU to share the 'burden' of asylum seekers and refugees with neighbouring third countries, such as Morocco.[137] Boswell puts it plainly and declares that the EU supports 'refugee protection in countries or regions of origin, so that they would not be obliged to seek asylum in Europe'.[138]

Mobility Partnerships have been criticised for achieving the EU's 'disguised' externalisation of migration control.[139] Stefan Brocza and Katharina Paulhart agree with

133 European Commission (n106) 5.

134 Interview 13 (n3).

135 Sandra Lavenex, 'Justice and Home Affairs and the EU's New Neighbours: Governance beyond Membership?' 89 in Karen Henderson (ed.), *The Area of Freedom, Security and Justice in the Enlarged Europe* (Houndmills, Basingstoke, UK: Palgrave Macmillan 2004) 94.

136 European Commission, 'Regional Protection Programmes' COM(2005) 388 final, Brussels 1 September 2005.

137 Sandra Lavenex and Nicole Wichmann, 'The External Governance of EU Internal Security' (2009) 31(1) *JEI* 83, 91.

138 Christina Boswell, 'The "External Dimension" of EU Immigration and Asylum Policy' (2003) 73 *Int Aff* 619, 624.

139 Euromed Rights, 'EU-Morocco Mobility Partnership: Border Control at the Expense of Human Lives?' (2014), available at: http://www.euromedrights.org/publication/eu-morocco-mobility-partnership-border-control-at-the-expense-of-human-lives (accessed 20 August 2017)

this argument and describe Mobility Partnerships' first interests as expanding the EU's migration scope of influence and externalising its borders.[140] In addition, the Regional Development and Protection Programme for North Africa (RDPP NA) was to be included in the Mobility Partnership in order to support migration management and asylum with third countries.[141] The RDPP NA 'aims at improving protection of refugees and migrants and providing alternatives to irregular migration by enhancing dignified living conditions and opportunities'.[142] According to a Moroccan migrant representative in France, as well as a Moroccan working in an NGO supporting migrants' rights in Morocco, the EU uses Morocco to do its 'dirty job'.[143]

The EU's support for Morocco's new NSIA can be seen as a way for the EU to externalise its migration management and refugees' reception, keeping Morocco in its usual role of 'gatekeeper'.[144] Accordingly, Spanish representatives in Rabat argue that, as the NSIA was not foreseen, all the projects proposed in the framework of the Mobility Partnership had to be changed, because Spain had a high interest in this strategy, as it avoided migrants from coming to Europe.[145] The Moroccan strategy, which regularises immigrants and improves their access to work and basic rights, such as minimal healthcare, access to the labour market and education, is a sign that Morocco recognises its role as a country of settlement,[146] and it could influence migrants to settle in Morocco.[147] These migrants initially may have only transited through Morocco in the hopes of entering Europe. According to the literature, as well as a migrants' representative in Morocco, the

140 Stefan Brocza and Katharina Paulhart, 'EU Mobility Partnerships: A Smart Instrument of the Externalisation of Migration Control' (2015) 3(15) *Eur J Futures Res* 1, 6.

141 This project was included in the scoreboard of July 2017.

142 RDPP NA General Info Sheet 27.12.2016, available at: https://tunisia.iom.int/activities/projet-rdpp-d%C3%A9veloppement (accessed 5 September 2017).

143 Interview 24, Red Chabaka, Tanger, 22 April 2016; Interview 61 (n9).

144 Fanny Tittel-Mosser, 'Mobility Partnerships: A tool for the Externalization of EU Migration Policy? A Comparative Study of Morocco and Cape Verde' 238 in Juan Santos Vara, Sergio Carrera and Tineke Strik (eds), *Constitutionalising the External Dimensions of EU Migration Policies in Times of Crisis: Legality, Rule of Law and Fundamental Rights Reconsidered* (Cheltenham, UK: Edward Elgar 2019).

145 Interview 17 (n3).

146 Hein de Haas, 'Morocco: Setting the Stage for Becoming a Migration Transition Country?' (2014) MPI, available at: https://www.migrationpolicy.org/article/morocco-setting-stage-becoming-migration-transition-country (accessed 27 December 2017); Mohamed Berriane, Hein de Haas and Katharina Natter 'Introduction: Revisiting Moroccan Migrations' (2015) 20(4) *The Journal of North African Studies* 503, 517.

147 On the argument that migrants move because of their need for secure livelihood opportunities, see: Prakash Adikhari, 'Conflict-Induced Displacement, Understanding the Causes of Flight' (2013) 57(1) *Am J Polit Sci* 82; Hein de Haas, 'Mediterranean Migration Futures: Patterns, Drivers and Scenarios' (2011) 21(1) *Glob Environ Change* S59; Karen Duke, Rosemary Sales and Jeanne Gregory, 'Refugee Resettlement in Europe' 105 in Alice Bloch and Carl Levy (eds), *Refugees, Citizenship and Social Policy in Europe* (Houndmills, Basingstoke, UK: Palgrave Macmillan 1999) 106. On the importance of the access to the labour market in the decision to settle, see: Interview 26, CEI, Rabat, 25 April 2016; Interview 27, Collectif des travailleurs migrants au Maroc, Rabat, 25 April 2016.

strengthening of borders combined with an improvement in immigrants' situations and rights may transform the transit situation into a more permanent settlement.[148]

The second interest of the EU lies in the conclusion of an EURA with Morocco including third country nationals. Morocco has rejected such an agreement for almost two decades.[149] Mobility Partnerships can be seen as tools to provide leverage in the negotiations of EURAs with third countries.[150] Indeed, they can propose a full set of initiatives, including migration and development and legal migration possibilities, to counterbalance the burden of an EURA including third country nationals. An EU official emphasises that the EU realised that they needed a more balanced approach to give the EURA a chance to work. He added that Member States did not want to give any positive incentive if Morocco had not accepted resumption of the negotiations of the EURA. While inversely, Morocco did not want to restart the negotiations, if no positive incentive were given from the Member States.[151] The Mobility Partnerships provided the Member States with the opportunity to give the negotiations of the EURA a more balanced perspective.

Moreover, the EU was criticised for striving to conclude an EURA with a country that neither respects migrants' rights, nor has proper procedures in place to receive asylum claims. The European Parliament highlighted the fact that EURAs, in some cases, do not conform with human rights obligations.[152] The NSIA can contribute to the development of a well-functioning asylum system that recognises the status of asylum seekers and refugees and recognises their rights. The new law on asylum will help materialise the strategy. This explains why the EU has an interest in supporting the NSIA, as it will enhance its legitimacy to negotiate such an agreement. The development of the new Moroccan law on asylum can be influenced by the support provided through the Mobility Partnership, as a specific project aims at supporting the three laws foreseen by the NSIA, including the one on asylum.

Sergio Carrera, Leonhard den Hertog and Joanna Parkin underline that the use of the 'more for more' conditionality approach might not be the most efficient way to conclude an EURA. The EU has attempted to conclude such an agreement for over a decade without success. It is doubtful that putting constant pressure on Morocco will favour cooperation. Moreover, the visa facilitation agreement does not seem a sufficient bargaining chip, as not everyone can benefit from it. For the time being, it does not seem that the package that constitutes all the different Mobility Partnership projects would

148 Myriam Cherti and Michael Collyer (n111) 597–598; Interview 26 (n143).
149 Sergio Carrera, Leonhard den Hertog and Joanna Parkin (n60) 14.
150 Fanny Tittel-Mosser (n119) 354.
151 Interview 29 (n4).
152 Paula García Andrade and Iván Martin, 'EU Cooperation with Third Countries in the Field of Migration', Study, DG for Internal Policies, Policy Department C, European Parliament, PE 536.469, 2015, available at: http://www.europarl.europa.eu/RegData/etudes/STUD/2015/536469/IPOL_STU(2015)536469_EN.pdf (accessed 1 February 2018).

be sufficient for Morocco to accept and sign such an agreement. Moreover, as the EU failed to conclude EURAs with Cotonou countries (except Cape Verde), Morocco is afraid of becoming the country of return by substitution for African countries that decline to re-accept their nationals.[153] Moreover, the importance for the EU of the inclusion of a clause in EURAs obliging third countries to accept returnees who only transited through their territory to reach Europe seems inconsistent with the actual number of returns[154] and might not be worth it.

A new programme of EUR 35 million aiming at supporting Morocco's migration policy and the NSIA was accepted in December 2016.[155] Part of the project's funding is conditioned by the EU on the adoption of the three new laws on migration, asylum and human trafficking. The condition was for Morocco to put its promises into practice, or else it would lose the EU's financial and political support.[156] Yet, as an EU official pointed out, since the EU was not able to make a credible threat due to limited political support, the conditionality mechanism was weak and ineffective.[157] The EUR 35 million was allocated to Morocco even though only one law out of three had been adopted. This contradicts Thomas Feige, the head of the Maghreb division at DG Devco, who argued that 'funds will no longer be granted … (and) … will be injected only depending on the results of reforms'.[158] This raises the question of the existence of a hierarchy of issues in which conditionality can be applied or not.

4.2.3 The use of reversed conditionality by Morocco

The analysis conducted in this chapter up to this point has been fairly Eurocentric and shows different methods used by the EU to impose policy changes or cooperation on irregular migration to third countries. In this subsection, I look at the other side of the coin and discuss how Morocco, a country with a high power of negotiation, can also push the EU to cooperate on its own interests. Michael Teitelbaum has argued for nearly three decades that countries of emigration could pressure destination countries by using migration as a threat in foreign policy talks.[159] Several other authors have argued that third countries can use consultations on migration issues to their

153 Niels Coleman, *European Readmission Policy: Third Country Interests and Refugee Rights* (Leiden: Brill 2009).

154 European Commission, 'Evaluation of EU Readmission Agreements' COM(2011) 76 final, 23 February 2011.

155 European Commission, 'Décision d'Exécution de la Commission du 15.12.2016 relative au programme d'action annuel 2016-partie 3 en faveur du Maroc à financer sur le budget général de l'Union' C(2016)8836 final, Brussels, 1 December 2016.

156 European Commission (n107); Mohamed Limam and Raffaella A. Del Sarto (n74) 11.

157 Interview 29 (n4).

158 Mohamed Limam and Raffaella A. Del Sarto (n74) 11.

159 Michael Teitelbaum, 'Immigration, Refugees, and Foreign Policy' (1984) 38(3) *International Organization* 429.

benefit.[160] Jean-Pierre Cassarino explains how negotiations on the EURA can empower third countries and give them the opportunity to use 'reversed conditionality', and Emanuela Paoletti uses the term 'migration of power'.[161]

It should be remembered that, for the externalisation of migration and asylum reception to work efficiently, Morocco must be willing to cooperate with the EU, which means that good relations with the country must be maintained. As such, accepting Morocco's 'reversed conditionality' is the price to pay. Morocco knows that it has a high negotiation power with the EU because of its 'gatekeeper' role, but also because it is a key trading partner and a country that cooperates on terrorism issues. In practice, Morocco's 'reversed conditionality' might even be stronger than the EU's conditionality. According to two EU officials,[162] the new programme of EUR 35 million, previously mentioned, should have been launched following the adoption of the three new laws (on migration, asylum and human trafficking), because the aim of the programme is to financially support their implementation. However, the project was launched without this EU condition ever being met. According to an EU official, Mobility Partnerships are a means of dialogue with third countries, and even though the results of the implementation of the NSIA are not major, it is necessary for the EU to keep supporting the strategy because of the signal that it conveys.[163] Another EU official also underlines the high importance of the political dialogue with Morocco.[164] Moreover, the EUR 35 million project has been unlocked in a tense climate between the EU and Morocco, which resulted from the *Polisario* ruling. It seems that the funds have been allocated in order to show the EU's 'goodwill' and desire to keep solid relations with Morocco.

Since 2013, Morocco shifted its migration policy towards a more 'humanist' and less repressive approach following harsh criticisms of their human rights abuses of sub-Saharan migrants.[165] The NSIA concluded in 2014 materialises this new policy orientation. Morocco has several interests in the development and

160 Jean-Pierre Cassarino, 'Informalising Readmission Agreements in the EU Neighbourhood' (2007) 42(2) *The International Spectator* 179; Nora El Qadim, 'La politique migratoire européenne vue du Maroc: contraintes et opportunités' (*Politique Européenne* no 31 2010); Ahmet İçduygu and Damla B Aksel, 'Two-to-Tango in Migration Diplomacy: Negotiating Readmission Agreement between the EU and Turkey' (2014) 16 *EJML* 337; Sarah Wolff (n56).

161 Jean-Pierre Cassarino, 'Dealing with Unbalanced Reciprocities: Cooperation on Readmission and Implications' 1 in Jean-Pierre Cassarino, *Unbalanced Reciprocities: Cooperation on Readmission in the Euro-Mediterranean Area,* Special edition, (Washington DC: Middle East Institute Viewpoints 2010); Emanuela Paoletti, *The Migration of Power and North-South Inequalities: The Case of Italy and Libya* (Houndmills, Basingstoke, UK: Palgrave Macmillan 2010).

162 Interviews 6 (n63) and 7 (n78).

163 Interview 30 (n53).

164 Interview 2, EEAS, Brussels (by phone), 15 October 2015

165 *Yabiladi*, 'Regularisations des étrangers au Maroc: analyse d'une décision historique mais surtout stratégique', 15 November 2013, available at: https://www.yabiladi.com/articles/details/20944/regularisation-etrangers-maroc-analyse-d-une.html (accessed 12 January 2018).

implementation of the NSIA. First, a Moroccan academic and a member of Expertise France put forth that the NSIA improves Morocco's image.[166] According to a Moroccan migrants' representative living in France, for Morocco its image is crucial.[167] The literature corroborates this argument, and Sakina Abushi and Hicham Arroud argue that the Moroccan policy shift was a way to gain a better image internationally, and show sub-Saharan countries that Morroco had improved the treatment of sub-Saharan migrants.[168] An EU official declared that 2013 was a dreadful year for sub-Saharan migrants.[169] There was a strong international mobilisation on the issue of the mistreatment of sub-Saharan migrants in Morocco, relayed by several reports from civil society and international organisations and by documentaries. Members of Expertise France and the Council of Europe in Rabat pointed out that having good relations with Africa is a new priority for Morocco, which wants to be a major interlocutor on African issues and strengthen its economic relations with the African continent.[170] In 2014, only a few months after the launch of the new immigration policy, Morocco concluded 17 economic agreements with sub-Saharan countries.[171] Moreover, in 2014, sub-Sharan Africa represented 6.4% of Moroccan international trade, compared to 4.4% ten years earlier.[172] This is in line with Morocco's 'Politique Africaine',[173] and it is also materialised by the fact that Morocco once again joined the African Union in 2017. According to a Moroccan academic and an EU official, improving relations with African countries of origin was one of the main reasons for the adoption of such a strategy in the first place.[174] Myriam Cherti and Michael Collyer also recognise Morocco's sudden policy turn as a more proactive policy that echoes Morocco's own political interests for Africa.[175]

Morocco is using 'reversed conditionality' to benefit from important amounts of EU and Member States' funding for the implementation of the NSIA. Morocco is taking advantage of the EU's interest in the implementation of the NSIA by influencing the EU and the Member States to propose projects that financially or technically support the NSIA as a condition to effectively implementing the strategy. They are also requesting funds in exchange for making progress in the strategy's implementation. The CNDH, from the beginning, highlighted the

166 Interview 5 (n7) and 10 (n3).
167 Interview 61 (n9).
168 Sakina Abushi and Hicham Arroud, 'A Migration Bubble? Reading the New European Neighbourhood Policy in the Moroccan Context' (2016) Heinrich Böll Stiftung, available at: https://eu.boell.org/en/2016/06/15/migration-bubble-reading-new-european-neighbourhood-policy-moroccan-context (accessed 13 August 2016).
169 Interview 6 (n63).
170 Interviews 10 (n3); Interview 12, Council of Europe, Rabat, 19 January 2016.
171 Myriam Cherti and Michael Collyer (n111) 601.
172 Ministère de l'Economie et des Finances, 'Relations Maroc-Afrique: l'ambition d'une nouvelle frontière' (2014) 1, 10.
173 Royal Institute for Strategic Studies, 'La Politique Africaine du Maroc', 26 Octobre 2015.
174 Interviews 5 (n7) and 6 (n63).
175 Myriam Cherti and Michael Collyer (n111).

necessity of financial aid from the EU and added that this should be a priority of the Mobility Partnership.[176] Since the launch of the NSIA, funding increased extensively as immigration issues became more policy relevant, but also because Morocco was in a better position to ask for funding.

One side of Morocco's aspirations in its relations with the EU on migration matters is often overlooked. Nora El Qadim exposes the fact that not only economic interests or an improved 'image' explain the shift towards a less security-oriented approach in Moroccan migration policy; 'dignity and (self-) respect' features are often presented as central aspirations.[177] This argument is interesting when used in the context of Morocco's negotiations with the EU, notably on visa issues. Nora El Quadim explains that Moroccans were pushing the EU to negotiate a visa facilitation agreement, because the process to apply for a visa to enter Europe is considered humiliating by Moroccans.[178] Some Moroccan officials talked about the lack of 'dignity and respect' in relation to the procedure to obtain a visa to Europe.[179] The Moroccan population and officials see the freedom of circulation as a 'symbol of economic and social privilege'.[180] Additionally, Moroccan officials find it unfair that EU citizens can enter Morocco without a visa, when Moroccans do not have the same right when it comes to entering Europe.[181] A Moroccan official argued that since Moroccans need to have a visa to travel to Europe, they tend to settle in Europe rather than travel back and forth according to European labour needs.[182] A representative of the MCMREAM added that, because Moroccan migration is becoming increasingly long term, requests for family reunification have increased. Moreover, Moroccan authorities would like the visa facilitation agreement to be non-conditional on the conclusion of an EURA.[183] The EU, which sees the visa facilitation agreement as a bargaining chip to conclude an EURA with Morocco, is not likely to accept this proposition. This scenario shows the dynamism in the power relationship between Morocco and the EU, as both sides use the conclusion of an agreement (EURA or visa facilitation) as a bargaining chip in relation to the other.

4.3 Administrative capacity of third countries

The last Section will present how the level of administrative capacity of a third country can explain the degree of legal and policy relevance of Mobility

176 CNDH, 'Foreigners and Human Rights in Morocco for a Radically New Asylum and Migration Policy' (2013) Rabat 1, 9.

177 Nora El Qadim, 'De-EUropeanising European Borders: EU-Morocco Negotiations on Migrations and the Decentring Agenda in EU Studies', 134, in Marc Woons and Sebastian Weier (eds), *Critical Epistemologies of Global Politics* (Bristol, UK: E International Relations 2017) 143.

178 Ibid.

179 Ibid.

180 Ibid 145.

181 Interview 13 and 16 (n3).

182 Interview 16 (n3).

183 Ibid.

Partnerships. I discuss how countries with a low administrative capacity can be influenced not only in the development of legal and policy-relevant projects, but also in the content of the policies and laws themselves.

4.3.1 Third countries as recipients of development aid

Development aid is mainly constituted of financial support from donors towards a third country called 'in development'.[184] Jean-Claude Berthelemy argues that development aid is classically given to countries where the donor has stronger ties or similar political orientations.[185] Capacity building is tightly related to development aid and will be analysed in the next sub-section. Development aid can cover many different areas, such as education, health, labour market development, and it is also closely linked to migration. The GAM/GAMM as a global approach links development aid to migration management. First, it is a tool to prevent migration, as it is believed that by developing the country of origin, fewer migrants will seek to come to Europe.[186] Second, it is a bargaining tool in order to push third countries to cooperate on restrictive migration policies in exchange for development aid. Cape Verde has been historically dependent on development aid as the country is not self-sustainable. One of the reasons for Cape Verde to seek closer ties with the EU is the fact that the EU is the biggest aid donor, and it would help Cape Verde to secure funding. Mobility Partnerships are seen as tools to attract more funding for projects, not only by both Morocco and Cape Verde officials, but also by Spanish representatives.[187]

It should be noted that the EU is not the only development aid donor in Cape Verde or Morocco. Other important international donors, such as the UN and USAID, for example, fund activities in these countries. In addition, some EU Member States have particular bilateral development aid programmes, such as, for example, Portugal and Luxembourg programmes with Cape Verde, and Spain, France and Germany programmes with Morocco. As we can see, postcolonial ties are not always the reason for a Member State to develop a strong bilateral development aid scheme. Moreover, there are a multitude of actors involved in the implementation of Mobility Partnerships, including international organisations, such as UNDP, IOM or ICMPD. Similarly as the Member States do, these

184 Moosa Elayah, 'Lack of foreign aid effectiveness in developing countries between a hammer and an anvil' (2016) *Contemporary Arab Affairs*, 9(1) 82, 83.

185 Jean-Claude Berthelemy, 'Bilateral donors' interest vs. recipients' development motives in aid allocation: Do all donors behave the same?' (2005) *Cahiers de la Maison des Sciences Economiques* 1, 9–10.

186 The argument according to which the development of third countries will lead to less migration towards Europe has been debunked, for example, in Stephen Castles, Hein de Haas and Mark J. Miller, *The Age of Migration: International Population Movements in the Modern World*, fifth edition (Houndmills, Basingstoke, UK: Palgrave Macmillan 2014) 25–29.

187 Interviews 13 (n3), 17 (n3), 34 (n33) and 39 (n34); Interview 33, Direção Geral das Comunidades, Praia, 23 February 2016.

international organisations cooperate with Morocco and Cape Verde in the framework of the Mobility Partnership, as well as outside of it.

When analysing the projects proposed in the Mobility Partnerships with Morocco and Cape Verde under migration and development topic, I noticed that they are not the most common initiatives. In the case of Morocco, most of the migration and development projects are pre-existing projects. However, some initiatives are worth a closer look. In Cape Verde, it is mainly Portugal and Spain that propose these types of projects. France also proposed one project. The other Member States party to the Mobility Partnership did not propose any at the time of its conclusion. An interesting point to raise concerns a project proposed by Cape Verde to foster cooperation between hospitals in Member States and Cape Verde. As a response to the Cape Verdean demand, Portugal launched a project to support the Cape Verdean national health system in the fields of haemodialysis and oncology. This development project had unintended consequences on migration. Before the creation of an hemodialyzer unit at the Hospital Agostino Neto in Praia, people needed to be evacuated, mainly to Portugal, in order to be treated. Since the creation of the unit, the Ministry of Health noted that the number of people that needed to receive health treatment in Portugal dropped. This example shows that appropriate development projects can have a 'positive impact' on migration issues. According to a Cape Verdean representative in Lisbon who works for an NGO dealing specifically with issues related to haemodialysis, the impact is more tenuous.[188] According to him, the haemodialysis unit was created in Cape Verde, but it is not functional. He argues that the Cape Verdean government prefers Cape Verdeans to go abroad to be treated, because the treatments undertaken in Portugal are financed by Portugal, not Cape Verde. In addition, the unit itself would be exorbitant to run and would require a large amount of clean water, which is a scarce commodity in Cape Verde. Moreover, Cape Verdeans themselves prefer to be treated in Portugal, because being haemodialyzed in Cape Verde would leave them *de facto* out of the donors' lists, according to the same migrant representative. In Cape Verde, projects related to migration and development are mainly conducted at a bilateral level, although sometimes they are at a multilateral, Member States level. When we look at the Annex to the Joint Declaration with Morocco, new migration and development projects are mainly proposed by France, and they include initiatives on skill development or auto entrepreneurship. It seems that most of the bilateral projects on migration and development have not been included in the Mobility Partnership.

In Cape Verde, the EU and the Member States are not the only donors supporting migration initiatives. The UN, for example, supported the Migration and Development Working Group included in the Ministry of Foreign Affairs.[189] The One UN Programme also supported child victims of irregular migration and helped to strengthen the government's capacity on child-protection issues.[190] The

188 Interview 66, Associação Girassol Solidario, Lisbon, 4 November 2017.
189 United Nations, 'Cape Verde, an Emerging Nation' (2010) 1, 27.
190 Ibid 32.

'Migration House' project of Cape Verde consists of migration data research and analysis to develop the government's capacities to address key problems associated with migration. It aims at enabling Cape Verde's government to answer the challenges posed by new migration trends on the islands. The 'Migration House' of Cape Verde is an IOM programme in cooperation with the United Nations Development Programme (UNDP) and the United Nations Population Fund (UNFPA). These projects usually are not included in the scoreboard. I argue that this is normal, as these projects are not Mobility Partnership-related projects (they do not involve the EU or a Member State).

When looking at Morocco, we can take the example of the NSIA to try to better understand the role of all parties and the extent of development aid. Out of the 27 specific objectives of the NSIA, 14 are supported by European projects.[191] Through the Mobility Partnership, the SPRING programme unlocked EUR 10 million, specifically for one new project to support the implementation of the strategy. According to an official of DG Devco, DG NEAR is coordinating this project,[192] which was divided into two sub-projects. The first is a budget-support programme, which aims at financing two primary areas of intervention of the NSIA: education and health. The second sub-project promotes migrants' integration in Morocco. It covers special capacity-building support provided to the newly developed MCMREAM (I discuss this project in more detail in the next sub-section, as it is related to capacity building), as well as an initiative called '*Parcours vers l'insertion*' (Path to insertion) and the '*Tamkine-Migrants*' initiative. The '*Parcours vers l'insertion*' initiative is organised in collaboration with the Office of Vocational Training and Work Promotion (*Office de la Formation Professionnelle et de la Promotion du Travail* (OFPPT)), and it aims to train at least 1,500 migrants on labour and market-access issues. This project is part of the broader '*Sharaka*' project, which aims to support the development of Moroccan employment agencies and access to labour markets in Morocco as well as in Europe. According to a representative of Expertise France, the agency in charge of the '*Sharaka*' project, the part of the '*Sharaka*' project that aims at supporting Moroccans' access to the French labour market, does not work because the border is closed, and with the migration crisis, it is no longer a priority.[193] This project is a problematic one. It exemplifies overlaps of initiatives and maladministration of funding, as the GIZ, the German development agency, conducted similar training courses in parallel to the ones organised by the OFPPT under '*Sharaka*' since no common ground between the different parties involved could be found. According to a member of Expertise France, the result was that every person in the projects' target group could benefit from the programme twice, leading to unnecessary spending.[194] Coordination between the Member States is poor.

191 MCMREAM, 'Stratégie Nationale pour les Marocains Résidant à l'Etranger', Bilan 2013–2016 (2016) 1, 91.

192 Interview 1, DG Devco, Brussels, 28 October 2015.

193 Interview 10 (n3).

194 Ibid.

'*Sharaka*' is the key project related to migration and development, even if it focuses mainly on access to the labour market. DG Devco, the development Directorate-General, is in charge of coordinating '*Sharaka*', and it is one of the only initiatives DG Devco has taken part in since the negotiation of the Mobility Partnership.[195] One of the activities of the project was to map all pre-existing activities related to migration and development, and see if the most successful ones could be replicated. This shows that migration and development initiatives proposed in the framework of the Mobility Partnership rely on past initiatives at the bilateral level. The '*Sharaka*' project also has a strong capacity-building component for Moroccan institutions in charge of migration issues.[196] The '*Tamkine-Migrants*' project aims at supporting access to health care for migrant women. This project is not new, and it existed prior to the Mobility Partnership.

Moreover, as noted already, a new programme with a budget of EUR 35 million aims to support Morocco's migration policy and the NSIA, which was accepted in December 2016. This project was included in the draft scoreboard of November 2017, and it is the continuation of the SPRING project ('*Promouvoir l'integration des Migrants au Maroc*'), which was listed in the previous scoreboard.[197] According to an EU official, this project supports activities outside of the Mobility Partnership.[198] This argument is questionable, because reinforcing the capacity of Moroccan authorities to implement the NSIA is in line with the objectives pursued in the Mobility Partnership. It is surely an unintended consequence of the Mobility Partnership, as this strategy was only presented by Morocco after the conclusion of the Mobility Partnership. But addition of the numerous new projects to the scoreboard, which are aimed directly or indirectly at supporting the implementation of the NSIA, shows not only the EU's interest in the implementation of the strategy, but also the relevance of the Mobility Partnership in its implementation.

Besides the Mobility Partnership, other actors have also intervened in the NSIA. IOM, for example, intervened in 12 specific objectives of the NSIA. IOM's main initiative is the 'integration of Migration in national development strategies' in partnership with UNDP, but it is not only aimed at Morocco.[199] Another initiative relates to the fight against human trafficking, and IOM was consulted by the MCMREAM for drafting the asylum law.[200] IOM, in collaboration with other UN agencies, such as UNDP, UNHCR and the United Nations Educational, Scientific and Cultural Organization (UNESCO), has developed a support programme for the implementation of the NSIA, including capacity building on migration matters for Moroccan authorities.[201]

In addition, several Member States implement bilateral cooperation. For example, the Belgian Development Cooperation (BTC) participates in the capacity

195 Interview 1 (n88).
196 MCMREAM (n187).
197 Interview 30 (n53).
198 Interview 2 (n160).
199 MCMREAM (n187).
200 Interview 15 (n32).
201 MCMREAM (n187) 92.

building of Moroccan authorities and NGOs on issues related to immigration, asylum and human trafficking, which are the themes of the three new laws that must be developed under the NSIA.[202] The German cooperation is dynamic. In relation to the NSIA, Germany has developed two projects. The first aims at strengthening the capacities of territorial communities on migration issues, and the second relates to asylum and refugee protection. A key initiative of this second project is the training of Moroccan authorities in asylum law, including the staff in charge of asylum claims at the BRA. Non-EU Member States are also implementing relevant initiatives at the bilateral level. For example, Switzerland is promoting the right of sub-Saharan migrants and sensitising its partners to asylum law, and the United States aims to counter terrorism by supporting the employability of young Moroccans as well as primary education.[203]

Many of the projects listed above, implemented in support of the NSIA, have capacity-building components. Let us now discuss how the different actors, mainly the EU and the Member States, support the development of administrative capacity in Cape Verde and Morocco.

4.3.2 The influence of capacity building on the legal developments in Morocco and Cape Verde

As previously discussed, many development aid initiatives include capacity building components because development aid and capacity development are strongly interconnected.

Morocco has long taken the opportunity to modernise its own equipment and benefit from foreign expertise by cooperating with the EU or individual Member States, particularly on border management.[204] In addition to pre-existing capacity building on border management (a type of capacity building still provided through the Mobility Partnership), through the Mobility Partnership Moroccan staff working in relevant ministries or civil services can benefit from training and capacity building financed by the EU on issues such as international law, refugee rights, and capacity building in order to acquire the tools to implement the three new laws following their adoption. The legal capacity building is mainly focused on human trafficking and asylum law. The law on immigration is not related to a project included in the Mobility Partnership. Rather, capacity building is aimed towards the development of institutions to deal with immigration and enhance cooperation between institutions, which mainly focuses on the capacity building of the MCMREAM.

Several actors are included in the legal capacity building provided to Moroccan authorities in order to help them develop and implement the three new laws, which are the cornerstone of the NSIA. Interestingly, the Council of Europe (CoE) is one

202 Ibid 93.

203 US Department of State, 'U.S. Relations with Morocco, Bureau of Near Eastern Affairs', Fact Sheet 20 January 2017, available at: https://www.state.gov/r/pa/ei/bgn/5431.htm (accessed 4 December 2017).

204 Sarah Wolff (n62) 138–139.

of the actors, even though the CoE is not officially part of the Mobility Partnership,[205] and it is never mentioned in the Annex or the scoreboard. The activities of the CoE in the field of human trafficking are complementary to the activities conducted by ICMPD under the MIEUX programme, which are included in the scoreboard. Moreover, the MIEUX programme, as well as the CoE activities on human trafficking, are financed by the EU,[206] however, nothing explains why one project figures in the Mobility Partnership and the other does not. An official from the Council of Europe in Strasbourg argues that because the CoE and ICMPD work on the same issues, some coordination is required.[207] Members of ICMPD and the CoE clarified that ICMPD participates to the drafting of the Protocol on Human Trafficking, and the CoE works on the harmonisation of the legislation and legal developments.[208] The ICMPD team is composed of French and Belgian experts. The project conducted by the CoE as well as the MIEUX project are both initiatives of Morocco. A representative of the MCMREAM agrees that there is a lot of work to be done on this issue, and that the Ministry of Justice and the Ministry of the Interior need support. Consequently, the development of the Law on Human Trafficking has been supported by the CoE, IOM, UNHCR. Some Member States are also involved in the legal development.[209] An EU official declares that the CoE supports Morocco in the development of their law on human trafficking.[210] The representative of the CoE in Morocco clarifies that, even though the CoE has been active on the issue of human trafficking for several years in Morocco, they have not been consulted on the draft of the new law on human trafficking; only IOM has been consulted.[211] The Council of Europe has worked on human trafficking in Morocco since 2012 (before the conclusion of the Mobility Partnership).[212] The Moroccan CoE representative explains that the process of drafting the law was faster than with the other two laws, because they had shared good practices with Morocco since 2012.[213]

Concerning the law on asylum, the projects with Belgium, France and Germany are being implemented individually by each Member State.[214] There is an important cooperation with France on the new asylum law, and the institutional support will be intensified once the law is adopted.[215] Germany will support Moroccan authorities once the law on asylum is concluded, and they already cooperate with the UNHCR on international law training provided to Moroccan officials.[216] Germany will support the Moroccan government in the implementation of the asylum law.

205 Interview 4 (n116).
206 Interview 2 (n160).
207 Interview 4 (n116).
208 Interviews 4 (n116) and 18 (n17)
209 Interview 16 (n3).
210 Interview 2 (n160).
211 Interview 12 (n166).
212 Interview 4 (n116).
213 Interview 12 (n166).
214 Interviews 16 (n3), 19 (n18) and 8 (n3).
215 Interview 8 (n3).
216 Interview 11 (n3).

Belgium is also supporting the strategy in its asylum component on the demand of the MCMREAM. They provide training for regularised migrants and refugees on access to self-employment opportunities. They also provide training on the three new laws and their implementation for ministries, local authorities and NGOs.[217] Belgium also participated in a brainstorming session during the conception of the law on asylum. Similarly, UNHCR, even though it is not directly a party to the Mobility Partnership, plays a significant role by providing training on asylum and international law to Moroccan authorities in order to support the implementation of the new law on asylum once it is adopted.[218] A MoU was conducted in 2015 between the MCMREAM and several UN agencies, including the UNHCR and IOM, the former asking the latter for help in the implementation of the NSIA, whereas neither the EU nor France, for example, were invited to provide support.[219] The UNHCR also made informal comments on the law on asylum.[220] Spain also worked on the development of the three laws and the development of the NSIA.[221]

An EU official said that Morocco has a limited capacity of absorption, because they are small teams, and many projects are already being financed.[222] According to members of two implementing organisations, there is a lack of coordination between ministries and inside the MCMREAM itself.[223] The MCMREAM is requesting a lot of funding, but it is questionable whether they have the capacity to act on all other ministries.[224] According to the staff of a technical organisation, the MCMREAM has difficulties using the technical assistance provided, because it lacks vision, and it does not always accept the adjustments proposed regarding the capacity building provided to reorganise the ministry.[225]

It should not be overlooked that civil society in Morocco was active in denouncing human rights abuses, which led to starting a process towards the new migration policy.[226] The CNDH works with civil society on asylum issues. For example, they drafted a document to remind Morocco of its obligations relative to the new migration policy and the NSIA.[227] Representatives of migrants' organisations criticised the EU because they did not involve grassroots organisations that have the experience to support migrants in Morocco.[228] Instead, the EU keeps funding the same influential NGOs, even though their results are questionable.[229] Moreover, a CNDH official declares that the EU needs to do much more for the implementation of the strategy, and they need to unlock more long-term funding

217 Interview 19 (n18).
218 Interview 9 (n104).
219 Interviews 16 (n3) and 9 (n104).
220 Interview 9 (n104).
221 Interview 17 (n3).
222 Interview 7 (n78).
223 Interviews 10 (n3) and 15 (n32).
224 Interview 15 (n32).
225 Interview 10 (n3).
226 Interview 21, CCSM, Rabat, 15 April 2016.
227 Interview 22 FASED, Rabat, 19 April 2016.
228 Interviews 22 (n223) and 27 (n143).
229 Interview 22 (n223).

in the form of budget support, rather than project-based funding. It seems that this demand was heard, because the allocation of the EUR 35 million budget support aims at supporting the implementation of the NSIA. Several NGOs agree that the EU needs to give more funds to Morocco, because they believe that, even if it has the political will to apply the strategy, Morocco does not have sufficient funds to do so.[230]

As discussed previously, since the launch of the NSIA, funding has increased extensively as immigration issues have become more policy relevant, but also because Morocco has been in a better position to ask for funding. As stated earlier, Morocco is a country with a high power of negotiation currently developing and implementing a strategy on immigration and asylum, which is of high importance for the EU and the Member States for several reasons previously explained. This puts Morocco in a situation where it has real weight in the negotiations with the EU on the content and amount of capacity building provided to them. Moroccan officials have more leverage to negotiate funding and capacity building in the areas of interest, needs and issues that they consider relevant, rather than only on issues relevant for the EU (even though both still seem to be going in the same direction). Using 'reversed conditionality', Morocco can argue that without the EU funding its projects, it could not implement the NSIA, which is not in the interest of the EU and, therefore, puts pressure on them. Morocco is able to ask for increased funding for capacity-building projects, because the interest in the implementation of the NSIA and Morocco's continuing cooperation on migration issues are key political interests in the EU and the Member States. This does not exclude, however, the influence of foreign experts in its legal and policy developments, for example, through advice given on draft bills or training provided on related issues.

In Cape Verde, fewer actors are involved in the legal capacity development than in Morocco, and the 'capacity building' provided is more direct than in Morocco. *More direct* in the sense that, rather than providing training for Cape Verdeans authorities to be better able to draft new legislation or giving advice on the legal drafts, as happened in Morocco, in Cape Verde new laws are usually fully drafted by the donor. For example, the new law on immigration as well as the asylum law were fully drafted by a Cape Verdean and a Portuguese expert in two MIEUX projects. ICMPD experts are also drafting the implementing decrees of the new law on immigration.[231] An ICMPD representative agrees that in Cape Verde, there is less training and capacity building and more 'full drafting' of the legal instruments; and because Cape Verde's capacities are limited, it is highly influenced by EU experts.[232] According to an EU official, the MIEUX projects were crucial in the implementation of the immigration policy and the creation of the legal framework.[233] The Mobility Partnership is still considered as being positive because the Ministry of the Communities has been able to develop its

230 Interviews 22 (n223) and 27 (n143).
231 Interview 18 (n17).
232 Ibid.
233 Interview 39 (n34).

competencies in order to better identify its own interests. It is because it has gained this knowledge that it has been able to implement new policies.[234] An official from the Ministry of the Communities declares that the reports made through the Mobility Partnership support government policies, helping them to identify issues that they could not have put forward without assistance.[235]

An EU official argues that the visa facilitation and readmission agreements gave a boost to the Mobility Partnership.[236] Representative on all sides (the EU, Cape Verde officials and ECOWAS migrants) argue that the readmission agreement was advantageous to Cape Verde because it helped it in managing migration flows coming from ECOWAS, which Cape Verde could not have managed in the long term.[237] The EU proposed technical assistance for the creation of a readmission facility following the conclusion of the EURA, but according to an official of the EU Delegation, Cape Verde did not ask for help until two years after the conclusion of the EURA.[238] The same representative declares that the lack of government resources makes everything proceed slowly. According to her, Cape Verde is not reactive, which explains why not much is done. She adds that sometimes the DUE just needs a request in order to proceed, but Cape Verde does not ask for their help.[239] An unintended effect arose from the conclusion of the visa facilitation agreement. Several migrants' representatives in Cape Verde and representatives of Cape Verdeans in France declared that it became easier to enter Europe from Cape Verde, rather than from another African country, leading several ECOWAS migrants to travel to Cape Verde and stay until they could acquire (somewhat easily compared to neighbouring countries) Cape Verdean citizenship, which helped them profit from the visa facilitation agreement.[240] The visa facilitation is not a way for everyone to get a visa to Europe, but if individuals do fulfil the conditions, then access to visa facilitation allows them to enter Europe. Most have the idea to settle, unless they know that they can easily circulate between the EU and Cape Verde, as pointed out by a Cape Verdean migrants' representative in Paris.[241] A Senegalese representative argued that Europe is no longer an attractive destination, and ECOWAS migrants now prefer staying in Cape Verde.[242]

In a context where a third country has a low administrative capacity and low power of negotiation, the EU can impose the type of capacity building the third country receives and adapt the delivered capacity building to its own interests. Cape Verde is a country of low geopolitical interest for the EU and, therefore, does not have a real power of negotiation when it comes to

234 Interview 33 (n183).
235 Ibid.
236 Interview 39 (n34).
237 Interviews 39 (n34) and 45 (n53); Interview 52, Associação dos Emigrantes Senegaleses Residentes em Cabo Verde, Praia, 2 December 2016.
238 Interview 39 (n34).
239 Ibid.
240 Interviews 49 (n45), 52 (n233), 54 (n82) and 59 (n25).
241 Interview 59 (n25).
242 Interview 54 (n82).

requesting capacity building in its own areas of interest. For example, as the prime interest of the EU is to avoid irregular migration coming to the EU, it may be tempting to provide capacity building primarily on border control in the third country. In Cape Verde, a high number of proposed projects are linked to capacity building relating mainly to border control and the fight against irregular migration. This could indicate that the capacity building provided to Cape Verde is influenced by the EU's priorities, not by the primary needs of Cape Verde. Border control is an issue highly relevant to the EU and the Member States, but it happens to be important for Cape Verde too as it shifts towards a more restrictive migration policy. According to a Portuguese official, the Mobility Partnership allowed funding for better border control in Cape Verde. The Mobility Partnership facilitated the cooperation between the Member States, the EU and Cape Verde, and without this framework, it would not have been possible to implement projects that important. According to a Portuguese official in Cape Verde, enhancing the border control capacity was needed in Cape Verde because it was becoming a transit country, with increasing immigrant arrivals that they had no capacity to manage.[243] Besides capacity building on border issues, Cape Verde needs capacity building in various other areas, including in their capacity to develop a sound legal framework on migration, asylum and human trafficking issues. By implementing projects that aim at drafting full legislations, rather than providing training, like in Morocco, the EU and the Member States do not allow Cape Verdean officials to build the necessary knowledge to draft these laws on their own. If no capacity building is provided to them, it can be argued that the relevant institutions also cannot properly implement these laws. Finally, as Cape Verde is not able to attract the required capacity building and funds to enhance their capacities in areas that need improvement, they stay in a constant state of dependence towards the EU and the Member States. Therefore, Cape Verde is more prone to be influenced by the EU and the Member States in their policy and legal developments.

4.3.3 The foreign influence on policy and legal developments

Mohamed Limam and Raffaella Del Sarto argue that the EU 'has been transferring its rules and practices to third countries through various cooperation and capacity building programmes'.[244] Jairzinho Lopes Pereira adds that the EU considers itself a normative power able to lead chief organisational changes in a third country.[245] First, I argue that both Morocco and Cape Verde, being developing countries, are lacking administrative capacity compared to the EU. However,

243 Interview 34 (n33).

244 Mohamed Limam and Raffaella A. Del Sarto (n74) 2.

245 Jairzinho Lopes Pereira, 'Theorizing the EU conditionality policy and its application in West Africcan countries: The case of Cape Verde' (2014) *European Scientific Journal*, Special Edition, 389, 395.

saying that the policy and legal developments in Morocco and Cape Verde are the sole fruit of either the EU and the Member States or the third country is simplistic. The reality is more complex and is based on the geopolitics between all actors involved. The situation in both Morocco and Cape Verde differs according to their negotiation potential.

According to a Cape Verdean official, the NIS started to be developed in 2008 (the year of the conclusion of the Mobility Partnership). At the time of conclusion of the Mobility Partnership, interest in immigration questions in Cape Verde had just started.[246] A resolution was made by the government in order to design a new immigration policy. In this resolution, the government underlines the augmentation of migration fluxes towards Cape Verde, which influenced the content of a new policy that was more restrictive towards immigration.[247] An official of the DGI argues that, even though the Mobility Partnership supported the creation of the new policy, it does not mean that the policy exists because of the Mobility Partnership.[248] However, the DGI official concedes the fact that the Mobility Partnership oriented the policy, as the policy was defined by the reports developed by Member States' experts in the framework of the Mobility Partnership.[249] A Cape Verdean official argues that, in general, they accepted the projects that the EU and the Member States proposed, but they always tried to turn them around in a way that also would be beneficial for Cape Verde.[250] Once Cape Verde built its knowledge on migration issues through the different Mobility Partnership projects, new projects established on the recently acquired knowledge were proposed. According to a Cape Verdean official, the NIS is supported by the EU and the Member States in various ways; financially, as the Mobility Partnership funds the projects developing and implementing the strategy, but also technically because of the expertise provided in the projects.[251] Accordingly, everything that leads to better administrative capacity and a better management of immigration will be financed by the EU.

I argue that the enhancement of technical capacities has not been provided outside of border control. For example, according to an ICMPD official, Mobility Partnerships usually help to improve national coordination on migration matters, which is a great achievement, but this was not really the case in Cape Verde.[252] There were no capacity building projects proposed to strengthen the capacity of the DGI or the coordination between different ministries, although the scattered migration competencies could have benefitted from such initiatives. This is also the case regarding legal capacity building, which would have given more autonomy on legislative matters to Cape Verdean authorities. The reasons not to provide this type of capacity building are multifaceted. It can be explained by the

246 Interview 38, IOM, Praia, 24 February 2016.
247 DGI, Praia, 23 February 2016.
248 Ibid.
249 Ibid.
250 Interview 33 (n183).
251 Ibid.
252 Interview 32 (n98).

interest, or rather disinterest, of the EU and the Member States towards Cape Verde several years after the conclusion of the Mobility Partnership and after projects aiming at securing its borders were completed. It can also be linked to the fact that the administrative capacity of Cape Verde at the launch of the Mobility Partnership was lower than the administrative capacity of Morocco, therefore Cape Verde needed more time to reach a level of administrative capacity in which they could effectively benefit from the same type of capacity building as Morocco.

According to a Cape Verdean academic who acted as an expert for MIEUX, the legal developments in Cape Verde are defined by the Mobility Partnership and the EU and the Member States that implement the related projects.[253] He adds that the MIEUX project aimed at revising the existing migration and asylum laws. Moreover, it is agreed by a Portuguese official in Cape Verde that Portuguese laws have highly influenced the content of new legal acts.[254] A former Cape Verdean Secretary of State for Foreign Affairs argues that legal developments are highly influenced by Portugal because Cape Verdeans are accustomed to transferred legal instruments and want to stay in this dependence.[255] According to a Cape Verdean academic from the diaspora, Cape Verdeans think that it is normal to use pre-existing laws, mainly from Portugal, because they have always seen this as common practice. They only gradually realise that this is not normal. He argues that the problem is that they have not yet been 'decolonised in their heads'.[256] He argues that the transposition of existing laws from Portugal to Cape Verde is an issue because the context is not the same. He points out that institutions are created when there is no trained staff to operate them and no need for such institutions in Cape Verde, for example, the creation of the Constitutional Court in 2015.[257] If this last statement is true, then the lack of legal capacity building can also be linked to the fact that Cape Verdean authorities do not see the need to enhance their capacities in this area, as they prefer staying in a state of dependency. External experts played a key role in the development of the legal framework in Cape Verde, and the influence of Portuguese law is notable. When comparing Law 66/VIII/2014 and Portuguese Law 23/2007,[258] it is undeniable that the content is similar. According to a representative of a migrant organisation in Cape Verde, most of the time Cape Verdean policies are strongly influenced by Portugal, even though they are not applicable to the situation of the country.[259] It is clear in the case of Cape Verde that postcolonial ties have an important influence

253 Interview 40 (n14).
254 Interview 34 (n33).
255 Interview 45 (n53); Interview 69, Congresso dos Quadros Cabo-Verdianos da Diaspora/Universidade do Minho, Braga, 5 December 2017.
256 Interview 69 (n251).
257 Ibid.
258 Lei 23/2007 de 4 de Julho Aprova o regime jurídico de entrada, permanência, saída e afastamento de estrangeiros do território nacional, Diário da República, 1.a série – No 127–4 de Julho de 2007, 4290.
259 Interview 46, Associação dos Serraleoneses Residentes em Cabo Verde, Praia, 17 November 2016.

on the content of the laws. The familiarity of Portuguese experts with the legal framework in Cape Verde (similar to the one in Portugal), as well as the sharing of a common language, makes them the most suitable to work on projects, such as the MIEUX project, that aim at fully drafting new laws. Portuguese experts are not, however, the only ones involved. The risk of legal transplantation is high due to the combination of different factors: a low power of negotiation, which does not give Cape Verdean officials the possibility to negotiate adequate capacity building or to influence the projects proposed in the framework of the Mobility Partnership; a low administrative capacity, which makes them easily influenced and makes legal transplantation attractive because of speed and cost efficiency (which is an additional perk for a poor country); lastly, it has strong bilateral ties with Portugal and is used to legal transplants from Portugal.[260]

I argue that when a third country has a low level of administrative capacity, the level of legal transplants is high because it is less costly to adopt, but also because the third country has less opportunity to develop its capacities in order to be able to draft the laws independently. This is less true for a country that has a low administrative capacity but a high power of negotiation, as it can benefit from the necessary capacity building and financial support to develop its legal framework. Being less true does not make the assumption false, however, as we will see; even in this case, the content of the legal and policy developments can be influenced by the EU and the Member States.

Let us now consider the case of Morocco. The NSIA significantly impacts the Moroccan policy and legal framework on migration and asylum issues. Legally, it does so because it aims at developing and adopting three new laws on migration, asylum and human trafficking. Practically, it does so through the modification of Moroccan authorities' policies and behaviour of towards immigrants and refugees. However, it is usually agreed that the adoption of these new laws is a crucial step forwards. As we saw previously, only the law on human trafficking has been adopted so far. Some interviewees argue that important legislative activity in Morocco is the reason for not adopting all of the laws yet, in particular the adoption of several organic laws before the elections of 2016.[261] On the other hand, the slow process is attributed to the fact that the government does not know concretely how the laws will be implemented, or if the government will have the means to apply them with a larger number of immigrants.[262] It should be noted that usually European interviewees are more optimistic than Moroccan ones. It is commonly agreed that if the King wants these laws to be adopted, it will occur. The representative from the CoE in Strasbourg explained that the problem with the development of the new Law on Human Trafficking, for example, came from the fact that it was not clear who in Morocco would manage the new policy on immigration launched in 2013,[263] which later led to the conclusion of the NSIA.

260 Interview 45 (n53); Interview 69 (n251).
261 Interviews 9 (n104), 4 (n116), 6 (n63) and 14 (n3).
262 Interviews 4 (n116), 5 (n7), 7 (n78) and 8 (n3).
263 Interview 4 (n116).

According to a French official and a member of Expertise France, Morocco backtracked from the NSIA in 2015.[264] There is a slowdown of the dynamic around the NSIA. A French official argues that it is not because of a lack of will, but rather the recognition that the situation in Morocco is more difficult than it was in 2013 because of the European migrants' crisis and the security context.[265] For the most pessimistic respondent, a UNHCR official, most of the NSIA is only on paper.[266] Seeing that the laws on asylum and migration still have not been adopted in October 2019, this last assumption might be the correct one.

When looking at the content of the law on human trafficking, I cannot argue that one country in particular influenced it. Yet, that does not mean that it was not influenced by foreign experts. As we saw previously, several Member States and International Organisations were included in the brainstorming, drafting and commenting on the law on human trafficking and the Bill on Asylum. The multitude of actors makes influence by only one of them less likely. The Protocol to Prevent, Suppress and Punish Trafficking in Persons Especially Women and Children also inspired the new law, supplementing the United Nations Convention against Transnational Organised Crime. For example, the definition of human trafficking is similar in the new law and in the Protocol. Moreover, Morocco benefited from many different training courses in relevant subjects, such as international law and asylum law, which give the authorities the knowledge to propose a legislative act to address their own realities and interests rather than relying on already drafted laws. It is also interesting to note, however, that the postcolonial relations between France and Morocco differ from those between Portugal and Cape Verde. First, decolonisation happened earlier in Morocco, which could lead to distended ties between the two countries and may urge Morocco to seek support and alliances with other countries. Then, the interference of France in legislative matters in Morocco is probably less welcome than the interference of Portugal in Cape Verde. With the law on immigration of 2003, the 'decolonisation' of the law was already saluted. The question of the 'prestige' of a foreign model that gives legitimacy and legal authority to transplanted law is also more present in Cape Verde than in Morocco, which always tries to distance itself from the former colonial power in this regard.

The last point of this sub-section provides an overview of other forms influence by the EU and the Member States through which Morocco and Cape Verde legal and policy developments can be shaped, even though they are more indirect. 'Overt diffusion', which arises from 'the physical presence of the EU in third states', can be one of these forms, such as with the EU Delegation and Member States' embassies.[267] Third countries' governments can increasingly become open to such influence as they grow used to working with foreign advisors or because of

264 Interviews 8 (n3) and 10 (n3).

265 Interview 8 (n3).

266 Interview 9 (104).

267 Iann Manners, 'Normative Power Europe: A contradiction in Terms?' [2002], *JCMS* 40(2) 235, 245.

strong relations with the Member States provide them with 'legislative support'. This situation can open the ground for legal transplants or transplant policies. In both countries, several EU and Member States actors are present and regularly interact with the local authorities. For example, Member States' embassies, the EU Delegation, Member States' development agencies, technical cooperation agencies, etc., are all present in the territory of the third country, and the cooperation and exchanges between them and the local authorities have been enhanced through the Mobility Partnership. The Mobility Partnership is a framework for cooperation and dialogue, bringing all parties together through the implementation of projects, but also through different monitoring meetings or specific negotiations. Third countries become accustomed to these foreign actors, because they interact with them recurrently and , therefore, they can be more open to foreign suggestions and direct or indirect policy orientation pushes.

Several other situations in which 'transplant policies' can occur have been discussed in the literature, and they might apply to the case of Mobility Partnerships. The EU can diffuse its norms to third countries by different means. For example, it can be through *contagion*, which is unintended. In this case, the EU does not really decide to transfer its norms, but third countries adopt them because they seem efficient or a 'model'. This seems to be more the case in Cape Verde with Portugal than in Morocco with France, as the bilateral ties of the first duo are stronger. However, I argue that in both cases the EU could play the role of the 'model' as both countries strive to have a good and close relationship with the EU and to keep their position of 'best student'. Then, procedural diffusion can be the consequence of the institutionalisation of a relationship through, for example, cooperation agreements. Mobility Partnerships aiming at institutionalising dialogue and cooperation between the EU and third countries can also be subject to subsequent procedural diffusion.[268] It is not possible to identify only one type of influence that Member States and the EU have in third countries, as several types can be combined and several reasons lead to more or less policy and/or legal transplant. Moreover, the influence can be linked to the existence of the Mobility Partnership, but it may also be related to pre-existing conditions, such as the existence of postcolonial ties. A Cape Verdean academic pointed out two last points that are often overlooked. The first one is that besides Portuguese experts, the Cape Verdean diaspora also has a lot of influence regarding the content of the laws in Cape Verde. They are engaged in discussions and provide advice to Cape Verdean legislators and the government. For example, the Cape Verdean Constitution was drafted by a member of the diaspora living in Portugal, Wladimir Augusto Correia Brito.[269] The second point that the Cape Verdean academic put forth is that the influence does not always go from the EU towards third countries, but the legal framework in Portugal can also be influenced by provisions existing in Cape Verde.[270]

268 Ibid 244.
269 Interview 69 (n251).
270 Ibid.

4.3.4 The consequences of administrative capacity development

Carmen Barros from the DGI argues that:

> some of the concrete results of the Mobility Partnership contributed to Cape Verde in the sense the country now has more knowledge about immigration. However, these results can also have contributed to the EU: a properly functioning immigration policy contributes to the objective of fighting against irregular migration, as well as a proper implementation of the readmission agreement.[271]

This sums up the situation. The consequences of administrative capacity development are double: it is beneficial for the EU because the third country will be able to more efficiently implement policies or other initiatives that are in the interest of the UE (such as border control, for example); and it is beneficial for the third country because it acquires knowledge and competencies, but also because it might give it a more strategic position towards the EU. I argue that the administrative capacity of both Morocco and Cape Verde improved to a certain extent with the implementation of the Mobility Partnership.

We saw that the EU and the Member States intervened through different methods in the development of the third country's administrative capacity: development aid in general and capacity building in particular. For example, institutions that oversee migration issues are financed and/or created by the EU and the Member States. In the case of Morocco, the MCMREAM was created by the new Policy on Immigration as the first Moroccan institution to work specifically on immigration issues (previously only emigration issues were targeted). Before the creation of the MCMREAM, there was no specific interlocutor in Morocco dealing with this issue. Since its creation, the MCMREAM has been substantially funded by the EU through the Mobility Partnership. It is in the interest of the EU to have a functioning institution working on migration as it will ensure a proper implementation of the Moroccan migration policy and NSIA, which are of high importance to the EU. Looking at Cape Verde, it is interesting to come back to one statement made by an EU official,[272] who said that the EUD was in favour of providing support and assistance to Cape Verde for the creation of a readmission facility. Since the conclusion of the EURA between the EU and Cape Verde, its implementation has been problematic because, as an IOM official and Cape Verdean representative pointed out, Cape Verde does not have existing readmission facilities and does not know what these readmission facilities should look like or if they even have the means to create such a facility on every (or even several) *island*(s).[273] The fact that, despite the loss of interest in the Mobility Partnership following the conclusion of this agreement, the EU was pushing to support the creation of such

271 Iann Manners (n263) 244.
272 Interview 39 (n34)
273 Interviews 45 (n53) and 38 (n242).

facilities could be explained by the necessity for Cape Verde to have the capacity to readmit irregular migrants sent back by the EU.

The second example is the funding and co-development of policies on migration. Coming back to Morocco, the example of the funding and support for the NSIA seems adequate. We saw previously that the EU is heavily funding this strategy because it is of high relevance for the EU and the Member States, in line with the policy of externalisation of migrants and refugees' reception. Even though the NSIA was not created by the EU, it supports its implementation and development by funding and proposing new projects of 'mutual' interest. However, it should be noted that, in this case, the development of Morocco's capacities in receiving immigrants and asylum seekers enhances their position towards the EU, making them even more geopolitically important and, therefore, increasingly able to require funding and tailored capacity building. In the case of Cape Verde, various proposed projects, which were implemented directly through the Mobility Partnership, aimed at developing and funding the implementation of the NIP and NIS. Through these initiatives, the Mobility Partnership raised awareness on immigration issues in Cape Verde, supported and directed the creation and development of an immigration policy and ensured that the strategy would set the ground to effectively implement this policy. In this case, a sufficient level of administrative capacity had to be reached in order to be able to implement restrictive immigration policies, but the geopolitical importance of Cape Verde seems to have decreased. Indeed, we saw that since the conclusion of the EURA, the interest of the EU and the Member States faded. I argue that the development of administrative capacity does not always lead to a better geopolitical position, nor does it increase the potential negotiation power of a country. This argument also counts for the EU's support of border control. We saw that in both Mobility Partnerships, the funding and capacity building related to border control were important. Border control is one of the first tools to fight against irregular migration, so this is not a surprise. However, the cases of Morocco and Cape Verde are again different due to their geopolitical situations. Morocco's border with the Spanish enclave is a key point for the EU, as it leads to direct entry into the EU's territory. The capacity of Morocco to guard this border is therefore key. But at the same time, the will of Morocco to be the 'gatekeeper' provides it with a high negotiation power, not only to attract more funding and capacity building for border control, but also to raise different issues of interest for Morocco. On the contrary, in Cape Verde, once the EU considered that Cape Verde's capacity to efficiently guard its borders had been reached, the EU did not feel the need to reward Cape Verde by supporting its other areas of interest.

As the Mobility Partnership is mainly implemented by the EU and the Member States, rather than by the third country, the importance of the administrative capacity for the implementation of the Mobility Partnership is only partial. It is important to ensure that the policies and laws pushed or supported by the EU and Member States are effectively and efficiently implemented in order to reach the 'positive' result foreseen by the EU. The improvement of administrative capacity is also necessary to ensure that the goals of the Mobility Partnership are being implemented sustainably. This means that the capacity of the third country's authority on border issues must be at least satisfactory, and the first aim of the Mobility Partnership is to provide tools to the third country to efficiently fight against irregular migration towards Europe. If, like the NSIA, the projects aim at creating circumstances for immigrants to want to permanently settle in the third country because they have access to enhanced rights and given the possibility for decent living conditions, it is a positive, though unintended, consequence that must be supported.

4.4 Conclusion

First, we clearly can see that the bilateral relations between a Member State and Morocco or Cape Verde are vastly preferred as a model of cooperation versus multilateral cooperation or cooperation directly with the EU. Even though the Mobility Partnership is an interesting framework for dialogue and some level of cooperation, it never managed to overpass the preference for bilateral cooperation. We see that postcolonial ties still play an important role, as former colonial powers generally implement a large number of initiatives through the Mobility Partnership. As in the case of Portugal, former colonial powers are influential in the legal and policy developments in the former colony. However, the importance of postcolonial ties is different in the cases of Morocco and Cape Verde. The relations between Portugal and Cape Verde are much stronger, and Portugal not only funds and implements several important projects, it also is actively involved in the drafting of new legal instruments. This fact is not only related to the existence of postcolonial ties, but also to the low level of administrative capacity and financial means of Cape Verde, making legal transplant an easy and cost-effective way to develop their legal framework. In the case of Morocco, things are different. Morocco still has strong bilateral ties with France and Spain, but it also developed strong bilateral ties with other Member States with which they do not share this type of tie.

The second major finding is that the negotiation power a third country can retrieve from its geopolitical situation can have a key impact on the types and content of projects implemented through the Mobility Partnership, and these projects can influence the content of the policies and laws developed in the framework of the Mobility Partnership. The study shows that the negotiation power of a third country is also related to the type of conditionality used by the EU to push a third country to implement some policies in the EU's interest. Starting with the case of Cape Verde, I found that it has a low power of negotiation, because it is not geopolitically important for the EU, and this importance even seems to have diminished since the conclusion of the EURA. Through the capacity building that has been provided to Cape Verde in terms of border control, Cape Verde has been able to strengthen its borders and more efficiently fight against irregular migration. Once the borders were better controlled and the EURA was concluded, the EU and the Member States seem to have lost interest in the Mobility Partnership with Cape Verde, which is unsuccessfully trying to start a new phase more focused on migration and development, which are Cape Verde's interests. From this analysis, I can conclude that a country with a low power of negotiation will not have much choice but accept the projects proposed by the EU, and it will not be able to negotiate projects that are in its interests. This also goes for the development of capacity building. Moreover, as Cape Verde has to accept projects that are proposed in the framework of the Mobility Partnership, the Member States and the EU can easily use this means to shape the policy and legal frameworks of the third country.

Several projects proposed and implemented through the Mobility Partnership have direct and intended policy and legal relevance, and I can say that the EU took a proactive position in these developments. The strong influence of the EU and the Member States does not mean that Cape Verde has no agency at all. Additionally, it should not be overlooked that other factors could lead a third country to cooperate. When a country has a low negotiation power, the EU can still use its traditional conditionality approach where the third country is dependent on the EU's aid and support, and it does not have much choice but to follow the EU's directions.

On the contrary, Morocco has a strong negotiation power, which puts it in a privileged position. The EU already changed its conditionality approach to a 'more for more' approach that proposed a more 'balanced' partnership. Then, throughout the development of the Mobility Partnership in Morocco, we can see that the EU takes mainly a supportive role and provides funding and capacity building in relation to Morocco's interests. Moreover, projects proposed in the framework of the Mobility Partnership with Morocco have a different nature than the ones in Cape Verde, as they are more focused on capacity building and training than on drafting full policies or legislation. Additionally, in order to ensure the effective implementation of the NSIA, Morocco has another key bargaining chip with the EU, the conclusion of an EURA. Because Morocco has a strong power of negotiation with the EU, I argue that they are using 'reversed conditionality' in order to attract more funding and develop projects according to their own interests.

The level of administrative capacity conditions mostly the influence on the content of legal and policy developments. First, a country with low administrative capacity will be more prone to legal and policy transplants. Moreover, if a country like Cape Verde has a low administrative capacity and low financial capacity, it can be interested in a quick and cost-effective way of developing its legal framework. Additionally, its strong postcolonial ties and familiarity with transplanting Portuguese legislation explain why the new laws developed in the framework of the Mobility Partnership are highly influenced by Portuguese law. The power of negotiation also plays a key role here. A country like Cape Verde that has a low negotiation power will not have the possibility to negotiate capacity building in areas of its interests, and, as we saw, it will not benefit from the required capacity building to develop its own legal framework, therefore it faces the imposition of projects that directly draft the policies and laws. On the contrary, Morocco, with its high negotiation power, can attract projects supporting its capacity building in relevant areas, such as international law and asylum law. Moreover, including various stakeholders in the capacity building and development of new laws makes Morocco less prone to be influenced by one country in particular. While it is normal that legal or policy developments are somehow influenced by other countries, the problem lies in the full transposition of legal acts from one legal system to another, as it usually does not fit the imposee's particular context. Finally, the EU is aware that a certain level of capacity building is necessary to be able to effectively implement policies that favour the EU, for example, to properly manage external borders, and it will, therefore, provide the required capacity building. A country like Cape Verde is not able to negotiate capacity building in areas other than border control, because it is not in the EU's interest, therefore, Cape Verde will not increase its power of negotiation. On the other hand, Morocco can gain even more negotiating power as it becomes more capable of effectively implementing restrictive policies.

5 Mobility Partnerships

The way forward

The European Union has had to face unprecedented challenges regarding migration. In order to meet these challenges, the EU has turned to and increasingly relied on third countries to support it in ensuring migration management and border control. Yet, the EU also recognised that third countries would expect to gain something in return for their collaboration. Ever since the Arab Spring uprisings and the 'migration crisis', the EU has increasingly needed third countries' assistance in order to manage migration flows. As a response, several major policy developments occurred in 2015. The Commission suggested in the European Agenda on Migration of 2015, that the EU and the Member States should work together with partner countries to put into place concrete measures to prevent hazardous journeys. Subsequently, several new instruments were put forth, such as the new Migration Partnership Framework with third countries under the European Agenda on Migration, which underlined the importance of providing capacity building to the host communities, and the Emergency Trust Fund for Africa, which substantially increased the funding capabilities of new initiatives. The European Agenda on Migration and the Migration Partnership Framework merit further discussion, as they are new parallel frameworks to the GAMM and Mobility Partnerships. The EU external migration policy framework has been noticeably altered since 2015, in parallel with the institutional landscape within the Commission, which has led to some ambiguities, as we will see throughout this chapter. We will analyse the current role played by the GAMM and its instruments in coexistence with the new instruments introduced, as well as the shifting of powers from DG Home to the External Action Services and DG Devco. Finally, I present what could be considered the next generation of Mobility Partnerships, the pilot projects. This evolution of the Mobility Partnership instrument can be seen as a return to the basics, with circular migration and new mobility schemes at its core.

5.1 The policy developments after the 'migrant crisis'

The start of the 'migrant crisis' in 2015 led the EU to attempt to take more effective action regarding the protection of its external borders and the return of irregular migrants. Following the drowning of several thousand migrants since February 2015, the European Council held an emergency meeting on April 23, during which the Member States agreed to follow a Ten-point Action Plan.[1] This Action Plan focuses on the migration crisis in the Mediterranean, and it was officially aimed at avoiding the loss of lives. When looking at the Action Plan, one notices a security aspect, rather than the humanitarian one. For example, points nine and ten focus on the externalisation of migrants and asylum reception, and they do not aim directly at saving lives. Rather, they focus on sharing the 'burden' of asylum seekers and immigrants with third countries. Following the extraordinary European Council meeting, the European Parliament adopted a Resolution on 29 April, wherein it called for the application of a temporary protection scheme and the enlargement of the mandate of the EASO, in order to increase its operational role in the processing of asylum applications.[2]

Shortly after, on 13 May 2015, the Commission published a 'European Agenda on Migration' aimed at designing a 'coherent and comprehensive approach to reap the benefits and address the challenges deriving from migration'.[3] Subsequently, the EU put forth a Communication Establishing a New Migration Partnership Framework (MPF) with Third Countries under the 'European Agenda on Migration', which states the need to address 'the root causes of irregular migration and forced displacement and to provide capacity building to the host communities and relevant institutions'.[4] The European Council of June 2015 requested that the Commission create a European Return Programme.[5] Thereafter, high-level political dialogues on readmission were launched to focus on return and readmission with specific countries.[6] Consequently, in September 2015, President Juncker presented the EU Action Plan on return. In the EU Action Plan on return, the Commission reiterated the idea of proposing visa facilitation agreements in exchange for the conclusion of readmission agreements, even though this seemed at times to be an insufficient bargaining chip.[7] But the EU Action Plan on return also benefited from an increase of funding, amounting to EUR 800 million dedicated to return in Member States' national programmes for the period 2014–2020.[8] The principal goals of the EU Action Plan on return were enhancing voluntary return, strengthening the role of FRONTEX and creating a system that would ensure a better enforcement of return.[9]

1 European Commission, 'Joint Foreign and Home Affairs Council: Ten point action plan on migration', Press release, IP/15/4813 Luxembourg, 20 April 2015.
2 European Parliament resolution of 29 April 2015 on the latest tragedies in the Mediterranean and EU migration and asylum policies 2015/2660(RSP), Strasbourg, 29 April 2015.
3 European Commission, 'A European Agenda on Migration' COM(2015) 240 final, Brussels, 13 May 2015, 1, 2.
4 European Commission, 'Establishing a New Partnership Framework with Third Countries under the European Agenda on Migration' COM(2016) 385 final, Strasbourg, 7 June 2016 1, 6.
5 European Commission, 'State of the Union 2015', Speech, 9 September 2015.
6 European Commission, 'EU Action Plan on return' COM(2015) 453 final, Brussels, 9 September 2015, 12.
7 Ibid 14.
8 Ibid 2.
9 Ibid 3–10.

Meanwhile, the EU-Turkey Joint Action Plan was concluded on 29 November 2015. Turkey agreed to take back all irregular migrants crossing the border to Greece from Turkey against the backdrop of the EU's financial support.[10] Additionally, the Valetta Summit took place in November 2015, during which European and African officials discussed the European migration crisis. At the conclusion of the Summit, a political declaration and an action plan were adopted. In this Action Plan there were five main objectives: address the root causes of irregular migration; enhance cooperation on legal migration and mobility; increase the protection of migrants and asylum seekers; fight against human trafficking and cooperate on return, readmission and reintegration.[11] Following the Summit, the EU created an Emergency Trust Fund to support development in Africa, in return for African countries' cooperation in the fight against irregular migration.[12] The Trust Fund, is presented as a complementary and novel tool to supplement the EU's current development cooperation tools, including Mobility Partnerships. The Joint EU-Africa Strategy, the Rabat Process and the Khartoum Process are used to oversee the execution of the action plan adopted during the Valetta Summit.[13] In the framework of the Joint Africa-EU Strategy, a programme supporting the Africa-EU Migration and Mobility Dialogue was launched in 2016. It aimed at enhancing the governance of migration and mobility within Africa and between Africa and the EU while improving migrants' rights.[14]

In March 2017, the Commission approved a renewed Action Plan on return[15] and a Recommendation[16] to better ensure the effective implementation of EU

10 European Commission, 'Fact Sheet: EU-Turkey joint action plan', Brussels, 15 October 2015, available at: http://europa.eu/rapid/press-release_MEMO-15-5860_en.htm (accessed 4 August 2017).

11 Valletta Summit, 11–12 November 2015, Action Plan, available at: https://www.consilium.europa.eu/media/21839/action_plan_en.pdf (accessed 17 October 2017).

12 Ibid.

13 Council of the European Union, Summary of discussions, High Level Working Group on Asylum and Migration, 5657/17, Brussels, 31 January 2017, 11. The Africa-EU Dialogue on Migration and Mobility includes the Rabat Process, which was launched in 2006 as the first Euro-African Ministerial Conference on Migration and Development. More information on the Rabat Process is available at: https://www.rabat-process.org/en (accessed 17 October 2017). The proposed goal of the Rabat Process is to develop dialogue and cooperation on migration more generally, including legal migration and mobility; prevention of irregular migration; measures to counteract irregular migration; migration and development and international protection. The Khartoum Process is also included in the Africa-EU Dialogue on Migration and Mobility, and it embodies in a way the East-Africa version of the Rabat process. More information about the Khartoum Process is available at: https://www.khartoumprocess.net (accessed 17 October 2017).

14 The Africa-EU Partnership, Support to the Africa-EU Migration and Mobility Dialogue (2016), available at: http://www.africa-eu-partnership.org/en/documents/support-africa-eu-migration-and-mobility-dialogue (accessed 4 August 2017).

15 European Commission, 'Communication on a More Effective Return Policy in the European Union – A renewed Action Plan', COM(2017) 200 final, Brussels, 2 March 2017.

16 European Commission, 'Recommendation on making returns more effective when implementing the Directive 2008/115/EC of the European Parliament and of the Council', C(2017) 1600 final, Brussels, 7 March 2017.

rules on return and significantly improve return rates. In May 2017, the Commission and the European External Action Service (EEAS) published proposals on future cooperation ten years after the launch of the Joint Africa-EU Strategy in a joint communication.[17] This communication aimed at setting the EU and Member States' objectives at the Africa-EU Summit, which was held at the end of November 2017.[18] These objectives mainly related to security and the development of the labour market in Africa, mostly targeting youth.[19] In October 2017, the European Parliament issued a report that included several recommendations for the Africa-EU Summit.[20] According to the report, an emphasis should have been put on economic development, good governance, human development, migration and mobility and environment.[21] Subsequently, on 16 November 2017, the European Parliament adopted a resolution setting their position for the Africa-EU Summit.[22]

5.2 From the Global Approach to Migration and Mobility (GAMM) to the European Agenda on Migration (EAM): a comparative analysis

5.2.1 Objectives and geographical scope

The objectives of the European Agenda on Migration (EAM) do not seem to differ much from those of the GAMM. The emphasis is increasingly put on enhancing third countries' migration management capacities, fighting against human trafficking and returning irregular migrants, much to the detriment of mobility. The main objectives of the MPF are similar to those of the Mobility Partnerships, as they cover irregular migration, legal migration and asylum. Moreover, the negotiation of a readmission agreement was a key prerequisite to the conclusion of a Mobility Partnership. Now, with the MPF, return remains one of the chief interests, as the MPF mentions that the relationship between the EU and third countries will be 'guided by the ability and willingness of the countries to cooperate on migration management, notable in effectively preventing irregular migration and readmitting irregular migrants'.[23] However, there is no longer any mention of a visa facilitation agreement, which was a key element in ensuring that Mobility Partnerships remained balanced instruments. The Partnership Framework puts a tougher accent on return, underlining that the 'EU's goal should now be

17 European Commission, 'Joint Communication for a Renewed Impetus of the Africa-EU Partnership' JOIN(2017) 17 final Brussels, 4 May 2017.

18 Joint declaration of 5th African Union-European Union Summit, 30 November 2017, available at: http://www.consilium.europa.eu/media/31991/33454-pr-final_declaration_au_eu_summit.pdf (accessed 14 January 2018).

19 Ibid 5.

20 European Parliament, 'EU-Africa strategy: a boost for development 2017/2083 (INI)', 24 October 2017 Committee report tabled for plenary, single reading.

21 Ibid 7–8.

22 European Parliament, 'Resolution of 16 November 2017 on the EU–Africa Strategy: A boost for development' (2017/2083(INI))

23 European Commission (n20) 6.

specific and measurable increases in the number and rate of return and readmission'.[24] The consistent difficulties in concluding binding readmission agreements with third countries arguably explains the shift towards a more operational cooperation on return. According to Juan Santos Vara, this marks a key step in the 'process of informalisation of EU external migration policy'.[25] He argues that this informalisation started in 2005, with the establishment of the Global Approach to Migration and the launch of soft law instruments, such as the Mobility Partnerships, but the MPF has led to a new level of informalisation, particularly of readmission, as now operational agreements with third countries have replaced legally binding readmission agreements.

While the GAMM is not restricted geographically, what does differ across regions is the 'intensity and degree to which the approach is applied, and the mix of instruments used'.[26] Moreover, the geographic scope of the EAM is more restrictive than that of the GAMM, as it focuses mainly on regions 'where most of the migrants reaching Europe originate from',[27] with the goal of curbing immigration from these regions to Europe. Moreover, the geographical scope of the MPF is different from that of the GAMM, because it identifies priority countries in advance, while Mobility Partnerships are meant to cover the EU's eastern and southern regions, and CAMMs have no geographical limitations at all. The priority countries for the MPF are Afghanistan, Algeria, Egypt, Ethiopia, Iran, Jordan, Lebanon, Libya, Mali, Morocco, Niger, Nigeria, Senegal and Tunisia. Jordan, Morocco and Tunisia are also covered by a Mobility Partnership, and the EU concluded CAMMs with both Ethiopia and Nigeria.

Furthermore, the Commission admitted that the creation of a common European Migration Policy was a failure, and it acknowledged that the EU needed to try a new method to connect internal and external policies on migration.[28] The Commission suggested in the European Agenda on Migration that the EU and the Member States should 'work together with partner countries to put in place concrete measures to prevent hazardous journeys'.[29] Moreover, the MPF is presented by the Commission as a 'coherent and tailored engagement where the Union and its Member States act in a coordinated manner'.[30] In these documents cooperation with third countries is again highlighted as the pivotal point of the EU response to migration flows. Additionally, bilateral relations between an EU Member State and a third country are put at the centre of the relationship. The

24 Ibid 7.
25 Juan Santos Vara 'Soft international agreements on migration cooperation with third countries: A challenge to democratic and judicial controls in the EU' 25 in Sergio Carrera, Juan Santos Vara and Tineke Strik (eds), *Constitutionalising the External Dimensions of EU Migration Policies in Times of Crisis* (Cheltenham, UK: Edward Elgar 2019).
26 European Commission (n9) 7.
27 European Commission (n19) 8.
28 Ibid.
29 European Commission (n162) 4.
30 European Commission (n50) 6.

Communication on establishing a new Partnership Framework underlines that 'the special relationships that Member States may have with third countries, reflecting political, historic and cultural ties fostered through decades of contact, should also be exploited to the full for the benefit of the EU. … The Member States with the most developed bilateral relationships with a particular country should be fully involved in the EU's discussions with it'.[31] On paper, Mobility Partnerships aimed at developing a more collaborative approach between Member States. The Commission called EU Member States to make more efforts towards ensuring coherency and integration in their strategies and programmes, yet, in practice, national migration policies were always at the heart of Mobility Partnerships. As we have seen throughout the book, postcolonial ties linking a Member State and a third country strongly influenced the conclusion and implementation of Mobility Partnerships.

5.2.2 The 'root causes' rationale

The EAM and the GAMM clearly diverge in their rationales. The EAM takes a 'root causes' approach, linking development assistance to the fight against irregular migration. This approach is in opposition with the GAMM, which takes a more positive stance on migration, seeing it as beneficial for the countries of origin and destination.

A parallel can be drawn with the Tampere programme launched almost two decades ago, which aimed at addressing the 'root causes' of migration. In order to address these root causes, the Tampere Programme aimed at fighting against poverty, ameliorating living conditions and access to the national labour market, deterring conflict and building up democracy.[32] Ernst Georg Ravenstein already looked at the 'root causes' of migration in 1885. He was one of the first scholars to argue that the major causes for migration are economic, and therefore migration and development are two inseparable concepts.[33] Based on Ravenstein's work, the push-pull theory was developed.[34] The push-pull theory looks at the context in the country of origin (root causes) and the context in the country of destination in order to explain migration from one country to the other. The Tampere Programme seemed to follow the push-pull theory, which stated that some factors determined whether people would migrate or not. These factors included the lack of economic opportunities and political repression.[35] The 'root

31 Ibid 8.
32 Council of the European Union (n78) Point 11.
33 Ernst Georg Ravenstein, 'The Laws of Migration' (1885) *J Royal Stat Soc* 48(2) 167; Ernst Georg Ravenstein, 'The Laws of Migration' (1889) *J Royal Stat Soc* 52(2) 241.
34 Everett S. Lee, 'A Theory of Migration' (1966) *Demography* 3(1) 47; Constantine Passaris, 'Immigration and the Evolution of Economic Theory' (1989) *Int Migr* 27(4) 525.
35 Stephen Castles, Hein de Haas and Mark J Miller, *The Age of Migration. International Population Movements in the Modern World* (Houndmills, Basingstoke, UK: Palgrave Macmillan 2014) 28; Thomas K. Bauer and Klaus F. Zimmermann, 'Causes

causes' addressed by the Tampere Programme correspond to the push factors, according to the push-pull theory. Ronald Skeldon, Stephen Castles, Hein de Haas and Mark J Miller have criticised this theory.[36] They claim that it is too simplistic, and it does not take several other factors into account, such as migrants' agency.[37] They also declare that push factors, such as demography or environment, should not be considered separately from other factors that can influence the living conditions of prospective emigrants. They give the example of Eastern European countries where, despite negative population growth, high emigration rates exist.[38] Stephen Castles, Hein de Haas and Mark J Miller argue that the push-pull theory is unsuccessful in explaining situations such as return migration or parallel emigration and immigration from and to a country.[39] Despite criticisms in the academic literature, the belief that the development of the country of origin can stop emigration seems to be vivid in policy makers' minds.

The 'more for more' approach relates to positive conditionality that utilises development cooperation aid as a 'carrot' for third countries that fulfil the EU's objectives. On the opposite end, there is negative conditionality, which implies the suppression of development aid when a third country does not deliver on the EU's agenda. It is also called 'less-for-less'. The Partnership Framework emphases the carrot and stick approach, a remarkable difference with the GAMM, which was based on the 'more for more' approach. The MPF states that:

> positive or negative incentives should be integrated in the EU's development policy, rewarding those countries that fulfil their international obligations to readmit their own nationals, and those that cooperate in managing the flows of irregular migrants from third countries, as well as those taking action to adequately host persons fleeing conflict and persecution. Equally, there must be consequences for those who do not cooperate on readmission and return.[40]

This approach marks the discontinuity with the EU's development standards, which concentrated aid on lower-income and less-developed countries with the goal of lowering poverty. Indeed, this policy approach transforms development aid into an instrument for supporting the EU's interests. This is contrary to the tenets of development cooperation, which condemns aid conditionality and argues that aid should be centred on needs, not on the fulfilment of the EU's external agenda.

of International Migration: A Survey' 95 in Cees Gorter, Peter Nijkamp and Jacques Poot (eds), *Crossing Borders: Regional and Urban Perspectives on International Migration* (Aldershot, UK: Ashgate 1998) 103.

36 Ronald Skeldon, *Population Mobility in Developing Countries: A Reinterpretation* (London: Belhaven Press 1990) 125–126; Stephen Castles, Hein de Haas and Mark J Miller (n201) 25.

37 Ibid.

38 Ibid 29.

39 Ibid.

40 Ibid 9.

With its current approach, the EU runs the risk of weakening development cooperation by making aid conditional on obedience to the EU's migration concerns, instead of aiming at reducing poverty and supporting populations in need. Moreover, making development aid conditional to third countries' obedience could have, in fact, an opposite result than the one expected. It could actually increase poverty and reduce prospects and, as a result, increase irregular migration flows to the EU rather than cutting them. There is a paradox between a root causes approach, which by definition entails long-term objectives, and the Valetta Action plan or a short-term emergency fund to tackle these root causes (the Emergency Trust Fund for Africa) and the EU's emphasis on the reduction of arrivals.[41]

These new tools, as well as the MPF, prescribe out-of-reach objectives in terms of long-term development. Additionally, a representative of a civil society organisation working on migration in the Sahel stated that the MPF and its 'development aid' instruments are considered by local African development actors as 'cynical attempt[s] to bribe African countries with aid', which wrecks the improvement that the EU has made in development cooperation over the last ten years.[42] EU Member States themselves are divided on the question of conditionality.[43] Central and eastern Member States, and those confronted with high numbers of migrant arrivals, are usually sympathetic towards using development aid as an instrument to tackle irregular migration. Whereas, Member States that are also significant bilateral donors tend to argue against it.[44]

5.3 The effects of the shift in the main actors on the GAMM and its instruments

An ICMPD representative explained that one of the big 'game changers' in terms of the dynamics between DG Home and DG Devco was linked to the launch of the EU Trust Fund for Africa. The exponentially larger amount of funding available gave DG Devco a completely different political weight and leverage.[45] DG Home and DG NEAR also contribute to the trust fund through their own instruments and wish to see projects linked to their own mandates implemented. He added that this is precisely the question of the mandate that is very important, because in this new constellation of institutional changes, DG Home has lost part of its mandate and its power. Until the introduction of the new instruments, there were significant disparities in the normative approaches taken by DG Home and DG Devco when it came to priorities guiding EU external migration policies. A major point of divergence between the two DGs was the emphasis DG Home put

41 Clare Castillejo, 'The European Union Trust Fund for Africa. A Glimpse of the Future for EU Development Cooperation' (2016) DIE Discussion paper 22 Bonn: Deutsches Institut für Entwicklungspolitik.

42 Clare Castillejo, 'The EU Migration Partnership Framework' (2017) DIE Discussion paper 28 Bonn: Deutsches Institut für Entwicklungspolitik 1, 15.

43 Clare Castillejo (n41).

44 Clare Castillejo (n42).

45 Interview, ICMPD, Brussels, 3 December 2019.

on return and readmission, which collided against DG Devco's focus on development. Rafaëlle Faure and others suggested that 'DG Home's outlook on migration tends to be short-term and focused on security threats inside the EU. This means that its actions aim, primarily, to restrict human mobility and stem irregular immigration'.[46] However, the difficulty of concluding and effectively implementing readmission agreements[47] through the GAMM and Mobility Partnerships led to the creation of more operational tools on readmission and return, which were embedded in the EAM and Migration Partnership Framework.[48] The mandate on return and readmission is now shared between DG Home and the EEAS, with DG Devco in charge of the implementation of these new projects. In addition, DG Home and DG NEAR are both involved in the implementation of projects related to labour migration, with DG NEAR focusing mainly on the Southern Partnership and DG Home on the Eastern Partnership. According to an ICMPD official, DG Devco and DG Home are still reflecting on their respective roles within this emerging landscape.[49]

5.3.1 Towards the end of the GAMM?

Sergio Carrera and others have argued that the EAM, which is a DG Home policy instrument, is most likely replacing the GAMM on migration issues.[50] The 'European Agenda on Migration' as well as the MPF are based on the principles of the GAMM, which was strictly linked to EU foreign affairs. The European Agenda on Migration is presented as being focused on third countries' interests and development, which does not seem to follow a purely migration-control focus. However, as mentioned in the previous section, that might be a question of rhetoric, rather than an actual political shift.

When analysing the content of the EAM, it is noticeable that no direct reference is made to the GAMM in relation to the external policy dimensions in the Agenda, other than in the EAM's footnote 47, which talks about Mobility Partnerships. In the same section, the EAM mentions the political priority given to 'maximizing the development benefits for countries of origin'[51] by supporting decent work, youth employment and salary- and social-protection policies, which can support countries of origin in improving their economic prospects. The EAM states that this will occur jointly with the work undertaken through Mobility

46 Raphaëlle Faure, Mikaela Gavas, and Anna Knoll, 'Challenges to a comprehensive EU migration and asylum policy' (2015) Overseas Development Institute 1, 16.

47 Sergio Carrera, 'Implementation of EU Readmission Agreements', Springer Briefs in Law 2016; Katharina Eisele, 'The EU's readmission policy: Of agreements and arrangements' 135, in Sergio Carrera, Juan Santos Vara and Tineke Strik (eds), *Constitutionalising the External Dimensions of EU Migration Policies in Times of Crisis* (Cheltenham, UK: Edward Elgar 2019).

48 Juan Santos Vara, (n25) 28.

49 Interview (n45).

50 Sergio Carrera, Raluca Radescu and Natasja Reslow, 'EU External Migration Policies: A preliminary Mapping of the Instruments, the Actors and their Priorities' (2015) EURA-net Report CEPS/University of Maastricht 1, 44.

51 European Commission (n19) 16.

Partnerships, which are DG Home instruments. With the EAM and the MPF, the EU strives to integrate migration issues into the wider external and development policies framework, enhancing the role played by DG Devco. Moreover, the influence of the EEAS is evident when the EAM states the need to 'step up' the role of the EU Delegations in third countries to guarantee greater coordination and information sharing as well as the need to mainstream migration issues into development cooperation.[52] The EEAS has earned political influence and now has a role in the coordination of external dimension components, which expands the role of the EU Delegations on migration-related issues. Arguably, the EAM has not yet fully replaced the GAMM, because the former is truly global while the EAM only refers to some strategic countries. However, according to an ICMPD representative, DG Home is currently cornered by the EEAS and DG Devco, which makes the GAMM much less relevant than it was.[53] Even though there has been no political courage to 'kill' the GAMM, nothing has been done to revive it either, relegating it being one tool among many included in much larger packages provided to partner countries.

5.3.2 Towards the end of the Mobility Partnerships and Common Agendas for Migration and Mobility (CAMMs)?

The GAMM is implemented through two specific instruments: the Common Agendas for Migration and Mobility (CAMM) and the Mobility Partnerships. A key component of the MPF is the EU compact. EU compacts resort to 'all means available' to fight irregular migration and externalise the reception of migrants and refugees to third countries; 'all means available' includes development aid policy tools. Compacts are tailored country packages, and they combine aspects from different EU instruments and policies. They are mainly meant to generate tangible results in curbing the flow of irregular migrants by boosting assistance for those in need in their countries of origin and transit.

Natasja Reslow and Juan Santos Vara argue that the Partnership Framework may be substituting Mobility Partnerships as the new tool for cooperation with third countries on migration issues.[54] This argument should be much more nuanced. First, Mobility Partnerships have not (yet) been replaced. In the eastern EU, partner countries are still very much attached to Mobility Partnerships, and most countries, such as Moldova or Belarus, for example, are still actively using them as frameworks for cooperation with EU Member States. Moreover, the 20 key deliverables for 2020 for the Eastern Partnership[55] still make direct reference to Mobility Partnerships in point 17, which

52 European Commission (n19) 8.
53 Interview (n45)
54 Natasja Reslow 'Transformation or continuity? EU external migration policy in the aftermath of the migrant crisis' 106 in Sergio Carrera, Juan Santos Vara and Tineke Strik (eds), *Constitutionalising the External Dimensions of EU Migration Policies in Times of Crisis* (Cheltenham, UK: Edward Elgar 2019); Juan Santos Vara (n25) 26.
55 European Commission, 'Eastern Partnership – 20 Deliverables for 2020 Focusing on key priorities and tangible results', SWD(2017) 300 final, Brussels 9 June 2017.

underlines the importance of the instrument for visa liberation dialogues. High-Level Mobility Partnership meetings are still being held in this region. However, in the south, the situation is much more problematic, because many new instruments, such as the Migration Partnership Framework and the Trust Fund for Africa, were put into place. Furthermore, the lack of progress related to the conclusion of readmission agreements within the framework of Mobility Partnerships in the Mediterranean region led, according to an ICMPD representative, to a 'crisis of purpose' within DG Home.[56] In 2017, DG Home decided to stop organising meetings supporting the governance of Mobility Partnerships and started an internal reflection on the future of the instrument. The ICMPD representative added that, just as with the GAMM, nobody took any political decision to bring Mobility Partnerships to an end, and currently there is no political courage to do so. He also added that, rather than putting an end to Mobility Partnerships, the decision was made to put them on hold, at least temporarily, until the next Commission proposes a new migration package in 2020,[57] with the hope that it will provide a bit of an impetus to Mobility Partnerships. Nevertheless, Mobility Partnerships are still being implemented. An ICMPD representative underlined that ICMPD was 'injecting a bit of life' into the instrument by financing the implementation of two new Mobility Partnership projects in Morocco and Jordan through the Mobility Partnership Facility.[58] Arguably, in the south, Mobility Partnerships have not been fully replaced by the Migration Partnership Framework or other new instruments, but they were side-lined while DG Home became politically weaker and the EEAS proposed a whole set of new instruments. Mobility Partnerships lost leverage, and they are no longer *the* main instrument of cooperation with third countries. Rather, they are one instrument among many others.

The CAMM is a soft law instrument designed as a substitute to Mobility Partnerships for third countries who are not yet ready to fully commit to collaboration on all areas required to conclude a Mobility Partnership, mainly the conclusion of a Readmission Agreement in return for a Visa Facilitation Agreement.[59] Moreover, the CAMM is not a static instrument, and it may evolve into a Mobility Partnership over time. Three CAMMs have been concluded: one with Ethiopia,[60] one with Nigeria,[61]

56 Interview (n45).

57 Florence Schulz, 'Von der Leyen promises new migration package in first half of 2020', *Euractive* 12 November 2019, available at: https://www.euractiv.com/section/future-eu/news/von-der-leyen-promises-new-migration-package-in-first-half-of-2020 (accessed 18 December 2019).

58 The Mobility Partnership Facility (MPF) is an EU-funded initiative contributing to the operationalisation of the Global Approach to Migration and Mobility (GAMM), available at: https://www.icmpd.org/our-work/capacity-building/european-and-global-initiatives/mobility-partnership-facility-mpf (accessed 15 December 2019).

59 Paula García Andrade and Ivan Martín (n181) 34.

60 Council of the European Union, 'Joint declaration on a Common Agenda on Migration and Mobility between the Federal Democratic Republic of Ethiopia and the European Union and its Member States', Brussels 11 November 2015.

61 Council of the European Union, 'Joint Declaration on a Common Agenda on Migration and Mobility between the Federal Republic of Nigeria and the European Union and its Member States', Brussels 12 March 2015.

and one with India.[62] All concluded CAMMs are built on the same model, including a preamble summarising the existing cooperation between the EU and the third country and a list of the main objectives of the tool. These objectives follow the four pillars structure of the GAMM. The areas of action of the CAMM are 'research, data collection, exchange of best practices and capacity building', but no specific projects were proposed in the CAMM's Joint Declaration.[63] All CAMMs have been concluded contemporaneously with the introduction of the set of new instruments following the 'migrants crisis' in 2015. For example, the CAMM with Ethiopia was signed at the end of the Valletta Summit, and it is funded through the EUTF.[64] Additionally, Ethiopia has been chosen as a pilot project for the MPF in the form of a 'compact'. In Nigeria, shortly following the conclusion of the CAMM, the MPF was introduced, also in the form of a compact, which focuses on combatting human trafficking and overlaps with the scope of action of the CAMM; the EUTF finances initiatives on return, reintegration and humanitarian support as well as the initiatives included under the compacts.[65] It becomes clear, again, that CAMMs coexist with and thanks to other key instruments, such as the Trust Fund. According to an ICMPD representative, CAMMs are dead, and no mention is of them directly anymore.[66] They have all been, at least in the facts, replaced by new instruments. The proliferation of all these instruments overlapping and working in parallel to each other has led to confusion on the partner countries' side. One Ethiopian official working on migration justifiably commented, 'We do not have clarity between these bilateral processes. It is not useful to have all these different names for what is, essentially, the same thing'.[67]

It is still uncertain to what extent the inter-DG relations are leading to collaboration or competition when it comes to cooperation between the EU and third countries on migration issues. According to Claire Castillejo, some observers see the MPF as being constructive in pressing various EU institutions to cooperate on migration and enhancing policy coherence.[68] I argue, on the contrary, that all of these instruments show a lack of coherence and clear divergencies of interests between the main actors, which has led to greater competition. The overlapping of instruments put forth by DG Home, on the one hand, and the EEAS and DG Devco, on the other, has led to a dilution of the channels of cooperation with third countries, as the different DGs and services push for their own rationales and use different types of conditionality.

62 Council of the European Union, 'Joint Declaration on a Common Agenda on Migration and Mobility between India and the European Union and its Member States', Brussels 29 March 2016.
63 Paula García Andrade and Ivan Martín (n181) 35.
64 Castillejo (n42) 26.
65 Castillejo (n41) 9.
66 Interview (n45).
67 Castillejo (n42) 20.
68 Ibid 19.

5.4 Legal pathways: the case of pilot projects

According to the Commission, improved and tailor-made cooperation on legal migration with third countries will support the reduction of irregular migration, contribute to filling gaps in particular areas of Member States' labour markets and encourage cooperation on migration management in general, including readmission and returns.[69] Following this idea, the Commission has developed, together with EU Member States, several pilot projects with African countries to encourage legal migration schemes for work or training reasons. The effective implementation of pilot projects relies on several stakeholders, including the engagement of the private sector.

Ten African countries were chosen to benefit from these pilot projects: Morocco and Tunisia, with whom the EU had concluded Mobility Partnerships; Ethiopia and Nigeria, with whom the EU had concluded CAMMs; Egypt, which is part of a comprehensive migration dialogue;[70] Guinea, The Gambia and Niger, who have cooperated with the EU on return and readmission issues; and Senegal and Ghana, who are priority sending countries.[71] Four pilot projects on legal migration are currently being implemented with Egypt, Morocco, Nigeria and Tunisia. The countries were selected based on Member States' feedback and the EU's interest in collaborating with these countries.

Pilot projects must be based on a comprehensive analysis of labour market offer and demand in EU Member States and countries of origin, with an inclination for temporary forms of migration, which might comprise circular migration schemes. It is interesting to note that this correlates with the original rationale behind Mobility Partnerships.[72] According to the Commission, thanks to Mobility Partnerships and circular migration schemes, the EU could solve the problem of labour market shortages by allowing legal labour migrants entry into the labour market proportionally to EU Member States' needs.[73] This explains why legal migration was presented as one of the main goals of Mobility Partnerships. However, with the economic crisis of 2008, the triple-win approach quickly lost its momentum as labour needs in Member States decreased.[74] Currently, the unemployment rate in the EU is the lowest since before January

69 European Parliament, 'Growing impact of EU migration policy on development cooperation', Briefing October 2016.

70 More information is available at: https://eeas.europa.eu/delegations/egypt_en/37530/1st%20Session%20of%20the%20EU-Egypt%20Migration%20Dialogue (accessed 15 December 2019).

71 Kate Hooper, *Exploring New Legal Migration Pathways: Lessons from Pilot Projects* (Washington, DC: Migration Policy Institute 2019) 1, 2.

72 Nicolas Sarkozy and Wolfgang Schäuble, 'New European Migration Policy, a Franco-German plan presented by Nicolas Sarkozy and Wolfgang Schäuble to G6 immigration ministers meeting in the UK', 26 October 2006 1.

73 Anna Triandafyllidou, 'Circular migration: Introductory remarks', 1 in Anna Triandafyllidou, *Circular migration between European and its neighbourhood: choice or necessity?* (Oxford: Oxford University Press 2013) 7.

74 Stephen Castles and Derya Ozkul (n85) 27; Piyasiri Wickramasekara, 'Circular Migration: A Triple Win or a Dead End' (2011) International Labour Organization.

2000.[75] Additionally, the pilot projects could also create longer term migration recruitment, should Member States be willing to do so and take into account third countries' worries about brain drain. There are examples of successful projects with more long-term perspectives, such as the German Triple-Win Programme.[76] This programme aimed at hiring nurses from Serbia, Bosnia and Herzegovina, the Philippines and Tunisia in order to palliate nurse shortages in Germany.

Through the Mobility Partnership Facility, ICMPD is currently in charge of supporting the implementation of pilot projects by providing funding to Member States. So far, they have funded four pilot projects. The first one is called 'Digital Explorers',[77] and it is implemented by Enterprise Lithuania in cooperation with Afriko, Diversity Development Group, Code Academy and Ventures Platform Foundation. In this project Enterprise Lithuania recruited 50 Nigerian ICT specialists who went to Lithuania to work in private ICT companies for up to one year. At the end of the year, the specialists will be reintegrated into the Nigerian labour market. The second pilot project, 'Pilot Project Addressing Labour Shortages through Innovative Labour Migration Models (PALIM)', is being implemented between Morocco and Enabel, the Belgian Development Agency. This is again an ICT related project, but, in this case, 80 young Moroccans without ICT experience travelled to Belgium in March 2019 in order to gain ICT skills. After the technical training programme, 30 of the Moroccan trainees will stay in Belgium to work permanently, while the other 50 will go back to Morocco, where they will be supported in finding jobs and applying the skills they learned in their national context.[78] The third project, High Opportunity for Mediterranean Executive Recruitment (HOMERe), is implemented between France, Egypt, Tunisia and Morocco. The project is not really a pilot, as it started over ten years ago and has been very successful, according to an ICMPD official. The goal of this project is to offer internships to up to 250 young graduates from Egypt, Tunisia and Morocco in French multinational companies that have branches in those three countries. First, the young graduates spend 18 months training in France, then they return to their countries of origin to work in the local branches of these companies. The sectors covered by this project are ICT, blue economy, tourism, climate, energy, entrepreneurship and administration.[79] Finally, the fourth pilot

75 Eurostat, 'Unemployment Statistics', October 2019, available at: https://ec.europa.eu/eurostat/statistics-explained/index.php/Unemployment_statistics (accessed 15 December 2019).

76 More about the programme is available at: https://www.giz.de/en/worldwide/41533.html (accessed 15 December 2019).

77 More information is available at: https://www.icmpd.org/fileadmin/ICMPD-Website/3._Digital_Explorers.pdf (accessed 15 December 2019).

78 More information is available at: https://www.icmpd.org/fileadmin/user_upload/Pilot_Project_Addressing_Labour_Shortages_through_Innovative_Labour_Migration_Models.pdf (accessed 15 December 2019).

79 More information is available at: https://www.icmpd.org/fileadmin/user_upload/High_Opportunity_for_Mediterranean_Executive_Recruitment.pdf (accessed 15 December 2019).

project, 'Young Generation As Change Agents', is implemented by the Spanish Ministry of Science, Innovation and Universities via the Spanish Service for the Internationalisation of Education in cooperation with the Spanish Ministry of Labour, Migration and Social Security; the Moroccan Ministry in charge of Moroccans Living Abroad and Migration Affairs; the Moroccan Ministry of Employment and Social Affairs and IOM. The project relates to the mobility of Moroccan Master's students who want to spend one year studying in Spain. At the end of the Master's degree, the project provides students returning to Morocco with mentorship and personalised, customised support to help them start their own businesses.[80]

Currently, the interest of the Commission for these pilot projects on labour migration are high, and EU Member States have realised that they need to cover gaps in their labour markets. According to an ICMPD representative, pilot projects will be on the new agenda.[81] He added that Eastern European countries have shown high interest in pilot projects through Mobility Partnerships, because they still consider Mobility Partnerships the backbone of their cooperation with the EU. In parallel, the Commission continues to urge Member States to continue to develop pilot projects, broadening the geographical focus beyond North Africa.[82]

5.5 Conclusion

This chapter gives a general overview of the place and relevance of Mobility Partnerships in the EU external migration policy framework as of the time of writing. The 'migrant crisis' led to a state of emergency, which required a strong response from the EU. Since 2015, the response has taken the form of a proliferation of migration management instruments. While it is true that, through the introduction of the new instruments following the 'migrant crisis', the GAMM and its instruments, Mobility Partnerships and CAMMs, have lost a lot of their momentum and attractiveness. The proliferation of instruments being implemented concomitantly has led to a situation where no instrument can be considered *the* key instrument for cooperation with third countries, ineluctably having a negative impact on the influence of each individual instrument. However, this issue has also affected instruments other than Mobility Partnerships, such as, for example, the MPF and the Compacts. The only key instrument currently in place is the EUTF, because of the resources allocated to it, which amount to several billion Euros, an all-time high in terms of EU funding. However, as it is an emergency instrument, its future remains unclear.

However, my analysis has found that Mobility Partnerships are not yet dead, although their influence varies significantly from one region to another. They have

80 More information is available at: https://www.icmpd.org/fileadmin/user_upload/Young_Generation_As_Change_Agents.pdf (accessed 15 December 2019).

81 Interview (n45).

82 European Commission, 'The Delivery of the European Agenda on Migration' COM (2017) 558 final, Brussels, 27 September 2017.

lost a lot of influence in the south because they are now in competition with a broad range of new instruments on similar issues. However, in the east, the situation is different. Indeed, Mobility Partnerships are still being used by Eastern Partnership countries as the main framework of cooperation with the EU, and the appetite for the instrument does not seem to have faded. This can be explained by the fact that the plethora of new instruments implemented since 2015 have focused only on Africa and the Mediterranean, meaning that no significant new instruments have been competing with Mobility Partnerships in the east. Additionally, it seems that a new type of instrument, the pilot project, comes as an extension to Mobility Partnerships, focusing on the development of legal pathways and based on the Mobility Partnerships' early model.

The findings in this research also provide insights into policy changes or, more accurately, revisits. When analysing the content of the new policy instruments, we can see that there are no major innovations. Addressing the root causes of migration brings us back 20 years, to the introduction of the Tampere programme, which took a very similar approach with very few results. Even though the literature has been quite vocal about the fact that more development usually leads to more, not less, migration, it seems to have been overlooked by policy makers. Moreover, this 'new' policy orientation does not actually bring much novelty in the EU external migration policy landscape as its (unstated) end goal is still the fight against irregular migration towards the EU. Another non-novelty is the idea of circular migration as a way to open legal pathways for migration. The new pilot projects are built on the same model as the Mobility Packages, which then became Mobility Partnerships. While the economic situation at the time of the first implementation of Mobility Partnerships led to the quick cessation of all projects focusing on circular migration, the current low unemployment rates and increased needs for specific categories of workers have helped revive the idea. Here again, one cannot help but wonder whether policy makers have taken into account the criticisms towards these types of schemes.

Finally, due to the fast-paced changes in the field of EU external relations, further analysis will be required. It will be interesting to see how Mobility Partnerships evolve with the start of the new Commission in early 2020, whether they manage to gain back some momentum, or they fully disappear from the policy landscape. It would also be interesting to see how pilot projects evolve, and whether they can complement Mobility Partnerships by creating new mobility channels for citizens of third countries.

Conclusion

In the preceding chapters, we examined the legal and policy relevance of Mobility Partnerships for the development and implementation of migration policies and laws in third countries and analysed what factors could influence this relevance. The three main factors that we looked at were: the state of relations between third countries and EU Member States, the power of negotiation of a third country and its level of administrative capacity. The book combined a comparative legal analysis of the development of the legal frameworks in Morocco and Cape Verde with an empirical study of the implementation of Mobility Partnerships' projects in relation to national migration strategies. The empirical findings in this study provide a new understanding of the implementation of Mobility Partnerships. Indeed, this book makes a considerable contribution to the understanding of the stage of implementation[1] of Mobility Partnerships, the interests of all parties in the implementation and the expectations of the actors for the future of these Mobility Partnerships.[2]

Before looking at the relevance of Mobility Partnerships, it was essential to know what Mobility Partnerships had managed to deliver so far. In Chapter 2, I first looked at the factors leading to the conclusion of the Mobility Partnerships with Cape Verde and Morocco. Then I conducted a thorough analysis of their implementation. With this analysis I gained interesting insights about the types of projects being implemented, the main policy areas covered by projects and, importantly for this research, I highlighted projects with potential legal or policy relevance. The analysis of the implementation of Mobility Partnerships also raised some criticism about the efficiency of the monitoring tool, the scoreboard. I argue that not only are these scoreboards insufficient to properly evaluate the implementation of the projects, but they are inadequate to present the dynamics in place. During the evaluation of the implementation of both Mobility Partnerships, I also noticed overlaps between projects as well as the lack of cooperation between different actors. The Court of Auditors, in its Special Report in 2016, pointed out similar pitfalls and suggested a continuous evaluation of Mobility Partnerships.[3]

1 Chapter 2.
2 Chapter 4.
3 European Court of Auditors, 'EU external migration spending in Southern Mediterranean and Eastern Neighbourhood countries until 2014', Special Report No 9/2016, Luxembourg, 2016.

Once the overview of the implementation of Mobility Partnerships was completed, I looked at their relevance. In Chapter 3, a comparative analysis of the legal and policy frameworks in Morocco and Cape Verde was conducted. A comparison of the legal and policy frameworks before and after the conclusion of the Mobility Partnerships contributed to highlighting the legal and policy developments that occurred since the conclusion of the Mobility Partnerships. I then examined whether these changes could be attributable to the implementation of the respective Mobility Partnership.

According to the EU, Mobility Partnerships 'will necessarily have a complex legal nature'.[4] Mobility Partnerships are usually presented as non-binding instruments, soft law instruments or as having a soft legal nature.[5] In Chapter 1, I examined the legal nature of Mobility Partnerships. I looked at how Mobility Partnerships fit in the EU legal architecture and what it means for Mobility Partnerships to be soft law instruments, in terms of relevance. Few studies have analysed the actual legal and policy implications of soft law instruments. The suggestion resulting from my analysis is that Mobility Partnerships are non-traditional EU instruments, which are non-binding.[6] In Chapter 3, I analysed whether or not Mobility Partnerships, while being soft law instruments, have relevance for the development of the legal and policy frameworks in Morocco and Cape Verde. I argue that Mobility Partnerships, despite their non-binding character, have legal and policy relevance for third countries regarding the regulation of migration, asylum, human trafficking and even labour law.[7] The first key finding of this book is that Mobility Partnerships are soft law instruments with potential legal and policy relevance for third countries. Mobility Partnerships may not be the only reason for changes, but they clearly play a role. Moreover, flexibility was one of the main reasons why the EU preferred Mobility Partnerships to be soft law instruments. The Annex is a living document that can easily be modified by all partners. In this book I found that Mobility Partnerships are flexible instruments that can be adapted to new political priorities.[8] This can be illustrated by the drastic change in policy orientations that occurred in Morocco between the

4 Commission of the European Communities, 'Circular Migration and Mobility Partnerships between the European Union and Third Countries COM' (2007) 248 final, Brussels, 15 May 2007, 1, 3.

5 Sergio Carrera and Raül Hernández I Sagrera, 'The externalisation of the EU's labour immigration policy: Towards mobility or insecurity partnerships?' (2009) CEPS Working Document 321, 1, 28; Sergio Carrera and Raül Hernández I Sagrera, 'Mobility Partnerships; 'Insecurity Partnerships' for Policy Coherence and Migrant Workers Human Rights in the EU', 97, in Rahel Kunz, Sandra Lavenex and Marion Panizzon (eds.), *Multilayered Migration Governance: The Promise of Partnership* (London, New York: Routledge 2011) 97. Panos Koutrakos, *European Foreign Policy: Legal and Political Perspectives* (Cheltenham: Edward Elgar Publishing 2011) 164–165; Bart Van Vooren, *EU External Relations Law and the European Neighbourhood Policy: A Paradigm for Coherence* (London, New York: Routledge 2012) 209–210.

6 Chapter 1.

7 Chapters 3 and 4.

8 Idem.

conclusion of the Mobility Partnership and the launch of the new global Policy on Immigration and Asylum a few months later. Therefore, they can play a role in continuing discussions between the EU and third countries. However, the soft law nature of Mobility Partnerships did not come without setbacks. The soft law nature of Mobility Partnerships has been criticised as being non-democratic because it excludes the European Parliament from the process and can be used as a tool to circumvent the legislative process.[9]

The legal framework on migration was inadequate in both countries before the conclusion of the Mobility Partnerships, and their migration related policies were either focused quasi-exclusively on emigration, in the case of Morocco, or almost nonexistent, in the case of Cape Verde.[10] Chapter 4 exposed how the administrative capacity of the third country has been instrumental in our understanding of the relevance of Mobility Partnerships, mainly in the development of the content of new policies and laws developed through Mobility Partnership projects. The chapter shows how development aid and capacity building can influence the legal and policy developments in Morocco and Cape Verde. In addition, it shows how the level of administrative capacity is detrimental to the effective implementation of the developed instruments and other EU priorities, such as border control. The power of negotiation of the third country plays a key role as it defines the level of capacity building and development aid that a third country can receive. I argue that, in terms of immigration, both countries were lacking administrative capacity when they concluded their respective Mobility Partnerships. This means that there was a need in both countries to develop their legal and policy frameworks on immigration, as they were facing a growing number of immigrants remaining in their territory rather than transiting through it. This is a critical point to be stressed. Even if the legal and policy developments seem to be pushed forth by the EU, they are occurring because third country officials are accepting the need to cooperate with the EU on these issues. While the Mobility Partnerships without a doubt played a role in both countries' legal and policy developments, arguing that the changes occurred only because of the projects implemented by the EU and Member States disregards the autonomy of Cape Verde and Morocco as political actors. Additionally, it does not consider the complex geopolitical framework in which the authorities of both countries developed their policies. Mohamed Berriane, Hein de Haas and Katharina Natter rightly urge academics to study migration in a more holistic way.[11] I followed this approach in this book, taking into account the interests and geopolitical position of Morocco and Cape Verde.

In the cases of Morocco and Cape Verde, the Mobility Partnership influenced the development of laws related to the entry and stay of foreigners, human trafficking and, to some extent, asylum.[12] Both Mobility Partnerships also influenced

9 Chapter 1.

10 Chapter 3.

11 Mohamed Berriane, Hein de Haas and Katharina Natter, 'Introduction: Revisiting Moroccan migrations' (2015) *The Journal of North African Studies* 20(4) 503, 517.

12 Chapter 3.

the implementation of National Strategies in relation to migration (and asylum in the case of Morocco) and, more precisely, to the integration of immigrants (and refugees). These strategies all led to the opening of exceptional periods of regularisation for migrants as well as improvements in the access to labour and labour rights for regular migrants in addition to other socio-economic rights.[13] The analysis illustrates how, in the Moroccan case, the Mobility Partnership provided important external support for the development and implementation of a new national strategy on immigration and asylum. The EU took a reactive position, by supporting its implementation *a posteriori*, rather than a proactive role.[14] In the case of Cape Verde, the situation was very different, and the EU clearly took a more proactive approach.[15] The development of the National Immigration Strategy[16] is the fruit of distinct phases in which the EU was involved since the conclusion of the Mobility Partnerships. As a matter of fact, these different steps have been linked to Mobility Partnership projects.

In Chapter 4, we examined to what extent and how the three factors: the state of relations between third countries and EU Member States, the power of negotiation of a third country and its level of administrative capacity influenced the relevance of Mobility Partnerships for Morocco and Cape Verde. The three factors are usually combined. Our conclusion is that Mobility Partnerships have a 'differentiated relevance'. Differentiated relevance means that, in some cases, legal and policy changes can be imposed by the EU, while in other cases the EU can support them according to the interests of the third country. The level of influence of the EU and Member States in the legal and policy developments as well as in the content of the new legal acts or policies can be differentiated depending on external factors. In the cases of Cape Verde and Morocco, the EU and Member States play very different roles in the legal and policy developments because the three factors are combined in different manners.

In the case of Cape Verde: a) strong postcolonial ties connect Cape Verde and Portugal, b) Cape Verde has a low power of negotiation and c) Cape Verde has a low level of administrative capacity (lower than Morocco). Consequently, the EU and Member States played a proactive role in the development and implementation of legally- and policy-relevant projects, 'building' Cape Verdean's NIS and drafting full legislation, such as, for example, Law 66/VIII/2014 on entry, stay, exit and expulsion of foreigners. This is because Cape Verde has a low power of negotiation and is in a position where it has to 'take or leave' projects proposed by the EU and Member States rather than a position where they can negotiate projects which are of their own interests (b). Moreover, Portugal played an important role, not only in proposing new legally and policy relevant projects, but also in influencing the content of the legal and policy developments (a). In this

13 Idem.

14 Chapter 4.

15 Chapters 3 and 4.

16 Estratégia Nacional de Imigração, Aprovada pela Resolução do Conselho de Ministros no 3/2012, de 23 de Janeiro, B.O.C.V., I Série, no 3, 23 de Janeiro de 2012.

configuration, Mobility Partnerships projects are influenced by the EU and Member States and so is the content of the new laws and policies. Because Cape Verde has a low level of administrative capacity combined with a low level of power of negotiation, it cannot negotiate adequate capacity-building projects to improve its level of administrative capacity, leaving it in a state of dependency upon foreign expertise (b and c). Additionally, legal transplants can seem advantageous because they are a cost-efficient way of developing legal frameworks (c). As Cape Verde is accustomed to transplanting Portuguese legislation, the influence of the former colonial power in the content of the laws developed is high (a and b).

The case of Morocco is very different, and the EU is taking a supportive role in legal and policy developments. In Morocco: a) the postcolonial ties are less strong than in Cape Verde, b) Morocco has a high level of negotiation and c) Morocco has a low administrative capacity (but higher than Cape Verde). Because Morocco has a high power of negotiation, it can negotiate the content of the Mobility Partnership and influence the EU and Member States to implement projects that support its own policy and legal needs (b). For similar reasons, Morocco can benefit from adequate capacity building to develop its administrative capacity in relevant fields and be less influenced in the content of its new laws and policies (b and c). Additionally, Morocco has looser ties to its former colonial power and can involve more actors in the capacity building that is provided to its officials, which limits the influence of only one country and, therefore, the risks of legal transplants (a, b and c).

In Chapter 4, the 'standard' conditionality used by the EU in its relations with third countries was described, showing that the EU can use conditionality to push third countries to follow and implement policies that are favourable to the EU and that often include the fight against irregular migration. The 'more for more' conditionality was discussed. It was included in Mobility Partnerships after the Arab Spring uprisings as the EU realised that they would need to propose more positive incentives to third countries in order to increase cooperation on migration. The third type of conditionality introduced in the chapter is 'reversed conditionality'. It is often assumed that Mobility Partnerships are unfair and driven by the EU's 'more for more' conditionality putting a high pressure on third countries. Drawing on Cassarino's notion of 'reversed conditionality',[17] this book advocates a more balanced view of EU-third country relations and argues that Mobility Partnerships are also instrumentalised as part of domestic agendas of third countries.[18]

The first Mobility Partnerships were concluded with third countries with weak leverage vis-à-vis the EU, and this pattern changed only after the Arab Spring. Reslow[19] highlights the 'take it or leave it' approach adopted in the cases of

17 Jean-Pierre Cassarino, 'Informalising Readmission Agreements in the EU Neighbourhood' (2007) *The International Spectator* 42(2) 179, available at: https://halshs.archives-ouvertes.fr/hal-01232695/document (accessed 13 January 2017).

18 Chapter 4.

19 Natasja Reslow, 'The Role of Third Countries in EU Migration Policy: The Mobility Partnerships' (2012) *EJML* 14(4) 395.

Moldova, Cape Verde and Senegal, where the EU unilaterally proposed the same Mobility Partnership text to these third countries with little room for negotiation. Nevertheless, the relations between different parties to a Mobility Partnership may be more dynamic than what is often assumed. More dynamic relations can be understood as relations that consider the interests of the third country, which is not only seen as a beneficiary. Morocco was the first country that refused the list of projects in the Annex to the Joint Declaration because it was not negotiated with them and simply imposed. It is interesting because it shows that Morocco had some leverage that prior countries concluding Mobility Partnerships did not have. Then, throughout the development of the Mobility Partnership in Morocco, we can see that the EU mainly took a supportive role and provided funding and capacity building in relation to Morocco's interests. As a case in point, with the launch in 2014 of the Moroccan National Strategy on Immigration and Asylum (NSIA),[20] the list of projects proposed by the EU and its Member States was considerably modified in order to support the Moroccan strategy. The EU should consider the idea of dynamic relations not only when negotiating and implementing Mobility Partnerships but also other instruments such as the EU Compacts. Third countries that are priorities for the EU in terms of migration management are the key to an effective implementation of the different tools. Agreements must be concluded that consider third countries' own needs to solve their national immigration challenges.

Morocco and Cape Verde are clearly different in terms of geopolitical importance for the EU. This book argues that Cape Verde has a low geopolitical importance for the EU because of, among other reasons, its geographical location, small population size and small emigration fluxes towards the EU. This low geopolitical importance confers a low power of negotiation to Cape Verde. On the other hand, Morocco has a high power of negotiation, mainly due to its role as 'gatekeeper', conferring the country a higher power of negotiation. A key finding to emerge from this study is that the power of negotiation that a country gains from its geopolitical importance for the EU influences the measure to which a Mobility Partnership is relevant for the development of the legal framework in that country. I argue that in locations with a low level of negotiation power, the Mobility Partnership is mainly used as a tool by the EU and Member States to impose their interests upon the third country. Whereas, in places with a high level of negotiation power, the Mobility Partnership is used as a tool by the EU and the third country to achieve both their objectives. In this configuration, the third country can influence the content of the Mobility Partnership. It is often forgotten that third countries have gained an important level of negotiation power because they are of key geopolitical importance for the EU in terms of migration control, and they are not passively implementing EU's migration policies. A third country can use the conditionality mechanism to its advantage by pushing the EU to

20 Stratégie Nationale d'Immigration et d'Asile, 2014, available at. http://www.marocainsdumonde.gov.ma/fr/le-minist%C3%A8re/affaires-de-la-migration/strat%C3%A9gie-nationale-dimmigration-et-dasile (accessed 19 January 2018).

cooperate on issues in the third country's interest. This is the case of Morocco, which became an extremely valuable ally of the EU in the fight against irregular migration through its role as 'gatekeeper' and close cooperation on border control.

In this book I argue that the power of negotiation influences the relevance of Mobility Partnerships in two ways.[21] First, it influences the content of the Mobility Partnership and, therefore, the projects that are being implemented. This means that a country with a high power of negotiation can influence the implementation of legally- and policy-relevant projects, whereas the EU and Member States can impose policy- and legally-relevant projects upon a country with a low power of negotiation. Secondly, the influence that the EU and Member States have on the content of new legal and policy developments is also differentiated according to the power of negotiation of a third country. In this case, the factors of administrative capacity and power of negotiation are combined. I argue that if a country has a low administrative capacity, it will be more likely to be influenced in its legal and policy development. It should be clarified that being influenced by foreign legislation in itself is not inadequate, and it is a common practice throughout the world.[22] What can be seen as more problematic is the transposition *ad litteram* of legal provisions which are not adapted to the needs of the receiving country.

As presented in Chapter 1, several reasons can explain the existence of legal transplants and policy transfer. The first one is the likelihood for foreign experts to replicate laws and policies in force in their own countries. In the case of Morocco, because experts from different nationalities are involved in the projects leading to legal and policy developments, this risk is minimised. But in the case of Cape Verde, the new laws on immigration and on asylum were fully drafted by a Cape Verdean and a Portuguese expert. In this case I argue that the risk of transposition *ad litteram* of legal provisions is high. The risk is enhanced by the fact that Portugal and Cape Verde have strong postcolonial ties and a long-standing tradition of legal transplant. I argue that the occurrence of legal transplants and policy transfer is higher where the country has a low power of negotiation.[23] This can be explained by the fact that a country with a higher level of negotiation power can negotiate relevant capacity-building projects to be included in Mobility Partnerships as well as involve more actors in the implementation of capacity-building projects. This way, the influence of a single actor is reduced, which makes legal and policy transplants less likely to occur. It does not mean that the different actors have no influence at all. It should also be noted that, even in the case of a low power of negotiation, the third country still has its own agency. While the officials of a third country with low power of negotiation might not be able to put

21 Chapter 4.

22 Alan Watson, *Legal Transplants. An Approach in Comparative Law* (Edinburgh: Scottish Academic Press 1974).

23 Chapter 4.

forth their interests in a successful manner, it does not mean that they are completely passive recipients.

When looking beyond the role of Member States in legal transplants and policy transfers, we can see that the EU can also play a role. Iann Manners argues that technical assistance can be a way for the EU to transfer its norms. In the case of Morocco, even though it seems that the country has more agency to direct the type of technical assistance or capacity building that it receives, it is not immune to this type of transfer of norms. The same argumentation can be applied to the existence of 'overt diffusion', 'contagion' or 'procedural diffusion'[24] in Cape Verde and Morocco. Both countries have benefited from development aid and technical support for decades, and they are accustomed to collaborating with EU officials based in their territories. Collaboration between the Moroccan and Cape Verdean governments and the EU delegations in these countries goes far beyond the question of migration. The processes and ideas developed and shared through this cooperation can lead to a transfer of norms that could lead to policy and legal change. It also should not be dismissed that many officials in Cape Verde and Morocco have studied in Europe and have been influenced by European or, more generally, Western norms.[25]

Another question that merits further discussion is the relevance of Mobility Partnerships to the enhancement of migrants' access to rights. The first pillar of the GAMM[26] covers mobility, legal migration and integration. The notion of circular migration has been closely related to the Mobility Partnership tool.[27] Mobility Partnerships were presented by the EU as tools that favour circular migration and, therefore, enhance legal migration options for third country nationals within the limits and conditions set by the Member States. Circular migration was perceived by the EU as 'an important shift in migration patterns' for countries of origin.[28] The negotiations of the first Mobility Partnerships, including the one with Cape Verde, were influenced by the idea of a triple win approach using circular migration.[29] However, with the conclusion of the first Mobility Partnerships, criticism started to raise.[30] The economic crisis that struck Europe, which started in 2008, had a negative impact on the implementation of Mobility Partnerships in terms of legal migration opportunities. It is often assumed that Mobility Partnerships are unfair tools created in favour of the EU and its Member States, and that they do not provide new opportunities for legal

24 Iann Manners, 'Normative Power Europe: A Contradiction in Terms?' (2002) *JCMS* 40(2) 235, 244–245.

25 Interview 13 Moroccan Ministry of Labour, Rabat, 19 January 2016.

26 European Commission, 'The Global Approach to Migration and Mobility', COM (2011) 743 final, Brussels, 18 November 2011.

27 Commission of the European Communities (n5) 4.

28 Global Commission on International Migration (GCIM), 'Migration in an Interconnected World: New Directions for Action, Report of the Global Commission on International Migration', 5 October 2005, 1, 31.

29 Chapter 2.

30 Sergio Carrera and Raül Hernández I Sagrera (n6) 28.

migration to third countries. In 2011, Carrera and Raül Hernández I Sagrera published an article in which they criticised circular migration opportunities provided by the Mobility Partnerships with Moldova, Cape Verde and Georgia.[31] They argued that these Mobility Partnerships give 'few tangible examples of effective 'circular migration' initiatives'.[32] Legal migration was presented as one of the novelties of the Mobility Partnership, however, in practice, very few projects have been implemented to develop legal migration channels for third country nationals. In Chapter 2, I found that the topic with the lowest implementation *ratio* pertains to mobility, legal immigration and integration. I argue that Mobility Partnerships do not deliver on their promises of increased mobility.

However, this does not mean that Mobility Partnerships are not relevant for enhancing migrants' rights. Both Mobility Partnerships played a significant role in the development and implementation of immigration and asylum strategies in Cape Verde and Morocco, which aimed to enhance the rights of immigrants living in these third countries and improve their integration. Sub-Saharan migrants in Morocco and Cape Verde directly benefit from the legal and policy changes supported by the EU and Member States through the Mobility Partnerships. Their access to rights was enhanced, even though this is not the Mobility Partnerships' primary aim. The focus should be put on migrants' rights in the third country, rather than on the limited access to the EU. Indeed, the legal framework for migrants' rights in the third country can be positively impacted by the implementation of a Mobility Partnership, as was the case in Morocco and Cape Verde. The legal and policy developments in Morocco and Cape Verde improved, to some extent, access to socio-economic and political rights for sub-Saharan migrants. These positive consequences of the Mobility Partnerships are often overlooked, as they were not foreseen at the time of the negotiation of the instruments. Mobility Partnerships often have a negative image as they are seen only as tools that fail to keep the promise of enhancing mobility. Mobility Partnerships are more than just opportunities for legal migration channels towards Europe (which they are not), and this should be underlined. Some academics wonder however whether the improvement of migrants' rights following the regularisation period constitutes a lasting change or only a brief interruption in Morocco's repressive policies against sub-Saharan migrants.[33] It should be noted that even though improvements are still needed in terms of migrants' access to rights, the fact that access has improved is already a positive step in the right direction. Morocco and Cape Verde are still developing countries with difficulties providing access to rights to their own nationals. Therefore, rather than analysing migrants' access to rights in comparison to Western standards, it would be more interesting to see if access to existing rights in Morocco and Cape Verde is the same for nationals and immigrants.

31 Ibid 97.

32 Ibid 101.

33 Myriam Cherti and Michael Collyer, 'Immigration and Pensée d'Etat: Moroccan migration policy changes as transformation of 'geopolitical culture'' (2015) *The Journal of North African Studies*, 20(4) 590, 602.

Besides, it is striking to see how much emphasis is put on the development and implementation of the NSIA and NIS compared to emigration strategies in Morocco and Cape Verde. It is striking because both Morocco and Cape Verde have large populations of emigrants living in Europe, whereas the percentage of immigrants living in the two countries is still very low. In 2014, immigrant populations represented 0.25% in Morocco and 3.2% in Cape Verde.[34] One could wonder why strategies on emigration targeting a much higher share of the population are not more developed, or why so much focus is put on a phenomenon (immigration) which is not numerically significant. When linking the development and implementation of both immigration and emigration strategies to the Mobility Partnerships, we can clearly see that the focus is exclusively put on supporting the development and implementation of immigration strategies. This not only demonstrates the interests of the EU and the Member States in the development and implementation of immigration strategies in third countries, but it also reveals third countries' growing need for such strategies as they become migration destination countries.[35] It can also show how the EU's priorities condition third countries' priorities. By having easier access to financial and technical support for strategies that are in the interests of the EU, the third countries are incentivised to develop immigration strategies rather than emigration strategies. Since emigration strategies are not able to attract the same level of financial support, they seem to be overshadowed.

Furthermore, we can discuss whether Mobility Partnerships enable the conclusion of other binding acts or the implementation of specific policies with third countries that support the externalisation of EU's migration policies. The book puts forward that the EU uses the Mobility Partnership tool, among others, to externalise the reception of migrants and refugees in neighbouring third countries.[36] The externalisation approach includes the development of asylum laws and reception capacities in third countries to involve them in the procedures of receiving asylum seekers and sharing the 'burden' of asylum seekers and refugees with neighbouring third countries. To fight the entry of irregular migrants in its territory, the EU also externalises some of its migration control to neighbouring third countries, converting them into EU's 'gatekeepers'. Strong border control capacities, the fight against human trafficking and the conclusion of Readmission Agreements are several ways put forth by the EU to 'support' third countries in successfully playing their gatekeeping roles. The analysis suggests that Mobility Partnerships do have relevance in the development of legal frameworks in third countries in the areas of migration, human trafficking and asylum law as well as the development of stronger border controls. The EU is using different strategies when implementing Mobility Partnerships in order to promote legal and policy

34 For Morocco: Haut-Commissariat au Plan, Les Résidents Étrangers au Maroc (selon RGPH 2014) 18 December 2017, 1, 4; For Cape Verde: Instituto Nacional de Estatística, Inquérito Multi-objectivo Contínuo 2014 Estatísticas das Migrações (2015) 1, 14

35 Mohamed Berriane, Hein de Haas and Katharina Natter (n12) 517.

36 Chapters 3 and 4.

developments in these fields. The EU's support for Morocco's National Strategy for Immigration and Asylum (NSIA) can be seen as a way for the EU to externalise its migration and reception of refugees. Indeed, the Moroccan strategy, by regularising immigrants and improving their access to work and basic rights, such as minimum health care, access to the labour market and education, could influence migrants to settle in Morocco.[37] Initially, these migrants may have only transited through Morocco in the hope of entering Europe. However, the strengthening of borders, combined with improvements in immigrants' circumstances and access to rights, transformed the transit situation into a more permanent settlement.[38] Through Mobility Partnerships third countries can be involved in the fight against irregular migration and the externalisation of the EU's migration control. However, it is simplistic to believe that third countries have no say in the matter. The interests of the different parties, as well as their capacities to negotiate, are conditioning the EU's actions.

Finally, in Chapter 5, I discussed the future of the GAMM and Mobility Partnerships. The 'migrant crisis' led to a state of emergency, which required a strong response from the EU. The response took the form of a proliferation of migration management instruments since 2015. It is true that through the introduction of the new instruments following the 'migrant crisis', the GAMM and its instruments, Mobility Partnerships and CAMMs, have lost a lot of their momentum and attractiveness. The proliferation of instruments being implemented concomitantly led to a situation where no instrument can really be considered *the* key instrument for cooperation with third countries, ineluctably having a negative impact on the influence of each individual instrument.

I argue that Mobility Partnerships are not (yet) dead. Their influence varies a lot from one region to the other. They have lost a lot of influence in the South because they are now in competition with a broad range of new instruments on similar issues. However, in the East, the situation is different, which can be explained by the fact that the plethora of new instruments implemented since 2015 focused only on Africa and the Mediterranean, meaning that no significant new instruments are competing with Mobility Partnerships in the East.

Moreover, I argue that, even though many new instruments have been developed since 2015, there is no major change in the substance of EU migration policy. Addressing the root causes of migration brings us back 20 years to the introduction of the Tampere programme. Another non-novelty is the idea of circular migration as a way to open legal pathways for migration. The new pilot projects are built on the same model as the Mobility Packages, which then became Mobility Partnerships. While the economic situation at the time when Mobility Partnerships were first implemented led to the quick abortion of all projects focusing on circular migration, current low unemployment rates and the increased need for specific categories of workers helped revive the idea.

37 Chapter 4.
38 Myriam Cherti and Michael Collyer (n35) 597–598; Chapter 4.

Finally, due to the fast-paced changes in the field of EU external relations, further analysis will be required. It will be interesting to see how Mobility Partnerships evolve with the start of the new Commission in early 2020, whether they manage to gain back some momentum, or they fully disappear from the policy landscape. It will also be interesting to see how pilot projects evolve and whether they can complement Mobility Partnerships by creating new mobility channels for citizens of third countries.

Bibliography

'Cabo Verde Defende Aplicação Flexível dos Protocolos de Livre Circulação na CEDEAO' *RadioTelevisão Caboverdiana*, 21 May 2012, http://rtc.cv/index.php?paginas=21&id_cod=4221 (accessed 16 April 2017).

'Cabo Verde e EUA assinam memorando que regula deportação de cidadãos' *Expresso das Ilhas*, 24 January 2017, www.expressodasilhas.sapo.cv/politica/item/51790-cabo-verde-e-eua-assinam-memorando-que-regula-deportacao-de-cidadaos (accessed 7 December 2017).

'Cabo Verde: Isenção de vistos para a UE' *Observador*, 5 May 2017, http://observador.pt/2017/05/05/cabo-verde-isencao-de-vistos-para-a-ue (accessed 7 December 2017).

'A Casablanca, des propriétaires tentent d'interdire la location aux Africains' *France24*, 18 July 2013, http://observers.france24.com/fr/20130718-casablanca-proprietaires-interdire-location-africains-discrimination-raciale (accessed 10 March 2017).

'Texte Intégral du Discours Adressé par SM le Roi à la Nation' *Maroc.ma*, 19 March 2013, www.maroc.ma/fr/discours-royaux/annonce-des-r%C3%A9formes-constitutionnelles-texte-int%C3%A9gral-du-discours-adress%C3%A9-par-sm-le (accessed 10 September 2017).

'Discours de SM Le Roi À L'occasion Du 38ème Anniversaire de La Marche Verte' *Maroc.ma*, www.maroc.ma/fr/discours-royaux/discours-de-sm-le-roi-loccasion-du-38eme-anniversaire-de-la-marche-verte (accessed 25 July 2016).

'France/Africa: Remaking an Old Relationship' (2009) 50(18) *Africa Confidential* 4.

'Isenção de vistos aos cidadãos da União Europeia e Reino Unido vai ser discutida na sessão parlamentar de Junho 18 May 2017' *Inforpress*, 18 May 2017, www.inforpress.publ.cv/isencao-de-vistos-aos-cidadaos-da-uniao-europeia-e-reino-unido-vai-ser-discutida-na-sessao-parlamentar-de-junho (accessed 6 December 2017).

'Une Nouvelle Opération de Régularisation de Migrants au Maroc' *h24info.ma*, 13 December 2016, www.h24info.ma/maroc/une-nouvelle-operation-de-regularisation-de-migrants-au-maroc/49045 (accessed 8 February 2017).

'Politique Migratoire: Adapter les Lois, un Passage Obligé' *La Vie éco*, 20 December 2015, http://lavieeco.com/news/politique/politique-migratoire-adapter-les-lois-un-passage-oblige.html#FbpHJsL5ubaZY25Q.99 (accessed 8 December 2017).

'Press Release: 7e Réunion de Dialogue Politique entre le Cabo Verde et l'UE au Niveau Ministériel et Signature d'un Accord Bilatéral entre le Luxembourg et le Cabo Verde en Matière de Migration' Luxembourg Government, 14 October 2015, www.gouvernement.lu/5329991/13-dialogue-politique (accessed 9 February 2018).

'Projet de Loi: les Marocaines Pourront Transmettre la Nationalité à leurs Conjoints Etrangers' *bladi.net*, 29 December 2014, www.bladi.net/marocaines-nationalite-conjoints-etrangers,40882.html (accessed 27 March 2017).

'USA to Deport 400 Immigrants to Cabo Verde' *Cabo Verde Network*, 26 January 2017, http://cvnetworktv.com/u-s-a-to-deport-400-immigrants-to-cabo-verde (accessed 7 December 2017).

Abbott, K et al., 'The Concept of Legalization' (2000) 54(3) *Int Organ* 401.

Abbott, K and Snidal D, 'Hard and Soft Law in International Governance' (2000) 54(1) *Int Organ* 421.

Aboulfaraj, Z and Mahmoud, M, 'Les réfugiés peuvent à nouveau obtenir des titres de séjour au Maroc' *Telquel*, 12 December 2018, https://telquel.ma/2018/12/12/les-refugies-peuvent-a-nouveau-obtenir-des-titres-de-sejour-au-maroc_1621607/?utm_source=tq&utm_medium=normal_post (accessed 13 October 2019).

Abushi, S and Arroud, H, 'A Migration Bubble? Reading the New European Neighbourhood Policy in the Moroccan Context' (Brussels: Heinrich Böll Stiftung 2016) https://eu.boell.org/en/2016/06/15/migration-bubble-reading-new-european-neighbourhood-policy-moroccan-context (accessed 13 August 2016).

ACVZ (Advisory Committee on Migration Affairs), '*The Strategic Country Approach to Migration. Between Ambition and Reality. Advisory Report Addressed to the Minister for Foreign Trade and Development Cooperation and the State Secretary of Security and Justice* (2015) www.adviescommissievoorvreemdelingenzaken.nl/binaries/adviescommissievoorvreemdelingenzaken/documenten/publicaties/2015/7/20/the-strategic-country-approach-to-migration-between-ambition-and-reality/Strategic_country_approach_to_migration_ACVZ_advisory_report_20150720.pdf (accessed 13 August 2016).

Addison, HJ, *Is Administrative Capacity a Useful Concept? Review of the Application, Meaning and Observation of Administrative Capacity in Political Science Literature* (LSE Research Paper) (London: London School of Economics and Political Science 2009).

Adikhari, P, 'Conflict-Induced Displacement, Understanding the Causes of Flight' (2013) 57(1) *Am J Polit Sci* 82.

Akesson, L, 'Under the Cover of Partnership' (2011) 16*NAI Annual Report*.

Alecmo, CCSM, GADEM and Mission Catholiquede Nouadhibou, *Situation des Migrants dans le Sud du Maroc: Mission d'Observation Conjointe* (2014) https://www.lacimade.org/wp-content/uploads/2014/10/20141014_Rapport_mission_sud_VF.pdf

Alemazung, JA, 'Post-Colonial Colonialism: An Analysis of International Factors and Actors Marring African Socio-Economic and Political Development' (2010) 3(10) *JPAS* 62.

Alioua, M, 'Régularisations des Etrangers au Maroc: Analyse d'une Décision Historique mais surtout Stratégique' *Yabiladi*, 15 November 2013, www.yabiladi.com/articles/details/20944/regularisation-etrangers-maroc-analyse-d-une.html (accessed 12 January 2018).

Aman, A, 'Why Morocco Really Wants Back in the African Union' *AL Monitor*, 27 July 2016, www.al-monitor.com/pulse/originals/2016/07/morocco-join-african-union-western-sahara-dispute-egypt.html (accessed 13 August 2016).

Amnesty International, 'EU: Action not Words Needed to End Suffering of Thousands', 14 September 2015, www.amnesty.org/en/latest/news/2015/09/eu-action-not-words-needed-at-jha-to-end-sufferingof-thousands (accessed 12 October 2017).

Anderson, R, 'Frontex y la Creación de la Frontera Euroafricana: Golpeando la Valla Ilusoria' (2011) 28(9) *Revista de Derecho Migratorio y Extranjería* 177.

Andrade, PG, 'The legal Feasibility of the EU's External Action on Legal Migration: The Internal and the External Intertwined' (2013) 15(3) *EJML* 263.

Andrade, PG, and Martín, I, 'EU Cooperation with Third Countries in the Field of Migration' (study, PE 536.469) (DG for Internal Policies, Policy Department C, European Parliament, (2015) www.europarl.europa.eu/RegData/etudes/STUD/2015/536469/IPOL_STU(2015)536469_EN.pdf (accessed 1 February 2018).

Andrès, H, 'Réciprocité et Droit de Vote des Etrangers en Espagne et au Portugal' (2013) *P@ges Europe* (La Documentation française, DILA), 4 March 2013.

Angenendt, S, 'Circular Migration: A Sustainable Concept for Migration Policy?' (2007) *SWP Comments* 11.

Angenendt, S, 'EU Mobility Partnerships: The "Most Innovative and Sophisticated Tool" of European Migration Policy?' (2014) *Migration Strategy Group Policy Brief.*

Arrach, A, 'The Moroccan New Immigration Policy and the Constitutional Protection of Fundamental Human Rights of Migrants' (2014) www.jus.uio.no/english/research/news-and-events/events/conferences/2014/wccl-cmdc/wccl/papers/ws6/w6-arrach.pdf (accessed 9 February 2018).

Bache, I and George, S, *Politics in the European Union* (Oxford: Oxford University Press 2006).

Baert, P, 'Unintended Consequences: A Typology and Examples' (1991) 6(2) *Int Sociol* 201.

Balch, A and Geddes, A, *Connections Between Admission Policies and Integration Policies at EU-level and Given Linkages with National Policy Making* (Promoting Sustainable Policies for Integration WP1) (ICMPD 2012) http://research.icmpd.org/fileadmin/Research-Website/Project_material/PROSINT/Reports/WP1_CompRep_Final_Submitted.pdf

Baldwin-Edwards, M, 'The Emerging European Immigration Regime: Some Reflexions on Implications for Southern Europe' (1997) 35(4) *JCMS* 497.

Balfour, R, '*EU Conditionality after the Arab Spring*' (European Institute of the Mediterranean 2012).

Balfour, R, and Raik, K, 'The European External Action Service and National Diplomacies' (2013) 73*EPC Issue Paper.*

Baracani, E, 'The European Neighbourhood Policy and Political Conditionality: Double Standards in EU Democracy Promotion?' 133 in Balzacq, T (ed.), *The External Dimension of EU Justice and Home Affairs Governance, Neighbours, Security* (Basingstoke, UK: Palgrave Macmillan 2009).

Battjes, H, *European Asylum Law and International Law* (Leiden, The Netherlands; Boston, MA: Nijhoff 2006).

Baxter, R, 'International Law in "Her" Infinite Variety' (1980) 29(4) *ICLQ* 549.

Belguendouz, A, *Le Maroc Non Africain, Gendarme de l'Europe? Alerte au Projet de Loi n° 02–03 Relative à l'Entrée et au Séjour des Etrangers au Maroc, à l'Emigration et l'Immigration Irrégulière* (Rabat: Imprimerie Beni Snassen, 2003).

Belguendouz, A, 'Immigration et Emigration: la Nouvelle Loi Marocaine' 11 in El Yazami, D (ed.), *Un siècle de migration Marocaines*, 24*Migrance* (2005).

Belguendouz, A, '*Le Maroc et la Migration Irrégulière – une Analyse Sociopolitique*' (Florence, Italy: CARIM – module socio-politique 2009).

Belguendouz, A, '"Stratégie National pour les Marocains Résidant à l'Etranger", une "Fake news"' *Wake up Info*, 6 February 2018, www.wakeupinfo.fr/2018/02/strategie-nationale-pour-les-marocains.html (accessed 8 February 2018).

Belouas, A, 'Casablanca: 2,500 à 3,000 personnes vivent dans la rue!' *La Vie écho*, 19 January 2017, http://lavieeco.com/news/societe/casablanca-2-500-a-3-000-personnes-vivent-dans-la-rue.html (accessed 3 December 2017).

Berriane, M, de Haas, H and Natter, K, 'Introduction: Revisiting Moroccan Migrations' (2015) 20(4) *The Journal of North African Studies* 503.

Berthelemy, JC, '*Bilateral Donors' Interest vs. Recipients Development Motives in Aid Allocation: Do All Donors Behave the Same?* (Paris: Cahiers de la Maison des Sciences Economiques 2005).

Biad, A, 'La Construction du Maghreb au Défi du Partenariat Euro-Méditerranéen de l'Union européenne' (2013) IX*L'Année du Maghreb* (En ligne) http://anneemaghreb.revues.org/1866 (accessed 23 November 2017).

Boswell, C, 'The "External Dimension" of EU Immigration and Asylum Policy' (2003) 79 (3) *International Affairs* 619.

Bothe, M, 'Legal and Non-Legal Norms – A Meaningful Distinction in International Relations?' (1980) 11*NYIL* 65.

Borchardt, G and Wellens, K, 'Soft Law in European Community law' (1989) 14(5) *Eur L Rev* 267.

Börzel, TA and Lebanidze, B, '"The Transformative Power of Europe" Beyond Enlargement: the EU's Performance in Promoting Democracy in its Neighbourhood' (2017) 33 (1) *East European Politics* 17.

Boyle, A, 'Dispute Settlement and the Law of the Sea Convention: Problems of Fragmentation and Jurisdiction' (1997) 46 *ICLQ* 37.

Boyle, A, 'Some Reflections on the Relationship of Treaties and Soft Law' (1999) 48 *ICLQ* 901.

Boyle, A, 'Soft Law in International Law Making' 118 in Evans, MD (ed.), *International Law* (Oxford: Oxford University Press 2005).

Bradford, A, 'The Brussels Effect' (2012) 107(1) *Northwest. University Law Rev* 1.

Brocza, S and Paulhart, K, 'EU Mobility Partnerships: A Smart Instrument for the Externalization of Migration Control' (2015) 15(3) *Eur J Futures Res* 1.

Buckland, B, 'Neither Seen not Heard: The Unintended Consequences of Counter-Trafficking and Counter-Smuggling' in Daase, C and Firesendorf, C (eds) *Rethinking Security Governance: The Problem of Unintended Consequences* (London: Routledge 2010) 137.

Bunyan, T, 'Europol and the European State' 1 in Bunyan, T (ed.), *Statewatching the Bew Europe: A Handbook on the European State* (London: Statewatch 1993).

Burlyuk, O, 'The "Oops!" of EU Engagement Agroad: Analyzing Unintended Consequences of EU External Action' (2017) *JCMS* 1.

Carling, J, 'Migration in the Age of Involuntary Immobility: Theoretical Reflections and Cape Verdean Experiences' (2002) 28(1) *J Ethn Migr Stud* 5.

Carling, J, and Akesson, L, 'Mobility at the Heart of a Nation: Patterns and Meanings of Cape Verdean Migration' (2009) 47(3) *Int Migr* 123.

Carrera, S, 'The EU Border Management Strategy: Frontex and the Challenge of Irregular Migration to the Canary Islands' (2007) 261*CEPS Working Document.*

Carrera, S, *The EU's Dialogue on Migration, Mobility and Security with the Southern Mediterranean: Filling the Gaps in the Global Approach to Migration* (Brussels: CEPS Liberty and Security in Europe 2011).

Carrera, S, and den Hertog, L and Parkin, J, 'EU Migration Policy in the Wake of the Arab Spring What Prospects for EU-Southern Mediterranean Relations?' (2012) *MEDPRO Technical Report.*

Carrera, S, and den Hertog, L and Stefan, M, 'It wasn't me! The Luxembourg Court Orders on the EU Turkey Refugee Deal' (2017) *CEPS Policy Insights 2017–2015.*

Carrera, S, and Hernández, I and Sagrera, R, 'The Externalisation of the EU's Labour Immigration Policy: Towards Mobility or Insecurity Partnerships?' (2009) 321*CEPS Working Document.*

Carrera, S, and Hernández, I and Sagrera, R, 'Mobility Partnerships: "Insecurity Partnerships" for Policy Coherence and Migrant Workers Human Rights in the EU' 97 in

Kunz, R, Lavenex, S and Panizzon, M (eds), *Multilayered Migration Governance: The promise of partnership* (London, New York: Routledge 2011).
Carrera, S, et al, 'Labour Immigration Policy in the EU: A renewed Agenda for Europe 2020' (2011) 240 *CEPS Policy Brief.*
Carrera, S, et al, 'EU-Morocco Cooperation on Readmission, Borders and Protection: A Model to Follow?' (2016) *CEPS Papers in Liberty and Security in Europe.*
Casas, M, Cobarrubias, S and Pickles, J, 'Stretching Borders Beyond Sovereign Territories? Mapping EU and Spain's Border Externalization Policies' (2011) 2(1) *Geopolítica(s), Revista de estudios sobre espacio y poder* 71.
Casas, M, Cobarrubias, S and Pickles, J, '"Good Neighbours Make Good Fences": Seahorse Operations, Border Externalization and Extra-territoriality' (2016) 23(3) *Eur Urban Reg Stud* 231.
Cassarino, JP, 'Informalising Readmission Agreements in the EU Neighbourhood' (2007) 42(2) *The International Spectator* 179 https://halshs.archives-ouvertes.fr/hal-01232695/document (accessed 13 January 2017).
Cassarino, JP, *EU Mobility Partnerships: Expression of a New Compromise* (Migration Policy Institute 2009).
Cassarino, JP, 'Dealing with Unbalanced Reciprocities: Cooperation on Readmission and Implications' 1 in Cassarino, JP (ed.), *Unbalanced Reciprocities: Cooperation on Readmission in the Euro-Mediterranean Area* (Washington, DC: Middle East Institute 2010).
Cassarino, JP, 'A Reappraisal of the EU's Expending Readmission System' (2014) 49(4) *The International Spectator* 130.
Castillejo, C, *The European Union Trust Fund for Africa. A Glimpse of the Future for EU Development Cooperation*, DIE Discussion paper 22 (Bonn: Deutsches Institut für Entwicklungspolitik 2016).
Castillejo, C, *The EU Migration Partnership Framework*, DIE Discussion paper 28 (Bonn: Deutsches Institut für Entwicklungspolitik 2017).
Castles, S, de Haas, H and Miller, MJ, *The Age of Migration: International Population Movements in the Modern World* (Basingstoke, UK: Palgrave Macmillan 2014).
Castles, S, de Haas, H and Miller, MJ, and Ozkul, D, 'Circular Migration: Triple Win, or a New Label for Temporary Migration?' 27 in Battistella, G (ed.), *Global and Asian Perspectives on International Migration. Global Migration Issues 4* (London: Springer 2014).
CCDH – PNUD, 'Le Droit au Développement au Maroc. Entre Pacte International relatif aux Droits Economiques, Sociaux et Culturels et Objectifs du Millénaire pour le Développement' (2010) *juillet.*
Chatzistavrou, F, 'L'usage du Soft Law dans le Système Juridique International et ses Implications Sémantiques et Pratiques sur la Notion de Règle de Droit' (2005) http://leportique.revues.org/591 (accessed 17 January 2018).
Cherti, M and Collyer, M, 'Immigration and Pensée d'Etat: Moroccan Migration Policy Changes as Transformation of "Geopolitical Culture"' (2015) 20(4) *The Journal of North African Studies* 590.
Chou, MH, *EU and the Migration-Development Nexus: What Prospects for EU-Wide Policies?* (Center on Migration, Policy and Society, University of Oxford, Working Paper 37) (Oxford: Oxford University Press 2006).
Chou, MH, *European Union Migration Strategy Towards West Africa: the Origin and Outlook of "Mobility Partnerships" with Cape Verde and Senegal*, EUSA Working Paper (2009).
Chou, MH, and Gibert, M, 'The EU-Senegal Mobility Partnership: From Launch to Suspension and Negotiation Failure' (2012) 8(4) *JCER* 408.

CNDH, *Conclusions et Recommandations du Rapport: 'Etrangers et Droits de l'Homme au Maroc: Pour une Politique d'Asile et d'Immigration Radicalement Nouvelle'* (2013).

CNDH, *Foreigners and Human Rights in Morocco for a Radically New Asylum and Migration Policy* (2013).

CNDH, *Avis du Conseil National des Droits de l'Homme sur le Projet de Loi no 27.14 Relatif à la Lutte Contre la Traite des Personnes* (2016).

CNDH, 'Secteur de l'Habitat et le Droit au Logement', www.cndh.org.ma/fr/bulletin-d-information/secteur-de-lhabitat-et-le-droit-au-logement (accessed 12 September 2017).

Coleman, N, *European Readmission Policy: Third Country Interests and Refugee Rights* (Boston, MA: Nijhoff 2009).

Collyer, M et al, 'Migration and Development: The Euro–Moroccan Experience' (2009) 35(10) *J Ethn Migr Stud* 1555.

Comissão Nacional para osDireitos Humanos e a Cidadania e o PNUD, *I Relatório Nacional De Direitos Humanos* (Praia, Cape Verde: Comissão Nacional para os Direitos Humanos e a Cidadania e o PNUD 2010).

Commission EC, 'Guidelines for a Community Policy on Migration, Commission Communication Transmitted to the Council on March 1985' (COM(85) 48 final), 7 March 1985, *Bulletin of the European Communities*, Supplement 9/85.

Commission EC, *On Immigration and Asylum Policies'* (COM(94) 23 final), Brussels, 23 February 1994.

Commission EC, *Action Plans and Scoreboards: Scoreboard to Review Progress on the Creation of an Area of Freedom, Security and Justice in the European Union* (COM(2000) 167), Brussels, 24 March 2000.

Commission EC, *A Community Immigration Policy* (COM(2000) 757 final), Brussels, 22 November 2000.

Commission EC, *Biannual Update of the Scoreboard to Review Progress on the Creation of an Area of 'Freedom, Security and Justice' in the European Union (First half of 2001)* (COM(2001) 278 final), Brussels, 23 May 2001.

Commission EC, *An Open Method of Coordination for the Community Immigration Policy* (COM(2001) 387), Brussels, 11 July 2001.

Commission EC, *European Governance: A White Paper* (COM(2001) 428), Brussels, 25 July 2001.

Commission EC, *Integrating Migration Issues in The European Union's Relations with Third Countries* (COM(2002) 703 final), Brussels, 3 December 2002.

Commission EC, *Integration and Employment* (COM(2003) 336 final), Brussels, 3 June 2003.

Commission EC, *European Neighbourhood Policy: Strategy Paper* (COM(2004) 373 final), Brussels, 12 May 2004.

Commission EC, *Area of Freedom, Security and Justice: Assessment of the Tampere Programme and Future Orientations* (COM(2004) 401 final), Brussels, 2 June 2004.

Commission EC, *Green Paper on an EU Approach to Managing Economic Migration* (COM(2004) 811 final), Brussels, 11 January 2005.

Commission EC, *Regional Protection Programmes* (COM(2005) 388 final), Brussels, 1 September 2005.

Commission EC, *Priority Actions for Responding to the Challenges of Migration: First Follow-up to Hampton Court* (COM(2005) 621 final), Brussels, 30 November 2005.

Commission EC, *Policy Plan on Legal Migration* (COM(2005) 669 final), Brussels, 21 December 2005.

Commission EC, *Thematic Programme for the Cooperation with Third Countries in the Areas of Migration and Asylum* (COM(2006) 26 final), Brussels, 25 January 2006.

Commission EC, *The Global Approach to Migration One Year on: Towards a Comprehensive European Migration Policy* (COM(2006) 735 final), Brussels, 30 November 2006.

Commission EC, *On Circular Migration and Mobility Partnerships Between the European Union and Third Countries* (COM(2007) 248), Brussels, 16 May 2007.

Commission EC, *On the Future of Relations between the European Union and the Republic of Cape Verde* (COM(2007) 641 final), Brussels, 24 October 2007.

Commission EC, 'Press Release: 'The European Union and Cape Verde Enter into a Mobility Partnership' Luxembourg/Brussels, 5 June 2008.

Commission EC, *A Common Immigration Policy for Europe: Principles, Actions and Tools* (COM(2008) 359 final), Brussels, 17 June 2008.

Commission EC, *Strengthening the Global Approach to migration: increasing coordination, coherence and synergies* (COM(2008) 611 final), Brussels, 8 October 2008.

Commission EC, 'Press Release: The European Union and Georgia enter into a Mobility partnership', Brussels, 30 November 2009.

Commission EC, *Mobility Partnerships as a tool of the Global Approach to Migration* (SEC (2009) 1240 final), Brussels, 18 September 2009.

Commission EC, *Delivering and Area of Freedom, Security and Justice for Europe's Citizens: Action Plan Implementing the Stockholm Programme* (COM(2010) 171 final), Brussels, 20 April 2010.

Commission EC, *Evaluation of EU Readmission Agreements* (COM(2011) 76 final), Brussels, 23 February 2011.

Commission EC, *A Partnership for Democracy and Shared Prosperity with the Southern Mediterranean* (COM(2011) 200 final) Brussels, 8 March 2011.

Commission EC, *Joint Statement by EU High Representative Catherine Ashton and Commissioner Štefan Füle on Morocco's Future Constitutional Reform* (MEMO/11/155), Brussels, 10 March 2011.

Commission EC, *Dialogue for Migration, Mobility and Security with the Southern Mediterranean Countries* (COM(2011) 292 final), Brussels, 24 May 2011.

Commission EC, *Proposal for a Regulation of the European Parliament and of the Council establishing the Asylum and Migration Fund* (COM(2011) 751 final), 15 November 2011.

Commission EC, *The Global Approach to Migration and Mobility* (COM(2011) 743 final), Brussels, 18 November 2011.

Commission EC, *Delivering on a New European Neighbourhood Policy* (JOIN(2012) 14 final), Brussels, 15 May 2012.

Commission EC, 'Press Release, Migration and Mobility Partnership signed between the EU and Morocco', Brussels, 7 June 2013.

Commission EC, 'Press Release, Mobility Partnership signed between the EU and Azerbaijan', Brussels, 5 December 2013.

Commission EC, 'Press Release, EU and Tunisia establish their Mobility Partnership', Brussels, 3 March 2014.

Commission EC, *Service Juridique, Quality of Legislation team, Complexity of EU Law in Domestic Implementing Process*, Brussels, 3 July 2014.

Commission EC, 'Press Release, EU-Jordan: A New Partnership to Better Manage Mobility and Migration', Brussels, 9 October 2014.

Commission EC, 'Presse Release, New EU Regional Development and Protection Programme for Refugees and Host Communities in Lebanon, Jordan and Iraq', Brussels, 16 December 2013.

Commission EC, *An Open and Secure Europe: Making it Happen* (COM(2014) 154 final), Strasbourg, 11 March 2014.

Commission EC, 'Press Release, Joint Foreign and Home Affairs Council: Ten Point Action Plan on Migration' (IP/15/4813), Luxembourg, 20 April 2015.

Commission EC, *A European Agenda on Migration* (COM(2015) 240), Brussels, 13 May 2015.

Commission EC, 'State of the Union 2015' (Speech), 9 September 2015.

Commission EC, '*Fact Sheet: EU-Turkey Joint Action Plan*', Brussels, 15 October 2015.

Commission EC, *Establishing a New Partnership Framework with Third Countries under the European Agenda on Migration* (COM(2016) 385 final), Strasbourg, 7 June 2016.

Commission EC, *Evaluation of the Cotonou Partnership Agreement* (SWD(2016) 250 final), Brussels, 15 July 2016.

Commission EC, 'Press Release, EU Launches Mobility Partnership with Belarus', Luxembourg, 13 October 2016.

Commission EC, *Communication on a More Effective Return Policy in the European Union - A renewed Action Plan* (COM(2017) 200 final), Brussels, 2 March 2017.

Commission EC, *Recommendation on Making Returns More Effective when Implementing the Directive 2008/115/EC of the European Parliament and of the Council* (C(2017) 1600 final), Brussels, 7 March 2017.

Commission EC, *Joint Communication for a Renewed Impetus of the Africa-EU Partnership* (JOIN(2017) 17 final), Brussels, 4 May 2017.

Commission EC, *The Delivery of the European Agenda on Migration* (COM(2017) 558 final), Brussels, 27 September 2017.

Committee for Development Policy Expert Group Meeting, Review of the List of Least Developed Countries, Monitoring the Progress of Graduated Countries: Cape Verde, New York (16–17 January 2011).

Conseil Consultatif des Droits de l'Homme, La Protection Des Refugies Au Maroc, Table ronde 14 février 2008, Rabat-Maroc (Série 'Séminaires').

Council of the European Union, Edinburgh 11–12 December 1992: Conclusions of the Presidency (SN 456/1/92 REV 1).

Council of the European Union, *Terms of Reference of the High-Level Working Group on Asylum and Migration: Preparation of Action Plans for the Most Important Countries of Origin and Transit of Asylum Seekers and Migrants* (5264/99), Brussels, 13 January 1999.

Council of the European Union, *Action Plan for Morocco* (11426/99 LIMITE JAI 75 AG 30), Brussels, 30 September 1999.

Council of the European Union, Presidency Conclusions, Tampere European Council, 15–16 October 1999.

Council of the European Union, Africa-Europe Summit under the Aegis of the OAU and the EU, Cairo Declaration, (Conseil/00/901), Cairo, 4 April 2000, http://europa.eu/rapid/press-release_PRES-00-901_en.htm (accessed 5 August 2017).

Council of the European Union, Presidency Conclusions, European Council Meeting in Laeken, Laeken, 14 and 15 December 2001, (SN 300/1/01 REV 1).

Council of the European Union, Presidency Conclusions of the Seville European Council, Seville, 21–22 June 2002, (13463/02), Brussels, 24 October 2002.

Council of the European Union, *Council Conclusions on Migration and Development*, (8927/03), Brussels, 5 May 2003.

Council of the European Union, 2618th Council Meeting Justice and Home Affairs, Brussels, 19 November 2004, (1415/04 (Presse 321)).

Council of the European Union, *The Hague Programme: Strengthening Freedom, Security and Justice in the European Union*, (2005/C 53/01 OJ C 53/1), 3 March 2005.

Council of the European Union, Presidency Conclusions of the Brussels European Council, 15 and 16 December 2005, (SN 15914/01/05, 30 December 2005, 2 (III Africa)).

Council of the European Union, *On Refugees and Exiles, Report on the Application of the Dublin II Regulation in Europe*, (AD3/3/2006/EXT/MH) (2006).

Council of the European Union, *The EU and Africa: Towards a Strategic Partnership – The Way Forward and Key Achievements in 2006*, (16630/06), Brussels, 11 December 2006.

Council of the European Union, Brussels European Council. Presidency conclusions, 14–15 December 2006, (16879/1/06), Brussels, 12 February 2007.

Council of the European Union, Council Conclusions on Extending and Enhancing the Global Approach to Migration, Luxembourg, 17–18 June 2007.

Council of the European Union, Brussels European Council 14 December 2007: Presidency Conclusions (16616/1/07 REV 1), Brussels, 14 February 2008.

Council of the European Union, *Draft Council Conclusions on Mobility Partnerships and Circular Migration in the Framework of the Global Approach to Migration* (16283/07) Brussels, 7 December 2007.

Council of the European Union, *Joint Declaration on a Mobility Partnerships between the European Union and the Republic of Moldova*, (9460/08 ADD1), Brussels, 21 May 2008.

Council of the European Union, *Joint Declaration on a Mobility Partnership between the European Union and the Republic of Cape Verde*, (9460/08 ADD2), Brussels, 21 May 2008.

Council of the European Union, *European Pact on Immigration and Asylum*, (13440/08 ASIM 72), Brussels, 24 September 2008.

Council of the European Union, Brussels European Council 18–19 June 2009: Presidency Conclusions, (112252/2/09), Brussels, 10 July 2009.

Council of the European Union, *Commission Staff Working Document – Mobility Partnerships as a Tool of the Global Approach to Migration*, (13489/09), Brussels, 21 September 2009.

Council of the European Union, *The Stockholm Programme: An Open and Secure Europe Serving and Protecting the Citizens*, (17024/09), Brussels, 2 December 2009.

Council of the European Union, *The Stockholm Programme: An Open and Secure Europe Serving and Protecting the Citizens*, (2010/C 115/01), Brussels, 4 May 2010.

Council of the European Union, *Joint Declaration on a Mobility Partnership between the European Union and Armenia* (14963/11 ADD1), Brussels, 6 October 2011.

Council of the European Union, *Joint Declaration Establishing a Mobility Partnership Between the Kingdom of Morocco and the European Union and its Member States*, (6139/13 ADD 1 REV 1), Brussels, 12 April 2013.

Council of the European Union, *Extract from the 26–27 June 2014 European Council Conclusions Concerning the Area of Freedom, Security and Justice and some Related Horizontal Issues*, (OJ C 240), 24 July 2014.

Council of the European Union, *Joint Declaration on a Common Agenda on Migration and Mobility between the Federal Republic of Nigeria and the European Union and its Member States*, Brussels, 12 March 2015.

Council of the European Union, *Joint declaration on a Common Agenda on Migration and Mobility between the Federal Democratic Republic of Ethiopia and the European Union and its Member States*, Brussels, 11 November 2015.

Council of the European Union, *Summary of Discussions, High Level Working Group on Asylum and Migration*, (5657/17), Brussels, 31 January 2017.

Craig, P and de Búrca, G, *EU Law, Text, Cases and Materials* (Oxford: Oxford University Press 2012).

Creta, S, 'Number 9 – Stop violence at the borders!', https://www.youtube.com/watch?v=w67k5MkUEWQ (accessed 6 February 2016).

Curzi, CL, 'The Externalization of European Borders: Steps and Consequences of a Dangerous Process' Open Migration (12 July 2016) http://openmigration.org/en/analyses/the-externalisation-of-european-borders-steps-and-consequences-of-a-dangerous-process (accessed 12 October 2016).

D'Amato, A, 'Softness in International Law: A Self-Serving Quest for New Legal Materials, A Reply to Jean d'Aspremont' (2009) 20*EJIL* 897.

Dandashly, A, 'The EU Response to Regime Change in the Wake of the Arab Revolt: Differential Implementation' (2014) 37(1) *J Eur Integr* 37.

D'Aspremont, J, *Formalism and the Sources of International law* (Oxford: Oxford University Press 2011).

D'Aspremont, J, 'Softness in International Law: A Self-Serving Quest for New Legal Materials' (2008) 19(5) *EJIL* 1075.

De Bel-Air, F, 'Migration Profile: Morocco' (2016) *MPI Policy Brief.*

De Búrca, G, 'The Principle of Proportionality and its Application in EC Law' 105 in Barav, A and Wyatt, DA (eds), *YBEL 13* (Oxford: Oxford University Press 1993).

De Búrca, G, and Scott, J (eds), *Constitutional Change in the EU: From Uniformity to Flexibility* (Oxford: Bloomsbury 2000).

De Haas, H, 'Migration, Remittances and Regional Development in Southern Morocco' (2006) 37*Geoforum* 565.

De Haas, H, 'Mediterranean Migration Futures: Patterns, Drivers and Scenarios' (2011) 21 (1) *Glob Environ Change* S59.

De Haas, H, ' Morocco: Setting the Stage for Becoming a Migration Transition Country?', Migration Policy Institute (19 March 2014) www.migrationpolicy.org/article/morocco-setting-stage-becoming-migration-transition-country (accessed 24 March 2017).

Delcour, L, 'The EU: Shaping Migration Patterns in Its Neighbourhood and Beyond' 261 in Kochenov, D and Amtenbrink, F (eds), *The European Union's Shaping of the International Legal Order* (Cambridge: Cambridge University Press 2013).

Den Hertog, L, 'Money Talks: Mapping the Funding for EU External Migration Policy' (2016) 95*CEPS Paper in Liberty & Security in Europe.*

Dercaci, A, 'European Neighbourhood Policy: New Models of External Governance' 287 in Pérez de las Heras, B, *Democratic Legitimacy in the European Union and Global Governance: Building a European Demos* (Cham, Switzerland: Springer 2016).

De Witte, B, Hanf, D and Vos, E (eds), *The Many Faces of Differenciation in EU Law* (Antwerp, Belgium: Intersentia 2001).

DGI, *Balanço e Avaliação da Implementação do Plano de Acção da ENI de 2013 a 2015* (2016).

DIDH, 'Conseil national des droits de l'Homme, Bureau de l'Organisation Internationale pour les Migrations, argumentaire du séminaire régional "Gouvernance des migrations et droits de l'Homme"', *Rabat*, 15 July 2013.

Do, U and Huddleston, T, '"Negotiating Migration" 277 in the Euro Mediterranean. The Potential for EC Mobility Partnerships' (*IEMed-CIDOB Mediterranean Yearbook*2009) www.migpolgroup.com/public/docs/163 NegotiatingMigrationintheEuro Med.pdf (accessed 8 January 2018).

Dobbin, F, Simmons, B and Garrett, G, 'The Global Diffusion of Public Policies: Social Construction, Coercion, Competition, or Learning?' (2007) 33*Annu Rev Sociol* 449.

Douglas-Scott, S, 'A Tale of Two Courts: Luxembourg, Strasbourg and the Growing European Human Rights Acquis' (2006) *Common Mark Law Rev* 629.

Duke, K, Sales, R and Gregory, J, 'Refugee Resettlement in Europe' 105 in Bloch, A and Levy, C, *Refugees, Citizenship and Social Policy in Europe* (Basingstoke, UK: Palgrave Macmillan 1999).

Dupuy, RJ, 'Declaratory Law and Programmatory Law: From Revomutionary Custom to "Soft Law"' 247 in Akkerman, R, van Krieken, P, and Pannenborg, C (eds), *Declarations on Principles: A Quest for World Peace* (Leiden, The Netherlands: Sijthoff 1977).

Dupuy, PM, 'Soft Law and the International Law of the Environment' (1991) 12*Mich J Int'l L* 420.

EFG Consulting, *Imigração em Cabo Verde: Subsídios para a Política Nacional de Imigração Relatório Final da Comissão Interministerial para Estudo e Proposição das Bases da Política de Imigração* (2010).

Eisele, K, *The External Dimension of the EU's Migration Policy: Different Legal Positions of Third-Country Nationals in the EU, A Comparative Perspective* (Leiden, The Netherlands; Boston, MA: Nijhoff 2014).

Eisele, K,'The EU's Readmission Policy: Of Agreements and Arrangements' 135, in Carrera, S, Vara, JS and Strik, T, *Constitutionalising the External Dimensions of EU Migration Policies in Times of Crisis* (Cheltenham, UK: Edward Elgar 2019).

Ellis, J, 'Shades of grey: Soft Law and the Validity of Public International Law' (2011) 25 (2) *LJIL* 313.

El Moussaoui, H, 'Maroc – Carte RAMED: Couverture Médicale Gratuite ou Chèque en Bois?' *Libre Afrique* (8 February 2016) www.libreafrique.org/ElMoussaoui-RAMED-maroc-080216 (accessed 22 March 2017).

El Qadim, N, 'La Politique Migratoire Européenne Vue du Maroc: Contraintes et Opportunités' (2010) 31*Politique Européenne*.

El Qadim, N, *Le Gouvernement Asymétrique des Migrations: Maroc/Union Européenne* (Paris: Dalloz 2015).

El Qadim, N, 'De-EUropeanising European Borders: EU-Morocco Negotiations on Migrations and the Decentering Agenda in EU Studies' 134 in Woons, M and Weier, S, *Critical Epistemologies of Global Politics* (Bristol, UK: E-International Relations Publishing 2017).

Enders, A, *Histoire de l'Afrique Lusophone* (Paris: Chandeigen 2013).

Epstein, R and Sedelmeier, U, 'Beyond Conditionality: International Institutions in Post-communist Europe after Enlargement' (2008) 15(6) *J Eur Public Policy* 795.

Escoffier, C, *Droits Economiques et Sociaux des Migrants et des Réfugiés dans le Région Euromed: Accès aux Soins de Santé et au Marché du Travail* (Euro-Mediterranean Human Rights Network 2008).

Euro-Mediterranean Human Rights Network, *Analysis of the Mobility Partnership Signed Between the Kingdom of Morocco, the European Union and Nine Member States on 7 June 2013* (February 2014).

Euromed Rights, 'EU-Morocco Mobility Partnership: Border Control at the Expense of Human Lives?' (2014) www.euromedrights.org/publication/eu-morocco-mobility-partnership-border-control-at-the-expense-of-human-lives (accessed 20 August 2017).

European Court of Auditors, *Special Report No 9/2016, EU External Migration Spending in Southern Mediterranean and Eastern Neighbourhood Countries Until 2014* (Luxembourg2016).

European Migration Network, *Circular and Temporary Migration* (Luxembourg: National Contact Point 2011).

European Migration Network, *National Contact Point Luxembourg 2016 Annual Report on Migration and Asylum 25th April 2017 – Final Version 1*, (Luxembourg: National Contact Point 2017).

European Parliament, *EU-Africa Strategy: A Boost for Development* (2017/2083(INI), Committee report tabled for plenary, single reading), 24 October 2017.

European Training Foundation, 'Migration Support Measures from an Employment and Skills Perspective: Georgia' (2015) http://cadmus.eui.eu/bitstream/handle/1814/36841/MISMES_Georgia.pdf?sequence=1&isAllowed=y (accessed 10 August 2017).

European Training Foundation, 'Migration Support Measures from an Employment and Skills Perspective: Tunisia' (2015) www.etf.europa.eu/webatt.nsf/0/2938DD5003574A3EC1257E9A002BF071/$file/MISMES%20Tunisia.pdf (accessed 10 August 2017).

European Union, 'Conclusions on Countries in Which There is Generally No Serious Risk of Persecution (Conclusions on safe countries of origin)', 30 November 1992.

European Union, Joint Africa-EU Declaration on Migration and Development, Tripoli, 22–23 November 2006, (2006).

Fassmann, H and Munz, R, 'Patterns and Trends of International Migration in Western Europe' (1992) 18(3) *Popul Dev Rev* 457.

Faure, R, Gavas, M, and Knoll, A, *Challenges to a Comprehensive EU Migration and Asylum Policy* (London: Overseas Development Institute 2015).

FIDH and GADEM, *Maroc: Entre Rafles et Régularisations, Bilan d'une Politique Migratoire Indécise* (2012).

Fierro, E, *European Union's Approach to Human Rights Conditionality in Practice* (The Hague, The Netherlands; London; New York: Nijhoff 2003).

Finnemore, M and Toope, S, 'Alternative to "Legislation": Richer Views of Law and Politics' (2001) 55*Int Organ* 743.

Frattini, F, *Migration and Development: Time for Creative and Courageous Approaches, Speech to the EU-Africa Ministerial Conference on Migration and Development* (Tripoli22 November 2006).

Gabrielli, L, *Corridor Report on Spain: The Case of Ecuadorian and Moroccan Immigrants* (Interact Research Report 2015) (2015).

GADEM, *Rapport sur l'Application au Maroc de la Convention Internationale sur la Protection des Droits de Tous les Travailleurs Migrants et des Membres de leur Famille* (2013).

Geiger, A, '"Barcelona Process: Union for the Mediterranean" Readjusting the Euro-Mediterranean Partnership' (EU Office of the Friedrich-Ebert-Stiftung in Brussels 2008) http://library.fes.de/pdf-files/bueros/bruessel/05364.pdf (accessed 5 August 2017).

Geiger, M and Pécoud, A, 'The Politics of International Migration Management' 1 in Geiger, M and Pécoud, A (eds), *The Politics of International Migration Management* (Basingstoke, UK: Palgrave Macmillan 2010).

General Affairs and External Relations Council, *2463rd Meeting of the General and External Relations Council*, (14183/02), Brussels, 18 November 2002, V.

Gibert, M, 'The New European Security Architecture: An Example of "Messy Multilateralism"?' 179 in Chafer, T and Cumming, G (eds), *From Rivalry to Partnership? New Approaches to the Challenges of Africa* (Aldershot, UK: Ashgate 2011).

Global Commission on International Migration, *Migration in an Interconnected World: New Directions for Action. Report of the Global Commission on International Migration* (5 October 2005).

Goodwin-Gill, GS, 'The Right to Seek Asylum: Interception at Sea and the Principle of Non-Refoulement' (2011) 23(3) *IJRL* 443.

Gruchalla-Wesierski, T, 'A Framework for Understanding "Soft Law"' (1984) 30*J McGill Law* 37.

Guedes Vieira, AV and Ferreira-Pereira, LC, 'The European Union-Cape Verde Special Partnership: The Role of Portugal' (2009) 42(1) *PJIA* 42.

Guiraudon, V, 'European Integration and Migration Policy: Vertical Policy-making as Venue Shopping' (2000) 38(2) *JCMS* 251.

Guth, J, 'Transforming the European Legal Order: The European Court of Justice at 60+' (2016) 12(1) *JCER* 455.

Guzman, A and Meyer, T, 'International Soft Law' (2010) 2(1) *JLA* 171.

Haddad, E, 'The External Dimension of EU Refugee Policy: A New Approach to Asylum?' (2008) 43(2) *Gov Oppos* 190.

Haddadi, S, 'Two Cheers for Whom? The European Union and Democratization in Morocco' (2002) 9*Democratization* 149.

Hampshire, J, 'European Migration Governance since the Lisbon Treaty: Introduction to' (2016) 42(4) *J Ethn Migr Stud* 537.

Hampshire, J, 'European Migration Governance since the Lisbon Treaty: 'Speaking with One Voice? The European Union's Global Approach to Migration and Mobility and the Limits of International Migration Cooperation' (2016) 42(4) *J Ethn Migr Stud* 571.

Hartley, TC, *The Foundations of European Union Law* (Oxford: Oxford University Press 2010).

Hatton, TJ, 'European Asylum Policy' (2005) 194*Rev Natl Inst Econ* 106.

Henson, P and Malhan, N, 'Endeavours to Export a Migration Crisis: Policy-Making and Europeanisation in the German Migration Dilemma' (1995) 4(3) *German Politics* 128.

Hillgenberg, H, 'A Fresh Look at Soft Law' (1999) 10(3) *EJIL* 499.

Hooghe, M et al, 'Migration to European Countries: A Structural Explanation of Patterns, 1980–2004' (2008) 42(2) *Int Migr Rev* 476.

Hooper, K, *Exploring New Legal Migration Pathways: Lessons from Pilot Projects*, (Washington, DC: Migration Policy Institute 2019) 1.

Hyndman, J and Mountz, A, 'Another Brick in the Wall? Neo-Refoulement and the Externalization of Asylum by Australia and Europe' (2008) 43*Govt & Opposition* 249.

İçduygu, A and Aksel, DB, 'Two-to-Tango in Migration Diplomacy: Negotiating Readmission Agreement between the EU and Turkey' (2014) 16*EJML* 337.

ICMPD and IOM, *A Survey on Migration Policies in West Africa* (2015).

Ikeda, R, *The Imperialism of French Decolonisation: French Policy and the Anglo-American Response in Tunisia and Morocco* (London: Palgrave Macmillan 2015).

Ilhéu, F, 'The Role of China in the Portuguese Speaking African Countries: The Case of Mozambique'. 84*Documentos de Trabalho*, (Centro de Estudos sobre África e do Desenvolvimento Instituto Superior de Economia e Gestão da Universidade Técnica de Lisboa 2010).

IOM, *Migração em Cabo Verde: Perfil Nacional* (2009).

IOM, 'The European Union-Moldova Mobility Partnership 2008–2011: Evaluation Report' (2012) www.mfa.gov.md/img/docs/eu-moldova-mobility-partnership-evaluation.pdf (accessed 31 October 2017).

IOM, *Estrategia Nacional de Emigraçao e Desenvolvimento* (2014).

IOM, *Maroc, Bilan 2016*, (*Edition* 31, January–December 2016).

IOM, *Perfil Migratório de Cabo Verde* (2017 Draft).

IOM, 'Migração em Cabo Verde: Perfil Nacional' 'Migration and the Economic Crisis in the European Union: Implications for Policy' (2010) www.labourmigration.eu/resea

rch/report/12-migration-and-the-economic-crisis-implications-for-policy-in-the-europ ean-union (accessed 28 August 2017).

Jacobsson, K, 'Between Deliberation and Discipline: Soft Governance in the EU Employment Policy' 81 in Mörth, U (ed.), *Soft Law in Governance and Regulation: An Interdisciplinary Analysis* (Cheltenham, UK: Edward Elgar 2004).

Jans, J, 'Proportionality Revisited' (2000) 27(3) *Legal Issues of Economic Integration* 239.

Jerónimo, P, 'Imigração e Cidadania na União Europeia: o Estado de Residente de Longa Duração' 325 in Silveira, A (ed.), *Direito da União Europeia e Transnacionalidade* (Lisbon: Quid Juris 2011).

Jerónimo, P, 'A Cidadania comoIinstrumento de Inclusão: Significado e Alcance da Promessa de uma Cidadania Cívica da União Europeia' 182 in Freitas da Rocha, J (ed.), *Anuário Publicista da Escola de Direito da Universidade do Minho – Tomo I, Ano de 2012 – Responsabilidade e Cidadania* (Departamento de Ciências Jurídicas Públicas Escola de Direito da Universidade do Minho 2012).

Jerónimo, P and Vink, M, 'Os Múltiplos de Cidadania e os seus Direitos' 23 in Costa Lobo, M (ed.), *Portugal e a Europa: Novas Cidadanias* (Fundação Francisco Manuel dos Santos e União Europeia 2013).

Jetschke, A and Murray, P, 'Diffusing Regional Integration: the EU and Southeast Asia' (2012) 35(1) *West Eur Politics* 174.

Joppke, C, 'Immigration Challenges the Nation-State' 5 in Joppke, C (ed.), *Challenge to the Nation-State: Immigration in Western Europe and the United States* (Oxford: Oxford University Press 1998).

Juncker, JC, *A New Start for Europe: My Agenda for Jobs, Growth, Fairness and Democratic Change, Political Guidelines for the next European Commission*, Opening Statement in the European Parliament Plenary Session, Strasbourg, 15 July 2014.

Juss, S, 'The Decline and Decay of European Refugee Policy' (2005) 25(4) *Oxf J Leg Stud* 749.

Justice and Home Affairs Council, *Action Plan of the Council and the Commission on How Best to Implement the Provisions of the Treaty of Amsterdam Establishing an Area of Freedom, Security and Justice*, (1999/C 19/01), 3 December 1998.

Kassim, H and Le Galès, P, 'Exploring Governance in a Multi-Level Polity: A Policy Instruments Approach' (2010) 33(1) *West Eur Politics* 1.

Kelley, J, 'New Wine in Old Wineskins: Promoting Political Reforms through the New European Neighbourhood Policy' (2006) 44(1) *JCMS* 29.

Keukeleire, S and MacNaughtan, J, *The Foreign Policy of the European Union* (London: Palgrave Macmillan 2008).

Khachani, M, 'La Migration Circulaire: Cas du Maroc' (2008) *CARIM Analytic and Synthetic Notes.*

Khachani, M, 'La Migration Irrégulière au Maroc: Un Etat des Lieux' 43 in Haut-Commissariat du Plan (ed.), *Les Cahiers du Plan no 29* (2010).

Khrouz, N, 'De la Respécification de la Notion de Transit' 103 in Khrouz, N and Lanza, N (eds), *Migrants au Maroc: Cosmopolitisme, présence d'étrangers et transformations sociales* (Rabat: Centre Jacques-Berque 2015).

Klabbers, J, 'Informal Instruments before the European Court of Justice' (1994) 31*Common Mark Law Rev* 997.

Klabbers, J, 'The Redundancy of Soft Law' (1996) 65(2) *NJIL* 167.

Klabbers, J, 'Informal Instruments before the European Court of Justice''Law-making and Constitutionalism' 81 in Klabbers, J, Peters, A and Ulfstein, G (eds), *The Constitutionalization of International Law* (Oxford: Oxford University Press 2009).

Kohstall, F, 'Strenghtening Autocracy: The World Bank and Social Reform in Egypt' in Daase, C and Firesendorf, C (eds), *Rethinking Security Governance: The Problem of Unintended Consequences* (London: Routledge, 2010).

Kotlok, N, 'Le "Développement Solidaire" une Politique Migratoire au Service du Développement des Pays Africains?' (2010) *Hommes et migrations* 268.

Koutrakos, P, *European Foreign Policy: Legal and Political Perspectives* (Cheltenham, UK: Edward Elgar 2011).

Kunz, R, Lavenex, S and Panizzon, M, 'Introduction: Governance Through Partnerships' 1 in Kunz, R, Lavenex, S and Panizzon, M (eds), *Multilayered Migration Governance: The Promise of Partnership* (London, New York: Routledge 2011).

Kuptsch, C, 'The Economic Crisis and Labour Migration Policy in European Countries' (2012) 37(1–2) *Comparative Population Studies* 15.

Kuzel, A, 'Sampling in Qualitative Inquiry' 33 in Crabtree, B and Miller, W (eds), Doing Qualitative Research (Newbury Park, CA: Sage 1992).

Lahlou, M, *Le Maghreb dans son Environnement Régional et International: Un Schéma Migratoire Reconfiguré, dans les Faits et dans l'Approche Politique* (Paris: Ifri-Programme Migrations, identités, citoyenneté 2011).

Lambert, H, 'Asylum Seekers, Refugees and the European Union Case Studies of France and the UK', 112 in Miles, R and Thränhardt, D, *Migration and European Integration: The Dynamics of Inclusion and Exclusion* (London; Madison, NJ: Fairleigh Dickinson University Press 1995).

Lavenex, S, 'Justice and Home Affairs and the EU's New Neighbours: Governance Beyond Membership?' 89 in Henderson, K, *The Area of Freedom, Security and Justice in the Enlarged Europe* (Basingstoke: Palgrave Macmillan 2005).

Lavenex, S, 'Shifting Up and Out: The Foreign Policy of European Immigration Control' (2006) 29(2) *West Eur Politics* 329.

Lavenex, S, '*Multilayered Migration Governance: The Partnership Approach in the EU and Beyond*', UNRISD Conference: Regional Governance of Migration and Socio-Political Rights – Institutions, Actors and Processes, 14–15 January 2013, Geneva, Switzerland.

Lavenex, S, and Kunz, R, 'The Migration–Development Nexus in EU External Relations' (2008) 30(3) *J Eur Integr* 439.

Lavenex, S, and Schimmelfennig, F, 'EU Rules Beyond EU Borders: Theorizing External Governance in European Politics' (2009) 16(6) *J Eur Public Policy* 791.

Lavenex, S, and Stucky, R, 'Partnering for Migration in EU External Relations' 116 in Kunz, R, Lavenex, S and Panizzon, M (eds), *Multilayered Migration Governance: The Promise of Partnership* (London: Routledge 2011).

Lavenex, S, and Uçarer, EM, *Migration and the Externalities of European Integration* (Lanham, MD: Lexington Books 2003).

Lavenex, S, and Uçarer, EM, 'The External Dimension of Europeanization: The Case of Immigration Policies' (2004) 39(4) *Cooperation and Conflict* 417.

Lavenex, S, 'and Wichmann, N, 'The External Governance of EU Internal Security' (2008) 31(1) *J Eur Integr* 83.

Lee, ES, 'A Theory of Migration' (1966) 3(1) *Demography* 47.

Leech, BL, 'Asking Questions: Techniques for Semi-Structured Interviews' (2002) 35(4) *PS Political Sci Politics* 665.

Lefébure, A, 'Qui sont les Sans-Abris au Maroc?' *HuffPost Maroc* (2 October 2017) www.huffpostmaghreb.com/2017/10/02/qui-sont-les-sans-abris-au-maroc_n_18161064.html (accessed 3 December 2017).

Lehne, S, 'The Big Three in EU Foreign Policy' (2012) *Carnegie Europe*http://carnegieeurope.eu/2012/07/05/big-three-in-eu-foreign-policy-pub-48759 (accessed 27 December 2017).

Lelieveldt, H and Princen, S, *The Politics of the European Union* (Cambridge: Cambridge University Press 2015).

Lenz, T, 'Spurred Emulation: The EU and Regional Integration in Mercosur and SADC' (2012) 35(1) *West Eur Politics* 155.

Limam, M and Del Sarto, R, 'Periphery under Pressure: Morocco, Tunisia and the European Union's Mobility Partnership on Migration' (2015) *EUI Working Paper RSCAS* 75.

Mack, N et al, *Qualitative Research Methods: A Data Collector's Field Guide* (USAID 2005).

Maiani, F, *The Reform of the Dublin III Regulation*, Study for the Civil Liberties, Justice and Home Affairs Committee, Directorate General for Internal Policies, Policy Department C Citizens' Rights and Constitutional Affairs, European Parliament, (PE 571.360) (2016).

Maisenbacher, J, 'The Political Economy of Mobility Partnerships – Structural Power in the EU's External Migration Policy' (2015) 20(6) *NPE* 871.

Mananashvili, S, 'The Diffusion of the EU Asylum Acquis in the Eastern Neighbourhood: A Test for the EU's Normative Power' (2015) 20(2) *EFAR* 187.

Manners, I, 'Normative Power Europe: A contradiction in Terms?' (2002) 40(2) *JCMS* 235.

Marinaro, F, *Report Drawn Up on Behalf of the Committee on Social Affairs and Employment on the Communication from the Commission of the European Communities to the Council (Doc. C2–6/85- COM(85) 48 final) on Guidelines for a Community Policy on Migration Together with a Draft Council Resolution*, Working Documents 1985 1986, Document A2–4/85, 1 April 1985.

Martin, M, 'Extension of Mobility Partnerships with Euro-Mediterranean Partners' (2012) *Panorama, Culture and Society* 279.

Martinez, LF, 'Les Migrations en Transit au Maroc: Attitudes et Comportement de la Société Civile face au Phénomène' (2009) *L'année du Maghreb*https://anneemaghreb.revues.org/611 (accessed 3 February 2018).

Martiniello, M, 'The New Migratory Europe: Towards a Proactive Immigration Policy?' 298 in Parsons, C and Smeeding, T, *Immigration and the Transformation of Europe* (Cambridge: Cambridge University Press 2006).

Massey, DS et al, 'Theories of International Migration: A Review and Appraisal' (1993) *Popul Dev Rev* 431.

Massey, DS et al, *Worlds in Motion: Understanding International Migration at the End of the Millennium* (Oxford: Clarendon Press 1998).

May, P, 'Policy Design and Implementation' 223 in Peters, BG and Pierre, J, *Handbook of Public Administration* (London: Sage 2003).

Mayall, J, 'The Shadow of Empire: The EU and the Former Colonial World' 292 in Hill, C and Smith, M (eds), *International Relations and the European Union* (Oxford: Oxford University Press 2005).

MCMREAM, 'Stratégie Nationale d'Immigration et d'Asile' (2014) www.marocainsdumonde.gov.ma/fr/le-minist%C3%A8re/affaires-de-la-migration/strat%C3%A9gie nationale-dimmigration-et-dasile (accessed 13 August 2016).

MCMREAM, *Guide des Marocains Résidant à l'Etranger* (2015).

MCMREAM, *Politique Nationale d'Immigration et d'Asile: 2013–2016* (September 2016).

MCMREAM, *Stratégie Nationale pour les Marocains Résidant à l'Etranger, Bilan 2013–2016* (2016).

McNair, A, *The Law of the Treaties* (Oxford: Oxford University Press 1961).

Médecins Sans Frontières, 'Violences, Vulnérabilité et Migration: Bloqués aux Portes de l'Europe' (13 March 2013) www.msf.fr/actualite/publications/violences-vulnerabilite-et-migration-bloques-aux-portes-europe (accessed 6 February 2016).

Melotti, U, 'Migratory Policies and Political Cultures in Europe: Is there Something New?' (Heinrich Böll Stiftung 2008). https://heimatkunde.boell.de/2008/03/01/migratory-policies-and-political-cultures-europe-there-something-new (accessed 17 January 2017).

Merton, R, 'The Unanticipated Consequences of Purposive Social Action' (1936) 1(6) *Am Sociol Rev* 894.

Meyns, P, 'Cape Verde: An African Exception' (2002) 13(3) *JoD* 153.

Migreurop, 'In Morocco, the Hunt for Foreigners Kills, and While this is Going On, the EU Negotiates and Keeps Quiet', Press Release (2 August 2013) www.migreurop.org/article2272.html?lang=fr (accessed 8 March 2017).

Miller, J, 'A Typology of Legal Transplants: Using Sociology, Legal History and Argentine Examples to Explain the Transplants Process' (2003) 51(4) *Am J Comp L* 839.

Ministère de l'Economie et des Finances, *Relations Maroc-Afrique: l'Ambition d'une Nouvelle Frontière* (2014).

Ministère de l'Emploi et des Affaire Sociales, *Stratégie Nationale pour l'Emploi', Comité de pilotage de la SNE du 24 février 2015* (2015).

Ministère de l'Intérieur, 'L'Admission au Séjour: Les Titres de Séjour (statistiques)' www.immigration.interieur.gouv.fr/Immigration/L-admission-au-sejour-Les-titres-de-sejour-statistiques (accessed 7 December 2017).

Ministério dos NegociosEstrangeiros, *Balanço da Presidência Portuguesa do Conselho da Uniao Europeia, 1 de Julho a 31 de Dezembro de 2007* (2007).

Monar, J, 'Justice and Home Affairs: The Treaty of Maastricht as a Decisive Intergovernmental Gate Opener' (2012) 34(7) *J Eur Integr* 717.

Mörth, U, *Soft Law in Governance and Regulation: An Interdisciplinary Analysis* (Cheltenham, UK: Edward Elgar 2004).

Müller, P, 'EU Foreign Policy: No Major Breakthrough despite Multiple Crises' (2016) 38 (3) *JEI* 359.

Natter, K, 'The Formation of Morocco's Policy Towards Irregular Migration (2000–2007): Political Rationale and Policy Processes' (2014) 52(5) *Int Migr* 15.

Nuno, M, *Migration Policies of the European Union with its Mediterranean Partners: Need for Greater Mobility*, Study (PE 457.131), (Directorate-General for External Policies of the Union, Directorate B, European Parliament 2014).

Nuno, M, and Souiah, F, 'Les Politiques Mises en Place par le Maroc Envers ses Ressortissants' (2013) 1303*Hommes et migrations* 147http://hommesmigrations.revues.org/2574 (accessed 2 January 2017).

OECD, *The Challenge of Capacity Development: Working towards Good Practices* (2006).

Olivier, M, 'The Relevance of "Soft Law" as a Source of International Human Rights' (2002) 35(3) *Comp Int Law J South Afr* 289.

Orb, A, Eisenhauer, L and Wynaden, D, 'Ethics in Qualitative Research' (2000) 33(1) *JNS* 93.

Özler, Z, 'Breaking the Vicious Circle in EU-Turkey Relations: Visa Negotiations' (2012) 11(1) *TPQ* 121.

Paxton, J, *The Statesman's Year-Book 1974–75: The Encyclopaedia for the Businessman-of-the-World* (London and Basingstoke, UK: Springer 2016).

Panara, C, *The Sub-National Dimension of the EU: A Legal Study of Multilevel Governance* (Heidelberg, Germany: Springer 2015).

Papastavridis, E, 'Enforcement Jurisdiction in the Mediterranean Sea: Illicit Activities and the Rule of Law on the High Seas' (2010) 25 *IJMCL* 569.

Parkes, R, *Mobility Partnerships: Valuable Addition to the ENP Repertoire?* (SWP Working Papers FG 1 2009/03), (Berlin: Stiftung Wissenschaft und Politik 2009).

Parkes, R, 'EU Mobility Partnerships: A Model of Policy Coordination?' (2009) 11(4) *EJML* 327.

Passaris, C, 'Immigration and the Evolution of Economic Theory' (1989) 27(4) *Int Migr* 525.

Pattenden, R, 'The Discretionary Exclusion of Relevant Evidence in English Civil Proceedings' (1996) 1 *Int'l J Evidence & Proof* 361.

Palgrave Macmillan Staff, *The Statesman's Yearbook 2012: The Politics, Cultures and Economies of the World* (New York: Springer 2011).

Patrick, SM, 'The EU's Migration Crisis: When Solidarity and Sovereignty Collide' (2015) Council on Foreign Relationswww.cfr.org/blog/eus-migration-crisis-when-solidarity-and-sovereignty-collide (accessed 27 December 2017).

Pauwelyn, J, 'Is It International Law or Not, and Does it Even Matter?' 125 in Pauwelyn, J (ed.), *Informal International Lawmaking* (Oxford: Oxford University Press 2012).

Peers, S, 'Building Fortress Europe: The Development of EU Migration Law' (1998) 35 *Common Mark Law Rev* 1235.

Peers, S, 'Legislative Update: EU Immigration and Asylum Competence and Decision-Making in the Treaty of Lisbon' (2008) 10(2) *EJML* 219.

Peers, S, *EU Justice and Home Affairs Law* (Oxford: Oxford University Press 2011).

Pennell, CR, *Morocco since 1830: A History* (New York: New York University Press 2000).

Pereira, JL, 'Theorizing the EU Conditionality Policy and its Application in West African Countries: The Case of Cape Verde' (2014) *ESJ Special Edition* 389.

Perrin, D, *Immigration and Citizenship Law in the Maghreb: Turning Aliens into Citizens*, (EUI Working Paper RSCAS 2011/40), June 2011.

Perrin, D, *Country Report: Morocco*, (RSCAS/EUDO-CIT-CR 2011/42), October 2011.

Pfetsch, FR, 'Power in International Negoiations: Symmetry and Asymmetry' (2011/2012) *Négociations* 16.

Pina-Delgado, J, 'La Regulación Internacional de los Flujos Migratorios entre Cabo Verde y la Unión Europea (en especial hacia España)' (2011) 28 *Revista de derecho migratorio y extranjeria* 121.

Pina-Delgado, J, 'O Cruzamento entre a Política Migratória Cabo-Verdiana para a Europa e a Política Migratória Cabo-Verdiana para a África Ocidental' 523 in Costa, S and Sarmento, C (eds), *Entre África e a Europa: Nação, Estado e Democracia em Cabo Verde* (Coimbra, Portugal: Almedina 2013).

Portuese, A, 'The Case for a Principled Approach to Law and Economics: Efficiency Analysis and Genreal Principles of EU Law' 275 in Mathis, K (ed.), *Law and Economics in Europe: Foundations and Applications* (Dordrecht, The Netherlands: Springer 2013).

PRO Asyl, 'Out of Sight, out of Mind: Externalisation of Migration and Refugee Policies' (5 August 2016) www.proasyl.de/en/news/out-of-sight-out-of-mind-externalisation-and-regionalisation-of migration-and-refugee-policie (accessed 12 October 2017).

Raimundo, A, 'Mapping the Agency of a Small, Former Colonial Power. Portugal and EU Political Conditionality in Sub-Saharan Africa' (2014) 15(4) *Perspectives on European Politics and Society* 589.

Ramos, MC, 'Some Ethical Implications of Qualitative Research' (1989) 12(1) *RNH* 57.

Ravenstein, EG, 'The Laws of Migration' (1885) 48(2) *J Royal Stat Soc* 167.

Ravenstein, EG, 'The Laws of Migration' (1889) 52(2) *J Royal Stat Soc* 241.

República de Cabo Verde, Governo de Cabo Verde, 'Programa do Governo VIII Legislatura 2011–2016' para A (2011).

República de Cabo Verde, 'Programa do Governo, IX Legislatura (2016)' (2016) http://peds.gov.cv/sites/default/files/2018-06/Programa%20do%20Governo%20da%20IX%20Legislatura%202016-2021.pdf (accessed 11 February 2018).

Reslow, N, 'Migration and Development? An Assessment of Recent EU Initiatives' (2010) 6(1) *JCER* 3.

Reslow, N, 'Deciding on EU External Migration Policy: The Member States and the Mobility Partnerships' (2012) 34(3) *JEI* 223.

Reslow, N, 'The Role of Third Countries in EU Migration Policy: The Mobility Partnerships' (2012) 14*EJML* 393.

Reslow, N, *Partnering for Mobility? Three-level Games in EU External Migration Policy* (Maastricht, The Netherlands: Datawyse/Universitaire Pers 2013).

Reslow, N, 'EU "Mobility" Partnerships: An Initial Assessment of the Implementation Dynamics' (2015) 3(2) *Politics and Governance* 117.

Reslow, N, '"Not Everything that Counts can be Counted": Assessing "Success" of EU External Migration Policy' (2017) *Int Migr* 1.

Reslow, N, 'Transformation or Continuity? EU External Migration Policy in the Aftermath of the Migrant Crisis' 106 in Carrera, S, Vara, JS and Strik, T, *Constitutionalising the External Dimensions of EU Migration Policies in Times of Crisis* (Cheltenham, UK: Edward Elgar 2019).

Reslow, N, and Vink, M, 'Three-Level Games in EU External Migration Policy: Negotiating Mobility Partnerships in West Africa' (2014) 53(4) *JCMS* 857.

Ritchie, J and Lewis, J, *Qualitative Research Practice: A Guide for Social Science Students and Researchers* (London: Sage 2003).

Roger, B, 'Manuel Valls à Rabat: la France Souhaite Faciliter l'Obtention de Visas pour les Marocains' *Jeune Afrique* (26 July 2012) www.jeuneafrique.com/175018/politique/manuel-valls-rabat-la-france-souhaite-faciliter-l-obtention-de-visas-pour-les-marocains (accessed 17 October 2016).

Roos, C, *The EU and Immigration Policies: Cracks in the Walls of Fortress Europe?* (Basingstoke, UK: Palgrave Macmillan 2013).

Rosas, A, 'The European Union and Mixed Agreements' 200 in Dashwood, A and Hillion, C (eds), *The General Law of EC External Relations* (London: Sweet and Maxwell 2000).

Royal Institute for Strategic Studies, *La Politique Africaine du Maroc*, 26 October 2015.

Sarkozy, N and Schäuble, W, *New European Migration Policy: A Franco-German Plan Presented by Nicolas Sarkozy and Wolfgang Schäuble to G6 Immigration Ministers Meeting in the UK*, 26 October 2006.

Santos, O, 'A Livre Circulação de Pessoas e Bens na CEDEAO está em Debate em Cabo Verde' *RFI Português* (24 May 2010) http://pt.rfi.fr/africa/20100524-livre-circulacao-de-pessoas-e-bens-na-cedeao-esta-em-debate-em-cabo-verde (accessed 16 April 2017).

Sayad, A, *The Suffering of the Immigrant* (Cambridge: Wiley 2004).

Schimmelfennig, F, Engert, S and Knobel, H, 'Costs, Commitment and Compliance: The Impact of EU Democratic Conditionality in Latvia, Slovakia and Turkey' (2003) 41(3) *JCMS* 495.

Schimmelfennig, F, Engert, S and Knobel, H, and Sedelmeier, U, 'Governance by Conditionality: EU Rule Transfer to the Candidate Countries of Central and Eastern Europe' (2004) 11(4) *J Eur Public Policy* 661.

Schermers, HG, 'A Typology of Mixed Agreements' 23 in O'Keeffe, D and Schermers, HG (eds), *Mixed Agreements* (Deventer, The Netherlands: Kluwer 1983).

Schulz, F, 'Von der Leyen Promises New Migration Package in First Half of 2020', *Euractive*12 November 2019www.euractiv.com/section/future-eu/news/von-der-leyen-promises-new-migration-package-in-first-half-of-2020 (accessed 18 December 2019).

Scott, J, 'Extraterritoriality and Territorial Extension in EU Law' (2013) 62(1) *Am J Comp Law* 87.

Seddiki, N, 'Place du Droit International dans le Système Juridique des Etats' (2013) *Revue Maroco-Espagnole de Droit International et Relations Internationales* 153.

Seeberg, P, *Mobility Partnerships and the EU, Part I: Where are we Regarding Implementation and what will be the Consequences?* (Odense, Denmark: Center for Contemporary Middle East Studies 2014).

Senden, L, *Soft Law in European Community Law Modern Studies in European Law* (Oxford: Bloomsbury 2004).

Senden, L, 'Soft Law, Self-regulation and Co-regulation in European Law: Where do they Meet?' (2005) 9(1) *EJCL* 1.

Serviço de Estrangeiros e Fronteiras, *Temporary and Circular Migration in Portugal: Facts, Policies and Strategies* (European Migration Network 2010).

Serviço de Estrangeiros e Fronteiras, *Relatório de Imigração, Fronteiras e Asilo*, 2014.

Sidiguitiebe, C, 'Campagne de Régularisation des Migrants: ce qu'il Faut Savoir' *Telquel.ma* (13 December 2016) http://telquel.ma/2016/12/13/campagne-regularisation-migrants-ce-quil-faut-savoir_1527188 (accessed 8 February 2017).

Silva, N and Chantre, A, 'Cape Verde: A Large Diaspora and Low Turnout by External Voters' 200 in International IDEA and IFE, *Voting from Abroad: The International IDEA Handbook* (2007).

Simmons, BA and Steinberg, RH, *International Law and International Relations. An International Organization Reader* (Cambridge: Cambridge University Press 2007).

Shaffer, G and Pollack, M, 'Hard vs Soft Law: Alternatives, Complements and Antagonists in International Governance' (2010) 94*Minn Law Rev* 706.

Skeldon, R, *Population Mobility in Developing Countries: A Reinterpretation* (London; New York: Belhaven Press 1990).

Smartt, U, *Optimize Public Law* (Oxford: Routledge 2014).

Smith, KE, 'The Use of Political Conditionality in the EU's Relations with Third Countries: How Effective?' (1998) 3*European Foreign Affairs Review* 253.

Snyder, F, 'Soft Law and Institutional Practice in the European Community' 198 in Martin, S (ed.), *The Construction of Europe* (Dordrecht, The Netherlands; Boston, MA: Springer 1994).

Snyder, F, 'Interinstitutional Agreements: Forms and Constitutional Limitations' 453 in Winter, G (ed.), *Sources and Categories of European Union Law: A Comparative and Reform Perspective* (Baden-Baden, Germany: Nomos 1996).

Sokol, D, 'International Antitrust Institutions' 187 in Guzmán, AT, *Cooperation, Comity, and Competition Policy* (Oxford: Oxford University Press 2011).

Sorensen, G, *Political Conditionality* (London; New York: Routledge 2013).

Statewatch, 'Frontex: Cooperation with Non-EU States' *March Briefing*2017.

Ştefan, OA, 'European Competition Soft Law in European Courts: A Matter of Hard Principles?' (2008) 14(6) *ELJ* 753.

Ştefan, OA, 'European Soft law: New Developments Concerning the Divide between Legally Binding Force and Legal effects' (2012) 75(5) *Mod Law Rev* 879.

Ştefan, OA, 'Soft Law and Enforcement of EU Law' 200 in Jakab, A and Kochenov, D (eds), *The Enforcement of EU Law and Values: Ensuring Member States' Compliance* (Oxford: Oxford University Press 2017).

Stent, GS, *Paradoxes of Free Will* (Philadelphia, PA: American Philosophical Society 2002).

Stern, M, 'The Karthoum Process: Critical Assessment and Policy Recommendations' (2015) *IAI Working Papers* 15/49, December 2015, www.iai.it/sites/default/files/iaiwp1549.pdf (accessed 25 November 2017).

Stunkel, L et al, 'Comprehension and Informed Consent: Assessing the Effect of a Short Consent Form' (2010) 32(4) *IRB* 1.

Tanzi, A, 'Problems of Enforcement of Decisions of the International Court of Justice and the Law of the United Nations' (1995) 6*EJIL* 539.

Tarver, HM and Slape, E, *The Spanish Empire: A Historical Encyclopedia* (Santa Barbara, CA: ABC-CLIO 2016).

Teitelbaum, MS, 'Immigration, Refugees, and Foreign Policy' (1984) 38(3) *Int Organ* 429.

Temperman, J, *State-Religion Relationships and Human Rights Law: Towards a Right to Religiously Neutral Governance* (Leiden, The Netherlands: Brill 2010).

Terpan, F, 'Soft Law in the European Union—The Changing Nature of EU Law' (2015) 21*ELJ* 68.

Thielemann, ER, 'Why Asylum Policy Harmonisation Undermines Refugee Burden-Sharing' (2004) 6*EJML* 47.

Thies, CG, 'A Pragmatic Guide to Qualitative Historical Analysis in the Study of International Relations' (2002) 3(4) *Int Stud Perspect* 351.

Thirlway, H, *The Sources of International Law* (Oxford: Oxford University Press 2014).

Thürer, D, The Role of Soft Law in the Actual Process of European Integration 131 in Jacot-Guillarmod, O (ed.), *L'avenir du Libre-Echange en Europe: Vers un Espace Economique Européen?* (Zürich, Switzerland: Schultess Polygraphischer Verlag 1990).

Tittel-Mosser, F, 'Mobility Partnerships: A Tool for the Externalization of EU Migration Policy? A Comparative Study of Morocco and Cape Verde' 238 in Carrera, S, Vara, JS and Strik, T (eds), *Constitutionalising the External Dimensions of EU Migration Policies in Times of Crisis Legality, Rule of Law and Fundamental Rights Reconsidered* (Cheltenham, UK: Edward Elgar 2019)

Tittel-Mosser, F, 'The Unintended Legal and Policy Relevance of EU Mobility Partnerships: A Comparative Implementation Analysis of Morocco and Cape Verde' (2018) 20*EJML* 314.

Tittel-Mosser, F, 'Reversed Conditionality in EU External Migration Policy: The Case of Morocco' (2018) 14(4) *JCER* 349.

Toepoel, V, *Doing Surveys Online* (London: Sage 2015).

Tolentino, AC, Rocha CM and Tolentino NC, 'A Importancia e o Impacto das Remessas dos Immigrates em Portugal no Desenvolvimento de Cabo Verde', *Observatório Da Imigração*, April 2008.

Tomasevski, K, *Between Sanctions and Elections: Aid Donors and their Human Rights Performance* (London: Pinter 1997).

Trauner, F and Kruse, I, 'EC Visa Facilitation and Readmission Agreements: Implementing a New EU Security Approach in the Neighbourhood' (2008) 290*CEPS Working Document*.

Triandafyllidou, A, 'Circular Migration: Introductory Remarks' 1 in Triandafyllidou, A (ed.), *Circular Migration Between European and its Neighbourhood: Choice or Necessity?* (Oxford: Oxford University Press 2013).

Trubek, DM, Cottrell, P and Nance, M, '"Soft Law", "Hard Law", and European Integration: Toward a Theory of Hybridity' (2005) 1002*University of Wisconsin Law School Legal Studies Research Paper Series*.

Trubek, DM, Cottrell, P and Nance, M and Trubek, L, 'Hard and Soft Law in the Construction of Social Europe: The Role of the Open Method of Co-ordination' (2005) 11 (3) *ELJ* 343.

Trusted, J, *Moral Principles and Social Values* (London: Routledge & Kegan Paul 1987).

Tusalem, RF, 'The Colonial Foundations of State Fragility and Failure' (2016) 48(4) *Polity* 445.

UCI, *Plano de Acção 2013–2016 da Estratégia Nacional de Imigração* (2013).

UCI, *Estudio Diagnostico: Identificação das Necessidades dos Imigrantes no Processo de Integração Social em Cabo Verde* (2014).

United Nations, Department of Economic and Social Affairs, 'Recommendations on Statistics on International Migration Revision', 58*Statistical Paper Series M*, (Rev 1), United Nations, Human Rights Committee (HRC), New York, 1998.

United Nations, Department of Economic and Social Affairs, 'CCPR General Comment No. 28: Article 3 (The Equality of Rights between Men and Women)' (29 March 2000), CCPR/C/21/Rev.1/Add.10.

United Nations, Department of Economic and Social Affairs, *Report of the Human Rights Committee A/60/40 Volume I* (2004).

United Nations, Department of Economic and Social Affairs, Economic and Social Council, 'Definition of Basic Concepts and Terminologies in Governance and Public Administration' (E/C.16/2006/4), New York, 27–31 March 2006.

United Nations, Department of Economic and Social Affairs, *Cape Verde an Emerging Nation* (2010).

United Nations, Department of Economic and Social Affairs, *Rapport du Rapporteur Spécial sur la Torture et autres Peines ou Traitements Cruels, Inhumains ou Dégradants sur sa Mission au Maroc*, 15–22 September 2012 (A/HRC/22/53/Add.2).

United Nations, Department of Economic and Social Affairs, Human Rights Office of the High Commissioner, 'Declaration by Joy Ngozi Ezeilo after her visit in Morocco', Rabat, 21 June 2013, http://newsarchive.ohchr.org/EN/NewsEvents/Pages/DisplayNews.aspx?NewsID=13481&LangID=F (accessed 6 February 2017).

United Nations, Department of Economic and Social Affairs, HCR, *Morocco Factsheet*, 1 April 2015.

United Nations, Department of Economic and Social Affairs, UN Habitat, Conferência das Nações Unidas sobre a Habitação e o Desenvolvimento Urbano – Habitat III Relatório de Cabo Verde, 2016.

United Nations, Department of Economic and Social Affairs, HCR, *Rapport de Fin d'Année 2016* (2017).

United Nations, Departement of Economic and Social Affairs, United Nations, DESA, 'Population Division: International Migrant Stock 2005 and 2015', www.un.org/en/development/desa/population/migration/data/estimates2/estimates15.shtml (accessed 26 October 2016).

United Nations Human Rights Office of the High Commissioner, 'Declaration by Joy Ngozi Ezeilo after her visit in Morocco', Rabat, 21 June 2013, http://newsarchive.ohchr.org/EN/NewsEvents/Pages/DisplayNews.aspx?NewsID=13481&LangID=F (accessed 6 February 2017).

Urbano de Sousa, C and Pina-Delgado, J, *Estudo Sobre o Quadro Legislativo da Politica de Migração e Asilo na Republica de Cabo Verde* (MIEUX/ICMPD 2013).

US Department of State, Bureau of Democracy, Human Rights, and Labor, 'Country Reports on Human Rights Practices, Cape Verde Report 2012', 19 April 2013, www.state.gov/j/drl/rls/hrrpt/2012/af/204100.htm (accessed 8 December 2017).

US Department of State, Bureau of Democracy, Human Rights, and Labor, 'U.S. Relations with Morocco, Bureau of Near Eastern Affairs, Fact Sheet', 20 January 2017, www.state.gov/r/pa/ei/bgn/5431.htm (accessed 4 December 2017).

Van Criekinge, T, *The EU-Africa Migration Partnership: A Case Study of the EU's Migration Dialogue with Ghana and Senegal* (Florence, Italy: EUI Migration Working Group, European University Institute 2010).

Van Hüllen, V, *EU Democracy Promotion and the Arab Spring: International Cooperation and Authoritarianism: Governance and Limited Statehood* (New York: Palgrave Macmillan 2015).

Van Nuffel, P, 'The Protection of Member States' Regions Through the Subsidiarity Principle' 55 in Panara, C and De Becker, A (eds), *The Role of the Regions in EU Governance* (Heidelberg, Germany: Springer Science and Business Media 2010).

Van Selm, J, 'Immigration and Asylum or Foreign Policy: The EU's Approach to Migrants and Their Countries of Origin' 143 in Lavenex, S and Uçarer, EM (eds), *Migration and the Externalities of European Integration* (Lanham, MD: Lexington Books 2002).

Van Stokkum, LK, *More Mobility for Development! Policy Coherence for Development in Practice: Making the EU Mobility Partnership a Tool for Development in Cape Verde* (Foundation Max van der Stoel 2015).

Van Vooren, B, *EU External Relations Law and the European Neighbourhood Policy: A Paradigm for Coherence* (London and New York: Routledge 2012).

Vara, JS 'Soft International Agreements on Migration Cooperation with Third Countries: A Challenge to Democratic and Judicial Controls in the EU' 25 in Carrera, S, Vara, JS and Strik, T (eds), *Constitutionalising the External Dimensions of EU Migration Policies in Times of Crisis* (Cheltenham, UK: Edward Elgar 2019).

Varela, O, 'Readmitidos e/ou Repatriados? Uma Re-leitura do Acordo de Readmissão de Cabo Verde com a União Europeia' 61 in Evora, I, *Diaspora Cabo-Verdiana: Temas em Debate* (Centro de Estudos sobre Africa, Asia e America Latina 2016) https://issuu.com/comunicacao_cesa/docs/livro_diaspora-cabo-verde_final (accessed 16 April 2017).

Vaz, LH, 'O Acordo para Evitar a Dupla Tributação entre Portugal e Cabo Verde – Um Cabo das Tormentas?' *Jornal de Negocios*, www.jornaldenegocios.pt/opiniao/detalhe/o_acordo_para_evitar_a_dupla_tributaccedilatildeo_entre_portugal_e_cabo_verde___um_cabo_das_tormentas (accessed 5 December 2017).

VerLoren van Themaat, P, *The Changing Structure of International Economic Laws: A Contribution of Legal History, of Comparative Law and of General Legal Theory to the Debate on a New International Economic Order* (The Hague, The Netherlands; Boston, MA; London: Brill 1981).

Vezzoli, S, *The Role of the State in International Migration: Exploring the Transition from Colony to Independence* (Oxford: International Migration Institute, University of Oxford: Working Papers Series (102) (2014).

Vogt, WP, *Dictionary of Statistics and Methodology: A Nontechnical Guide for the Social Science* (Thousand Oaks, CA: Sage 2005).

Ward, N, 'Facilitating the Temporary Movement of Natural Persons: Economic Partnership Agreements Versus Bilateral Migration Agreements and Mobility Partnerships' 143 in Kunz, R, Lavenex, S and Panizzon, M (eds), *Multilayered Migration Governance: The promise of partnership* (London: Routledge 2011).

Ward, N, '*Comparing EU-Mobility Partnerships and the Provisions for Temporary Movement of Labour in the Cariforum-EC Economic Partnership*', Paper presented at the conference Swiss migration and EU mobility partnerships: Unveiling the Promise, Bern, 12–13 December 2008 (as cited) in Reslow, N, *Partnering for Mobility?: Three-Level*

Games in EU External Migration Policy (Maastricht, The Netherlands: Datawyse/Universitaire Pers 2013).

Watson, A, *Legal transplants: An approach in Comparative Law* (Edinburgh, UK: Scottish Academic Press 1974).

Weil, P, 'Towards Relative Normativity in International Law?' (*1983*) 77*Am J Int Law* 413.

Weinar, A, 'Improving EU and US Immigration Systems' Capacity for Responding to Global Challenges: Learning from Experiences' *EU–US Immigration Systems* (2011/02) (Florence, Italy: Robert Schuman Centre for Advanced Studies, San Domenico di Fiesole (FI): European University Institute 2011).

Weinar, A, 'Mobility Partnerships – What Impact do they have on Legal Migration and Mobility?' *The Migration Policy Centre* (The Migration Policy Centre, European University Institute, Florence, Italy2012) www.migrationpolicycenter.eu/publication/mobility-partnerships-what-impact-do-they-have-on-legal-migration-and-mobility (accessed 25 August 2017).

Wickramasekara, P, *Circular Migration: A Triple Win or a Dead End* (International Labour Organization 2011).

Williams, C, 'Research Methods' (2007) 5(3) *JBER* 65.

Wihtol de Wenden, C, 'Révolutions Arabes et Migrations: Schengen face aux Accords Bilatéraux de Contrôle des Frontières', 8 (August/September) *Esprit*2011.

Wheeler, DL and Walter, CO Jr, *Historical Dictionary of Portugal* (Lanham, MD; Toronto, Canada; Plymouth, UK: Scarecrow Press 2010).

Wolff, S, *The Mediterranean Dimension of the European Union's International Security* (Basingstoke, UK: Palgrave Macmillan 2012).

Wolff, S, 'The Politics of Negotiating EU Readmission Agreements: Insights from Morocco and Turkey' (2014) 16*EJML* 69.

Woods, J and Gabbay, D, 'Relevance in the Law: A Logical Perspective' 261 in Gabbay, D et al (eds), *Approaches to Legal Rationality* (Dordrecht, The Netherlands: Springer 2010).

World Bank, *Migration and Development Brief 21* (Washington, DC: The World Bank 2013).

World Markets Analysis, 'Government to Request EU Membership for Cape Verde', 9 May 2005.

Wouters, K and Den Heijer, M, 'The Marine I Case: A Comment' (2010) 22*IJRL* 1.

Wunderlich, D, 'The Limits of External Governance: Implementing EU External Migration Policy' (2012) 19(9) *J Eur Public Policy* 1414.

Wunderlich, D, 'Implementing EU External Migration Policy: Security-Driven by Default?' (2013) 11(4) *Comp Eur Politics* 406.

Wunderlich, D, 'Towards Coherence of EU External Migration Policy? Implementing a Complex Policy' (2013) *Int Migr* 51.

Youngs, R, 'Ten Years of the Barcelona Process: A Model for Supporting Arab Reform?' (2005) 2*FRIDE Working Paper*.

Zaireg, R, 'MRE: Pas de Vote Direct ni de Représentation Parlementaire cette Année' *HuffPost Maroc* (11 April 2016) www.huffpostmaghreb.com/2016/04/11/mre-vote-maroc _n_9658110.html (accessed 7 February 2018).

Index